2-08

The Unknown Dead

THE
UNKNOWN DEAD
Civilians in the
Battle of the Bulge

Peter Schrijvers

The University Press of Kentucky

Publication of this volume was made possible in part by a grant
from the National Endowment for the Humanities.

Scholarly publisher for the Commonwealth,
serving Bellarmine University, Berea College, Centre College of Kentucky,
Eastern Kentucky University, The Filson Historical Society, Georgetown
College, Kentucky Historical Society, Kentucky State University,
Morehead State University, Murray State University, Northern Kentucky
University, Transylvania University, University of Kentucky, University of
Louisville, and Western Kentucky University.
All rights reserved.

Editorial and Sales Offices: The University Press of Kentucky
663 South Limestone Street, Lexington, Kentucky 40508-4008
www.kentuckypress.com

Maps by Dick Gilbreath

ISBN 0-8131-2352-6 (hardcover : alk. paper)

Manufactured in the United States of America.

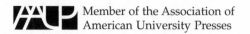 Member of the Association of
American University Presses

For my grandparents—

All in their own way
marked by the Second World War.

For there is no folly of the beast of the earth
which is not infinitely outdone
by the madness of men.

—Herman Melville, *Moby Dick*

Contents

Photographs follow page 206

Maps

Preface

For Joe Waddle from Tennessee the first day of 1945 was to be one of the worst of his life. Early that morning, his and another infantry company of the 11th Armored Division received orders to capture Acul, a hamlet some six miles west of Bastogne. At first the soldiers made good progress, hampered only by snow-covered snipers and mines. As they reached the last hill in front of Acul, however, enemy fire intensified furiously. To the east, Joe Waddle could see many American tanks on fire and others stopped dead in their tracks or retreating. But the infantry did what they had been told: they stormed the hamlet and captured what was left of it. They hurriedly positioned their antitank guns, hunkering down amidst the shell holes, the ruined farms, the dead cattle and horses. The German counterattack was not long in coming and proved devastating. Tanks blasted the hamlet from up close and soon sent the Americans scurrying for the nearest hill. Joe Waddle even left his helmet behind. He and his shaken comrades later that day derived satisfaction only from the fact that their artillery was now punishing the Germans in Acul mercilessly, setting much of the small farming community ablaze.

Acul was where Joe Waddle for the first time in his life killed a human being: a young and handsome German soldier whose face he would never be able to forget. For the Tennesseean that memory was perhaps as much the reason for revisiting Acul in April 1997 as was his own close escape. More than half a century after the battle, the veteran's thoughts as he loafed about the Belgian hamlet's streets and farmyards were those of men in uniform. Of comrades who had died too young. Of those who had survived and were now fading away. Of the German soldier he had killed and always imagined as having had blond hair though the coalscuttle helmet had in fact kept his head completely hidden.

Nothing in Joe Waddle's memory of Acul prepared him for his encounter with Mrs. Duplicy that spring day in 1997. Had she lived here all her life? The woman nodded. But where had she been during the battle? In Acul, the woman insisted. Joe Waddle was incredulous.

Acul had been razed to the ground by both sides. He had presumed that the inhabitants were gone and had never let them enter his mind. Where exactly had she been then? In the cellar of a stable that was now gone, Mrs. Duplicy explained, with nearly thirty others of the hamlet's inhabitants. As if by miracle, none of them had been killed or injured. Joe Waddle and Mrs. Duplicy continued to reminisce about the battle for quite some time. The flabbergasted veteran left Acul that spring day with civilians on his mind more than soldiers.[1]

This book is about people like Mrs. Duplicy. It is a book about the Battle of the Bulge and what it meant for the inhabitants of the region to be caught in the middle of it. Readers of these pages will look in vain, however, for the story of Marthe Monrique. Belgian journalists in the immediate postwar years succeeded in molding Mrs. Monrique into somewhat of a celebrity. They portrayed the woman from Celles as having single-handedly halted the German armored spearhead that got closest to the Meuse River. She was said to have done so on Christmas Eve by feeding the enemy a false story about roads mined all the way to Dinant. The information was said to have made the Germans decide on an alternative route that led to their demise and the end of the steamroller offensive.

Before long, a billboard next to a disabled Panther tank in Celles was proudly claiming this to be the place where Marthe Monrique had brought the German offensive to a halt. No reference here to the Americans who had taken the steam out of the German juggernaut by Christmas Eve or of the British troops guarding the Meuse. No mention either of the crucial role of the Allied air forces in savaging the 2nd Panzer Division's spearhead in view of the Meuse when the skies finally cleared. Still, no matter how implausible the story, Marthe Monrique became a local legend, and photos have been preserved of Mrs. Monrique posing next to the Panther for visitors right after the war.[2]

The point is that people needed to believe the story of Marthe Monrique. They found comfort in the knowledge that at least one civilian had been able to stand up to the enemy and, without help from foreign troops, had changed the course of battle. Marthe Monrique thus came to embody everything that the average civilian in reality had not been during the offensive. For many civilians the trauma caused by suffering was deepened by a humiliating feeling of impotence in the face of the overwhelming military power that both warring sides unleashed at them. The fate of the civilians inside the salient was determined by military decisions that they could neither control nor influence. Military people coldly decided what towns and villages were important enough to attack, besiege, or wipe away. Other than fleeing or hiding there was little the civilians could do in response to the military moves. "We feel like we are in God's hand," a villager wrote when caught in a furious artillery duel in Assenois on Christmas Day 1944, "and we surrender ourselves to it."[3]

To say that the civilians were reactive in the context of a military operation, however, is far from saying that they were merely passive victims. For those who were given the chance in this surprise offensive, the very decision to flee or hide, for example, was the first of many tough calls that could make the difference between life or death. Equally momentous were such decisions as when and where to shelter, how to procure water and food, how to care for the sick and wounded, how to deal with troops taking over their homes, and whether to care for injured soldiers or hide deserters. Soldiers who caught glimpses of the civilians through the fog of battle regularly expressed admiration for the courage they displayed as well as for their resilience, defiance, and solidarity. All of them qualities they shared with the combatants.

It is because of the reactive nature of civilians in the path of war that I have organized the experiences of the salient's inhabitants into chapters reflecting the raw military logic of the Battle of the Bulge. That battle resulted from Hitler's decision in September 1944 to try and regain the initiative in the war following the substantial retreat in the east and west. Hitler eventually opted for a major counteroffensive in the west. Harking back to the success of May 1940, he again ordered his generals to plan a major strike through the densely wooded Ardennes of Belgium and Luxembourg. The objective of the counteroffensive was to cross the Meuse as soon as possible and then to break into the open and capture Antwerp. As Hitler saw it, this would mean the loss of a vital port and logistical hub while at the same time dividing British and American armies north and south of the salient. These combined blows might convince the Allies to quit the war, enabling Germany at last to concentrate entirely on defeating the Soviet troops in the east.

Blinded by the belief that the Germans had become too weak by the end of 1944 to launch a major offensive, American commanders smugly ignored overwhelming evidence to the contrary filtering in from the area behind the Ardennes. They continued to use the

Ardennes as a training ground for new divisions and a resting area for badly battered ones. The Germans, meanwhile, were refitting divisions pulled off the western and eastern fronts and rebuilding them with new conscripts and convalescent soldiers backed up by tanks and artillery that continued to roll from factories inside the *Reich* in considerable numbers. When the German offensive started on the morning of December 16, 1944, it took the Allies completely by surprise. Moreover, the Germans now "enjoyed a three-to-one advantage in manpower, a two-to-one advantage in tanks, and general superiority in artillery."

The attack caused shock and havoc in American ranks. Small units nevertheless succeeded in delaying the enemy long enough on crucial roads and bridges to sap his momentum and allow the Allied command to pour in all available reserves. Though the German force was impressive, it was no longer comparable to that which had smashed through the Ardennes in May 1940. What had changed most was that the Germans lacked fuel and were at a serious disadvantage in air power, the latter explaining why Hitler had launched the offensive during bad weather. The Allies managed to contain the salient by Christmas, when the skies began to clear. They slowly began rolling it back at the start of the new year. A month later the Germans were back at the West Wall where they had started. The failed counter-offensive cost the Germans approximately 100,000 casualties. The British counted 200 dead and 239 wounded. The Americans, who had borne the brunt of the offensive, suffered 19,000 killed, 15,000 captured, and 47,000 wounded.[4]

None of the military histories of the battle, official or unofficial, that I have consulted in the course of my research mentions the number of civilian casualties, as if these are unrelated or, worse, insignificant. In fact, some battle histories make it appear as if there were no civilians present to begin with. Stephen Ambrose, for example, in the chapter on the Bulge in his best-selling book *Citizen Soldiers* claims: "If a village had been or was the scene of a battle, its civilian population was usually gone." Yet the most reliable estimates put the number of civilians who perished during the Battle of the Bulge at around 3,000. This means that for roughly every six American soldiers killed in this battle, one Belgian or Luxembourg noncombatant suffered a similar fate. Even more revealing is the fact that this battle caused such a large number of civilian casualties in a rural area that was only sparsely populated.

One official estimate in September 1945 put the number of Belgians who lived in the invaded area at 82,663. That would mean that the battle reduced the civilian population in the Belgian Ardennes by no less than 3 percent.[5]

About as many civilians lost their lives in the Battle of the Bulge in 1944–45 as did in the attacks against the Twin Towers in New York on September 11, 2001. The fate of the victims lost to terrorism in a matter of hours has been mourned by people around the world ever since. That of the civilians killed in the Battle of the Bulge in a span of six weeks barely registered with a public opinion inured to death in a largely conventional war that would ultimately cost the lives of some fifty million people, more than half of whom were noncombatants. But none of those in the salient who stayed behind without their loved ones could ever be asked to find comfort by putting things in historical perspective. This therefore is the story of the civilians who perished in the Battle of the Bulge. It is a story not of numbers, but of individuals with names and faces. A story that repeated itself in various shapes and forms on the battlefields of World War II and in many wars since.

Acknowledgments

My sincere gratitude goes to the families Maus and Schröder in Möderscheid, for their hospitality during unforgettable summer vacations in the Belgian East Cantons and for their willingness to speak frankly of fear and suffering during the Battle of the Bulge. It is their harrowing stories that convinced me of the need for a book on the cruel and little known fate of the Belgian and Luxembourg civilians in the winter of 1944–45.

It is impossible to mention everyone who in the course of this research provided me with valuable information, help, and advice. I am prepared, however, to run the risk of singling out some of the most important people: Richard Boijen, Alain Colignon, Robert Fergloute, Roland Gaul, Luc Hanegreefs, Sylvie Hilgers, Jean-Pierre Kever, K. D. Klauser, Christian Limbrée, Dirk Luyten, Eddy Monfort, Luc De Munck, Luc Nollomont, Reg Perkins, Niko Pfund, Chris Plant, J. Pothen, Bernadette Rensonnet, J. Bryan Sperry, Sophie Vandepontseele, Michel Vanderschaeghe, Emiel Vantongelen, and Cyriel Vleeschouwers. Charles Hilgers on a perfect summer afternoon in Eupen in 2002 was kind enough to speak to me at length about his painful experiences of dark winter weeks as a boy.

A special word of thanks goes to Caroline Finch in England for agreeing to scrutinize the English manuscript of a Belgian she knew merely as the brother of her daughter-in-law. Her comments in real ink on real paper delivered by a real person have proved to be of great value in this virtual age.

My father, Urbain Schrijvers, was reminded once again that children are a job for life as he agreed to take on the laborious task of indexation just when he thought he could sit back and enjoy retirement.

My sister Karin, with whom I have been sharing the lifestyle of the urban nomad, never abandoned me as she continued to read chapters even while transplanting from San Diego to Singapore.

An author should only be so lucky to find a publishing team like the one that makes the University Press of Kentucky tick. Director Stephen Wrinn consulted time zones on the Internet just to make sure he could catch me on the phone at acceptable hours as I moved from Belgium to Australia. His interest in the project as well as in the writer behind it, his professional advice, and his firm assurances have been much appreciated. So too are the diligence and cheerfulness of acquisitions editor Gena Henry, the painstaking work of editing supervisor Nichole Lainhart and freelance copyeditor Robin Roenker, the meticulous mapmaking of Dick Gilbreath, and the creative marketing of Leila Salisbury and her team. Thanks also to Craig Wilkie for his detailed replies to my questions of a more administrative nature.

I owe another large debt to my enthusiastic publishers in Belgium and the Netherlands for creating an excellent Dutch translation of this American book.

A whole batch of new colleagues at the School of History enabled me through their kindness to feel at home straight away at the University of New South Wales in Sydney. Their professional drive and Aussie humor at the same time provided me with sufficient energy to complete this project even while starting a new job and new courses.

Finally, I can never say enough thanks to my wife, Elle, my parents, brother, sisters, niece, and family-in-law. For many years they were willing to accept that even while I was with them part of me would leave and wander off to the bitter Ardennes.

Part I

Deluge

Chapter 1

The Northern Shoulder

"She cries and cannot understand."

The *SS-Obergruppenführer* was short, burly, and fat-faced. He looked the stereotypical butcher. In fact, Sepp Dietrich had been one in a previous life. But that was before he had met Adolf Hitler. Dietrich, discharged from the army as a sergeant at the end of the Great War, had become part of Hitler's inner circle when the former corporal was still no more than an aspiring politician. Throughout those uncertain years he had served Hitler loyally, first as his chauffeur, then as his bodyguard. When Hitler finally managed to seize total power in 1933, Dietrich was rewarded with a stellar career for his loyalty. At home, as head of the Führer's bodyguard, the *SS-Leibstandarte Adolf Hitler*, Dietrich played a key role in Hitler's notorious purge of Nazi ranks in 1934. By the time of the Russian campaign, he was heading a full-fledged division, the 1st SS Panzer Division. In the summer of 1944, SS-Gen. Sepp Dietrich had stood in Normandy with an entire panzer corps under his control. Now, in December 1944, the even bigger Sixth Panzer Army was entirely his, lurching behind the West Wall, poised to deal the main blow in the Führer's daring counteroffensive.[1]

Some admired Dietrich for his bravery and the utter ruthlessness with which he had waged war on the eastern front. Army generals worried about his drinking habits and rated him capable at best of commanding a division. They had thought it wise to team him up with the smart and experienced Fritz Kraemer as the Sixth Panzer Army's chief of staff. All that mattered to Hitler, however, was Dietrich's unwavering loyalty, a quality the Führer had come to appreciate even more in his "old fighters" since the failed attempt against his life orchestrated by army officers in the summer of 1944. Hitler

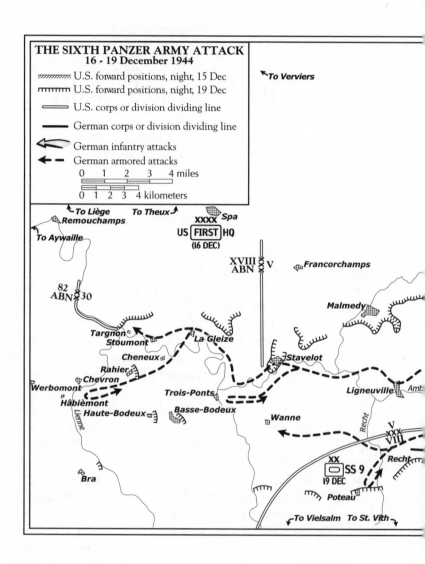

THE SIXTH PANZER ARMY ATTACK
16 - 19 December 1944

〰〰〰 U.S. forward positions, night, 15 Dec

ⅢⅢⅢ U.S. forward positions, night, 19 Dec

━━━ U.S. corps or division dividing line

━━━ German corps or division dividing line

◄━━━ German infantry attacks

◄━ ━ German armored attacks

0   1   2   3   4 miles

0 1 2 3 4 kilometers

To Verviers

To Liège

Remouchamps

To Theux

Spa

XXXX

US FIRST HQ

(16 DEC)

To Aywaille

XVIII
ABN   V

Francorchamps

82
ABN   30

Malmedy

Targnon
Stoumont

La Gleize

Cheneux

Stavelot

Rahier
Chevron

Werbomont

Trois-Ponts

Ligneuville   Amb

Hàbièmont

Haute-Bodeux

Basse-Bodeux

Wanne

Recht

Lienne

V
VIII

Bra

XX
SS 9
19 DEC

Recht

Poteau

To Vielsalm   To St. Vith

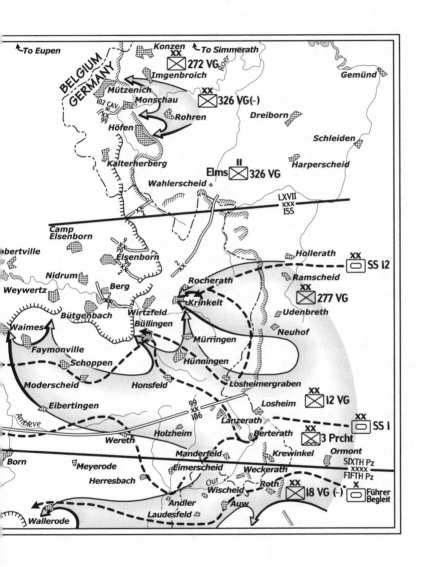

had been adamant that the main effort of the counteroffensive should be assigned to his crony. Sepp Dietrich's Sixth Panzer Army would form the crucial northern prong. It was to jump off between Monschau in the north and the Losheim Gap in the south, waltz across the Elsenborn Ridge and the Hautes Fagnes plateau, cross the Meuse River on both sides of Liège, and capture the richest prize: the Belgian port and Allied logistical hub of Antwerp.[2]

To accomplish all this, Hitler made sure to equip Dietrich with a formidable iron fist, making his by far the strongest of the three armies designated for the Ardennes. Dietrich was given command over all the SS panzer divisions available for the offensive, four crack divisions in all: the 1st and 12th would bear the brunt; the 2nd and 9th would form the second wave. These panzer divisions would operate in combination with a parachute division and the infantry of one *Panzergrenadier* and four *Volksgrenadier* divisions. Counting attached separate units, the Sixth Panzer Army fielded no fewer than eight hundred assault guns and tanks (including most of the *Königstiger* or King Tigers) and, with one thousand pieces, more artillery and rocket launchers than the Fifth Panzer and Seventh Armies combined.[3]

1 Dietrich's iron fist was to smash a hole through the middle section of the German-Belgian border. In doing so, his troops would immediately spill into that part of Belgium known as the *Ostkantone*. From north to south, the East Cantons were made up of Malmedy, Eupen, and St. Vith. Spread out across gently rolling hills cupping a marshy plateau, the region was home to a people made up mostly of farmers scattered across a patchwork of small, tightly knit communities. Dense forests, a stubborn earth, and hard winters had taught them diligence as much as humility. Taciturn faces bespoke a leaden past. For the East Cantons were a typical borderland, marked by torn identities and divided loyalties.

The population of the Belgian Ardennes is composed primarily of French-speaking Walloons. But if Malmedy cherished its ancient Romanic roots and spoke a Walloon dialect, Eupen and St. Vith displayed a distinct Germanic heritage in customs and language. Before the age of leviathan nations, Malmedy had been happy to form a minuscule abbatial principality with sister-city Stavelot. St. Vith had belonged to the duchy of Luxembourg, Eupen to the modest duchy of Limbourg. But revolutionary winds had swept away the ancient order and, one by one, the principalities had been swallowed up by

France in 1795. When Napoleon's empire collapsed in 1815, people in the three territories woke up to learn that they had been made subjects of the king of Prussia. Reorganized into *Kreise* they would remain part of Germany for more than a hundred years. A long century of assimilation left an indelible imprint on the region, and even in Malmedy French had grudgingly begun to make way for the German language. But then the Great War had erupted, sucking the newly formed Germans of this borderland into a maelstrom that in 1920 would spit them out as Belgians.[4]

Belgium had been quick to make political capital out of its fame as the Great War's "martyr country." In the grip of feverish nationalism and expansionism when it emerged from the war victorious, Belgium's representatives at the Versailles Conference lined up a battery of arguments to justify annexation of the Kreise on its eastern border. If the ethnic argument carried some weight where it concerned Malmedy, historical arguments were distorted to make Eupen and St. Vith, too, fit the Belgian mold. Much more straightforward was Belgium's claim to the region as compensation for huge damages suffered during the war. Moreover, control over the Hautes Fagnes plateau and the Elsenborn Ridge would provide Belgium with a strategic edge over Germany, thus—it was hoped—preventing history from repeating itself. The upshot had been Article 34 of the Versailles Treaty: Belgium was awarded the German borderland it had claimed, but on the condition that a majority of the region's inhabitants declared themselves in favor of the annexation. Officials so manipulated the 1920 plebiscite in their country's favor that the vote became known as "the little Belgian farce." Overnight some sixty-four thousand frontier Germans were transformed into as many borderland Belgians. The Kreise were duly reorganized into cantons.[5]

How bitterly divided the people in the East Cantons became over the annexation in the next two decades was best demonstrated in the Belgian parliamentary election of April 1939. On the eve of the war, slightly more than 45 percent of people in the border region voted for the *Heimattreue Front*, which advocated return to the Reich. The others cast their ballot for a mixture of largely pro-Belgian parties, with 38 percent of the total vote going to the Catholic party. To complicate matters further, a vote for a pro-German party in this deeply Catholic region did not necessarily entail support for a Nazi ideology that the inhabitants knew to possess a suspiciously anticlerical, if not antireligious, streak. Nevertheless, with Hitler's Germany growing stronger by the day, many in the East Cantons were irresistibly drawn to their mighty neighbor. They were lured by jobs that beckoned across the border while Belgium was still depression-ridden. Many even brought home good money from work on the West Wall (the Siegfried Line) when construction started along the right bank of the Rhine in 1936. Young German-speaking Belgians felt humiliated by the fact that they were made to serve in their new country's army but were relegated to auxiliary units where they could not carry arms. By late 1939 they were deserting in droves, finding a much warmer welcome in military units on the other side of the border.[6]

When Hitler's troops, in some cases spearheaded by reconnaissance troops composed of men from the Ostkantone, invaded Belgium in May 1940, large parts of the population in the border region enthusiastically cheered them. On May 18, ten days before Belgium had even capitulated, Hitler announced the Reich's annexation of the border areas. "Inwardly," the Führer noted in his decree, "they have always remained connected with Germany." The decree declared the region part of the German *Rheinprovinz*, and its cantons were once more organized into Kreise; the *Reichsmark* was introduced as early as June. Yet, even though they had been part of Belgium for less than a generation, people quickly noticed they were now being treated like second-class citizens in their newly found fatherland, too. They were referred to slightingly as *Rucksackdeutsche* to indicate the transitory nature of their nationality. Disappointingly few of the leading figures in the Heimattreue Front were trusted with key posts in the new German administration installed in the frontier Kreise. Moreover, people learned what it meant to have returned not just to Germany but to Nazi Germany. Anti-Catholic attitudes were soon creating friction. Those voicing opposition to the totalitarian regime disappeared into concentration camps like so many others across Europe. Nothing would cause more pain and unrest, however, than the conscription laws that began whisking away increasing numbers of young men after Hitler launched his war against Russia in June 1941. The small community would see no less than 8,700 men march off in German uniform. Two thousand of them would never return; another 1,600 would come back invalids. Some 1,000 draft dodgers went into hiding, many fleeing to Belgium, many joining the resistance. Left behind with too few hands to continue all of the backbreaking farm work and with increasing numbers of them in mourning, people in the former Ostkantone by the time of the

Normandy invasion in June 1944 were looking forward to yet another liberation.[7]

Liberation would come even before the summer of 1944 was over. Late in August the Allied armies broke free at last from the hedgerow shackles of Normandy. The breakout was followed by a hot pursuit of German troops who seemed to have in mind just one more goal: to find safety behind the immense West Wall protecting the mother country. Already early in September, after a breathtaking race across northern France, Allied armies were crossing the Belgian and Luxembourg borders. The Germans put up little resistance, allowing both small countries to be liberated with minimum destruction and bloodshed. Within days, and after some resistance at Dinant, American troops of Collins's VII Corps were crossing the Meuse, the last natural barrier of significance in front of the West Wall. Nothing remained to slow the advance but the lack of fuel and the crowds of near hysterical civilians. People in Liège climbed on the tanks of the 3rd Armored Division begging for guns. Meanwhile, Gerow's V Corps jumped the Meuse without difficulty on September 5; then marched through the Ardennes in southeastern Belgium and Luxembourg as if with seven-league boots. American troops were about to rub up against the West Wall.[8]

Though many had helped build it, the German-speaking former Belgians fell outside the West Wall. Caught between Allied armor and German concrete, there was nothing the people of the former Ostkantone could do but wait and hope for the best under what would be yet another alien regime. Many of the local party faithfuls had joined German-bound convoys. The overwhelming majority of the people, however, had stayed put. What was there to be found in Germany but death and destruction wrought by Allied bombers? Anyway, inhabitants of this border region were hopelessly rooted in their particular stretch of land for livelihood as much as identity.[9]

2 In Bütgenbach, barely three miles south of Elsenborn, Mrs. von Monschaw had waited for the arrival of Allied troops with a nervous mixture of trepidation and anticipation. She was German in blood and bone. But her husband had also been the first mayor of St. Vith after the area's annexation by Belgium. The Nazis had deemed this sufficient reason for them to seize her possessions in St. Vith and force her, at the age of sixty-one, into a home for the elderly in Bütgenbach, some eleven miles north of her hometown. Later she was at least given permission to move into a modest home in Bütgenbach. Though Mrs. von Monschaw realized that because of her language and roots the Allies would consider her one of the enemy, she could not help but wish for their speedy arrival.

The first tangible signs of her wishes being answered materialized on Saturday, September 2, 1944, when long columns of German vehicles began roaring through town on their way back from France. Day after day the retreat continued unabated, tanks and trucks chasing after one another as if afraid of being left behind, turrets and roofs camouflaged with foliage in vain attempts to outwit an enemy air force reigning supreme. At night exhausted German soldiers bellowed at people to get out of their beds and onto the streets, threatening to shoot those who lingered. Long military trains stood for hours in Bütgenbach station, hissing impatiently, the soldiers inside clamoring for food. On September 9 a mixture of horse-drawn wagons rumbled by loaded with old men and loot. Allied fighter-bombers specked the air, diving and climbing "like butterflies." Refugees began arriving from Malmedy and St. Vith. Many people in Bütgenbach took to their cellars; others joined the refugees. On September 11 Russian auxiliary troops limped by on foot. In the morning smoke billowed from Rocherath; in the afternoon dark clouds mushroomed over Elsenborn. The next day heavy artillery salvos boomed back and forth over Bütgenbach from morning till night. Then the Germans blew the bridges. The power was cut. Bütgenbach slid into darkness.

The first American vehicles appeared in town on the morning of September 13. "They were all remarkably silent," a surprised Mrs. von Monschaw jotted in her diary, "even the tanks rolled by on rubber wheels." Given the fact that the Americans had just entered German-speaking territory, the inhabitants found them remarkably amiable. They immediately proceeded to smash the busts of Hitler in Bütgenbach's town hall and to remove all of the Führer's portraits from the town's schools. They also imposed a curfew, prohibited large gatherings, and announced a series of additional security measures. Other than that, however, American troops caused the inhabitants no serious nuisance.[10]

Throughout the Ostkantone people had similar experiences with the GIs. Not even the *Frontläufer*, Gestapo agents infiltrating the newly occupied Kreise in search of military intelligence and news of the mood among the civilian population, could deny that the relationship with the American occupation forces was, in general, remarkably good. They had won the people's hearts and minds in a matter of days, so the reports to the *Sicherheitsdienst* read, by showering children with chocolate and generously distributing foodstuffs and cigarettes among the general populace. Most importantly, one agent claimed, time and again people told him that "under American rule they had again acquired a free life, whereas under the Germans everything had been dealt with too strictly and harshly." The same agent could not but conclude—his report corroborated by fellow spies—that "the population in the American-occupied territories were absolutely besotted with the Americans."

Already by October, however, Gestapo reports were signaling that the infatuation had started to wear off. Civilian food distribution remained a problem throughout much of Belgium and was even more of a headache in the isolated Ardennes. American military authorities appeared unable or unwilling to clamp down on the internecine feuds that had flared up again between pro-Belgian and pro-German factions. Civilians, the Reich's agents noted, were ratting on those who had collaborated with German occupation forces, people were being arrested or falling victim to mob justice, and so-called resistance groups were terrorizing communities with exorbitant requisitioning demands.[11]

Still, the most disheartening events by far were to take place early in October. In the heady days of September, when troops were steamrolling toward the Rhine, soldiers and civilians alike had been convinced that nothing would be able to stop the Allied momentum, not even the West Wall's bunkers and dragon teeth. By mid-September, Collins's VII Corps had been deployed along a front from Herve, eleven miles east of Liège, to Malmedy, while Gerow's V Corps had taken up positions on a line running from St. Vith to Echternach in Luxembourg. The West Wall was in sight, and behind it was the enemy's lair. Victory seemed at hand. But the long pursuit had left Allied troops thoroughly exhausted. Logistical lines were stretched to the breaking point. Lack of maintenance and repair had worn down equipment. Meanwhile, troops probing West Wall positions reported stiff resistance: the Germans appeared to have decided to make a stand. With German soil within reach, the pursuit had ground to a halt.[12]

This also meant that large numbers of civilians in the Ostkantone now lived dangerously close to what threatened to remain a front line for quite some time. German shells lobbed into villages near the West Wall were constant reminders of the fact that the war was not over yet. Military authorities were concerned about noncombatant casualties, but they also feared that the presence of civilians might hamper operations. Above all, they regarded the German-speaking inhabitants as security risks. Even if they did not actively engage in spying or sabotage, the population inevitably formed a sea in which enemy agents could move about unnoticed by counterintelligence. So thin were American lines in this sector, for instance, that German soldiers from the Ostkantone occasionally slipped through to spend time with their family and girlfriends. Gestapo infiltrators wheedled information from unsuspecting civilians by pretending to be German deserters.[13]

For all these reasons, American military authorities by the end of the first week of October announced a decision that sent shock waves through the region: the civilian population was to be evacuated. Between October 5 and 9 people in the Ostkantone closest to the West Wall at very short notice were told to pack some clothing, assemble at town halls and churches, and climb onto trucks that would carry them to the rear, sometimes as far away as Spa and Verviers. In the area north of the Losheim Gap alone, an estimated ten thousand people were evacuated to areas further west. Only a carefully selected handful of people were allowed to stay in each village to take care of the animals and what remained to be harvested. Emotional scenes unfolded in the assembly areas on the mornings of departure. No one knew what would happen to home, cattle, and field. No one knew who would take care of them or where they might be going. No one could tell when they would be back. Military authorities assured them that it would only be a few days or weeks. By mid-December, on the eve of the German counteroffensive, many still had not received permission to return home.

3 In the heart of the Losheim Gap, in the village of Afst, the early morning hours of Saturday, December 16 were cold as death. No one had bothered to send out patrols. A sprinkling of American soldiers were fast asleep in three of the village's abandoned houses. Nearly 90 percent of the area's inhabitants had been evacuated the previous month, leaving only ten civilians in Afst. Peter Jenniges, his wife, and their two children—the only youngsters left in the village— were tucked in beneath their warm down blankets. The family had returned to the upstairs bedrooms some time ago. The cellar, filled with potatoes, had been much too cramped and uncomfortable. Besides, they had convinced themselves that a direct hit on the house would leave them not much safer in the cellar. Like most nights, they slept a restless sleep, tossing and turning nervously. Ever since the Americans had arrived, Afst had come under German artillery fire from behind the West Wall for at least half an hour every day. Most houses had received damage of some kind.

That morning, around 5:30, the Germans added yet another day to their routine. But this time Peter Jenniges noted straightaway that they were putting remarkable energy in their shelling. He was wide awake even before an explosion shook their house. While his family rushed to the cellar, he quickly assessed the damage. The kitchen windows had been shattered. Smoke and an acrid powder were sucked in by an icy draft. Then he suddenly noticed a bright light dance through one of the windows. He was outside in the blink of an eye. The hay, stacked in a loft attached to the house, was on fire. Water from a couple of buckets made no difference. Within minutes the house itself was ablaze. Mrs. Jenniges darted in and out to save some belongings. Peter Jenniges hurried to drive the cows from the stable, the thunder of explosions drowning out the animals' fearful bellowing. As their home turned into a torch, they bolted to the nearest building, escaping American machine-gun fire by a hair's breadth.[14]

By noon the Jenniges home and several other buildings in Afst were nothing but smoldering ruins. Large numbers of German troops continued to pour into the Losheim Gap. That gap, a seven-mile-wide valley north of the Schnee Eifel, was Germany's historical passage to the west. German armies on their way to France had invaded Belgium through this corridor in 1870, in 1914, and again in 1940. At a time when most Allies were convinced that the enemy was too weak to launch a major counteroffensive anywhere in the west, no one had expected the Germans to come down this corridor once again. The 14th U.S. Cavalry Group formed a thin line in the gap, leaving virtually wide open the two northernmost miles that stretched toward the 99th Infantry Division. It was in part because of these weak defenses that Hitler had gambled on sending some of his best divisions through the Losheim Gap for a fourth time in recent memory. While the extreme right flank of von Manteuffel's Fifth Panzer Army poured through the corridor near the tip of the Schnee Eifel, poised to turn southwest toward St. Vith, troops forming Dietrich's left flank somewhat further north ripped through the gap on their way west.[15]

Although men of the 99th Division managed to delay a column of the 12th SS Panzer Division long enough to get Dietrich fuming, his other divisions—the 3rd Parachute, 12th Volksgrenadier, and 1st SS Panzer—smashed through the Losheim Gap, throwing the 14th Cavalry Group totally off balance. As the Americans beat a hasty and disorderly retreat on the afternoon of December 16, the narrow streets of Manderfeld, a village just west of Afst, jammed with vehicles. "Hysterical civilians ran alongside, begging to be taken along. Others, German at heart, stood by smiling and nodding." As American troops scrambled to fall back on the next village, they "set fire to several buildings solely in order to burn important papers." Several miles to the west, in Holzheim, GIs found the villagers "cool, almost hostile, clearing their houses of all traces of American occupation."[16]

Amidst the commotion in Manderfeld, Mathias Heinzius and his sister decided to stay put so as to keep an eye on the family farm. Earlier that Saturday their father and uncle had grabbed a knapsack, stuffed it with ham and bread, and hurried to the road leading west. By dusk the refugees had vanished from the roads. "We are the last ones," GIs abandoning the village warned Mathias that evening, "you are now in no-man's-land." For Mathias and his sister the hours that followed would be the worst of the offensive. Shell fire during the day had killed five villagers, three of them small children. At night terrifying artillery barrages continued to pound Manderfeld from all sides, rocking the village like the spasms of a quake. Only at dawn did things quiet down. Mathias stole a blurred glance through the kitchen window. He saw nothing but cratered fields and blackened snow. Then through the ringing in his ears he detected a monotonous clanking. He crept to another window and in the grayish morning light made out the contours of half-tracks and tanks. The vehicles crept past the farm, grating and squeaking as if no one had bothered to oil them. The metallic grind was punctuated by gruff cries and orders. "It was all so different from the Americans," Mathias thought. It was Sunday, December 17, and the Germans had just returned to Manderfeld.[17]

For several days, Heinrich Maus in Holzheim had been closely watching the German troops passing through from Manderfeld. First, assault troops had roared by; then supporting units had begun arriving. He knew it could only mean that Krewinkel, a village in the heart of the Losheim Gap, on the crossroad just south of Afst, was firmly back in the hands of Hitler's army. Heinrich Maus had been living in Holzheim since the Americans had forced people in Krewinkel to evacuate early in October. With Christmas now only a few days away, he decided it was time to go home. He hitched the animals to the wagon, helped his wife and three children onto it, and set off in the direction of the West Wall.

Maus, a wiry forty-one-year-old with vivid eyes, was glad to be heading for familiar surroundings. This was the second time he had been forced to abandon his beloved village for Holzheim in barely four months. Following the annexation by Germany in 1940, he had accepted the post of *Ortsbauernführer* for Krewinkel and vicinity. He had not taken on the role of local farm leader for ideological reasons. In fact, he had steadfastly refused to become a member of the Nazi Party. But he had reasoned that the post would enable him to keep an eye out on behalf of the community by the time the inevitable German demands for agricultural contributions came pouring in, as he remembered they had during the Great War. For nearly four years he had played the vital but thankless task of moderating between farmers and occupiers. Then, as the Allies raced toward Belgium in the late summer of 1944, the Germans had given him an order he could not possibly obey. To prevent anything in the former Ostkantone from falling into the hands of Allied troops, the Ortsbauernführer were to lead the villagers, their belongings, and their cattle into the Reich behind the West Wall. Like many others, Heinrich Maus had ignored the order. Instead, he and a number of neighbors had fled west. They had tended their cattle in the woods near Holzheim until they were satisfied the Americans were thoroughly in charge of Krewinkel.

As Heinrich Maus entered Krewinkel on that cold December day, he was surprised to see how drastically the fortunes of war had altered the appearance of his village in less than a week. The sleepy spot that had housed no more than a handful of GIs was now bustling with vehicles and bursting at the seams with soldiers. His own farm had been taken over by SS troops. They were kind to the farmer and his family, offering them some sausage and hot drinks. Thinking that the family had returned home from behind the West Wall, on the heels of their German liberators, they were curious to learn where in the Reich Heinrich Maus had stayed all that time. When the Germans looked Holzheim up on their map and realized that the farmer had just returned from the American side, the mood turned uncomfortably cool.

The following morning two officers came to get Heinrich Maus for questioning at the presbytery. For close to three hours he was grilled by five members of the Gestapo as to why he had chosen to flee in the direction of the enemy rather than follow German troops across the West Wall. When asked where the other villagers had gone, Heinrich Maus could only answer that they, too, were hiding out west. "Ah, all on the side of the Americans!" a Gestapo officer remarked sardonically. Another agent wanted to know if the village's Ortsbauernführer had not been ordered to ensure the entire community's withdrawal behind the West Wall? Heinrich Maus turned cold. Who, the agent insisted, had held that post in Krewinkel? More villagers were on their way back to Krewinkel, and Heinrich Maus knew he would be found out sooner or later. With pounding heart, he stammered out that he had been the Ortsbauernführer. The agents jumped up. The confession so enraged the incredulous Gestapo that they told him they had the right to shoot him on the spot. For the moment, however, they decided to send him home pending their verdict.

For several days they left him to think things over in mortal fear. As his house was crawling with SS, escape was impossible. Anyway, he could not leave his family behind. Then one morning the Gestapo came to get him. He was told to take a spade and an axe. They were going to the cemetery, they said, to bury the dead. Heinrich Maus knew he would be digging his own grave, for Krewinkel did not have a cemetery of its own. As they neared the church, however, he felt a rush of relief. Dozens of Germans lay dead in a nearby field. They had fallen in the opening days of the offensive. Together with Russian auxiliary troops, who had already stacked the corpses in neat rows, Heinrich Maus was to provide the soldiers with a decent resting place. The farmer's punishment for disloyalty was hard and morbid labor, but he would live.[18]

4 The Gestapo was never given a chance to settle in Krinkelt-Rocherath. Like the Losheim Gap, control of this area several miles further north was critical to the success of Dietrich's Sixth Panzer Army. The 12th and 277th Volksgrenadier Divisions were to gain control over a number of forest trails leading to the frontier villages, thus gaining access for the SS panzer divisions to routes beyond the villages, especially those in Bütgenbach, leading all the way to Liège and the Meuse.[19]

The carefully designed German plans would never be executed beyond the bloody fight for Krinkelt-Rocherath. Wedged between the Elsenborn Ridge and the West Wall, some eight miles northwest of

Krewinkel, the twin villages lay so close to each other they had become entangled. They had suffered more than others when the Americans arrived in September 1944. As the Germans tried to hold on to the villages for several days, four homes were reduced to ashes. On September 20, two inhabitants were blown up by a mine. From behind the West Wall, German artillery continued to harass the villages daily, and on October 7 American authorities decided to have the people evacuated. A small number of inhabitants (some seventy-four men and fourteen women) received permission to stay behind to take care of some three thousand head of cattle. So many animals had been killed or wounded by German shells that the Americans had allowed an inhabitant to perform emergency slaughters and transport the meat to the evacuees further west. There the uprooted had been as happy with the news from home as with the meat.

The news that an American lieutenant brought back to Krinkelt-Rocherath on the afternoon of December 16 from his foxhole in the forest to the east was much less welcome. "The Germans," he announced with a grave face, "are on their way back." Enemy artillery had been booming throughout the day, but then again it had been doing so off and on for the past three months. But the lieutenant soon turned out to be right: this time things were different. "Mama, Hedwig, Papa," a frantic GI yelled to the Josten family in their beds upstairs, "hurry to the cellar, the Germans are shelling." It was four in the morning on Sunday, December 17. Two of the GI's comrades were already dead. Krinkelt-Rocherath was under attack.

German and American fire that Sunday rocked the houses on their foundations. In the evening, Franz Halmes nervously asked an officer for a document that would provide him safe passage through American lines on his way to Elsenborn. But the American calmed him down, promising that if his troops were to leave, they would take all civilians with them. When Mr. Halmes emerged from his cellar the following morning, not a single soldier remained in the house. Some bandages and first-aid kits were all the GIs had left behind.[20]

The front line now ran right through the village. American soldiers were falling back from certain houses, but they were not abandoning Krinkelt-Rocherath. For that the stakes were too high. Inexperienced as they were, soldiers from the 99th Infantry Division were to make a stand at the hamlets in order to help save the crack "Indianhead" division. Some four miles further north, at the Wahlerscheid crossroads, the 2nd Infantry Division had launched an offensive on December 13 aimed at breaching the West Wall. The only way back for the division was a long and narrow forest road leading into Krinkelt-Rocherath. If the Germans took the hamlets, the famous division would be cut off.[21]

As wave upon wave of German troops threw themselves against the American defenses in and around the Belgian frontier villages, the remaining civilians found themselves trapped in the full fury of combat. First, the 277th Volksgrenadier Division stormed the villages. Then the steel force of the 12th SS Panzer Division was unleashed. Americans turned even the Krinkelt church into a fort, their Sherman tanks hiding behind the thick stone walls. Two German Panthers retaliated by firing point blank into the ancient masonry. In the cellar of number 65 on Rocherath's main street, Johann and Maria Droesch and their daughter Hedwig huddled together as enemy tanks systematically blasted houses suspected of harboring GIs. The family shuddered to think what would happen if the Germans took control of the villages. They were ardent anti-Nazis and in September the Americans had made one son, Paul, mayor of Krinkelt-Rocherath and nearby Wirtzfeld. Paul Droesch had been an active member of the resistance during the occupation and had served as a guide to American patrols probing the West Wall.[22]

During a lull on Monday morning, Hedwig decided to risk having a look upstairs. The German wounded were spread out on the ground floor. Gas masks, helmets, shell fragments, and debris littered the street. Houses were burning left and right. There was nothing left to eat. Even as her father darted to the stable to milk a cow, a new wave of violence rolled across the street. They tumbled back into the cellar, crying and praying with some of the neighbors.[23]

Across the street, two women, Thelka Palm and Suzanne Faymonville, were doing exactly the same. Then suddenly an American rifleman ambushed an SS officer. The victim, bleeding profusely, fled in the direction of the Palm house. Excited soldiers burst into the cellar, threatening to kill the two women if their officer was not found right away. As the SS recovered their commander, the women bolted out of the door and across the street, swelling the Droesch cellar to close to a dozen overwrought civilians.[24]

People in and around Krinkelt-Rocherath could now think of only one thing: escaping in order to save their own lives. That was easier said than done. In the confusion of battle many who thought they were heading for the American lines ran straight into the arms of German troops. The agitated soldiers did not make light of their ethnic brethren's disloyalty. Trying to slip away from their cellar in Rocherath, one group of civilians under a hail of fire crawled across the street, only to bump up against a row of tanks. Annoyed SS crews demanded to know what civilians were still doing in the combat zone. "Why aren't you a soldier?" an SS officer questioned one of the men. "What would you say," he taunted, "if we took you with us?" The group hurried on to where they suspected the Americans to be, but a German again barred the way. "You can't get through," he barked. "In the next house, fifty meters from here, there are Americans." The civilians just stared at him. "If you go there," he warned, "I'll shoot you in the back!" The group turned on their heels, once again running a gauntlet of fire, bursting out at the village's other end and into German-held Mürringen.[25]

The American lines were also fraught with danger. At five o'clock on Monday morning, with the enemy on the outskirts of Mürringen, two men and two women stole away from their village in the direction of Wirtzfeld. GIs manning an advance post, their nerves on edge, fired before asking questions. They hit Peter Hepp in the head. As his companions dropped to the ground, all they could do was listen to him whisper, "I am dead." Guilty of nothing more than having come from the German side, the surviving civilians were treated with suspicion rather than compassion. They were led away to Krinkelt and then carried off to Elsenborn. There they were subjected to a thorough interrogation, only to be released again still further to the rear, in Robertville.[26]

In Rocherath on Tuesday, people in the Droesch cellar were unable to hold out any longer. Eleven destroyed German tanks littered the streets in a radius of no more than 220 yards. Around noon GIs stumbled down the basement steps with news that the wooden shed was ablaze and that the fire was spreading to the house. The inhabitants were told to make a run for it to Wirtzfeld. Under the cover of small-arms fire, seven women and four men, with their heads down, catapulted themselves out of the house. Breathless they reached the approaches to Wirtzfeld along which the hardened 2nd Infantry Division was digging in. A morose American snapped at them to get the hell back to where they had come from. As they desperately tried to explain to him that they couldn't, that their house was on fire, a lieutenant stepped forward, reprimanding the soldier for his insensitivity. "Can't you see the state these poor people are in?" he glowered. Then the officer asked the civilians in fine French where they were from. "Rocherath," Hedwig Droesch stammered. She noticed that the troops were preparing hot drinks. When she begged for some coffee for her mother, seven or eight GIs obliged, thronging around them with their cups. It was the first warm liquid the villagers had tasted in three days, but they could not drink. So shot were their nerves that their trembling hands failed to bring the cups to their lips. The soldiers, tears in their eyes, made them sip like children.[27]

Despite constant German hammering, the "Indianhead" soldiers held on to the Krinkelt-Rocherath-Wirtzfeld area long enough to allow 99th Division troops to begin falling back to the Elsenborn Ridge. Late on Tuesday, they themselves followed suit. Civilians filtered into the new defense line together with the Americans. They joined some thirty inhabitants of Elsenborn village who had been allowed to remain behind in October. Most were men who were responsible for tending animals and harvesting potatoes. But a handful of women, too, had stayed to care for the very old, including a blind man who was too infirm to be transported. The people in Elsenborn were jittery. Already in September, troops had decided to have it out near their village in two frightful days that had claimed civilian casualties. Bewildered refugees trickling in from the villages that had just been abandoned to the Germans made an already tense atmosphere worse. Those who had escaped from Rocherath spoke of a Wirtz Creek red with the blood of soldiers.[28]

Tension rose in Elsenborn with each passing hour. As ever more German shells began to find their way into the village, American troops grew increasingly suspicious of the civilians in their midst. An order came down prohibiting civilians from leaving their cellars after sundown. With water mains ruptured, this meant that the few farmers left had to scoop or pump enough water for thousands of animals before five o'clock in the afternoon, all the while dodging artillery fire. GIs in Elsenborn found it hard to believe civilians who claimed they had escaped from the hell of Krinkelt-Rocherath. They began suspecting German infiltrators everywhere. One morning everyone hiding in the cellar of Nikolaus Schommers's home was rounded up and taken to an Elsenborn inn for interrogation. They were accused of having sent light signals to the Germans at night from the upstairs windows. Closer investigation revealed that the light had, in fact, come from careless GIs. Wilhelm Marx another day found himself under arrest for incitement, only to be released three days later. All he had done was plead with the GIs to have the civilians evacuated before it was too late. On Christmas Day the Americans decided Wilhelm Marx had been right after all. They hurriedly trucked all civilians still in Elsenborn to the rear.[29]

German shells reached Elsenborn, but German soldiers never did. Aware of the tremendous importance of jamming the offensive's northern shoulder to prevent the Bulge from widening, American troops from all sides rushed artillery reinforcements to the Elsenborn Ridge. More than three hundred guns of various types were amassed on or near the escarpment. They were strengthened by tanks and tank destroyers plus a battalion of chemical mortars. "The booming of guns grew ever louder and continued throughout the night," a villager in Nidrum, one mile southwest of Elsenborn, wrote in his diary on December 19. "Ever more guns are being lined up to as close as one hundred meters from our house." Before long, German troops in the Krinkelt-Rocherath-Wirtzfeld area were blasted to a halt. Within days American artillery batteries from the Elsenborn Ridge were capable of laying ferocious concentrations of fire on objectives across the northern rim of the Bulge, turning into deathtraps villages as far away as ten miles.[30]

In the days following Christmas it became clear to people living in the shadow of the Elsenborn Ridge that the Germans would never be able to penetrate the deadly wall of steel the Americans had thrown up around them. Though this made them breathe more easily, it did not mean they were spared all of war's miseries. So many Americans were stationed in Nidrum, for example, that each house was estimated to hold between thirty and forty soldiers. Careless GIs rigged makeshift heating devices in every room and even in the stables. On the last day of the year one of the village's farmhouses caught fire. The death toll, a villager noted, was "something to cry over." "Four high-quality cows in calf are burned," he detailed. "Two sows, in farrow for January, and one fat hog are also burned." In the dead of winter, with food supplies cut off, his was just one of many families who saw their means of subsistence wiped out. In the early days of the new year, the first farmers brave enough to return to Elsenborn from evacuation beheld a spectacle that cut right through their hearts. In homes that had escaped shelling, American combat troops had rampaged. Much of what had not been looted had been destroyed or thrown into the streets. Soldiers had fed the cattle with fodder that had been at hand, but they had not found the time to haul water to the stables. Many animals lay dead, their necks twisted in chains.[31]

5 The Americans were stonewalling the enemy at Krinkelt-Rocherath. But Gen. Sepp Dietrich was, if anything, stubborn. On Monday, December 18, he decided to try to get access to the Bütgenbach roads by launching the main thrust slightly farther south. That evening he ordered the badly mauled 12th SS Panzer Division to move down to the crossroads at Losheimergraben and from there to swing northwest to Bütgenbach via Hünningen and Büllingen.[32]

Like so many other villages close to the West Wall, Hünningen had been evacuated on a soft and sunny autumn morning. By noon of Thursday, October 5, of about four hundred inhabitants only eight remained in an eerily quiet village. The six men and two women had found it impossible, however, to take care of the livestock of close to sixty farms. In response to the cattlemen's pleas, the Americans had allowed another seventy villagers to trickle back by the day the Germans unleashed their counteroffensive.[33]

Though the village was startled by sporadic shell fire in the early hours of December 16, the rest of the day remained fairly calm. In late afternoon, however, rumors began flying back and forth of German troops advancing on Honsfeld, just southwest of Hünningen. At dark the shelling so increased in intensity that the villagers decided to sit out the night in their cellars. Dawn found Mathias Jouck in a state of panic. He and some neighbors decided it might still be possible to outrun the Germans. They were wrong. They had just left Hünningen when German machine-gun fire from the Honsfeld-Büllingen road took them for targets. They fled to a nearby mill where they found two dozen other villagers who had failed in their escape. One of them had been shot in the leg. The group weighed their options. On one hand they were afraid to leave their hiding place, but on the other hand they could not stay in the freezing mill much longer the way they were. The following morning a group of four women and five men rose, their joints stiff with cold. They were heading back for Hünningen to get food and extra clothing.

A wintry silence hung over the road leading into the village. Hünningen appeared utterly deserted. Then suddenly, as the villagers rounded the last curve, they heard loud yells. No one understood what had been said. As they were deciding what to do, machine guns opened fire. The villagers scurried to safety. Johann Lux lay dead in the street. Next to him, his brother Egidius hugged the ground. He weakly signaled to the others that he, too, had been hit. After minutes of mayhem, the firing abruptly halted. Two German tanks, soldiers riding on the decks, rumbled toward the villagers who stood with their hands above their heads. The Germans allowed the civilians to carry the wounded Egidius into a nearby house where he lived for another half hour. After they had placed the dead brothers on biers, the villagers were eager to continue into Hünningen. But the soldiers told them to wait until the village was cleared of the enemy. An hour later, the Germans rang the church bells. Hünningen was theirs.[34]

American artillery on the Elsenborn Ridge had no trouble finding Hünningen's range. Aware that tanks from the 12th SS Panzer Division had begun moving through the village on Monday night, they blasted away. Some forty-five civilians were still stuck in the village. On Wednesday one of many shells destined for Hünningen exploded right in the Jost courtyard, killing three German soldiers as well as sixty-two-year-old farmer Josef Schmitz. Shell fragments so mauled Mathias Jouck, who just days earlier had been lucky to survive German bullets, that a military ambulance had to rush him to Germany.

The following day Josef Schmitz still lay where he had fallen. In the rain of shells it took German soldiers to help civilians dig a grave and drag the body to the cemetery on a piece of canvas. An attempt to bury Johann and Egidius Lux could not be undertaken before Saturday, almost a week after they had been killed. While three men hewed graves from the frozen earth, three others used a horse-drawn wagon to carry the corpses along a distance of slightly more than a mile. The group of six labored the better part of the day. Countless times the work of both teams had to be interrupted to seek cover. Only when dark set in did the brothers find rest deep in their village's hallowed ground.[35]

In Büllingen, too, the Americans had allowed the number of civilians to increase again in the weeks following the early October evacuation so as to better enable people to take care of their farms. Within the first hours of the offensive on Saturday, one of the town's houses received a direct hit. On Sunday morning the fire increased to the point where farmer Albert Kohnenmergen needed an hour and a half to traverse the 330 yards from his home to the neighbor's stables. By noon a *Kampfgruppe* of the 1st SS Panzer Division dashed through the town on its way west. The following day troops of the 12th SS Panzer Division began arriving for the push against Bütgenbach. The Americans made sure to lay down a curtain of fire. On Tuesday, December 19, the roar of explosions was deafening. One civilian counted 3,500 rounds. In Josef Jouck's basement, people said their prayers sobbing and crying.[36]

Trapped in Büllingen, small groups of GIs joined the civilians in their cellars, putting them at risk even more. In the large basement shared by Emma Reuter and other civilians, several dozen Americans were hiding. German soldiers on Tuesday moved down the rows of houses determined to flush the enemy from their hiding places. Before long, hand grenades rolled down Mrs. Reuter's stairs, forcing the GIs to give themselves up within seconds, yelling: "Don't shoot! *Kameraden*, don't shoot!" In similar fashion close to a hundred Americans were driven into the open from neighboring houses. When in another street a German tank blew a track on an American mine, an NCO snarled at the inhabitants of a nearby home from which GIs were emerging with hands raised, "One should shoot civilians, too."[37]

American shelling of Büllingen would continue unabated for weeks. The town was punished with dreadful incendiaries of white phosphorus. In the early morning of December 27, a German soldier warned Mathilde Jouck that the church was burning. She was the town's sexton and hurried to the church to rescue the most sacred relics. Though the interior was ablaze when she arrived, the girl managed to reach the tabernacle and wrap chalice, consecrated wafers, and monstrance in one of the Mass vestments. Mathilde Jouck braved the searing heat while awaiting a pause in the firing. By the time she bolted from the church it had become a roaring ball of fire hot enough to melt even the giant bell. By early January German soldiers were speaking of "the hell of Büllingen."[38]

The ultimate goal of Dietrich's 12th SS Panzer Division as it swung away from Krinkelt-Rocherath was not Büllingen, but Bütgenbach's road net some three miles to the northwest. The American evacuation order of October had permitted only a few scores of farmers to stay behind in this town. They had been too few to keep the cows milked on schedule and American authorities had had to install several butchering stations to get rid of excess cattle. Though it pained the farmers, they were glad to know the meat was at least being transported to the evacuees in the rear. The cattlemen in Bütgenbach were joined by several women. They were to take care of Bütgenbach's old and infirm, most of whom the military authorities had brought together in the town's convent, which also served as a geriatric hospital. American troops made sure to keep close tabs on the civilians in this important garrison town. Remaining inhabitants were to carry special papers and stay indoors after dusk. They were prohibited from entering a 550-yard radius around the 99th Division headquarters. Many a worried farmer who had tried to slip back to Bütgenbach illegally had been caught by MPs and, after interrogation, sent back to the rear or taken into custody.[39]

On Sunday, December 17, when news spread that SS troops had been sighted as close as Büllingen, and refugees from this town and Krinkelt-Rocherath hurried by on their way to Malmedy, cold panic gripped those civilians still in Bütgenbach. Klara Kirch had worked closely with the town's Civil Affairs Detachment. But when the Americans started packing to make room for combat troops and the men asked her to come along, she refused. She simply could not bear the thought of leaving home. As refugees thanked her for allowing them to take in the warmth of her stove before moving on again, they whispered, "May God protect you from the SS!" Klara Kirch wondered what would happen to people the SS considered enemy collaborators.[40]

Refugees were still trickling through Bütgenbach on Sunday when the first shells started falling. Power lines were cut. On Monday the first buildings went up in flames. Putting out the fires was all but impossible as the water mains had been ruptured. Jittery American troops insisted on enforcing strict security measures even as civilians darted back and forth trying to safeguard each other's possessions. On Monday evening, Jakob Thomas, the town's secretary, was on his way to help at the smithy as it was burning out of control in the middle of town. He was promptly arrested for being out on the street during curfew hours.[41]

Had the 12th SS Panzer Division decided to outflank stubborn American resistance at Krinkelt-Rocherath on Sunday, it would still have found the road from Büllingen to Bütgenbach only lightly defended by small groups of stragglers. When its tanks began arriving in Büllingen late on Monday, however, crucial American reinforcements had already dug in. When Klara Kirch confided to an American officer that she was scared to death of the SS troops gathering in the neighboring town, he quickly reassured her: "Don't be afraid and stay calm, our SS is on the way." The reinforcements the officer knew were coming belonged to the 26th Infantry. Late on December 16 the regiment had started south from near Eupen where the entire division was licking its wounds after the terrible battle for the Hürtgen Forest. That division was the Big Red One, one of the most experienced in the U.S. Army. The men of the 26th Infantry had been ordered to bar the way to Bütgenbach. German and American crack troops were about to clash.[42]

On November 20 Mrs. Mertens had returned from evacuation in Malmedy to her home in Büllingen. On December 20 Germans were drinking coffee in her kitchen. She lived somewhat removed from the town, close to the manor house on the road midway between Büllingen and Bütgenbach. She pointed from her window and asked if the men she could see in the fields higher up belonged to their unit also. "Oh, no," they replied, "those are Americans." Mrs. Mertens instantly barricaded herself in the cellar. A father and his daughter who tried to flee the front line were back within minutes. They were all trapped. The battle surged back and forth for three days. Above Mrs. Mertens's head the house changed hands seven times. Each time she hurried to the well in a nearby field to draw some badly needed water, the guns remained silent. Yet each time she tried to build a fire, shells zeroed in on the smoky chimney for fear that the enemy was being afforded the luxury of warmth.[43]

A full-blown tank battle raged at Bütgenbach on December 21 and 22 as the frustrated 12th SS Panzer Division tried to force a breakthrough with all the armor it could muster. The situation was critical now, and the Americans quickly herded most of the remaining civilians into the town's convent. Americans even brought food to the citizens, as they were prohibited from leaving the convent's cellars under any circumstance. "It can't be that we will be killed here just like that!" Klara Kirch begged the town doctor who sat next to her in the basement. "If it is our fate," the Great War veteran calmly replied, "then we will have to accept it." On both days of the attack several tanks broke through, some hiding within the walls of the geriatric hospital before being picked off by bazooka teams. Fighter-bombers in search of German tanks on December 22 dropped bombs on the town, their force catapulting a cow onto the roof of the Zaun farm and killing at least one civilian. But it was artillery that pummeled the town day after day. American guns in support of the 26th Infantry fired more than ten thousand rounds on December 21 alone. During more than two weeks it was too dangerous to bury civilian dead. For lack of coffins, they were wrapped in blankets and temporarily laid to rest in the church next to the beleaguered convent. It was early January when some twenty-one casualties could finally be laid to rest in a mass grave. Almost all of them were infirm residents from the nursing home whom it had been impossible to evacuate.[44]

6 While soldiers of the 26th Infantry were refusing the 12th SS Panzer Division access to Bütgenbach, some three to four miles further west the Big Red One's 16th Infantry was beating off attacks by the 3rd Parachute Division at Waimes. The division, elite in name, was only a shadow of its former self. Virtually destroyed in Normandy, it had hastily been reconstructed by drawing heavily on the *Luftwaffe*'s support ground troops. Most of the division's officers and men were inexperienced. Many of its soldiers were no more than boys.[45]

Peeling away from the 1st SS Panzer Division's fast-moving Kampfgruppe Peiper, whose right flank they were supposed to protect, the paratroopers on Monday, December 18 were in control of Schoppen, a village roughly three miles southeast of Waimes. From Schoppen they managed to fight their way into Faymonville, the final village on the road to Waimes. Once inside the village, however, American artillery from the Elsenborn Ridge firmly pinned them down. Hard as they tried, the German soldiers never made it into Waimes. The stalemate placed Faymonville in the middle of the front line. Though its population had been evacuated on October 8, pleas from the evacuees and the fact that the village was reasonably far removed from the West Wall had made Civil Affairs agree to return all of them to their homes twelve days later. The village in December counted slightly more than six hundred people, most of them women, children, and older men. Most of the young men who during the occupation had not fled or gone into hiding were serving in the German army (some nineteen villagers wearing the uniform had already been killed; several others were missing).[46]

So unbearable became the shelling during the offensive's first week that on several occasions Faymonville's priest, Josef Breuer, begged the Germans to arrange a cease-fire to allow the inhabitants to leave. Two civilians had already been killed when, at around three or four in the morning of Saturday, December 23, a runner brought a message from a German officer. Through it, Josef Breuer learned that the Germans had tried—so they claimed—to negotiate a cease-fire with the Americans but had failed. They now expected the priest to assemble his flock at dawn and evacuate in the direction of German-held Schoppen before noon. Soldiers had been ordered to shoot any civilians moving in another direction. Josef Breuer thought the plan insane. The people would never be ready by noon. Worse, there was no cease-fire in place: the villagers would be moving targets. He flew off to the officers in the presbytery's shelter. But the Germans were in no mood to listen to the priest's arguments. "And what," Josef Breuer challenged them, "if the people refuse to go?" "Then," said the officer who had sent him the written order, "we will put five or six against the wall, and the matter is resolved."

At eleven o'clock that morning a long, weary column slogged through snow and dirt on their way to Schoppen. The day was crisp and, for the first time since the start of the offensive, frighteningly clear. American spotter planes instantly reported what were thought to be enemy troops. The column dissolved into chaos as the first shells kicked up earth and ice. When Josef Breuer ran to the German lines to beg them to radio the Americans for a firing pause, three of his flock were already dead, many more badly wounded. The Germans bluntly told the priest there was nothing they could do. Groups of terror-stricken civilians continued to filter into Schoppen throughout the day, filling every nook and cranny of its cellars. At least eight of those who left Faymonville that morning never lived to see their village again.[47]

German troops from Faymonville never managed to gain control over Waimes. Neither did they get a hold of Weywertz further to the north. But they got close enough to the village to make the few American defenders nervous. On Sunday, December 17, the 16th Infantry reinforcements had not yet arrived. In the morning sporadic enemy fire could be heard, but nothing else happened. Then, early in the afternoon, a tremendous explosion rocked the village. The roar was heard as far as Nidrum. All of Weywertz's windows were shattered. A malicious black cloud rose from fields just west of the village. A nearby farm was blown away like a house of cards; cows, a horse, a sheep were cut to pieces. Flying glass ripped into the head of a three-year-old boy. GIs rushed a blinded nine-year-old girl to a hospital in Eupen. Without a warning, American soldiers, afraid that the enemy would get a hold of it, had just blown up Weywertz's huge ammunition depot.[48]

On Monday, Big Red One infantrymen arrived just in time to dig in south of Weywertz. Hubert Küpper in the evening found himself brewing coffee for a bunch of weary combat soldiers. The GIs had entered his house just hours ago. One of the first things the veterans had done was remove the light bulbs to avoid drawing fire. A couple of hundred yards to the south, Maria Sarlette cooked potatoes until deep in the night. Dirty, disheveled Germans had invited themselves in earlier that day. One paratrooper had asked for a pair of pliers to remove a hobnail from his foot. The men were starving and an officer had asked her to prepare whatever food was available. Many soldiers never tasted the potatoes. They fell asleep were they sat.[49]

The GIs in Weywertz remained jittery for several days. Not even Doctor Hilgers, slipping in from Bütgenbach from time to time to visit patients, could move about without an American escort. GIs on Christmas Eve combed all of the village's houses in search of hidden weapons and ammunition. Several German refugees were arrested on suspicion of having cut telephone cables. At the start of the new year, Civil Affairs personnel organized a count of all people residing in Weywertz, issuing men and women official documents, and making it mandatory for all male residents aged twelve and older to have the new papers on them at all times.[50]

7 The exhausted troops of the 3rd Parachute Division never made it past the American foxholes south of Weywertz. The dugouts there were only part of a long defensive line facing south between Waimes and the Bütgenbach-Büllingen road and east where it stretched northward of the latter town. Hardened infantry and awesome firepower had made this northern shoulder impossible to crack even for the powerful Sixth Panzer Army. Ten days after the start of the offensive, Dietrich's SS panzer divisions were being siphoned off to the south to help exploit the successes of von Manteuffel's Fifth Panzer Army. The offensive's main effort, the *Schwerpunkt*, thus dramatically shifted to the center of the Bulge. The northern shoulder henceforth would be manned by second-line troops only.[51]

Artillery and, on clear days, aircraft continued to pound these troops mercilessly day and night until ground troops would finally push them out of the salient in January. Civilians trapped on the battlefield, meanwhile, had no choice but to share the fate of the German soldiers. To get at enemy supply lines, American guns not only pounded villages squarely up front, but also communities out of sight in the northern shoulder's hinterland.

Even those in the sturdiest hideouts lived in constant fear of a direct hit. On Wednesday, December 20, American artillery for the first time homed in on Eibertingen, a tiny village nearly eight miles southwest of Elsenborn. Already around three in the afternoon, a shell tore into the house of Martin Heyen. The explosion instantly killed a thirteen-year-old boy. The badly mangled grandfather Heyen died of his wounds two weeks later. In Mirfeld a direct hit on Christmas Eve killed Helene Spahn and the one-and-a-half-year-old girl she was holding in her arms; another one gutted the Zansen house, burying nineteen-year-old Marga Brülls under rubble and heavy beams. And so, by ones and twos, the total death toll stealthily climbed even in places where Americans in the autumn had taken the precaution of evacuating most civilians.[52]

Even in villages as far removed from the American batteries in Elsenborn as Ligneuville, ten miles to the southwest, artillery fire proved so devastating that German troops eventually ordered the remaining civilians to abandon their homes. At nearby Ondenval things were at least as bad. During the day Americans tore up the fields and woods surrounding the village; at night they pummeled Ondenval itself to get at soldiers seeking the relative warmth of houses. Farmers learned to take care of cattle during the briefest of morning lulls that soon were known as the Americans' *Kaffeepause*. Not a single house was spared. Fourteen shells hit the church; no less than eighteen landed on the presbytery. By some counts, ten thousand shells had exploded in and around Ondenval by the time the Americans retook the village in January.[53]

Civilians could see increasing signs of the frightful toll the constant pounding was exacting from the German troops along the northern shoulder. For a while the Germans continued to feel sufficiently self-assured to see to it that disloyal civilians received their just due. A man in Hünningen accused of sympathies for the Allies was arrested and disappeared into a concentration camp never to return. At Ligneuville—known as Engelsdorf by the Germans—a customs official who had been posted at what had been the new Nazi-German border with Belgium and who had decided to stay behind when the Americans arrived in September 1944, was swiftly taken into custody by the SS. As late as January 4 a draft dodger was arrested in Montenau and carried off by the *Feldgendarme*. Another suspected collaborator, caught halfway between Büllingen and Bütgenbach, was hung from the nearest tree.[54]

But as Allied firepower cut the sinews, the German grip inevitably weakened. Inexperienced replacements were hastily thrown into battered units of which they sometimes did not even know the names. Even in the elite Sixth Panzer Army so much of the artillery and supplies was horse-drawn that farmers became alarmed at the rate at which the animals made their winter feed dwindle. Gradually, however, even German horses came to be in short supply. In Valender, farmers and their horse-drawn wagons were commandeered to form part of a dangerous transport to fetch ammunition stacked somewhere in the Losheim Gap.[55]

Food stopped coming through in sufficient quantities to the point that even the deprived villagers took pity on the soldiers. People in Schoppen gave what milk and butter they could spare to the hungry Germans. "With the young soldiers," Anna Dollendorf noted compassionately, "we shared so to speak our last piece of bread and last drop of coffee." "Many of them had frozen limbs," Felix Fagnoul remembered of the German wounded assembled in his house in Iveldingen, southwest of Schoppen, "and all were grateful for any hot drink, any kind word." Grumpy German soldiers in Heppenbach ordered butcher Joseph Heyen to slaughter wounded cattle and supply them with enough meat at least to celebrate Christmas Eve.[56]

As they got weaker with each new day, Dietrich's troops could only dream of matching the awesome American firepower amassed at the Elsenborn Ridge. In the end the lone German replies to the incessant enemy tirade came to be irrelevant in the sound and fury of war on the northern flank. But they sufficed to shatter the lives of still more families in the Ostkantone. On Christmas Day, the Gronsfelds in Weywertz, close to Elsenborn, at last felt safe enough to come up from the cellar and eat upstairs again. Seated at the kitchen table on this ravishing day, they blinked at the sun-drenched snow. Then, out of the blue, a German shell exploded behind the neighbor's house. A fragment shot through the window. It cut deep into Elfriede Gronsfeld's neck. American medics came to her aid, but there was nothing they could do. The girl was buried on December 29. She was five years old. "What can one say to the mother?" one of the village's women mourned in her diary. "She cries and cannot understand."[57]

Chapter 2

The Peiper Breakthrough

"I saw them flee, those who had taken away the nightmare."

The Sixth Panzer Army's offensive on the northern flank of the salient was not a total failure. In the morning of Sunday, December 17, Dietrich could report to Hitler that at least one combat group had succeeded in penetrating deep behind American lines and was fast gaining momentum. Kampfgruppe Peiper was a powerful force. It was made up of about 4,000 soldiers and 130 tanks, assault guns, and self-propelled tank destroyers from the elite 1st SS Panzer Division, known also as the Leibstandarte Adolf Hitler.

Joachim Peiper, the combat group's commander, was barely twenty-nine. Yet he brought with him from the eastern front a well-known reputation for bravery and ruthlessness. The remarkable esprit de corps of his band of young and arrogant soldiers, too, had been forged in the savage Russian war. The experience on the eastern front, however, had also forced the division's veteran troops through a process of barbarization. As Omer Bartov has shown, a series of "criminal orders" had presented the soldiers in Russia "with a blank cheque for the mass killing of civilians on the slightest suspicion of resistance to the army, and often without even that."[1]

Spearhead of the formidable Sixth Panzer Army, Peiper's force was assigned what his superiors termed "the decisive role in the offensive." So rapidly was Peiper's column to rush to the Meuse and surprise the enemy that his engineers were to carry no bridge construction equipment. Yet, on the first day of the offensive, bridge repair problems, traffic jams, and the lackluster performance of the 12th Volksgrenadier and 3rd Parachute Divisions in opening the way, caused Kampfgruppe Peiper serious delays near Losheim. Late in the afternoon a frustrated Peiper ordered his column to start rolling anyway. Shoving horse-drawn artillery from the roads and taking shortcuts even when they led through minefields, his tanks finally poured into the Losheim Gap. They reached Lanzerath by midnight.[2]

In the early hours of Sunday, December 17, Peiper impatiently ordered a parachute battalion in Lanzerath to join his men. Then he unleashed the keyed-up Kampfgruppe for the final run to the Meuse. Honsfeld was the first objective. Like so many other villages in German-speaking Belgium, Honsfeld had been evacuated by the Americans early in October. Only a small number of people had been allowed to stay. Crossroads in and near the village had been shelled on and off throughout the first day. Shortly after midnight, however, a sudden silence fell. The quiet lasted almost two tense hours. It was shattered by the metallic shrieks and roaring motors of tanks. Loud orders and the particular smell of exhaust fumes told villagers that German troops were moving through.

By noon on Sunday famished SS troopers and parachutists were combing Honsfeld in search of enemy soldiers and food. Father Signon was one of the villagers the Americans had permitted to stay behind in October. The village priest had cared for several of the sick and dying. Now he was ordered to look after the SS officers who burst into the presbytery. They demanded food and coffee and told him to make sure the rooms stayed heated. Meanwhile they ransacked his house from top to bottom, seizing all of the clothing they could find. Neighbors who had sought refuge in the presbytery hastily withdrew to the basement. German threats and bellows chased them back into the windswept streets. Sleet, ruptured water mains, and tanks grinding the surface had turned Honsfeld's roads into rivers of mud. The villagers were to scrape away the slush.[3]

To Father Signon's dismay a group of SS troopers thought nothing even of making themselves at home in the sacristy of Honsfeld's thick-walled chapel. They showed not the least respect for the sacred space and tore up Mass vestments for practical purposes. Then suddenly a shell happened to hit a nearby tree. The explosion showered jagged fragments through the chapel window. The freak incident felt like divine retribution. It "killed one of the desecrators," the village priest noted with barely disguised satisfaction, "and tore off another's arm."[4]

Such losses did not, however, suffice to slow the armored task force down. Neither did Peiper's men intend to have any prisoners hold them up. Flabbergasted civilians in Honsfeld saw SS troopers kill at least a few dozen GIs who tried to surrender. They also shot several prisoners in cold blood as they marched past the German vehicles on their way to the rear. For reasons that remain unclear, the SS added two civilians to the group of American prisoners taken in Honsfeld. As the POWs reached Lanzerath further to the rear, SS soldiers led both villagers into a barn next to the café Palm. They made them face the wall; then they shot them in the back of their heads.[5]

SS troops had also reached Büllingen on Sunday morning. An elderly man with a swastika band around his arm emerged from his house. He welcomed every passing tank with a Nazi salute. Then he directed the Germans to where the enemy had stored their supplies. Peiper's men took about two hundred American prisoners in and around the town and forced them to help fuel their vehicles with captured gasoline. SS troopers finished one wounded GI with a shot in the head. Other than that they treated the POWs correctly and allowed them to make it to the rear.[6]

As soon as the Kampfgruppe had refueled, it was on its way again. Peiper's tanks rumbled into Schoppen just as people were ready to sit down for Sunday lunch. The distant thunder of heavy guns had kept villagers on edge since Saturday morning. But if anyone had thought the Germans would return, they had certainly not expected them to arrive so soon. Mrs. Düchers saw people quickly pull in a Belgian flag that fluttered from the windowsill of their house. At the village chapel, an unsuspecting Mrs. Dollendorf, on her way to her sister's to share a meal, bumped into a giant tank. The hatch swung open and an officer impudently asked her, "How does one get to the coast from here?" "If you had wanted to be at the coast," Anna Dollendorf shot back, surprised at her own boldness, "you should have done better to stay there." Then she suddenly noticed the morbid runes on the officer's black collar. In a wholly different tone, Mrs. Dollendorf hurriedly told the SS trooper how to get to Faymonville.[7]

A couple of nights later, five SS soldiers in Honsfeld called down to André Schroeder's cellar from the top of the stairs. They needed someone, they claimed, to show them the way to the Jost farm. The frightened families pressed closer together. Mr. Schroeder volunteered to lead the way. But the SS troopers had already spotted sixteen-year-old Erna Collas, a beautiful girl who had made many a boy's heart in the village beat faster. The soldiers insisted that she show them the way. Erna never made it back to the safety of the cellar. It was May when her body was discovered in a foxhole near the road to Büllingen. Seven bullets had entered the girl from the back. There was no way to tell what else the SS soldiers had done to her.[8]

2 Peiper's spearhead late on Sunday morning passed just south of Faymonville and then roared through Ondenval and Thirimont. As it continued its way west, Kampfgruppe Peiper spun into a column that would eventually stretch across fifteen miles of roads. At Thirimont it swung sharply northwest to get onto the N-23 highway via a junction at Baugnez, some two and a half miles southeast of Malmedy. When Peiper's troops approached the junction shortly after noon, they were totally unaware that the last vehicles of one of the two large columns of the 7th U.S. Armored Division had just rumbled by on the N-23 to help reinforce St. Vith, a key town in the American defense farther south.

A small convoy transporting some 140 GIs of Battery B, 285th Field Artillery Observation Battalion, trailed the armored column by just a few minutes. As the battery passed through the center of Malmedy, civilians motioned and yelled, "Boches! Boches!" They pointed in the direction the Americans were heading. The men of Battery B made nothing of it. The convoy continued its way down the N-23. It was about to clash head on with Peiper's Kampfgruppe at the Baugnez crossroads.[9]

Baugnez was a collection of no more than eight or nine houses. Peiper's troops penetrated the hamlet that Sunday to find it almost deserted. Situated far enough from the West Wall, it had not been evacuated, but most inhabitants had left for church in Malmedy. Only a handful of civilians remained to witness the carnage that was to follow. As the unsuspecting men of Battery B entered Baugnez, their column was suddenly raked with German fire. GIs rushed from their vehicles. They jumped into ditches and crawled toward crevices however small.[10]

Peter Lentz was fifteen years old and was trying to make his way back to Hepscheid, a village further east from which he had been evacuated by the Americans in October. The boy happened to be at the crossroads with his bike when firing erupted. He threw himself into a ditch with two Americans who had jumped out of a jeep. An enemy soldier, not much older than Peter, forced them out of the ditch with their hands over their heads. Without the least hesitation the German shot the GIs one after the other. As the Americans slumped back into the ditch, the SS trooper reloaded his gun to eliminate the Belgian boy. "My brother is a German soldier," Peter quickly cried out in German, "and now German soldiers want to kill me." The soldier hesitated. Then he ordered the boy to disappear from sight in the nearest farmhouse. He sauntered back to the GIs in the ditch and fired a couple of additional bursts into the bodies.[11]

Battery B never stood a chance against the Kampfgruppe. The firing ceased not long after it had begun. American survivors of the ambush slowly emerged from the ditches with their hands in the air. SS troopers robbed them of rings, watches, cigarettes, and, above all, gloves. They roughly herded together more than 130 Americans (men from Battery B as well as prisoners taken earlier) in a field a hundred yards south of the road junction and café Bodarwé. As the POWs waited, their numb hands above their heads, tanks took up position near the soggy field. Then, suddenly, the tanks' machine guns opened fire on the Americans. The field erupted into pandemonium. Some prisoners tried to run. Others burrowed into the ground. Comrades tumbled on top of them, spilling blood from gaping wounds. Men from the 3rd SS Pioneer Company moved into the field and fanned out. They finished off survivors in cold blood. Here and there they kicked a lifeless soldier in the head or groin to make sure he was dead. Then they abandoned the job and drifted away. Silence enveloped the blood-stained field like a shroud.[12]

By diving for cover, pretending to be dead, or hiding under the corpses of fellow prisoners, several Americans managed to survive the massacre, many of them badly wounded. Twenty men tried to make a run for it even before dark set in. SS troopers immediately responded with furious machine-gun fire. Twelve GIs made it as far as café Bodarwé. When the Germans saw this, they set fire to the place. American soldiers who tried to get away from the searing flames were mowed down. Mr. Pierry, a neighbor, rushed to the scene to try and put out the fire. But the SS shoved him out of the way and warned they would kill him if he continued. Of Mrs. Bodarwé, who ran the café and had witnessed much of the carnage, no one ever found a trace.[13]

Still before dark, three more GIs tried to seek refuge in a house along a dirt road behind the café. But the frightened people refused to let them in and bolted their doors. Under cover of darkness, however, more survivors began to grope their way to safety, leaving eighty-three bodies behind on and near the killing field. While trying to make their way down the hill to Malmedy, several of the escaped prisoners ran into civilians willing to offer help at the risk of their own lives. Franz and Clément Xhurdebise, their bicycles in hand, watched as two figures emerged from a dark wood near the Baugnez field. The shadows swayed on their feet. One was Ted Flechsig. He had four bullets in his back, leg, and arm. The other was George Fox, who had bad wounds in his hand and shoulder. As well as they could, the GIs quickly sketched to the brothers what had happened. Franz Xhurdebise was in great danger himself. He was a draft dodger from Malmedy who had joined the maquis and had lived hidden in the forests for years. The return of the Germans had made him flee his hometown once again. He knew what his fate would be if the SS caught him aiding the enemy. But he decided to help anyway. Franz and Clément lifted the wounded GIs onto their bikes. They decided to head for Stavelot, some seven miles west of Baugnez. It took the brothers two strenuous hours to transport the wobbly American soldiers all the way to safety.[14]

Close to nine o'clock that same evening someone knocked on the door of the Martin farm in Florihé, a hamlet just south of Malmedy. The four Martin sisters—Bertha, Ida, Marie, and Marthe—were startled when a "wild-eyed" and "blood-spattered" American staggered into their home. The women were alone with their aging father. For a moment, they did not know what to do. Then they sprang into action. They carried Lt. Virgil Lary to a chair near the kitchen stove. He had been shot in the left foot twice. They carefully cleaned the wounds, then bandaged the mangled limb. The warmth had barely revived the officer when he insisted on continuing his way to Malmedy. The women obliged. They hurriedly improvised a crutch. Shortly after midnight one of the Martin sisters and her friend, Marthe Marx, started for town with the lieutenant. They all but carried him down the slope. The women arrived at the 291st Engineer Combat Battalion, on the edge of Malmedy, two hours later. They had brought in the sole surviving officer of the Baugnez massacre, the worst crime committed against American troops during the war in Europe.[15]

On Tuesday morning, in Géromont, a cluster of modest houses barely one mile northwest of Baugnez, Anna Blaise was staring at Sgt. William Merriken. She had tears in her eyes. With the help of his comrade, Pfc. Charles Reding, the badly wounded GI had arrived at her farm on Monday night. He was fortunate to have made it that far. Though Mrs. Blaise was no doctor, it was painfully clear to her that the young American's condition was getting worse by the hour. An agitated Reding tried to tell her something, but the slender sixty-two-year-old widow did not understand a word of what he said. In desperation, the American scribbled some words on a piece of paper and handed it to her. Mrs. Blaise knew that his message needed to reach the American lines as soon as possible if his injured comrade was to live. She hurried to the neighbors and explained the problem to Mr. and Mrs. Jamar in front of their seven children. The Jamars' fifteen-year-old son volunteered to help even before she had finished her story. Emile argued that he knew a smattering of English. What was more, since he delivered newspapers in the area, he was familiar with every road and shortcut in what was now no-man's-land south of Malmedy.

The boy hid the American message in the sole of his shoe and was on his way before ten o'clock on Tuesday morning. At the foot of the hill sloping into town, the road and shoulders were strewn with brownish metallic plates. Emile picked his way through the mines with agonizing slowness. His heart was still pounding against his chest when two American soldiers popped up from behind a roadblock on the edge of Malmedy. He failed to understand their questions. Before he knew it, he was in a jeep on his way to Francorchamps. From that town he was rushed to Hockai. There, at last, Emile was able to explain his story to an officer who spoke French. He took the note from his shoe and handed it to the American. The officer smiled. He rattled off commands in English. The other GIs in the room now also smiled at Emile.

Several anxious hours later, Mrs. Blaise was beside herself with joy when she saw an American ambulance make its way down the path to her house. Emile was in it, too. In his lap he held three of the giant GI breads that tasted like cake and made Belgian mouths water. Medics placed Sergeant Merriken on a stretcher and carried him out of the house. Before they could slide the sergeant into the ambulance, Anna Blaise leaned over her patient and kissed him goodbye.[16]

3 Even while some of its troops were committing the crimes at Baugnez, Kampfgruppe Peiper's spearhead had plunged down the steep slope of the N-23 with its sights on Stavelot. Crazy stories of an enemy counteroffensive and German troops heading straight for them had kept the inhabitants of Stavelot on edge since Sunday morning. It was in the afternoon, however, that Jean-Marie Grégoire and many others realized that the wild rumors had become a brutal reality. The most painful proof of this was the American columns withdrawing through Stavelot in nervous disorder. "As I left the movie theater Le Cercle Ouvrier, close to the bridge over the Amblève," the then nine-year-old later recalled, "I saw them flee, those who had taken away the nightmare, those whom we thought invincible."[17]

The withdrawal of the Americans was the signal for many of Stavelot's inhabitants to pack their bags and leave the town behind as soon as possible. The horrible events that had taken place in the days preceding the liberation late in the summer of 1944 were all too fresh in their minds. In the vicinity of Werbomont, a couple of miles to the west, German troops and their Russian auxiliaries had killed some twenty-two men and women in reprisal for what they described as the actions of "bandits." German soldiers in the night of September 4, 1944, had executed four people, one of whom was a priest, in the woods of Stavelot, on mere suspicion of involvement with the resistance. By late afternoon on Sunday, December 17, so many inhabitants of Stavelot were joining refugees in their rush to the Meuse that American authorities decided to prohibit all civilian circulation as of six o'clock.[18]

Mr. Grégoire, Jean-Marie's father, was scared. He had been in the resistance and could not afford to fall into the hands of German troops who were bound to be more vindictive than ever. He finally managed to slip out of Stavelot right before dawn. Not long after, Jean-Marie, his four-year-old brother, and his mother were on the road to Trois-Ponts, squeezed in between the last American vehicles. They were trying to outrun Peiper's armored column with one bicycle and a single suitcase.[19]

Peiper's Kampfgruppe had already reached the heights overlooking Stavelot on Sunday evening. But the commander assumed there would be a tough fight for the crucial town, which counted some five thousand inhabitants in normal times. He decided to give his men some rest first. They had, after all, been on the road for several days with barely a halt. The attack on Stavelot was not to take place before the night was over. It was this fortunate pause that enabled the Grégoire family and others to escape Stavelot in time. The welcome delay also allowed the meager American forces remaining in town to dig in for the coming clash. Still, when dawn came on Monday, the few American defenders proved no match for the Kampfgruppe. Within hours they were falling back from the north bank of the Amblève River that cut Stavelot in two. In the chaos that followed, the Americans also failed to blow up the vital bridge. Peiper's troops were across it in a flash. Before the SS troops even had time to let their surprise success sink in, they were gaining speed on the road to Trois-Ponts.[20]

Thinking that reinforcements of the 3rd Parachute Division would soon arrive to hold Stavelot and the bridge over the Amblève, Peiper left only a small security detachment behind in the town. But the paratroopers were held up at Waimes and Faymonville to the east. Around mid-morning, instead of German comrades, experienced GIs of the 30th Infantry Division elbowed their way into town from the north. By nightfall on Monday they controlled a sizeable part of Stavelot again. The 117th Infantry fought to clear all of Stavelot north of the Amblève, the largest part of town by far, until Tuesday afternoon. The bitter fighting had dire consequences for civilians trapped in their cellars. Eighteen-year-old Henri de Backer hid in a neighbor's basement with his mother, his sister, and sixteen other people. There was little to eat and nothing to drink. Some took sips from a bottle of vinegar. Others rushed from house to house to drain the last drops from idle faucets. At regular intervals Henri slipped into a nearby building. From an overhead basin he scooped water that had been meant to flush the toilet. So jealously did he guard his find that he never even told his thirsty mother and sister about it. Others responded to hardship with exemplary selflessness. Henri watched as a young woman dashed from the cellar in a desperate attempt to find milk for a hungry baby. She got no further than ten yards before she was mowed down.[21]

Later on Tuesday, troops from the 2nd SS Panzergrenadier Regiment—a column of the 1st SS Panzer Division separate from Peiper's—launched ferocious attacks from Stavelot's south bank. They were under firm orders from the division commander to keep the route to the advance Kampfgruppe open. But the 117th Infantry held on, and later that night American engineers finally blew the bridge. The following day, the SS Panzergrenadiers, equipped with bridging material, resumed their desperate attacks from the south bank. Again, however, their efforts were to no avail. Kampfgruppe Peiper had plunged deep into enemy territory. But it was cut off now and on its own. The SS task force like a cornered animal was now to grow more vicious and unpredictable by the day.[22]

If the blind furor of battle claimed the lives of around thirty of Stavelot's inhabitants, SS troops murdered scores of civilians in and around the town in cold blood. The killings had started the moment Peiper's Kampfgruppe descended into Stavelot early on Monday. Even while the battle for the bridge over the Amblève was raging, SS men executed two women and a man in a nearby street for no apparent reason. Later that day, on two main roads leading to the bridge from the south, they put nine men against the walls of their homes and cut them down. One of the victims, Mr. Gonay, was accused of having fired at the Germans. The charge was ridiculous, for Mr. Gonay had never owned a gun.[23]

Once Peiper's column was across the bridge, it fought its way through the center of town and turned left on the main road to Trois-Ponts. An SS trooper in an armored vehicle laughed hysterically as he emptied his machine gun into the house that belonged to the Gengoux family. The fourteen-year-old son dropped to the ground. Blood gushed from his stomach. Moments later he was dead. A couple of houses farther down the road, a soldier stopped to ask Joseph Albert if he was hiding any Americans. Far ahead of their army's main body and feeling threatened all around, it was a typical question that Peiper's men would ask repeatedly in the days to come. Equally typical was that when Mr. Albert assured his interrogator there were no Americans at his place, the German shot him anyway. On the same road, closer to Trois-Ponts, SS troopers killed Mr. and Mrs. Warnier in similar circumstances.[24]

Across from the homes of the Gengoux and Albert families, some thirty neighbors were hiding in the spacious basement of the villa *Les Quartiers*. Throughout the day, burst after burst was fired into the building by passing tanks and half-tracks. Then, around three o'clock in the afternoon, Mr. Lambert saw two SS troopers walk to his home at a brisk pace. In their hands they held pistols. He calmed his frightened wife and went to open the door. The Germans shot him without saying a word. They entered the villa and asked if there were any Americans. "No one but civilians," a woman answered, "come and see for yourselves." "You never thought we would return, did you?" the SS men sniggered. "We will," they boasted, "retake Brussels and Paris." Mrs. Lambert had heard the shots, but remained unaware of her husband's fate. The Germans demanded drinks. Mrs. Lambert, helped by her daughter, brought beer and wine. One of the soldiers put his pistol on the girl's chest and demanded cognac. As Mrs. Lambert hurried to another room to get the liquor, she suddenly noticed the lifeless body of her husband through the windowpanes of a dividing door. More dead than alive, she served the Germans all the alcohol she had available. Even when the SS troopers had left, no one dared to recover the body from the doorstep for fear of drawing fire from the road. The family waited until night to drag the body inside and slam the door shut.[25]

Still on the fatal road to Trois-Ponts, SS troops commenced a veritable killing spree on Tuesday. Five irate soldiers burst into the Georgin home in mid-afternoon. They maintained that "bandits" were hiding in the house. Despite strenuous denials from the Georgin family and neighbors, the SS men ordered Louis Nicolay to follow them outside. They shot him by the edge of the road. Then they returned to the kitchen to fetch their next victim. But Mr. Georgin knew what was coming. The moment they approached the road, he tore himself loose from his captors. He heard rifles crack as he ran toward the river. He swam across, but as he pulled himself onto the far bank, a machine-gun burst nearly ripped off his right arm. Despite the wound, he got away. His arm had to be amputated several days later. Meanwhile, Mr. Georgin remained in the dark about the fate of those he had left behind. On Christmas Day, a neighbor found the bodies of Louis Nicolay, Mr. Georgin's wife, and three other people. All had been shot in the head.[26]

Five people in three different houses up and down the road to Trois-Ponts were murdered in similar fashion that Tuesday. One of them, a woman, was shot while lying in bed. The worst crime, however, took place in the Legaye home on Tuesday evening. Some twenty neighbors—mostly women and children—had found refuge in the large solid basement that belonged to Prosper Legaye, his wife, Marie, and their three daughters. An American soldier had come down the stairs around noon to make sure there were no enemy soldiers hiding. Another GI checked the cellar just after dark. He advised the civilians to keep as quiet as possible. Because Mr. Legaye's dog continued to bark, people in the cellar made the painful decision to put the animal down. Not long after, they were startled by shots fired from the floor above their heads. They heard the Germans return the fire. The skirmish lasted about an hour.

German soldiers appeared in front of the house shortly after eight o'clock. They forced a grenade into the cellar, then another. People dived for cover. Somehow the blasts wounded only Régine Grégoire, who grimaced as her fingers touched the ugly gash in her leg. People were screaming and crying. "Heraus!" the Germans bellowed through the cellar window. Her companions begged Mrs. Grégoire, who was from the East Cantons, to explain to the Germans in their own language that there were only civilians in the cellar. She did so, but the irate soldiers continued to yell, "Heraus!" Mrs. Grégoire was the first to leave the hiding place. She was accompanied by her two children. Outside, a dozen SS troopers were waiting, their patience wearing thin.

They told Mrs. Grégoire they wanted everyone out in the garden at once. She relayed the order to those still inside. One by one they filed out of the cellar. Five of them were children younger than ten years of age. Through Mrs. Grégoire, the SS made them all squat or sit against the hedge. They kept Mrs. Grégoire and her two children apart. The soldiers were convinced that civilians had fired from the house. One of the troopers was wounded. He sneered at Mrs. Grégoire and cursed her. Alarmed by their ugly mood, she assured the soldiers once again that all of these people were civilians and innocent of any wrongdoing. An SS hissed at her that the innocent would have to pay for the guilty. Two soldiers aimed their weapons. They fired long angry bursts at the people as they clung to each other. Allied authorities later discovered twenty-two entangled corpses along the hedge. On the street near the entrance to the garden lay the lonely body of a fourteen-year-old.

Mrs. Grégoire and her two children were the only ones to survive the massacre. The SS troopers kept them prisoner in a nearby cellar. They interrogated Mrs. Grégoire several times, maintaining that civilians had shot at them from the Legaye house and wounded one comrade. When the subject turned to GIs, one German boasted, "We don't take Americans prisoner, we kill them." Another SS trooper returned with the news that some of those who had been shot in the garden were still moving. He grinned and said they would soon bleed to death. American soldiers would save Mrs. Grégoire and her two children from the hands of their SS captors three days later.[27]

When Peiper learned that the Americans had taken Stavelot and cut off his Kampfgruppe from reinforcements and supplies, he immediately ordered the commander of his reconnaissance battalion to turn around and try to retake Stavelot from the west. On Tuesday the largest part of the battalion went to attack the town using the main road from Trois-Ponts. Meanwhile, a smaller detachment probed a back road hoping to sneak in behind the defenders through the hamlets of Parfondruy, Ster, and Renardmont on high ground west and northwest of Stavelot.[28]

From their cellars civilians in the western outskirts of Stavelot witnessed ferocious fighting as SS troops and men of the 117th Infantry clashed. On Tuesday afternoon, the 118th Field Artillery Battalion fired three thousand shells to help stop the Germans. Lt. Frank Warnock in the midst of battle received word that a large group of civilians appeared to be trapped in some villa or château across the railroad track. Warnock took six men and went to investigate. They found the cellar of a large house packed with between twenty and twenty-five scared women and children. One woman, however, seemed unperturbed and firmly in charge. Unfamiliar with each other's languages, she and the officer were unable to communicate. "There was no need," Lieutenant Warnock remarked admiringly. "She spoke to her people rapidly and just as rapidly we all moved back to the safety of my sector." There the officer advised her to continue to the center of town. The courageous woman thanked him, rallied her group, and hurried on to safety.[29]

Backed up by murderous artillery fire, stubborn American infantrymen refused to allow Peiper's reconnaissance battalion access to Stavelot. Without a shred of evidence, frustrated German officers and NCOs accused the civilian population of aiding and abetting the enemy. Bloodied and angered, the SS troops turned on the inhabitants in the hamlets west of Stavelot. Some of them would later claim their commanders had ordered them to "clean out" these places. Many of the soldiers who were to commit the most vicious war crimes against civilians had been thrown into battle after only a few weeks of military training and instruction. The majority of the perpetrators varied in age between sixteen and nineteen years.[30]

A group of at least one hundred SS troopers on Tuesday afternoon went on a rampage in Parfondruy. They moved through the hamlet's few streets raking the windows of every house in sight with gunfire. They kicked in doors and demanded to know of the inhabitants if there were any Americans around. Their answers mattered little. Six farms the Germans set on fire. In five different homes they shot Mr. Crismer, Mr. Desonnay, Mr. Denis, Mr. and Mrs. Georis, and Mr. Bolette and his son. Mrs. Kapchis begged to be spared as she explained that her husband served in the German army. The SS trooper shot her without listening to a word she said. As the woman's alarmed mother burst into the room, the soldier killed her, too. Then he chased the other daughter through the house, mortally wounding her. Only one other woman, Mrs. Breda, escaped and lived to tell the tale.[31]

While all this was happening, two SS men were driving about a dozen people out of the Hurlet farm and into a nearby garage. With the exception of the farmer, they were all women and children. Most of the children were between two and eight years old. One of the soldiers entered the garage and maliciously aimed his machine gun at the captives. Two desperate women approached him begging for mercy. He kicked them away. Then the SS trooper quickly fired several bursts, watching as one after the other tumbled to the ground. Their job done, the two soldiers walked away without casting another glance at the victims. Minutes later, Mrs. Hurlet disentangled herself from the corpses. Though she had been shot in the leg and shoulder, she managed to get away, taking two small children with her. She ran back to the main building to find her daughter-in-law and a servant girl dead in the kitchen of the burning house. Some time later she gathered enough courage to return to the garage to investigate. Much to her relief, she failed to find the body of her husband. She was to learn later that he had escaped with bullet wounds in the hand and foot. Meanwhile, an incredulous Mrs. Hurlet discovered that Monique Thonon, too, had survived the massacre. The two-year-old child, freezing and covered in blood, lay next to her dead mother who had been expecting to give birth to another baby in a couple of weeks.[32]

As the SS troopers continued their way through the ditches on both sides of the road to Ster, they kept their guns aimed at a group of men they forced to walk in front of them in the open road. They were hostages snatched from houses in Parfondruy. Kicking and beating them, SS troopers forced several other people in Ster to join the group. "They won't be needing them anymore, Madame," one German sardonically told a woman running after her husband and two sons with their identity cards. As the Germans led away her husband, too, Mrs. Delcour stormed into the courtyard, her one-month-old baby in her arms. One of the soldiers—he could not have been more than seventeen—coldly aimed his gun at the woman and her child. "Don't you have a mother?" Mrs. Delcour cried in anguish. The boy stared at her for a long time. Then he left. Terrorized, Mrs. Delcour grabbed a blanket and fled into the woods. She stayed there for three days and nights, melting icicles in her mouth to warm the water before giving it to her baby to drink. By the time she dared return to Ster, her child was dying from hypothermia.[33]

Ten minutes after they had left Ster, Germans and captives arrived in Renardmont. The SS rounded up more people. They ordered Mr. Desonnay to leave his house. When an old foot wound prevented him from walking fast enough, the Germans grew impatient and shot him in the kitchen. As he writhed on the floor in pain, his daughter begged the soldiers to help him. They laughed and stepped outside. Mr. Desonnay died the next day. A little farther down the road, his son and a friend were cut down trying to escape. Sylvie Leduc, a seventy-five-year-old widow, was later found shot behind her house in Renardmont. She lay next to the body of her daughter.[34]

The Germans marched their twenty-one prisoners—nineteen men and two women—to a large washhouse. It belonged to the Legrand farm but stood apart from the main building. There was a scuffle at the entrance as the scared people sensed that something terrible was about to happen. The SS used the butts of their guns to force them into the building. A man who continued to struggle was shot on the spot. A woman who tried to reason with the soldiers ended up the same way. Six or seven troopers surrounded the washhouse. In each of the building's two entrances a soldier appeared, one armed with a rifle, another with a machine gun. Both men dropped to one knee and carefully took aim at the stupefied people. Then they fired into the crowd again and again. When they were out of ammunition, one SS man drew his pistol. He picked his way through the tangled bodies. Victims who still showed signs of life, the executioner shot through the temple or head. Meanwhile, another soldier returned with branches and ferns. The Germans set fire to them. Then whistles blew and the soldiers disappeared. The flames struggled, releasing lots of smoke. The swirling clouds allowed eight wounded to escape from the building and into the nearby woods.[35]

Marcel Legrand, the thirty-five-year-old owner of the farm to which the washhouse belonged, had fled to the granary above his house the moment he had seen the German soldiers arrive with their victims. The farmer stayed out of sight until it was dark. For a long time he listened to make sure the enemy had gone. Then he climbed down the stairs to find his mother-in-law, wife, and two children dead. They had all been shot in the head. Perhaps because the German soldiers thought they had witnessed the brutal massacre in the washhouse. Perhaps simply because the soldiers had felt like it.[36]

After too many days of unbearable terror, people were delirious with joy when GIs of the 117th Infantry finally managed to push Peiper's men out of Stavelot's western rim. As she caught sight of the first Americans filing through her village, an older woman in Parfondruy stormed into her garden wailing and screaming. A medic finally had to inject her with a sedative to calm her down.[37]

The GIs were appalled by the evidence of war crime upon war crime in and around Stavelot. The story of atrocities against GIs had been quick to spread after the Baugnez massacre. Before long, it was prompting American soldiers across Europe to refuse taking SS troopers prisoner. But the sight of more than 130 innocent people executed in cold blood all over Stavelot—more than half of them women and children—left troops of the 117th Infantry infuriated. For quite some time their officers had the greatest trouble keeping the GIs from shooting prisoners who displayed the shameless skulls and runes.[38]

By Wednesday the 1st SS Panzer Division's attacks against Stavelot from the south and west had come to naught. The 117th Infantry was now firmly in control of the largest part of town, north of the Amblève. But the smaller section of Stavelot, situated on the south bank, would remain in German hands until January 13. Until then, both sides continued to engage in artillery duels from across the river. By the time the battle was over, 105 of Stavelot's 1,250 houses would be destroyed, another 115 uninhabitable, and 700 damaged.[39]

The inhabitants on the southern bank felt trapped like rats throughout those long weeks of stalemate. Out of food and water, in mortal fear of the SS, some 150 women, children, and elderly men in the German-controlled part of town finally decided to abandon the large cellars of the dairy factory they had been hiding in. Somehow they managed to ford the river, crossing it in small groups, the strongest carrying children and elderly on their backs into friendly territory. American troops on the north bank immediately subjected them to thorough security checks to prevent German infiltrators from slipping through with them. Meanwhile, the Germans forced the remaining civilians just south of the Amblève to move to the countryside west and northwest of St. Vith. They announced that those choosing to disobey the evacuation order would be considered "terrorists."[40]

Life was no less hard and dangerous in the American-held sector north of the Amblève. German shells kept everyone on edge day and night, forcing people to spend most of their time in dark and damp cellars. Though inhabitants were occasionally harassed by hard-drinking combat men, relations between the civilians and American soldiers were generally good. In some cellars GIs even took the time to introduce Belgians to what seemed one of their favorite games: bingo. On Christmas Day one of Stavelot's priests prepared to celebrate Mass on the ground floor of a badly pockmarked bank building. Word quickly spread through the grapevine. Civilians and GIs alike flocked to the service while shells intermittently rocked the street. The priest said Mass wearing woolen gloves. He continually rubbed the chalice to prevent the wine from freezing.[41]

By the end of December the Americans, too, thought it time to begin evacuating the civilians. Truck convoys were to carry between 700 and 750 people far west of the Meuse. The vehicles lined up behind houses to prevent drawing fire. From the labyrinthine cellars of the town's proud abbey, civilians rushed to the trucks in twos. In the chaos of the evacuation, however, families were brutally torn apart even as they drove away from battle. In the dark hours of Saturday morning, December 30, a truck carrying thirty-two civilians missed a turn and plunged into the Vesdre. The accident left two older men and three very young children from Stavelot dead. As late as the end of February the Belgian Red Cross was trying hard to locate Ghislaine Beauvois. The small child from Parfondruy, an official note claimed, "had disappeared in the course of the evacuation."[42]

4 While its own reconnaissance battalion and other troops of the 1st SS Panzer Division tried in vain to dislodge the 117th Infantry from Stavelot, Kampfgruppe Peiper continued its race to the Meuse without looking back. Just after eleven o'clock on Monday morning, December 18, the column's lead vehicles approached Trois-Ponts. The town was located on the juncture of the Amblève and the Salm and named for the three bridges its inhabitants had built across both rivers. Peiper knew that if his Kampfgruppe seized these bridges, moved out of the Amblève Valley and onto the highway to Werbomont and Huy, he could be at the Meuse that very night. But the Americans knew this, too, and this time they made sure that all three bridges blew up.[43]

Until December 16, forty-five children and a female staff of about half a dozen had been enjoying the perfect peace and calm of the Amblève Valley in the château of Petit-Spay. Overlooking the river just northeast of Trois-Ponts, the château served as a home for children whose parents had fallen victim to the war. In previous months they had been joined by little ones from Antwerp and Liège who had been evacuated to escape the destruction that Hitler's V1s and V2s were wreaking. Young and old alike were flabbergasted when German troops barged in on Monday morning and proceeded to claim the premises for themselves. Ignorant of the dramatic changes that had come over the Ardennes in a matter of days, a child pattered in the direction of an SS trooper, grabbed the soldier's hand, and beamed, "Bonjour, Monsieur l'Américain." The German threw a glacial stare at the fidgety staff.

The SS swarmed out and searched the château for food. They did not find much. Exhausted and irritated they asked if there were any men in the home. There was only a chaplain, the superintendent replied, but he was ill. The SS lifted the man from his bed and dragged him away. When a staff member cried that he was innocent and tried to stop them, one of the SS brandished a machine gun and yelled: "This is what your priests carry! This is what your priests do!" They took the chaplain outside, shot him, and dumped his body in the Amblève.

The Germans had barely taken possession of the château when heavy American artillery began pummeling the target. Staff and children fled to the cellars. They stayed there for thirteen days without heat or light. They threw mattresses against the cellar windows to keep the worst cold out, but explosions blew away the makeshift insulation and tore a gaping hole in one wall. Only at night could staff members slip out to empty the reeking buckets that served as toilets. On those occasions they also filled jerricans with water from a nearby stream. At one point, the staff managed to cook a thin soup from dried cabbage and peas. Some SS men, however, took perverse pleasure in spoiling it by dumping a huge clump of salt into the cauldron. The SS thought nothing either of assembling their wounded in the basement and administering first aid in full view of the children. When some of the little ones screamed at the scenes in horror, the soldiers simply snapped at them to shut up.

Peiper's men stayed at the château no more than a couple of days. Their places were taken by less aggressive Volksgrenadiers led by an elderly commander who was moved to tears when he stepped into the children's troglodyte world. As soon as he learned that they were without food, he had his men turn up with a hundred breads. By limiting meals to a bowl of water and a dry crust, the German manna allowed the colony to survive for another ten days. Even under the new regime, however, things easily spun out of control. One evening drunk soldiers stumbled into the cellar threatening to shoot some of the staff. An officer intervened just in time to prevent the worst. Finally, on the thirteenth night, two German trucks waited on a path about one and a half miles from the château. The children in a long line slid through the woods silent as ghosts. Then the Germans whisked them away to the relative safety of the château at Farnières, less than five miles south of Trois-Ponts. Although the Salesian Fathers were already burdened with the impossible task of caring for some eight hundred people who had sought refuge behind their institute's thick walls, they received the traumatized children with open arms.[44]

5 One look at his maps told Peiper that with the bridges of Trois-Ponts gone he would have to continue northwest through the Amblève Valley as far as La Gleize. There he was to swing southwest again, secure the bridge over the Amblève at Cheneux and, finally, cross the bridge over the Lienne at Hâbièmont. This loop would eventually take the Kampfgruppe back to Werbomont and onto the highway leading to Huy and the Meuse. Peiper ground his teeth as he calculated the delay the detour would cause. There was no time to lose. His men had to get going.

On the roads to La Gleize and Cheneux, civilian refugees hurried along with suitcases and bundles. They came from Trois-Ponts, from Stavelot, and from as far away as Malmedy. Many were young people who had been active in the resistance or who feared being sent to Germany as forced laborers under a new German occupation. But there were elderly on the icy roads, too, and families with children and babies. That the flight from the Ardennes stopped short of escalating into the mass exodus triggered by the German invasion in May 1940 was probably due only to the harshness of winter. In one of the American vehicles falling back to the Lienne, two soldiers shared their cabin with an exhausted elderly couple. The man and woman had begged the GIs to take them along. They were Jewish. "We lived through the Nazi occupation," they sobbed, "but we cannot stand any more."[45]

Peiper's armor came roaring through La Gleize early Monday afternoon. Just when the column plunged downhill to Cheneux and started crossing the Amblève bridge, sixteen P-47 Thunderbolts swooped down on the vehicles. In one of the rare appearances of the Allied air force in the cloudy first week of the offensive, the American pilots bombed and strafed Peiper's troops all the way back to Stavelot. The attack failed to halt the Kampfgruppe. But it wrought havoc on Cheneux's tiny community. At the village entrance the aircraft blew up a house and its two elderly inhabitants. On the bridge they strafed two women. Only the seven-year-old boy who was with them managed to survive. The villagers rushed to the cellars with the strongest vaults.[46]

As the Americans turned out to have blown up the bridge over the Lienne at Hâbièmont, the main part of the Kampfgruppe on Monday evening began retracing its steps to La Gleize. Its purpose now was to capture a bridge over the Amblève just west of the village, at Stoumont. A smaller detachment dug in at Cheneux to secure the bridge already captured. Once again the SS had been thwarted; once again they were in a foul mood. Two troopers commandeered the house of the Prince family. Had his father not been critically ill, Maurice Prince would have fled Cheneux with the other young men of his village. Now there was nothing he could do but endure the soldiers' taunts and threats. The Germans entered the kitchen, grabbed a cane, and in one big sweep wiped everything from the table. They yanked open drawers and cupboards, stuffing whatever took their fancy into their oversized pockets: money, father's favorite pipe, even Maurice's football shoes. They demanded the boy's passport and beat him with the cane, accusing him of being a "partisan." Then, suddenly, the power broke down. Maurice slipped away in the welcome dark. He hid in a hayloft until the Americans forced the Germans out later that week.[47]

On Tuesday things remained quiet in Cheneux. The 82nd U.S. Airborne Division assembled near Werbomont to help strengthen the northern shoulder and stop Peiper. Patrols of the 504th Parachute Infantry began probing in the direction of Cheneux on Wednesday. They made the atmosphere grow tense again. The SS flushed most inhabitants from their cellars and packed them in the local school. A first American attack materialized in mid-afternoon. People in the school building shivered and moaned as horrible noises bounced back and forth between walls and blackboards. The SS beat off the paratroopers. At dusk they relocated the civilians once again. This time they chased them into the village church in the company of their priest. Attack upon attack followed during the night and the long day that followed. The sounds reverberating through the church grew infernal. The noise of rifles, grenades, and flak wagons mingled with the cries of soldiers fighting man to man. Bullets shattered the church windows. People crawled over shards of glass in their haste to become invisible under pews.

The Americans were in control of most of Cheneux by the end of Thursday, but skirmishes and shelling continued until Friday night. It was Saturday when the paratroopers finally allowed the civilians to leave the church and seek refuge in neighboring villages. By that time they had spent two days and three nights in God's own fortress without food or water. Desperate with cold, people had smashed the furniture to burn some wood. Mothers had made their thirsty babies suck handkerchiefs wetted with holy water. Some of the elderly had gone insane when combat was at its worst.

Squinting against the light of day, the inhabitants of Cheneux barely recognized their village. There were ruins everywhere and houses were still smoldering. Battle had claimed the lives of two more villagers. One elderly man had been mortally wounded near his farm. Another farmer, a father of eight, was killed while trying to save his cows from a burning barn. Paratroopers had to take care of so many of their own casualties that for a while after battle they scarcely paid attention to the civilian dead in the street.[48]

6 While the battle for Cheneux raged, a bigger battle erupted a mile to the northwest, at Stoumont. Persistent rumors about a German offensive had begun to worry the people there as early as Sunday. They became scared when refugees started flowing through their streets on Monday morning. With mouths dry from fear the refugees shouted snippets of news at the inquisitive faces in Stoumont. Someone yelled that he had heard the Germans attack Stavelot that very morning. By noon many inhabitants of Stoumont were on the road themselves. They left too late. Within a few hours, one villager was dead, a victim of the fighter-bombers harassing Peiper's column near Cheneux. That evening, Peiper's men, regrouping after the setback at the Lienne near Hâbièmont, made their bivouac between La Gleize and Stoumont. They were to seize Stoumont and the Amblève bridge just beyond it before the break of dawn.[49]

GIs of the same division that was being rushed to Stavelot had poured into Stoumont on Monday. But on Tuesday morning the men of the 30th Infantry Division proved no match for the full furor of Kampfgruppe Peiper. By noon Stoumont was firmly in German hands. There were tense moments when SS troopers began dragging trapped American soldiers from their hiding places. The Germans appeared to be "in a fury of frustration." Rumors of the brutal killing of American POWs near Malmedy had already drifted as far as Stoumont. Ernest Natalis, the village's respected schoolteacher, feared for the lives of the captured GIs. Perhaps to defuse the situation, he walked up to an officer and asked for a doctor to have a look at a mortally wounded American. The officer exploded at the request, and in no time Mr. Natalis was hemmed in by snarling SS troopers. "All the people around here," snapped one of them, "are terrorists." They grabbed his hat and flung it to the ground. Mr. Natalis calmly picked it up. The enraged officer pointed a pistol at him. After much pushing and shouting, the SS troopers finally decided to leave the teacher alone. There was more important work to be done. The fate of Kampfgruppe Peiper itself was hanging in the balance.[50]

Although the 30th Division's 119th Infantry had fallen back from the village of Stoumont, the soldiers stubbornly clung to the area just west of it, including the railroad station and the crucial bridge. From this base, and with the support of the 740th Tank Battalion and units of the newly arrived 3rd Armored Division, the crack infantry prepared to counterattack the isolated SS spearhead and halt it once and for all. Peiper's men sensed that the enemy was pressing for a showdown. As troops on both sides checked their weapons, Stoumont's inhabitants took to the cellars. Most flocked to three large shelters. East of the village, some 30 people made themselves invisible in the basement of the Robinson home. Nearby, close to 150 civilians, organized around the village priest, thronged together in a building in the church's shadow. On the other side of the village at least 260 people packed the basement of the St. Edouard Sanatorium. The large four-storied brick building was home to a Catholic order. Two hundred of the people in the sturdy cellars were young girls and convalescing children in the care of two priests and a group of sisters. Forty others were evacuees from around Elsenborn who had already been guests for several weeks. Another twenty people came from the village itself.[51]

The St. Edouard Sanatorium was perched on a steep hillside from which it not only had a stunning view of the Amblève Valley, but it also looked down on the main road through Stoumont. It was clear to both sides that whoever held the imposing building would dominate the village. By noon on Tuesday it was the Germans who were firmly in control of the sanatorium. They took over the entire ground floor. Machine guns, artillery, and tanks surrounded the building. The Germans soon spoke of the place as *Der Festung St. Edouard,* or St. Edouard Fortress.[52]

SS troops snooped around in the cellars during the evening. "You have nothing to fear from us if you do not harm us," one of them assured the people. "But," he added casually, "we had to execute some people from Stavelot who fired at our troops from the windows of their houses." Such halfhearted assurances did nothing, however, to assuage the people's fears. Most Belgians were all too aware that the Germans had used the excuse of franc-tireurs to explain the horrible crimes committed in Leuven and Dinant during the Great War.[53]

Father Hanlet, the chaplain, assisted by another priest, held two Masses in quick succession in the calm of Wednesday morning. Long lines of frightened people shuffled by to receive Communion. American shells began to rock the building around noon. Bullets rattled against the walls like hail. As darkness fell the terrible noise of battle moved to the inside of the sanatorium. Firing, scuffles, and shouts resounded from rooms and halls upstairs. The refugees huddled closer together. Then, suddenly, the door to the basement burst open and the sound of fighting rolled down the stairs. "Civilians! Civilians!" the refugees shrieked. GIs crouched on the stairs, peeking down with their rifles at the ready. Pandemonium erupted. Relieved civilians cried out in joy at being liberated. They wept, laughed, sang. To calm them down Sister Superior led the crowd in reciting twelve rosaries for those fallen in battle. The Americans promised that they would evacuate all civilians as soon as daylight returned.[54]

At midnight, however, Peiper's troops counterattacked. German tanks came close enough to fire into the building through the windows. Dust and acrid smoke swirled into the basement. People dipped handkerchiefs in buckets filled with water and tied them over their mouths. SS troopers stormed into the basement. Barking with anger, they took disarmed Americans prisoner, smashed their guns, and hurled the pieces to the floor. They caught an American radio operator who was hiding behind mattresses at the far end of the basement. "We should burn everything here," an infuriated officer yelled at the trembling refugees.[55]

The following morning the Americans again launched a ferocious attack against the sanatorium, this time from three sides. The Germans returned fire with every tank and gun available. The din prevented Father Hanlet from celebrating Mass. In a corner he quickly administered Communion to a sick girl the sisters had brought to him.

In the afternoon American tanks were firing point-blank into the building. Explosion upon explosion rocked the sanatorium. The roof collapsed. Walls crumbled. Parts of the basement ceiling plunged down. People flung themselves to the floor. They begged and prayed. With tremulous voices the crowd mumbled rosary after rosary. Father Hanlet thought the time had come to give his people general absolution. He had just done so when a shell pierced a basement wall and slammed into a supporting arch. Somehow it failed to explode, but people panicked. They groped through the whirling dust in search of protection. One of the priests rushed up the stairs to beg the Germans to negotiate a cease-fire. But he was shot at and was fortunate to return to the cellar unharmed.

The fighting continued deep into the night. But with dawn came a silence so abrupt and total it was unsettling. Some brave souls returned from the ground floor with news that the Germans had gone. But the liberators were still nowhere to be seen. An artillery duel again erupted as the withdrawing Germans tried to prevent the Americans from getting near. One of the wounded GIs whom the Germans had left behind in the cellar crept up the stairs. He stuck a white flag, made from a curtain rod and towel, out of a window. Minutes later American troops were in control of the sanatorium again.[56]

As if by miracle, not one of St. Edouard's 260 refugees was seriously hurt during the two days and nights of savage battle that had razed the building. Several people were seriously ill, however, and the Americans decided to commence evacuation straightaway. The dazed people descended the steep hill in a long line. GIs carried many a child in their arms. One soldier took dry socks from his pocket and slipped them over the icy feet of a girl who had lost her shoes. At the foot of the hill jeeps rushed the elderly and the sick to Stoumont station. The others followed on foot. At the station, big trucks swallowed all of them and spat them out again at places far beyond the reach of the enemy.[57]

Civilians inside the village of Stoumont emerged from their hiding places no less dazed on Friday afternoon. Four people had been killed in the seesaw battle. Two days in a row the Americans had pounded the place mercilessly with all the guns at their disposal, including heavy 155mm artillery pieces. People in the building near the church had had almost nothing to drink since the beginning of the bombardment. Mrs. Dumont and her four children had fled their damaged house and escaped to the cellar of her in-laws. There, a dozen or more people had been forced to listen for what seemed an eternity to the moans and screams of the wounded and dying in a German aid post on the ground floor.[58]

The villagers were happy to see the GIs. But the Americans were cautious and distrustful. Trucks had driven the men from the 30th Division to the Ardennes from the front near Aachen so hurriedly that some believed they were still in Germany. They did not immediately know what to make of the civilians. Ernest Natalis rushed into the street with a bottle of wine he had kept for special occasions. The GIs joined in, but not before making Mr. Natalis take the first sip.[59]

7 As ever more American troops and armor converged to blunt the German spearhead, it became clear to Peiper's commanders that the Kampfgruppe could not hold out much longer without reinforcements and supplies. The lack of fuel, for example, was leaving Peiper's tanks practically immobilized. While the Kampfgruppe fought for its life at Stoumont, Sepp Dietrich ordered the commander of the 1st SS Panzer Division to do whatever it took to break through to Peiper. On December 21, SS troops again attacked Stavelot. They also hurled themselves against Trois-Ponts. At the same time they tried to get across the Salm River in the hamlets of Neuville and Grand-Halleux. None of these desperate attacks were successful.

It was in this atmosphere of utter frustration that enraged troops of the Leibstandarte Adolf Hitler committed still more war crimes, this time in the area immediately south of the Amblève. On December 20 and 21, for example, SS troopers who appeared to be out of control descended on the château Detilleux. They looted the place from top to bottom. Jewelry, silverware, wine, antique furniture, garden tools, even a large portrait, disappeared into trucks. All else was smashed or ripped apart. A day later, nine SS men entered a house in Refat and demanded food. Their stomachs satisfied, they forced everyone into the cellar. Three women were told to stay. The soldiers dragged them into the bedrooms and raped them.[60]

Still more crimes took place in Wanne, a tiny village nearly three miles south of Stavelot. SS troops had been in Wanne since noon on Monday, December 18. They had demanded bread, eggs, butter, and bacon at gunpoint. They had stolen anything else there was to eat, including cattle. Other than that, however, they had behaved. But on Wednesday they suddenly turned on the inhabitants. Some villagers later testified that the SS troopers had claimed civilians were giving away the position of their tanks and artillery. Was this a disingenuous way of explaining why their troops had stopped advancing? Whatever the reason, the consequences for the people of Wanne were dreadful. The Germans arrested Jean-François Counet, beat him to a bloody pulp, and then drove him to Aisomont where they shot him. They dragged Emile Henroulle, the local forester, to the church, put him against the wall, and executed him. Two other men, one of them the café owner, were taken to the priest's garden and cut down with a machine gun. The SS cornered Mr. Maréchal near his farm's stables and shot him in the head. Others shot Denise Manguette while she crossed the road on her way to what she thought was a better hiding place. Miss Manguette was a refugee from Liège. She was twenty years old. She lived another half hour before dying from her wounds.[61]

8 When the Americans moved into Stoumont on Friday, December 22, they found that Peiper, behind the screen of a rearguard force, had withdrawn his troops to the village of La Gleize the night before. It was at La Gleize, barely two miles northeast of Stoumont, that the Kampfgruppe would make its last stand.

As late as Sunday evening, December 17, the inhabitants of La Gleize had been blissfully ignorant of the juggernaut that had been heading their way since Saturday. They would have heard the rumble of battle approach from Stavelot had they not been deafened by the exuberant chatter and music at the Echo des Campagnes, the village hall. The people of La Gleize were having their long-awaited liberation ball. They were drinking and dancing to celebrate the end of the war that had at last come in September. Refugees from Stavelot, wrapped in blankets and holding small bundles, abruptly broke up the party. Smiles froze on startled faces. People rushed home. By midnight not a sound could be heard at the Echo des Campagnes.[62]

More and more refugees were pouring in from the east on Monday morning. A man on a bicycle yelled that the old castle at Stavelot was burning. Before long, young people, married men, and entire families from La Gleize were on the run, too. Some fled to isolated farms in nearby hamlets. Others joined the westbound columns. They were not allowed much of a head start. By noon, Peiper's troops, on their way to the bridge at Cheneux, had already reached the edge of La Gleize.[63]

Léon Nézer, a refugee from Stavelot, had just stopped at Roanne, a hamlet northeast of La Gleize, when SS troops overtook him. The Belgian immediately struck the Germans as suspicious. Soldiers brought him before an SS officer. The moment he had seen the Germans, Léon Nézer had thrown away all the papers he had on him regarding his involvement in the resistance. But parts of his clothing and scraps of paper in his pockets told the Germans that they had indeed laid their hands on a "partisan." They beat him up, broke four of his teeth, and prepared to hang him from the nearest tree. The SS officer continued to comb through Mr. Nézer's wallet. "What's this?" he asked abruptly, holding up a devotional picture. "It is a picture of Our Lady of Perpetual Aid," Mr. Nézer murmured, his voice catching in his throat. "My mother gave it to me when I was eight." Drawing deep breaths, the officer, fixated, stared at the picture for a long time. Léon Nézer braced himself for more beatings from the SS because of the religious find. Suddenly, in a strange voice that spoke German first and then French, the officer told him that he was free to go. Lost in thought, the German handed Mr. Nézer his wallet back. "Go, fast!" he insisted.[64]

Eager to get to Cheneux, Peiper's tanks gunned their way through La Gleize early on Monday afternoon, killing two women and the postman. In the evening, the column rammed its way through the village once again, this time heading for Stoumont. SS troopers were now swarming all over La Gleize. Some sixty civilians had refused to leave their village or had been unable to flee. They all took to their cellars in a hurry. Fifty evacuees from Mürringen, a village in the East Cantons, joined them. All kept their heads down in the hope of escaping the ire of the SS.[65]

But the German troopers, arrogant and irascible, refused to leave the inhabitants alone. The house of Albert Michel, like so many others, had been cut off from water. That would not do, however, for the soldiers who moved into the rooms above his head. They made Mr. Michel come out of the basement and told him to make sure they would have enough water throughout their stay. Twice a day Mr. Michel was forced to climb a hill to get water at a public fountain. Twice a day he risked his life as shells continued to pockmark the area. On Wednesday an explosion blew him off his feet. Water seeped from both buckets as from a sieve. Dazed, his clothing ripped and covered in blood, he staggered to a neighbor's cellar. He hid and never returned to the SS masters at his home. The day after, Albert Devenne and his wife stumbled into an American command post in Borgoumont, just northeast of La Gleize. Haggard and out of breath, they recounted how an SS trooper had stopped Mr. Devenne on his way to his chicken coop and had coldly announced that he would be shot for spying. Somehow the frightened villager had escaped, made it to his home to get his wife, and broken out of La Gleize.[66]

By that time the Germans at La Gleize were referring to the village as *Der Kessel*, or the cauldron. As the Americans tightened the noose, the shelling increased. On Thursday morning SS troopers in search of a safer refuge for their wounded chased seventeen people from the cellar of the Dewez home. Not knowing where to hide next, the exposed civilians stumbled toward the hamlet of La Venne. There, however, SS troops brusquely cut them off and pushed them back. In a panic the refugees hurried from hamlet to hamlet, but each time were driven back. Trapped, and mad with fear, they fell back to the village again. Several houses were ablaze. A German officer finally rushed the desolate people to the church.[67]

The church was being converted into a first-aid station. At dark the building rapidly filled with wounded SS men and American prisoners evacuated from Stoumont. The injured were white as chalk and moaned and cried. Straw on the floor soaked up the blood. Soldiers died before the eyes of the villagers who crept into a corner afraid to move. On the other side of the thick church wall a German tank blasted away at regular intervals. The civilians prayed with their priest that they might live for just a few more hours; they did not hope for more. An SS soldier from Nuremberg who spoke French brought the villagers some coffee. He also gently put down a bucket with water so that they would have something to drink during the long night ahead.[68]

If the night with its eerie flashes and deep rumble was nerve-racking, the day that followed proved to be devastating. By noon on Friday punishing concentrations of American artillery fire were reducing La Gleize to rubble. Phosphorus shells set house upon house on fire. Explosions hammered the village hour after hour. Ignoring the large red-cross flag the Germans had hung from the church, shells tore into the spire and roof. Dust and stone rained down from the ceiling. The giant bells came crashing down with an earsplitting noise. The helpless wounded screamed. The villagers inside the church had had enough. They fled the crumbling refuge and drifted to the school. But SS troops in nearby trenches again chased them away. Darkness had fallen. Clinging to the walls, the villagers slowly made their way to a stable. Thunderous shelling continued throughout the night. Men leaned against the stable door to prevent it from being blown off its hinges. At dawn the wanderers again abandoned their shelter. Crouching in ditches and behind hedges, ever fearful of mines, they finally sneaked their way to the American lines. Inexplicably, all those who had been driven from their cellar on Thursday survived the two-day ordeal without serious harm. Seven other villagers, however, perished in the battle. A man and a boy later died of illnesses contracted in damp and drafty hideaways.[69]

On Saturday night Peiper ordered all those of his Kampfgruppe who were still able to walk to pull out of the cauldron. They were to try to reach the German lines further east. For the better part of a week the armored SS fist had sowed fear in the ranks of Allied soldiers and civilians alike. Peiper had started out with 4,000 troops who had later been joined by some 1,800 reinforcements. Now the remnants of his once cocky combat group numbered barely 800 men. On their way out of La Gleize they ordered two farmers to accompany them as guides. Under cover of darkness the weary civilians led the SS troopers to a small wooden bridge across the Amblève. As soon as dawn came the once haughty soldiers sneaked out of sight and hid in the woods. Peiper told the two Belgians to go home.[70]

9 Kampfgruppe Peiper had at last been stopped. It had taken the combined effort of units belonging to the 30th Infantry, 3rd Armored, and 82nd Airborne Divisions to do so. Together these three American outfits extended westward the defensive shoulder of the 1st, 2nd, and 99th Infantry Divisions that had stonewalled the rest of Dietrich's Sixth Panzer Army not far from its jump-off line. As at Elsenborn, heavy concentrations of American firepower played a vital role in the western part of the shoulder. One such artillery base had coalesced around Chevron, a village of no more than eight hundred people. With Stoumont and La Gleize situated, respectively, four and six miles to the northeast, airborne artillery as well as heavy 155mm batteries had quickly dug in on Chevron's high north-south ridge. Eagle-eyed radio operators in the church tower continually scanned the east.[71]

Chevron also served as the nerve center of the 82nd Airborne Division. Headquarter units and military police joined the cannoneers in the village. Because German agents were rumored to have been dropped from the skies north of the salient, the Americans decided on radical measures to prevent them from infiltrating the civilian population. The day after Christmas all of Chevron's male inhabitants between the ages of sixteen and sixty were loaded onto American trucks and driven to the rear. "The Germans were phobia-stricken by terrorists," observed Mr. Jamar, the village's seventy-eight-year-old notary, "the Americans have a phobia for German paratroopers." Many other villagers, fearful that the Germans might take over Chevron despite the many American reinforcements, left their houses voluntarily. Paratroopers swiftly claimed the abandoned houses for themselves.[72]

The SS troops never made it to Chevron. Instead, the agony of war for the remaining villagers was in the earsplitting furor of the American artillery that seemed never to stop. Heavy guns were as close to Mr. Jamar's house as fifty-five yards. On December 21, when they had been aiming for Stoumont, they had shattered the doors and windows. When they had directed their full wrath toward La Gleize two days later, the noise had been so horrendous it had made Yvonne, Mr. Jamar's daughter, burst into tears. On Christmas Day and the day after, the batteries trained massive firepower on German troops threatening the positions at Chevron from the south following the collapse of defenses at St. Vith. Bright flashes lit the rooms night after night and hour after hour. The angry salvos made the house tremble. The maddening noise finally drove a shell-shocked Yvonne Jamar into the closet where the old clothes were kept.[73]

The guns pounded the ears and frayed the nerves, but they also blasted the fear from people's hearts. Once the crisis of the Christmas days had passed, the inhabitants of Chevron never again worried about a German breakthrough near their village. They felt safe behind the steel wall of artillery. Those suffering a second German occupation had their faith in the Americans thoroughly shaken. But people in Chevron, like other witnesses of the buildup on the edges of the Bulge, knew that the Germans were heading for defeat. Not only did the Americans have too much artillery, they had too much of everything. On December 31 Mr. Jamar noted in his diary: "When seeing these American soldiers, the huge trucks, the enormous tanks, the large number of little jeeps driving at high speed, all these vehicles loaded with food, ammunition, equipment of all kinds . . . one can only be astounded, thinking that all this has come from America, across the sea on big ships!"[74]

Though most communication had to take place by means of sign language, relations between the rearguard troops and the remaining civilians were generally excellent. With most men gone, paratroopers volunteered to milk the cows and even made sure to carry some of it to people in the cellars. As rural Chevron had not yet been connected to any waterworks, GIs also helped take cattle to the watering troughs. The aged Mr. Jamar watched with approval how a GI urged a woman to hand over her yoke and its two buckets and then went to get water for her at the public fountain. It was, Mr. Jamar was pleased to note in his diary, "a little idyllic scene in the midst of the agony of war."[75]

For people who had not eaten well for four years, however, it was the mountains of food piling up in the American rear that impressed them most. While GIs in foxholes subsisted on tasteless rations and civilians inside the Bulge went hungry, rearguard troops in Chevron spoiled civilians with the amounts and the kinds of food they had almost forgotten existed. Mr. Jamar studded his diary with inventories and descriptions of American gifts of food to his family: ham, tomatoes, bacon, applesauce, chicken, lemon juice, turkey, rice, biscuits, jam, peaches, white bread, syrup, porridge, "mixed fruits from Africa," candy, coffee. "Truly," the notary wrote on the last day of 1944, "I talk now more often of eating than of the war."[76]

10 Had they been able to read the diary entry being written in Chevron that day, Mr. Jamar's comment would have struck the inhabitants of Malmedy, a town some fifteen miles northeast of the village, as highly ironic and painful. For it was exactly in the last days of 1944 that more suffering had came upon them than any they had experienced in four years of war.

At the outbreak of the German offensive it looked as if Malmedy would fall prey to enemy troops. Shells began to hit the town in the morning hours of Saturday, December 16. They killed thirteen civilians and three GIs in no time, leaving many more injured. Charles Hilgers, a twelve-year-old refugee from Wirtzfeld, witnessed one of many horrible scenes. A teenage girl lay in the street in a puddle of blood. She gazed at her severed legs. Charles knew the girl. He would remember for the rest of his life the red laced boots she had been wearing that day. In the afternoon more explosions echoed from the heights north of town: jittery American troops were blowing up ammunition and fuel depots. Civilians hastily removed Belgian flags from their houses. On Sunday Dietrich's troops were hammering the area east of Malmedy while Peiper's men were advancing along roads just south of the town. Withdrawing American troops poured through Malmedy all day long. The town's U.S. Civil Affairs unit was also given the order to pull out. Local Belgian administrators quickly followed suit. So did the local section of the Belgian Red Cross, which allowed only one doctor, Cécile Van Ackere, a female volunteer, to remain behind.[77]

The sight of military and civilian authorities abandoning them caused the population to panic. "Civilians joined the exodus with bicycles, pushcarts, wheelbarrows, baby carriages, anything in which to transport a few pitiful belongings." Malmedy was a fair-sized town of some 5,300 people. Complicating matters, some 6,000 refugees lived in the area, most of them in the care of American authorities. Almost half their number had found shelter in the town itself. The majority were evacuees from Belgian communities close to the West Wall. Some 400 were German displaced persons. That almost all of these people spoke the enemy's language did nothing to calm the nervous atmosphere. Some civilians actually thought it safer to leave town in columns protected by armed policemen. They feared reprisals on their way out from townspeople who had remained loyal to Germany in this largely French-speaking part of the East Cantons. To solve congestion and increase security the Americans finally halted all civilian circulation on Sunday afternoon. By that time, however, close to 4,000 inhabitants and evacuees had already fled from the town.[78]

Malmedy's remaining inhabitants were fortunate that Peiper's Kampfgruppe was interested in the Meuse and not in their beloved town. Dietrich's other troops, meanwhile, never made it to Malmedy. It was not for want of trying, however. On December 21, as part of Dietrich's order to break through to Peiper, the 150th Panzer Brigade launched a frontal assault on Malmedy in the hope of gaining control over vital roads leading to the Kampfgruppe. But by that time, the town, like Stavelot, had been reinforced with infantry from the 30th Division. The German attack petered out that same day, never to be followed by another. Enemy artillery fire did, however, continue to harass Malmedy day after day. Five hundred civilians sought refuge in a large cave dug into a hillside; two hundred people thronged together in the caves of the old town abbey; hundreds of others flocked to the solid cellars of the town's tanneries, factories, and main stores. There they lived in abominable conditions as American authorities and an ad hoc civilian government struggled to get sufficient quantities of water and food to the subterranean refugees.[79]

Yet, despite all that, GIs and civilians were generally optimistic after the failed attack of December 21. Malmedy had been shown to be firmly in the hands of the Americans on the ground. Moreover, as the skies began to clear, the air appeared to belong to the Allies for as far as the eye could see. On Saturday, December 23, the people of Malmedy stretched their necks to have a better view of the giant bomber formations that sliced through the sky on their way east. For the people in Chevron the aircraft were just another comforting show of force. For the inhabitants of Malmedy they were the beginning of a nightmare that would last three days.[80]

That Saturday more than six hundred medium bombers of the Ninth U.S. Air Force were heading for German bridges, crossroads, and railheads near the base of the Bulge to disrupt enemy supply lines. Zülpich was the target of twenty-eight B-26 "Marauders" of the 322nd Bomber Group. They had taken off from a base in France at 1:20 P.M. On their course to the target the bombers were to pass just south of Eupen, some fifteen miles north of Malmedy. But cloud formations and German antiaircraft batteries soon threw the formation into disarray and off course. At 3:25 P.M. only six B-26s were still heading for what their crews thought to be Zülpich or a town east of it. At 3:26 P.M. the pilots were over their target and dropped eighty-six bombs weighing 250 pounds each. The bombs whistled their way not to Zülpich but to American-held Malmedy.

At 3:27 P.M. GIs and civilians, who moments earlier had been admiring the mighty Allied machines, were sucked into a vortex of unimaginable destruction. Within seconds the center of town was obliterated. Fires raged out of control. Soldiers and civilians did not know where to begin offering help. Americans rushed to display large identification panels on the highest buildings and in the hills above the town. Over radio and phone they frantically signaled higher authorities that a tragic mistake had been made.[81]

With water mains ruptured, pumps frozen, and the fire brigade not equipped to deal with a crisis of such magnitude, fires were still burning the next day. Search teams dragged ever more bodies from under the rubble. American bulldozers cleared streets to allow ambulances to get through. While the desperate rescue operations continued in Malmedy that afternoon, the first of two thousand Allied heavy bombers from England reached the continent over Ostend, Belgium. Eighteen American B-24 "Liberators" headed straight for the stricken Malmedy. At 2:30 P.M. they released a bomb load almost four times as destructive as that of the day before.[82]

Even today there is no clear explanation for the second bombing error. To the people in Malmedy that Sunday afternoon the explanation did not matter. The only thing they could think of was to get away from what felt like a volcanic eruption in the middle of town. Dust and debris mushroomed high into the sky. Rapidly spreading fires engulfed entire blocks. Many never made it out of the cauldron. Joseph Marly, nine years old, was playing football with some friends when he heard the planes. His grandfather and mother plucked him from the street and rushed him to the cellar. They were on the stairs when a bomb exploded. The cellar went black. Only the burning sensation in his leg caused Joseph to come to again. A stove had turned over and red-hot coals were burning his flesh. His upper body was covered by a mattress, which had probably saved his life. Many others in his cellar had been less fortunate. His mother and sister were wounded. His grandfather, grandmother, aunt, and six-year-old brother were dead. Another of his aunts died after the Americans transported her to a hospital in Verviers.[83]

In the basement of the town abbey, Maria Blaise, two years older than Joseph, survived an ordeal that was no less frightening. She was an orphan of a kind. Her mother had died when she was eight. Her father had been forced into the German army. A woman from Düsseldorf was looking after her. At two o'clock in the afternoon, Ferdinand Hilgers, one of the town's priests, dropped by to console people and offer the crowd general absolution. Many older people wept. A half an hour later the earth suddenly rumbled. The lights went out. The walls trembled. The ceiling shook and caved in. The burners in the boiler room exploded. People gasped for air. They stumbled over suitcases and folding beds. Just as she thought she would suffocate, Maria grabbed the jacket of a passing man. He towed her behind him all the way to the coal chute. A frantic hand pulled her into the light and fresh air. At least forty corpses stayed behind in the dark.[84]

Smoke was still rising from Malmedy on Christmas Day. American engineers had fought throughout the night to tame the blaze. They had been able to reign in some of the runaway fires only by dynamiting and bulldozing houses into firebreaks. It was no longer possible to count the corpses. The morgues were full. Frozen bodies were piled up at the cemetery. Many others were laid out on stretchers and under blankets in school playgrounds. As some semblance of organization returned to Malmedy early in the afternoon, three groups of medium bombers belonging to the Ninth Air Force took off from a base near Paris. Their orders were to obliterate the road center of St. Vith and the Germans who had just captured it. Four B-26s drifted off course as a result of faulty instruments. They mistook Malmedy for St. Vith. Convinced that the smoke over the town was that from damage in St. Vith caused by planes that had preceded them, they dropped another sixty-four bombs, of 250 pounds each, right on target. As the dust over Malmedy settled once again late in the afternoon, incredulous soldiers and civilians returned to the rubble. Like automatons they resumed the digging.[85]

The bombardments of Malmedy were not the only cases of fratricide that occurred during the Battle of the Bulge. Allied planes also mistakenly bombed Verviers and the railroad yards at Arlon in their efforts to rupture German supply lines, causing military and civilian casualties in both towns. But the fate of Malmedy was by far the worst. Thirty-seven American soldiers were killed and close to one hundred were injured. A total of 225 civilians lost their lives in the three successive bombardments. Most of them were older people, women, and children. More than 140 victims were from Malmedy, the others were refugees. Many of the refugees had been evacuated from Belgian villages near the West Wall, and others had escaped from war-ravaged German cities like Aachen, Bonn, and Düsseldorf. But all of them had fled one danger only to perish in another. Much of the town was reduced to a mass of rubble. According to some estimates, nearly half of Malmedy's 1,160 houses had been destroyed or made uninhabitable. American military authorities, the Belgian Red Cross, and the National Work for Children tried to supply as many people as possible with food, clothing, and shelter. They failed to cope, however, especially with German artillery continuing to wreak havoc. On December 28 American trucks began evacuating large numbers of people to neighboring villages and refugee centers in the interior.[86]

The destruction that aircraft released over Malmedy was never meant to separate combatants from noncombatants, let alone make a distinction between nationalities. The explosives took the lives of American soldiers, Belgian civilians, and German refugees with equal greed. For those thrown together in the cauldron, the bombers were the only enemy. Count de Kerchove of the Belgian Red Cross in a letter to the mayor of Malmedy on April 18, 1945, pleaded in favor of Mrs. Sacha Epp. Mrs. Epp was thirty years old and German. She had lost her parents and had arrived in Malmedy as a refugee in October 1944. She volunteered as a nurse straightaway. During the bombardments and in the weeks that followed she worked day and night with de Kerchove's Belgian team to save lives. Now Belgian authorities insisted that she, like all other German refugees, return to her own country. Before leaving Malmedy himself, de Kerchove begged the mayor to intervene on Mrs. Epp's behalf and "to let her stay here, in this good town that she loves the way we love it." "She deserves it," the count wrote emphatically, "she has been perfect and is perfect . . . I cannot give her better praise." Sacha Epp never left Malmedy again.[87]

Chapter 3

Closing in on St. Vith

"If we have to die, we might as well stay here."

If the Sixth Panzer Army constituted the Schwerpunkt in Hitler's sweeping counteroffensive, the Fifth Panzer Army on Sepp Dietrich's left was to offer vital support for the main effort. Half of its eight divisions were panzer outfits; some of them—like the *Panzer Lehr* and *Windhund*—were veteran divisions of great renown. The man who was to take armor and infantry across the Meuse near Namur, past the Belgian capital of Brussels, and all the way to the Scheldt River that fed the Antwerp harbor, was a general of even greater fame. Hasso Eccard von Manteuffel was born into one of the oldest noble families of Prussia. Although a professional soldier, he was so small and fragile-looking that his friends nicknamed him *Kleiner*, or "Little One." As commander of the elite panzer division *Grossdeutschland*, on the eastern front, he had so impressed the Führer that he was called to Germany and promoted not to corps commander but to leader of the entire Fifth Panzer Army.[1]

Since all SS troops for the offensive were entrusted to Dietrich, von Manteuffel's army consisted entirely of Wehrmacht troops. The Fifth Panzer Army was made up of three separate corps, each of which was to operate in a clearly delineated corridor of advance. The 66th Corps was assigned the northern swath of von Manteuffel's sector. Its commander, Gen. Walter Lucht, was under orders to capture the key road and railroad center of St. Vith, one of the main towns in Belgium's East Cantons. The 66th Corps was nonetheless one of von Manteuffel's weakest. It was made up of only two divisions, both of them infantry. Except for assault guns and tank destroyers, the corps lacked armor. It was also quite weak on artillery.[2]

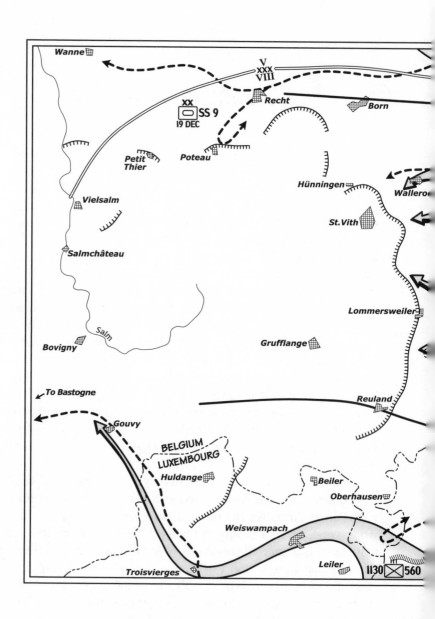

Wanne

V XXX VIII

XX SS 9 19 DEC

Recht

Born

Poteau

Petit Thier

Hünningen

Walleroe

Vielsalm

St. Vith

Salmchâteau

Salm

Lommersweiler

Bovigny

Grufflange

To Bastogne

Reuland

Gouvy

BELGIUM
LUXEMBOURG

Huldange

Beiler

Oberhausen

Weiswampach

Troisvierges

Leiler

1130 ⊠ 560

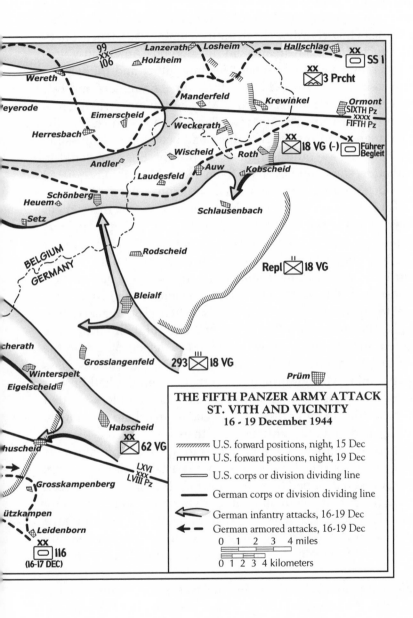

THE FIFTH PANZER ARMY ATTACK
ST. VITH AND VICINITY
16 - 19 December 1944

🟆🟆🟆🟆🟆🟆	U.S. forward positions, night, 15 Dec
🏚🏚🏚🏚🏚🏚	U.S. forward positions, night, 19 Dec
▭▭▭▭▭	U.S. corps or division dividing line
▬▬▬▬▬	German corps or division dividing line
◁══	German infantry attacks, 16-19 Dec
◀━ ━	German armored attacks, 16-19 Dec

```
0   1   2   3   4 miles
0 1 2 3 4 kilometers
```

1 The Hoffmann family slept in fits and starts during the early morning hours of December 16. Their farm lay on the outskirts of Weckerath, a village in the southern folds of the Losheim Gap, just inside the Belgian border. The irritating rumble of distant artillery fire kept puncturing their dreams. So did nervous American voices and the moaning sounds of vehicles rushing hither and thither. Mr. Hoffmann tossed and worried about their three daughters and two foster children sleeping under his roof. Mrs. Hoffmann's waking moments went to her sons. Johann and Klemens had been sent to the front in German uniforms. Both of them had been reported missing: one in Normandy, the other on the eastern front. She wondered if, against all odds, she would ever see them again. Then things quieted down outside and the Hoffmanns at last sank into a deep sleep.

Dawn at Weckerath broke with the usual slowness on this somber winter day. When it came at last, it brought cruel tidings. Villagers were banding together in the street. The rumor was that German forces under the cover of darkness had broken through the thin lines of the American 14th Cavalry. Some claimed that the Germans had already pushed past their village. Mr. Hoffmann, a veteran of the Great War, was about to dismiss the news as ludicrous when a shot cracked over their heads. The Hoffmanns fled to the first floor of their farmhouse. They peered through the window but failed to detect soldiers in the village or the surrounding fields. Then, suddenly, the window glass was blown to bits. Mrs. Hoffmann cried that something had hit her. She collapsed onto the floor. Catharina, one of her daughters, spotted a few GIs crouching in the garden and begged them to help her mother. But they signaled that the Germans were there and took off.

Less than an hour later German troops in white camouflage suits and a hodgepodge of vehicles were streaming past the Hoffmann farm. A military surgeon dropped by in the evening. The German had been told in the village that a civilian in an outlying farm had been badly wounded. He quickly bandaged Mrs. Hoffmann's wound and gave her a tetanus shot. Then he, too, moved on. He left behind a family with no electricity or water and a mother with a bullet in her chest.[3]

The soldiers responsible for shattering the lives of the Hoffmanns that Saturday morning belonged to the 18th Volksgrenadier Division, an outfit created from a Luftwaffe field division. They had no time to contemplate the fate of civilians in their path. Their orders were to make contact as soon as possible with the rest of the division that was swinging around the Schnee Eifel from the south. They were to meet up in the village of Schönberg, close off the escape route from the plateau, and seal the fate of the bulk of the 106th Division that was dug in on its heights. To do that, they first had to capture Andler, a village straddling the Weckerath-Schönberg road that dutifully followed the Our, a small but swift river.

American troops delayed the Germans just long enough to afford people in Andler time to weigh their options. However, agitated refugees from villages just to the east quickly made the decision for them. They claimed the Germans intended to round up all men and women more than eighteen years old as laborers. Andler had all but emptied of its inhabitants by mid-afternoon, but they were too late to outrun the Germans. Jakob Peterges and another couple of men from the village got as far as Valender, some five miles northeast of Andler. On Sunday when they pushed off for Malmedy they learned that SS troops were already in control of the roads south of the town. Not knowing what to do next, the men slowly drifted back to where they had come from. Haggard refugees from Herresbach warned them, however, that battle, meanwhile, had already spread to Andler. Again the men retraced their steps. They lingered forlornly in villages near Amel for the rest of the day. It was in Amel that German tanks overtook them even before Sunday had come to an end.

Jakob Peterges returned to Andler on Monday to find his farm transformed into a military barrack. All the agricultural tools that he had made sure to place under roofs in autumn had been dragged away and dumped in the surrounding fields. They had made room for scores of enemy horses. And nothing much remained of the farmer's carefully stored hay and oats. Large heaps of it had been scattered in front of the animals and between their sore hoofs. A large shell crater made the road in front of his farm impassable. A handful of troops from the 1st SS Panzer Division, who had crossed into the Fifth Panzer Army's sector on their way west, impatiently motioned Mr. Peterges to the gaping hole. They wanted to build a corduroy road around it with his firewood and told the farmer to help them search the surrounding farms for pickaxes and shovels. Mr. Peterges said he did not think such a road would hold. He also pointed out that he was not the village mayor and that they were perfectly capable of searching the farms by themselves. Enraged by the farmer's cheek, an SS officer pulled his pistol. "Beat it," he roared, "or I'll shoot you, you damned frontier brat." Mr. Peterges took to his heels as fast as he could. He watched from a safe distance as the SS troopers hauled wagonload after wagonload of firewood and building materials from his farm and dumped them into the hole thwarting their advance.[4]

While the stray SS in Andler stooped to road construction, troops of the 18th Volksgrenadier Division were busy strengthening their hold on Schönberg. The village that blocked the escape of two of the 106th Division's regiments from the Schnee Eifel and sent two roads into the heart of St. Vith had fallen into German hands on Sunday. As people recovered from the German artillery bombardment and the house-to-house battle that had followed it, a soldier showed up on the doorstep of Schönberg's presbytery. He told Maria Schmitz, the housekeeper, that he was a chaplain. Miss Schmitz eyed him with suspicion. The embarrassed German produced some papers confirming his religious function in the Wehrmacht. He claimed he had lost his Mass equipment. He admitted to having scrounged certain articles from bombed-out churches, but said he was still looking for a chalice to celebrate Mass with the troops. Maria did not know how to help. Americans had rushed Father Schumacher, the village priest, to safety just hours before the Germans captured the village. He had taken the chalice and consecrated wafers with him. Then she remembered the American officer who had stood on her doorstep two weeks earlier. He had not asked for a chalice, but had presented her with one. He had taken it from one of his soldiers who had owned up to stealing it from a church in the German town of Bleialf, not far from the West Wall. The officer had wanted a priest to have it. Maria went back inside and returned with the chalice. Because it had been taken from a German church anyway, she was convinced the American would not have objected to a German priest having it. Not even one in enemy uniform.[5]

The Americans had not only abandoned Schönberg, they had also failed to demolish the village's critical bridge. Long columns of German infantry and vehicles were soon pouring across the Our, capturing village after village. On Monday Father Koob thought it time to return to the presbytery in Atzerath. He noticed that among the German vehicles rumbling through the hamlet were some mechanized guns but even more horse-drawn artillery, bicycles, and pushcarts. "So what do you think of our offensive?" an officer asked. The priest wanted to know if he could speak freely. The officer nodded. "I have seen the Germans during the retreat and I have just seen the equipment they are taking into battle," Father Koob said. "I have also seen the tremendous war materiel of the Americans. I wonder what it is you want to accomplish." Yet, ill-equipped as the 18th Volksgrenadier Division was, the few American troops remaining between the Our and St. Vith were no match for them. Within forty-eight hours of the start of the surprise counteroffensive, less than five miles remained between the Germans and the key road center in the northern part of von Manteuffel's sector. More than seven thousand American soldiers of the 106th Division and supporting units were cut off on the Schnee Eifel east of the Our. Most of them would surrender within days, the worst defeat for the Americans during the war in Europe. No more than a thin screen of anxious and disoriented GIs remained between the river and St. Vith. They hurriedly withdrew to St. Vith where a defensive perimeter was gradually taking shape.[6]

In Wallerode, a village less than two miles northeast of St. Vith, those inhabitants who, after agonizing deliberation, had decided not to leave, were tracking the German offensive with their ears. On Saturday morning they had woken up to the booming of guns in the east. Now, on Sunday, they listened as the fracas of battle spread through the Our Valley southeast of them. Fifteen-year-old Josef Theissen had hardly had time to digest the events of the past two days. For him and his friends the three months since the liberation of September had been the most exhilarating of their lives. First the Germans had beaten a retreat on horses and bicycles; then the Americans had hummed through the village with column after column of modern motorized vehicles. In their wake had followed Belgian resistance fighters bent on revenge. They had broken into the homes of collaborators who had packed their bags and left with the Germans. Beds, mattresses, and furniture had been dumped into the streets. The villagers had breathed a sigh of relief when after a few days they finally moved on.

As calm settled over Wallerode again, the village boys had forged friendly relations with many GIs. Josef himself had found a buddy in a soldier from Maine who served as the village translator. The wealth of the Americans had astounded the teenagers. From a distance, ammunition boxes stacked in fields looked like houses. Troops received so much gasoline that they could afford to use it in burners for heating their tents. GIs had literally given away armloads of cigarettes and cigars. So much discarded clothing did the boys receive that they were sporting even GI underwear. And then, on Saturday, December

16, without the least warning, the happy bubble had burst. The Americans had disappeared so fast, his friend from Maine with them, that Josef could have sworn the alien creatures from overseas had existed only in his imagination.

The weary soldiers in gray who arrived on Sunday evening seemed much more real to war. Josef had no way of knowing that the Germans belonged to the 18th Volksgrenadier Division's Mobile Battalion. Neither could he know that von Manteuffel himself had ordered them away from the main road through Schönberg and Setz and onto the open ground around Wallerode so that they would have more room to maneuver for the final assault against St. Vith. But Josef could not ignore the grim *Nebelwerfer* battery beside his house, its multiple barrels pointing southwest.[7]

The 18th Volksgrenadier Division had closed up for the decisive blow against St. Vith. In Meyerode, a village two and a half miles northeast of Wallerode, a distressed Father Leuffen on Monday, December 18, added a brief entry to the parish chronicle. "Yesterday," he scribbled nervously, "the Americans withdrew to St. Vith from the West Wall. Now the villages around St. Vith will be turned into battlefields. What will happen to us?"[8]

2 While American troops at St. Vith were bracing themselves for a blow from the 18th Volksgrenadier Division from Wallerode and the Schönberg road, the first serious penetration of the town's defenses materialized not in the east but the northwest. And the challenge was posed not by Wehrmacht infantry but by a combat group belonging to the 1st SS Panzer Division. Having extricated itself from the Losheim Gap somewhat later than Peiper's column, the 1st SS Panzergrenadier Regiment formed the southern column of the Leibstandarte Adolf Hitler. For its drive to the Meuse, military planners had assigned it a route through Recht and Vielsalm. The route ran north of St. Vith but at Recht bent southwest into von Manteuffel's zone of advance and straight toward Poteau and Vielsalm. The SS troops had their eyes on the Meuse, not St. Vith. But the Americans had no way of knowing that. Moreover, whatever the designs of the Kampfgruppe were, if the Germans got a hold of Vielsalm they would block the major road that vital reinforcements were using to reach St. Vith. The 106th Division's headquarters in St. Vith ordered American troops near Recht and Poteau to halt the SS battering ram at all costs.[9]

Civilians in the villages northwest of St. Vith were to share the cost of hard military logic. Like so many other communities in the East Cantons, Born, a village some three miles east of Recht, had been forced to make terrible sacrifices for the privilege of annexation by Nazi Germany. In four years of war almost all of its able-bodied men had been gobbled up by the German army. More than thirty men on the eve of the counteroffensive were reported missing or killed in action, almost all of them at the eastern front. As the Americans withdrew from Born on Sunday morning, December 17, rumor had it that the Germans would impress into the *Volkssturm* every remaining man and boy capable of holding a weapon. By Sunday afternoon panicked refugees from Born were streaming toward Recht in droves.[10]

The alarmist rumors being spread by refugees from as far away as Schönberg caused many of Recht's inhabitants to join the exodus. They arrived in Poteau, a village astride the St. Vith–Vielsalm road, to find "a traffic jam of epic proportions." While columns of the 7th Armored Division were creeping toward St. Vith to help defend it, many more American vehicles were desperately trying to get away from the town. To complicate matters further, the 7th Armored Division's reserve, together with some smaller units, was hurriedly organizing a defense of the Poteau crossroads against the Kampfgruppe heading its way. Around six in the evening the Americans refused to let more refugees into Poteau. Those who had already made it into the village settled down for the night. Some families were offering hospitality to as many as seventy people in a single home.[11]

SS troops arrived in Recht at dusk on Sunday. A small group of American defenders in the village fought throughout the night in an attempt to delay the Germans. Some of the civilians who had refused to flee earlier that day now withdrew to the nearby slate quarries that had lain abandoned since the Great War. The old pits were cold and drafty, and water seeped from ceilings and walls. Such horrid conditions were nonetheless preferable to what was happening in the village itself. Duels between American tanks and German assault guns gutted most of the houses. Tracer fire ignited haylofts, setting ablaze at least two farms. All of the cattle driven from the smoking Mettlen farm were cut down by shell fire. Two SS troopers who approached the house of the Lorch family in search of something to drink were fired at by American machine gunners in a jeep. One German was killed; the other was badly wounded and lost consciousness. Comrades who rushed to the scene thought the shots had come from the house and held the inhabitants responsible. The Lorch family was able to breathe a sigh of relief only when the wounded soldier finally came to and explained what had really happened.[12]

It was the fate of border people to suffer the distrust of combatants on both sides. "This was old Germany or new Belgium," a sergeant of the 7th Armored Division wrote to his wife about his stay at a farmhouse not far from Recht. "These people were German. On the walls were pictures of husbands, brothers, and sons all in the uniform of the German army." "It was fear more than hospitality," he claimed, "that caused them to bring out bread, jam, and jellies and to sit up all night making coffee for us." Even while the American sergeant was writing these words, Mrs. Müsch and Miss Lejeune were standing up to an SS lieutenant in an embattled Recht. The officer had warned them in no uncertain terms to care only for the wounded men under his command. But the two women insisted that the POWs in their house deserved equal treatment. With calm determination they continued to serve coffee and sandwiches to both Germans and GIs.[13]

Recht fell to the SS before dawn on Monday. The Kampfgruppe pushed on to Poteau, a village on the border between the German-speaking and French-speaking parts of Belgium, and the major obstacle that remained on the road to Vielsalm. The Germans clashed with Poteau's American defenders as early as seven o'clock in the morning. The seesaw battle that followed was vicious. Most houses were thoroughly devastated. Burnt cattle stampeded from smoking farms.

Though many civilians had fled, scores of inhabitants and refugees remained behind. Ten villagers rushed to seek refuge in a solid stable that ended up holding more than thirty refugees from the East Cantons. There were some cows in the stable, but not enough to give milk to everyone. The children were hungry and thirsty. Three youngsters—two sisters and their brother—decided to take a risk: they would race to the farm opposite the stable and return with more milk. Just as they crossed the road, a shell exploded. Only when they reached the farm did the boy notice he was bleeding. Shrapnel had pierced his leather vest and gone through the wallet in his upper left pocket. People searched in vain for a surgeon among American and German combatants. By the time the Americans were in control of Poteau again and able to rush the victim to the rear it was too late. When GIs who had tried to save the boy at Petit-Thier learned later that day that he had died from internal bleeding, they gathered around his corpse. Some said their rosary; others cried.[14]

Few of the SS troopers escaped from Poteau. One wounded soldier, who claimed he had been forced into the SS, fled into Joseph Hugo's house. He changed into civilian clothes and hid among the refugees. When American troops regained the upper hand, the refugees were more than happy to deliver the SS trooper into their care. As soon as the GIs uncovered the SS tattoo on his arm, however, they clammed up and turned icy toward the civilian population. Only on Thursday had their distrust dissipated sufficiently for them to allow the civilians to leave the ruined village.[15]

The Americans had retaken Poteau. But two miles to the northeast German troops remained master of Recht. Barely two days after they had captured the village, the Feldgendarme arrived. They wanted to know where Willy Lejeune was. The twenty-three-year-old inhabitant of Recht had deserted from the Wehrmacht some time before. He was one of many German-speaking Belgians who had done so during the course of the war. After the defeat at Stalingrad in particular, increasing numbers of soldiers on leave in the East Cantons had gone into hiding at home or fled across the new border with Belgium where they had often joined the resistance. The German occupiers had treated their parents vindictively. They had subjected them to random searches, impounded their radios, and taken away their rationing cards. Willy Lejeune was in Recht when the Germans launched their counteroffensive, but he had refused to believe alarmist stories of their return. When at last he tried to sneak away to Poteau on Sunday night, he realized that he had become trapped. The Feldgendarme first took to grilling one of Recht's aldermen, warning him that it was his duty to hand over traitors like Lejeune. Then they marched to the slate quarries. Thanks to warnings from the villagers, Willy Lejeune had disappeared by the time they arrived. The Germans did, however, find his mother in the subterranean shelter. They subjected her to a harsh interrogation on the matter of her "poorly raised sons." But the aggrieved mother assured the men that she did not know where Willy was. And when she pointed out that her two other sons were doing their duty as Wehrmacht soldiers even as they were speaking, the interrogators relaxed their tone. Recht had received its first taste of the new occupation.[16]

3 Meanwhile, another threat to St. Vith had been building southeast of the town. The 62nd Volksgrenadier Division in the early hours of December 16 launched its attack south of the Schnee

Eifel, in support of the 18th Volksgrenadier Division's southern jab around the plateau. The division fought its way into the sector of the 424th Infantry, the only one of the 106th Division's three regiments to escape the German noose around the Schnee Eifel. If the men of the 424th Infantry were inexperienced, so were the Volksgrenadiers of the 62nd Division. Virtually destroyed on the eastern front, the division had been hastily rebuilt, in part by filling it with Czech and Polish conscripts who knew little or no German. Still, the American regiment stood little chance against an entire division. By the sheer weight of their numbers, the Volksgrenadiers deftly rolled the 424th Infantry back across the Our River. GIs blew half the span of the critical Our bridge at the Belgian frontier village of Steinebrück in the early afternoon of December 18. Later that day, a combat force of the 9th Armored Division, which had been rushed to the area to help plug the gap, was ordered to fall back from low ground along the river to a hill chain overlooking the main road connecting Steinebrück with St. Vith.[17]

Lommersweiler, about a mile west of Steinebrück, had remained untouched by the war in September 1944. Not a single bullet, bomb, or shell had disturbed the sleepy village's peace at the time of its liberation. Afterward, however, ever more heavy artillery had begun to build up on the high ground surrounding it. Over a period of three months Lommersweiler's inhabitants had learned to live with American batteries in their backs and German soldiers observing them from positions in the east no more than five miles away.

Weaker than elsewhere at the front, the artillery of the German 66th Corps had startled people in Lommersweiler on the morning of December 16 while doing little if any damage to their village. For their part, the Americans had responded to the challenge with furious barrages that made the village tremble. Although American batteries kept spewing fire the following day, the cracks and rattle of small-arms fire blowing in from Steinebrück became more and more pronounced. On Monday morning American artillery pieces were being withdrawn from their positions. The troops of the 9th Armored Division that returned from the Our hastily built a new defensive line just in front of Lommersweiler. That same day German shell fire damaged the church and several of the village's buildings.[18]

As the situation in Lommersweiler deteriorated on Monday, Gendarme Schreiber feared for his own safety and that of the men under his command. The Germans could be trusted to regard German-speaking gendarmes in Belgian uniforms as traitors, even more so because many gendarmes were known to have been recruited from the ranks of the resistance. Schreiber hurried to St. Vith for instructions. There he was flabbergasted to learn that all the gendarmes in the town had fled. An American officer informed him that the Germans could capture Lommersweiler at any moment and strongly advised against going back. But Schreiber knew he had to. The gendarmes in Lommersweiler were his responsibility, and he was determined not to let them fall into German hands.

Schreiber raced back to Lommersweiler and hurriedly organized the evacuation of his men. As soon as the name lists and other sensitive documents were hidden, the gendarmes took to their bikes. Sticking to the main road from Steinebrück, they pedaled the three and a half miles to St. Vith as fast as their legs allowed. After no more than a mile, one of the gendarmes was stopped by a flat tire. One of the many American vehicles zooming by stopped and picked him up. Some time later, Schreiber and his men passed a jeep at an American command post. On the hood sat their colleague. He looked dejected and was being guarded by a grim-faced GI who was holding a gun. Schreiber screeched to a halt and asked what had happened. The gendarme timidly told his commander he had fled to the woods when explosions had halted the vehicle that had picked him up earlier. Soon afterward he had run into MPs who had arrested him on the spot. His explanation in an English that was heavy with a German accent had made him look even more suspicious. Unfamiliar with the dark-blue uniform of the Belgian gendarmes, the MPs had mistaken it for the black outfit of an SS trooper. Schreiber knew it was not the first time this had happened. In no time he cleared the matter with the American officer in charge. The gendarmes found their hapless colleague a new bicycle and this time made it to St. Vith together. From St. Vith the exodus finally took the gendarmes all the way to Spa, where officials from all over the East Cantons were finding a safe haven.[19]

There were few if any safe havens, however, for civilians trapped in villages in the front line. Schreiber and his colleagues fled Lommersweiler shortly after noon on Monday. German soldiers captured the village on Tuesday night. The following morning Volksgrenadiers and civilians alike were pilfering the rich stocks of food that the GIs had left behind. By dusk American shells from batteries close to St. Vith were finding their way into the village. They wrecked house after house, pummeled the church with a vengeance, and drove the remaining inhabitants underground.[20]

With the Americans gone from the heights near Lommersweiler, troops of the 62nd Volksgrenadier Division continued their push along the Steinebrück–St. Vith road. On Wednesday, December 20, Anna Meyer was alarmed by the sudden silence that had come over Breitfeld. She grabbed her nine-month-old son and ran to her parents' house as fast as she could. Then, accompanied by her sister, she quickly returned to her own place to get warmer clothes. A vehicle dashed by on the road. It was German. Americans opened fire on it from a nearby house. German soldiers dragged a badly wounded comrade from the riddled vehicle and into a building. The din of battle echoed through the streets with increasing ferocity. But all Mrs. Meyer could think of was her son. Determined to make it back to the baby, she grabbed a white piece of clothing and she and her sister frantically waved the fabric over their heads like a flag of surrender. Breitfeld, the last obstacle on the road to St. Vith from the southeast, had fallen to the enemy.[21]

4 The defensive line taking shape in front of St. Vith stretched as far as Burg Reuland, some three miles southwest of Lommersweiler. The small farming community was made up of a handful of villages and hamlets that were hemmed into that corner of the East Cantons where the borders of Belgium, Luxembourg, and Germany meet. With utmost greed the war had reached into this corner, too. Most of the men in Burg Reuland by the end of 1944 were either boys or older men. Though some of the young men had volunteered to serve in the German army, most had not been given a choice. More than one hundred of Burg Reuland's men had been killed or gone missing wearing the German uniform. A handful had become casualties in France after D-Day; the others had been devoured on the eastern front. Some of Burg Reuland's people had resisted the hard-handed tactics of the Nazi regime. They, too, had been brusquely torn from their community, some never to return. Twenty-nine-year-old Michael Pick from Ouren had died in a concentration camp in 1943. The Gestapo in Lascheid had transported Peter and Johann Thelen to Germany as political prisoners. They were still alive when the Americans liberated their homeland, but they died in Dachau before the war was over.[22]

Although half the village of Auel near the Our River burned to the ground when German troops briefly resisted the American advance, on September 12, 1944, troops of the 28th Infantry Division captured the rest of Burg Reuland without much of a battle. At the end of the month the GIs from the 28th Division left Burg Reuland for positions nearer the West Wall. Their place was taken by the 174th and 402nd Field Artillery Groups and a number of other artillery units. The fresh American faces told the civilians they were to stay until spring. They aligned their batteries and built dugouts. Then they stocked coal, ammunition, and food for the long Eifel winter to come. The staff of the 174th Artillery installed their command post in a school in Lascheid. Reuland became the home of a large recreational center, complete with bar, bowling alley, and badminton facility. American Red Cross girls served coffee and doughnuts at the center, films were shown at least once a week, and occasionally even live shows could be enjoyed. Conditions in Burg Reuland resembled garrison life more than war that autumn in 1944. The contented artillerymen soon were referring to the area as "Sweet Valley."[23]

Youngsters flocked to the American installations in Sweet Valley like bees to honey. In stark contrast with the Germans, the GIs were refreshingly informal and talkative. They insisted on being called by their first names, wore their uniforms in a casual, sometimes even sloppy, manner, and appeared remarkably laid-back in whatever they were doing. If the GIs' optimism and can-do mentality were infectious, their army's wealth had an equally reassuring effect on youngsters who for four years had known nothing but want. Life remained hard for many in Burg Reuland. Those who had become dependent on pensions and other benefits paid by German authorities had not drawn a pfennig since the arrival of the Americans. Evacuees from all over had further swelled the ranks of the needy. Even farmers who were self-supporting had not seen items such as coffee, chocolate, or soap for many years. Children became the natural conduit for a brisk trade in various goods. They supplied the GIs with dark bread, eggs, and vegetables as well as the much sought after Nazi souvenirs. The GIs in turn sent the children home with bags filled with canned goods and other treats. Some youngsters became so familiar with the Americans that they accompanied them to the army dining halls, ogling the mounds of hot food awaiting them at the end of the line.[24]

Cella Kaut of Bracht was no longer a youngster; she was a thirty-one-year-old housewife with a baby daughter and a husband, who was at the eastern front. But she, too, had come to like the GIs. "The young artillerymen were," she noted, "with the exception of a few, generally good guys." Her father was no less enamored with them. It had all begun when a GI had struck up a conversation with Mr. Kaut in the very dialect of the Eifel. The flabbergasted farmer had learned that the GI's parents had emigrated to the United States from the region and had continued to speak the dialect in their home overseas ever since. From that moment on, Mr. Kaut, whose own son, Edmund, had gone missing near the Russian city of Smolensk in 1943, had given the GI and his comrades preferential treatment, at one time even supplying them with a wagonload of straw to make their dugouts more comfortable. The Americans returned the favors in any way they could, helping with, among other things, feeding the cattle. One day the soldiers made space for Cella and her father in a nearby barn where a movie was being shown. It was a story of love, separation, and faithfulness. When the movie was done, the GIs played some music and asked Mr. Kaut's daughter to dance. Halfway through one of the songs, Cella hid her face in her hands and burst into tears. The nostalgic melody had brought back memories of her husband and brother and all that the war had taken from her. The soldiers understood and let her cry. She felt much better afterward.[25]

In November the white GIs in Bracht were replaced by black soldiers who belonged to a battery of the 402nd Field Artillery Group. Few if any of the villagers had ever seen a black person in the flesh. Moreover, when the Allied troops had been closing in on Germany, Aryan propaganda had made sure to paint a picture of black American soldiers as drunks, rapists, and murderers of children. But Cella had gotten along so well with the Americans before them that she was determined not to let color spoil relations now. Taking along her two cousins, she walked up to the newcomers to introduce herself. The women said their names and tried to make conversation. The soldiers seemed surprised at the visit and ill at ease. Cella asked if any of them perhaps spoke some French. A young sergeant stepped forward and said he did. He spoke it well. That broke the ice. The black GIs did not allow the women to go home before they had looked at the tattered family photographs being pulled out from dozens of worn wallets. Bracht's black Americans quickly acquired the reputation of being even more generous than their white countrymen. Before long, people from all over the village came to trade with them, receiving anything from a pair of shoes to a woolen blanket for a chicken or a dozen eggs. Within weeks Cella was familiar even with the names of the wives and children of many of her black neighbors.[26]

Cella Kaut had the scare of her life later that month. In an unguarded moment her one-year-old daughter pulled a kettle of hot soup from the fire spilling some of it on her face. The child screamed horribly. In the panic that followed no one knew what to do. Someone daubed the skin with oil. Someone else dusted the blisters with flour. But the child continued to writhe with pain and finally refused to have anyone come near her. Desperate, Cella ran outside crying that her baby had burned herself. A GI rushed up to her and yelled something into a walkie-talkie. Minutes later a vehicle screeched to a halt at Cella's home. An artilleryman hurried inside to find a neighbor beside the suffering child; she was on her knees praying. The African-American soldier resolutely walked up to the child and picked her up. Then he began mumbling strange words to her that nobody understood. The girl instantly stopped crying. The soldier took her face into his hands and forced her to look straight into his eyes. The girl laughed, waved her arms, and held on to him. He told Cella to wash the girl's face with water and leave her alone. The child made a quick and full recovery. Cella afterward always wondered if the black soldier had possessed some kind of supernatural powers. Whatever the case, for the rest of the war her daughter was to trust blacks in uniform more than whites.[27]

Still, despite generally good relations, American troops could not afford an unconditional trust in the people who lived but a stone's throw away from the hated enemy, shared the enemy's language, and had sons serving in the enemy's army. When in Steffeshausen, for example, several fires broke out in a matter of days, killing one soldier, American authorities immediately suspected the civilians of arson, though the investigation later showed GI carelessness to be the cause. The fear of German infiltrators, such as the Gestapo Frontläufer, further complicated relations. Worried counterintelligence officers had civilian radio equipment smashed in Bracht, for example, and in several places in Burg Reuland arrested German spies disguised as refugees.[28]

The atmosphere in the border area was made more uncertain by treacherous shell fire that the enemy spasmodically brought down on American positions. Shells continued to be lobbed into Auel and Steffeshausen along the Our River at a rate of six to eight every three days. On November 15 they mauled three civilians. On November 21 they wounded two GIs and killed one in the local school. Two weeks later shrapnel snuffed out the life of a farmer in Reuland who was hauling fertilizer. A woman wounded in the village that same day died in an American hospital several months later.[29]

The American batteries in Burg Reuland, meanwhile, blasted the German positions with increasing fury. Windows in the villages were blown to bits and doors were shaken from their hinges. Plaster fell from walls and ceilings. Tiles slid from the roofs. Animals in their stables went wild with fear. People took to their cellars. They were told not to shut windows and doors and during each salvo to keep their mouths wide open. Even then people bled from their ears as the hellish blasts ruptured their eardrums.[30]

On the morning of Saturday, December 16, German artillery suddenly barked back at the Americans in Burg Reuland with inexplicable ferocity. Father Jakob Nols in Steffeshausen registered the incoming shells from the warmth of his bed. By six he had already counted around one hundred explosions, twenty of them near Steffeshausen. The next one was so close it sent hot, jagged shards straight through the bedroom's window and blackout curtains. Father Nols was up and about in the cold in no time.[31]

The American batteries responded to the challenge with even more fury. The 965th Field Artillery Battalion alone on December 16 fired more than a thousand shells at the Germans. Within hours, however, it was clear to the people of Burg Reuland that what was taking place was not just an intensified artillery duel. To their astonishment the Americans, with whom they had prepared to sit through the winter in expectation of a spring of peace, began withdrawing. And the withdrawal was not a scripted one, but a nervous, chaotic affair. Impatient American columns on Sunday were blocking Burg Reuland's streets from the direction of the West Wall. Artillery piece after artillery piece was being removed from the surrounding fields and squeezed into the traffic jams crawling toward Beho and St. Vith. Before pulling out of Auel, Americans set fire to heaps of documents in the garden next to their command post. Children in Lascheid stood on the sidewalks forlornly as the artillery troops they had known for so long ebbed west through the main street. "Don't worry!" a sergeant tried to reassure them. "We'll be back in a month!" The children said nothing.[32]

German artillery fire tapered off on Saturday but flared up again amidst the chaos of the American withdrawal on Sunday. Shortly after Mass, an explosion rocked the house of Hubert Maraite in Reuland. Shrapnel killed Elisabeth Hecker, a young woman expecting her first child. She was not a villager but a German refugee from a West Wall town. She had thought she would be safe in Reuland while her husband was risking his life at the eastern front. Rumors were now circulating of a major German offensive. But nobody seemed to know exactly what was going on, least of all the civilians. An American chaplain in Steffeshausen told Father Nols that the Germans had broken through and stood at less than three miles from the village. A lieutenant categorically dismissed this report as false and insisted the Germans had been beaten back. Yet the following morning the inhabitants awoke to find that the Americans had disappeared from Steffeshausen. They had taken with them four of the village's families who had proudly displayed the Belgian flag during the American occupation.[33]

More and more civilians joined the columns heading west. Almost all of Auel's inhabitants packed their bags, piling wagons high with belongings and taking even cattle with them on the road. In Lascheid a large group of men gathered to discuss a plan of action. Only when the artillerymen began to pull out of the village, however, did they at last decide to leave, too. In their hurry they grabbed nothing but food and identity cards. Few of the men knew French, but someone had thought of taking a Belgian flag to prove their loyalty to the Allied cause should the need arise. Others in the group objected to this, however, fearing that the German spearheads might overtake them soon. The flag was discarded. By the time they reached the Meuse, the German-speaking Belgians had been challenged by MPs over and over again and subjected to many harsh interrogations.[34]

GIs of the 424th Infantry who had fallen back from the Our River on Tuesday dug in along a line running straight through Burg Reuland. They now stood shoulder to shoulder with troops of the 9th Armored Division on their left. Together with the 28th Division's 112th Infantry on their right they formed the southernmost barrier defending St. Vith. Their respite would be brief. German troops were ferrying troops and assault guns across the Our as fast as they could. GIs in their foxholes hunkered down for the final assault on St. Vith. The people remaining in their cellars in Burg Reuland did the same.

5 St. Vith, a town with a population of some 2,800, had escaped most of the ravages of war during the Allied advance following the breakout in Normandy. The worst damage had been done on August 9, 1944, when bombers attacked the town's railroad station, destroying many buildings, including the St. Vithus Church, and killing fifteen people. By the early morning of September 13, only small groups of SS troopers continued to cling to St. Vith. Some drank er-

satz coffee in Mr. Feiten's kitchen while it was still dark. Then they, too, disappeared. Just hours later tanks pushed their way into St. Vith. Peter Feiten emerged from his cellar to have a look. American soldiers crouched in his garden, their rifles at the ready. An anxious Mr. Feiten showed himself with his arms in the air. "Zivil! Zivil!" he kept saying. One of the GIs turned to him and said, "Coffee? Coffee?" Mr. Feiten did not understand. The GI repeated the words. Suddenly Peter Feiten knew. "Kaffee!" he exclaimed. He signaled that he had understood and rushed to the kitchen. He returned with a cup of the coffee he had brewed earlier that morning for the SS. The GI emptied the cup and placed it on the windowsill. Then he and his comrades were gone. The town had been captured from the Germans with barely a shot.[35]

St. Vith had been a divided city before the war. Half the population had remained pro-German, some of whom had turned Nazi; the other half had embraced Belgium as their home, some even more so after the Nazis took control of the old fatherland. Years of German occupation had deepened the divisions into chasms. Those who had actively collaborated with the Nazi regime had not waited for the Allies to arrive. They had packed their bags early in September and joined convoys heading to the Reich behind the West Wall. In the wake of the American troops followed townspeople who had been refugees for years. Some had fled St. Vith because they had served as Belgian functionaries before the war, others because they had refused to serve in the German army. In particular, many of the latter had joined the resistance in Belgium and now returned as guides and liaison agents for the American troops. St. Vith's American Civil Affairs unit promptly rewarded many of them with posts in the town's administration or swore them in as policemen and gendarmes.[36]

If the resistance could not help being overbearing and at times even vengeful, relations between the inhabitants and the GIs in the town's loaded atmosphere remained "half friendly, half sullen." In stark contrast with other Belgian towns, the German-speaking people in St. Vith had not been out in the streets cheering the Americans as liberators. GIs inevitably remained ill at ease in a place that had baptized one of its avenues "Adolf-Hitler Strasse" and in which enemy billboards on the edge of town had assured it was *eine deutsche Stadt* (a German town). The inhabitants on their part never entirely surrendered to the disarming generosity and naive charm of the GIs. School did not resume for a long time, and children hung around the soldiers all day hoping for more candy. The Americans also bought loads of goodwill from the men with packs of Chesterfields and Camels. But when one of the town's girls accepted an invitation from a tank crew to take a ride through town, people whistled their disapproval when she reemerged from the turret some time later. They thought it most inappropriate for women to flirt with Americans while some of the town's men were still fighting them in the front line.[37]

Quite a few soldiers from St. Vith who had been given furloughs to visit their homes not long before the Americans arrived had changed into civilian clothing and failed to return to their German units. With almost one hundred of the town's men killed wearing the German uniform, most of them at the eastern front, these soldiers refused to risk their lives any longer in a war that appeared all but lost. Knowing that the measures would prove unpopular, American counterintelligence rounded up these deserters and early in October shipped most of them to a POW camp near Cherbourg. It was just one of many thorny issues facing American occupation forces in this border town. St. Vith also remained home, for example, to many *Reichsdeutsche*. Some had lived there since the annexation by Nazi Germany and had decided to stay behind. Others had arrived more recently as refugees from German towns and villages in the front line along the West Wall. They, too, were considered security risks. American authorities made them report to the police station every day and wear special armbands to set them apart from the local population. To complicate the matter of German-speaking Belgians and Reichsdeutsche, many Ukrainians lived in St. Vith. They had been brought to the area by German authorities to help on farms as forced laborers. The arrival of the Americans had set them free and on occasion tension between the former laborers and their onetime employers flared up. To keep things under control, American authorities imposed a curfew after dark during which only civilians with special responsibilities—interpreters, physicians, priests—could move about with official permits.[38]

Though the peace the Allies brought to St. Vith was at times uneasy, it was peace nonetheless. Whatever their nationality or political beliefs, the inhabitants had grown sick of years of war. Therefore, they were astonished when early on December 16 loud explosions shattered three months of fragile security in a matter of minutes. People failed to grasp what was happening right away. Some civilians at first thought the noise was caused by outgoing American shells. A flabbergasted mayor hurriedly quizzed the town's officials about the causes of the detonations. They had no clue either. An alderman was dispatched to the American Civil Affairs detachment. Had the Germans launched an attack? The Americans said they were not sure yet. But, they promised, if that proved to be the case, the population could count on being informed at the earliest time possible.[39]

The people of St. Vith never needed an official American confirmation to tell them that the Germans had gone over to the offensive from behind the West Wall. Nervous American convoys withdrawing through the town's streets had already told them that much early on Saturday. Panicky refugees who began to pour in from the east later that day quickly confirmed the picture. From one moment to the next the atmosphere in St. Vith turned grim. Many civilians began packing their bags. Resistance fighters and deserters alike feared for their lives. Those who had refused to obey the Nazi evacuation orders at the time of the Allied advance also feared reprisals. Young people were determined not to fall into the hands of the Germans as laborers or soldiers. But others in St. Vith were cheered by the prospect of renewed German rule. They sensed that revenge was imminent and were "quite obviously delighted." The Americans responded with increased suspicion. Staff of the 106th Infantry Division had stayed at Margret Doepgen's house in the Klosterstrasse since their outfit had replaced the 2nd Infantry Division on December 13. They had been courteous and kind and had spoiled Mrs. Doepgen and her mother with food and her two small children with toys. Now they suddenly turned cold and aloof. They took the maps from the living room walls and packed without saying a word. Even when prodded by Mrs. Doepgen about what was going on, the GIs remained silent.[40]

At four o'clock on Sunday morning two American officers and a Belgian gendarme woke up policeman Willy Genten. They wanted him to report to the Civil Affairs detachment as soon as possible. An hour later Willy Genten was making the rounds of St. Vith as town crier accompanied by two GIs. A big bell in one hand and American orders in the other, the policeman loudly proclaimed that a curfew was to go into effect immediately, that there would be no church services that day, and that even showing oneself at the window was prohibited. These were in part security precautions, but they were also measures intended to prevent a chaotic exodus and resulting traffic jams. The measures failed abysmally. Retreating military convoys swelled St. Vith's streets from the east. Meanwhile, American reinforcements tried to edge their way into town from the other side. A combat command of the 9th Armored Division managed to reach St. Vith as day broke. Snipers in civilian clothing took potshots at the column from a house near St. Joseph Kloster. American infantrymen stormed the building taking no prisoners. In the early afternoon the American Civil Affairs detachment decided the time had come to abandon St. Vith and leave it to the combat troops. The town's mayor, policemen, and gendarmes disappeared with them. Civil Affairs personnel made sure to take some families with them, too, especially those whose members had worked for Allied authorities. The Americans gave Günther Schütz and his family five minutes to grab some belongings and join them. The Schütz family left St. Vith without saying goodbye to the neighbors and without a chance to inform the grandfather of their hasty escape. Many other townspeople fled St. Vith that day, with or without American help. At dusk the first vehicles of the long-awaited 7th Armored Division entered the town to help defend it. Together soldiers and civilians created what one military historian has called "one of the most stifling traffic jams to beset the U.S. Army during the course of the war in Europe."[41]

Maria Heinen was just one of many civilians whose fate became entangled in the chaos on St. Vith's roads. She heard the town crier proclaim the curfew loud and clear that morning. But she was determined not to lose her husband to the German army at this late stage of the war, after he had escaped military service for more than four years. With heavy hearts she and her husband bundled up Heinz and Gerd, their two sons aged three and two. They placed the children and a few bags on their bicycles and pushed off in the direction of Ligneuville, northwest of St. Vith. They had covered barely a mile in the biting cold when GIs told them the Germans had already captured Ligneuville. It was dark when they finally reached Poteau after several miles of dirt trails through gloomy forests. A farmer was kind enough to offer the Heinen family a room. Maria undressed the boys and put them to bed. Early in the morning shells came crashing down all over Poteau. The 1st SS Panzergrenadier Regiment had launched its attack. There was no time for the Heinen family to get to their bikes. Mrs. Heinen grabbed her bags and the children's shoes and threw them in a wagon with refugees waiting for the horse to be hitched. She ran back to the bedroom and dressed the children as fast as she could. When she stepped outside again with the boys in her arms, the wagon was gone. Shells whistling over their heads, Mrs. Heinen and her husband fled to the woods. They convinced a refugee with a badly sprained ankle to let them have her little cart. In it Mrs. Heinen placed her two children. She promised to undertake a pilgrimage to Lourdes if they survived this. Then she and her husband were on the road again. On Tuesday morning they left Lierneux to get even farther away from the Germans. A GI on his way to the front gave Mrs. Heinen his woolen blanket. She used it to keep the shoeless children warm. Days later the Heinen family crossed the Meuse at Huy. Blind fear had made them outrun even the fastest German panzers.[42]

Many others in St. Vith had stayed behind. They either did not fear the Germans or dreaded the unprotected trek through biting cold weather more than the looming battle. "If we have to die," Mrs. Meurer's father-in-law had said, "we might as well stay here, no need to go far." Mrs. Meurer and her seventeen-year-old son, Erich, who risked induction into the German army, had decided to withdraw no farther than their cellar. By midnight of December 19 above their heads American reinforcements had formed a horseshoe-shaped defensive line around the town. It was roughly made up of armor from the 7th Armored Division on the northern flank, tanks of the 9th Armored Division facing east, and infantry of the 424th and 112th Regiments dug in looking southeast and south respectively. Only a sprinkling of miscellaneous troops extended the southern flank beyond the positions of the 112th Infantry. The opening of the U-shaped defenses gaped at the Salm River in the back of the defenders. All available American units had taken their positions on the St. Vith checkerboard. The next move was up to the Germans. St. Vith's inhabitants sat in their cellars like ghostly-white pawns—too scared to change places.[43]

Chapter 4

The Race for Bastogne

"Let's make certain not a single light can be seen."

At five thirty on Saturday morning, December 16, 554 artillery pieces and Nebelwerfers from behind the Our River all at once spewed their deadly charges into the Grand Duchy of Luxembourg. They continued to belch fire for about an hour and a half, churning some eight miles of front lines between Fischbach in the north and Wahlhousen in the south. The barrage accurately pummeled American positions from as far as six miles away. By late afternoon intrepid engineers had thrown bridges over the swollen Our River at Dasburg and Gemünd, and armor poured across in support of the Volksgrenadiers who had preceded them.[1]

These troops belonged to von Manteuffel's 47th Panzer Corps. They were to capture the Belgian town of Bastogne, a vital road center nineteen air miles west of the German frontier, and cross the Meuse upstream from Namur. To reach these objectives, they first had to cut through the Oesling, the northern third of the Grand Duchy of Luxembourg that is formed by a corner of the Ardennes Mountains and a plateau incised by deep valleys. Less densely populated than southern Luxembourg, the Oesling had long been a tourist magnet with its forested hills and romantic castles. The latter, many of them in ruins, bore testimony to the turbulent history of a region wedged between rival Germanic and Frankish territories.

The northern sector of the 47th Corps was the sole responsibility of the 2nd Panzer Division. Though the division had suffered heavy losses in Normandy, it remained a formidable and experienced force, rebuilt around a strong core of hardened veterans. Since

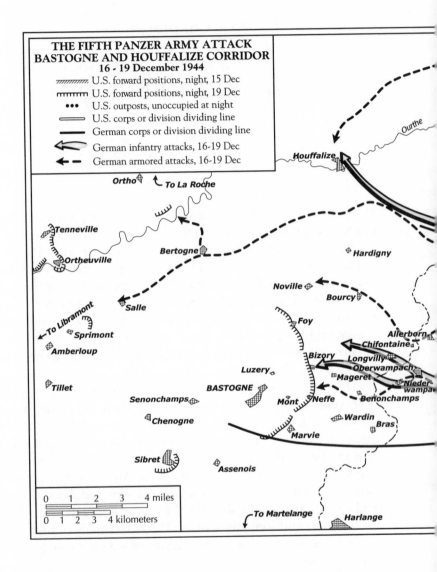

THE FIFTH PANZER ARMY ATTACK
BASTOGNE AND HOUFFALIZE CORRIDOR
16 - 19 December 1944

U.S. forward positions, night, 15 Dec
U.S. forward positions, night, 19 Dec
U.S. outposts, unoccupied at night
U.S. corps or division dividing line
German corps or division dividing line
German infantry attacks, 16-19 Dec
German armored attacks, 16-19 Dec

Ortho

To La Roche

Ourthe

Houffalize

Tenneville

Bertogne

Hardigny

Ortheuville

To Libramont

Salle

Noville

Bourcy

Foy

Allerborn

Chifontaine

Sprimont

Bizory

Longvilly

Amberloup

Oberwampach

Luzery

Mageret

Nieder-
wampa

Tillet

BASTOGNE

Senonchamps

Mont

Neffe

Benonchamps

Chenogne

Wardin

Bras

Marvie

Sibret

Assenois

0	1	2	3	4 miles

0	1	2	3	4 kilometers

To Martelange

Harlange

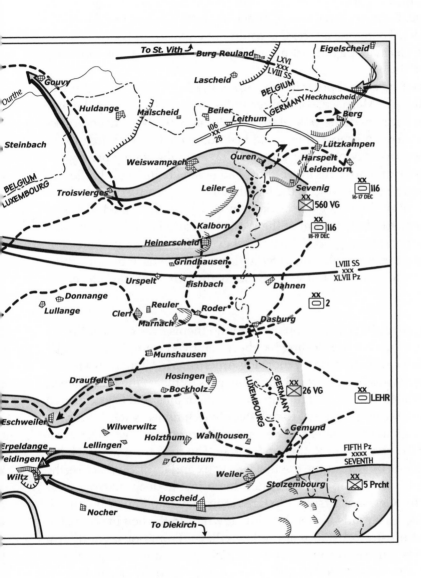

the entire 47th Panzer Corps faced nothing more than the 110th Infantry, a single regiment of the 28th Infantry Division, this meant that, on average, for every ten German attackers there was just one American defender. Therefore, all the GIs could hope to accomplish was to delay the German juggernaut by putting up resistance at the most crucial points.[2]

The first crucial point in the path of the 2nd Panzer Division was the village of Marnach, some three miles beyond the Our. By the time the Panzergrenadiers took Marnach late on Saturday, fifteen houses were ablaze and most others had been damaged. The church tower was destroyed; twelve direct hits had ravaged the stately presbytery. That none of Marnach's inhabitants had fallen victim to the battle was not due to luck, but due to the fact that the Americans had evacuated nearly all of them as early as September 29. As the Allied offensive had come to a halt in front of the West Wall early in the autumn, their removal had been part of the painful evacuation of many thousands of Luxembourgers who inhabited villages and towns in the four-mile-wide border—and frontline—area along the Our, Sûre, and Mosel rivers.[3]

American and German troops soon found themselves wishing that all of the civilians in the Oesling had been removed from the battlefield. By nine o'clock on Saturday morning Americans in Urspelt, just northwest of Marnach, were prohibiting villagers from leaving their homes. But German shell fire had ruptured the water mains, and GIs despaired of seeing farmers continue to risk their lives hauling water from public sources in the village square. Still more precarious was the situation of the civilians in Reuler on Sunday. The road from Marnach led to Bastogne by way of the town of Clervaux and its bridges across the Clerve River. To capture Clervaux down in the deep, narrow river basin, the Germans first had to fight their way into Reuler because it controlled the roads descending into town from the heights east of it. GIs put up stiff resistance at the key village. From houses and farm buildings American snipers and machine-gun teams wrought havoc on the attackers so persistently that German soldiers began to vent their anger on the inhabitants. In some instances they rounded up civilians, barricading them in cellars to keep them out of the way. Elsewhere they dragged the men into the streets, lined them up against walls with their hands above their heads, and threatened to shoot them if they moved. The Germans finally saw no other way of sweeping the village clean of enemy soldiers and presumed partisans than to set its farms on fire. One villager failed to escape from the blazing Heintz farm.[4]

Although Clervaux, a town with a population of about two thousand, lay almost six miles west of the German border, accurate shelling had driven its inhabitants into their cellars in the opening hours of the offensive. The surprise had been so total that flight for most became impossible. Joseph Geiben rushed his mother and sisters into their basement after an explosion unhinged the front door and blew in the window. The young townsman had even more reason to be scared than the women around him. He had deserted from the German army and shuddered to think what would happen to him if the Germans made it back to Clervaux before he could get out.[5]

Joseph Geiben was only one of many Luxembourgers who faced the same predicament. The Germans had occupied their miniature country (the grand duchy was home to no more than three hundred thousand people) in May 1940 and effaced its independence with the stroke of a pen, declaring it part of the Third Reich as the *Gau Moselland*. For four years the Nazis had worked to Germanize the Luxembourgers, prohibiting the use of Letzeburgesch, the duchy's native language, and converting all French-sounding place names into German. Though resistance to Nazi occupation had grown steadily since 1940, it had exploded in 1942 when the Germans began conscripting youths for work in the Reich's factories and farms and service in the Wehrmacht. Some six thousand Luxembourgers had dodged conscription or later deserted from their units. They had either gone into hiding in Belgium or disappeared in Luxembourg with the help of underground networks. Many had become active members of the resistance. All of them faced harsh punishment under German reoccupation.[6]

The first German troops managed to penetrate Clervaux in the dark hours of Sunday morning. The battle lasted throughout the day, raging most furiously around two of the picturesque town's most imposing landmarks. On Clervaux's southern edge, a sanatorium dominated the last curve of the main road winding into town from the heights to the east. Some 150 townspeople had flocked to the building as soon as the first shells had fallen on Saturday morning. In the afternoon of that first day, shells had pounded the structure so mercilessly that even its sturdy walls had failed to prevent jagged shards from tearing into the flesh of two of the civilians under its protection.

Somehow, Leonard Peters, bleeding profusely from a wound near his heart, had made it to an American aid station at the Villa Prüm; two medics had risked their lives rushing him in a jeep to a hospital in Wiltz. On Sunday morning and again in the afternoon, German troops launched ferocious attacks against the GIs in and around the sanatorium. Panzergrenadiers lobbed grenades through cellar vents and sprayed the windows with rifle fire. The refugees heard doors being kicked in late in the afternoon. Heavy boots tramped through the upstairs rooms. The sanatorium's nuns begged a little girl to accept a statue of the Holy Virgin and hold it high above her head to ward off danger for them all. Then, suddenly, the noise above their heads died down until only echoes could be heard of battle deep inside Clervaux.[7]

On Monday morning German troops were in control of all of Clervaux except its twelfth-century fortress. Manning its stone walls, turrets, and courtyard were some one hundred men of the 110th Infantry. In the dungeons beneath, eighteen German POWs and seventy-five civilians anxiously awaited their fates. Already on Saturday the civilians—mostly elderly men, women, and children—had climbed the road to the fortress like their forebears had done so often in the eight centuries past. Because the castle housed the kitchen of the regiment's Headquarters Company there was enough food and water to withstand a siege for several days. From behind the medieval apertures American snipers picked off enemy soldiers at will; only armored vehicles could cross the Clerve River with impunity. This so infuriated German soldiers that they forced civilians to carry the casualties away and bury them. Their commanders refused to let the situation drag on for days. Troops at seven o'clock on Monday morning received the order to torch the fortress. They readily obeyed by firing phosphorous bullets and shells into the ancient roofs. Liquid fire ran from the moss-covered slates while thousands of tiny flames dripped from the fortress walls, burning holes in the earthen moat. The ancient beams caught fire and the drafty buildings sucked in smoke. The civilians panicked: children screamed, mothers ran through the courtyard not knowing where to hide. A fortress window swung open shortly before noon. Someone slid a long pole through the opening. At the end of it dangled a limp white flag. Clervaux was German again. The soldiers and civilians who had been able to flee were few. Joseph Geiben had made sure he was one of them. He got out just in time. As early as Tuesday the Gestapo arrested two of its first victims in Clervaux, one of them a conscript. Both men were sent to Buchenwald.[8]

Even while some of the 2nd Panzer Division's troops were breaking into Clervaux's houses and conducting organized plunder (some of the loot was carried off in carts to areas behind the Our), its armored spearheads plunged onto the main and secondary roads leading to Bastogne. There remained only eight air miles between Clervaux and the Belgian border. Taken by surprise, many villagers in the area had only set out on Sunday, when they realized Clervaux was about to fall. Most were overtaken by the Germans even before they reached Belgium. People in Doennange had feverishly been packing on Sunday afternoon when five explosions near the church announced they were too late. Of those in the village who had managed to get away, Johann Breuer, father of five small children, was killed in sight of the border on Monday. Ferdinand Schon died on Belgian soil the following day.[9]

By the time people in Lullange had packed on Sunday, the early winter night had taken over. Accompanied by the village priest, an American sergeant made the rounds to dissuade people from leaving in the dark for fear that they might be mistaken for the enemy. As soon as dawn came on Monday, however, villagers stirred into action. Horse-drawn carts, loaded with boxes and baskets and freshly baked breads, rolled out of sight. Farmers released their animals from the stables, a man on a motorcycle chased the village herd westward. German troops in Doennange, meanwhile, were plundering everything they could use and smashing everything else. Nicolas Grasges, a Luxembourger forced into the German army, tried to intervene on behalf of a desperate countrywoman. A German officer gruffly dressed him down and told him to mind his own business.[10]

Also on Monday morning, Americans in Boevange urged the population to leave forthwith. They feared that the village, a junction of secondary roads three miles from the Belgian border, was about to become a battleground. The apprehensive Americans caused people to panic. Many did not bother to pack and quickly took off, barely making sure they had enough to eat on the way. Only a few farmers stayed behind to take care of people's animals. Like most other communities in Luxembourg, Boevange had had its fill of Nazi occupation. By the time the Allied liberators arrived in September 1944, a third of the inhabitants had been forced from their village. Most of the young men were in the German army or had gone into hiding. Males and females had been conscripted as laborers. Six households had been made to leave their farms as part of a much larger forced migration whereby more than 1,250 families were relocated from Luxembourg to Silesia or Poland. Twenty-eight villagers languished in prisons or concentration camps. Henri Scheer, the village mailman, had died in Mauthausen in May 1944. Battle was the last thing Boevange needed to add to war's heavy burden.[11]

In one of war's many twists of fate, however, battle that Monday bypassed Boevange and ravaged Hamiville instead. A village of no more than 180 inhabitants, Hamiville had the misfortune of sitting astride a knot of secondary roads right beside the Clervaux-Bastogne highway. If German tanks managed to capture the highway from their shortcut through Boevange, they would control one of the main roads into Bastogne at barely twelve miles from the town. American infantry, backed up by several tanks, were determined to prevent this from happening as long as possible. Hamiville was made to share the cost. Early on Monday morning the villagers were startled by a stream of refugees in wagons and an occasional car. Still more people followed on bicycles and on foot. Petrified mothers pushing baby carriages tried to keep up with the others. Even dogs had joined the refugees. By eight o'clock, Hamiville's alarmed inhabitants were packing; by ten o'clock, most were gone. Only a few dozen people stayed behind. Among them were Father Neser, several of the elderly, some farmers to watch over the animals, and a couple of refugees from other villages who were too tired to continue fleeing. Battle ignited around four o'clock in the afternoon. It burned out of control until two o'clock on Tuesday morning. By the time the Germans had wrested the village from the Americans, tank and artillery duels had set eight of Hamiville's farms ablaze, killed five civilians, and maimed several others.[12]

That same Tuesday morning, German tanks roared through Allerborn, the last Luxembourg village on the Clervaux-Bastogne highway. The 2nd Panzer Division had barely pushed its way into Belgium when the Gestapo started snooping around in the tiny village. They wanted to learn the whereabouts of the priest and schoolteacher. They also demanded to know who had erected the triumphal arch that had welcomed the Allies in September and continued to tower over Allerborn's main street.[13]

While the 47th Panzer Corps's other forces were to assault Bastogne, von Manteuffel wanted the 2nd Panzer Division to bypass the town and head straight for the Meuse. In keeping with orders, as soon as it entered Belgium from Allerborn, the division slightly veered to the northwest so as to stay clear of Bastogne. Just north of the town the Germans early on Tuesday captured Bourcy and then Rachamps without much of a fight. The regime they imposed on both communities was arrogant and strict, but humane. At Rachamps they summoned one of the village councilmen, warned him he would be held responsible for the villagers' behavior, and told him to report to the command post every morning. The councilman also received orders to provide food for the troops, and before long villagers were making daily contributions of meat, potatoes, eggs, and preserves from rapidly diminishing stocks. In addition, the Germans wanted the councilman to mobilize women to peel potatoes for the soldiers. They also demanded men to dig graves for comrades killed in battle.[14]

Within days the civilian burial details were working from eight o'clock in the morning until late in the afternoon without rest or food. The reason was that the 2nd Panzer Division had run into trouble at Noville. The village, two miles southwest of Rachamps, sat astride the main road leading into Bastogne from Liège. The Americans had sent an armored task force to block attacks from that direction. The 2nd Panzer Division, for its part, could not permit such a poisonous thorn to draw blood from its flank. The battle for Noville lasted from Tuesday morning to Wednesday afternoon. The remaining civilians spent that time in their cellars. They were not given so much as a break to grab some food, for the dazed Americans, fighting for their lives in a state of shock, brusquely threw them back as soon as they dared show themselves. By the time the surviving GIs withdrew to Bastogne, a surgeon of the 20th Armored Infantry Battalion could remember only two of the civilians, an old lady and her husband: they had been in a cellar reciting their rosary almost uninterrupted for two days.[15]

The battle for Noville was still raging when a special Gestapo unit descended on nearby Bourcy. On Wednesday, December 20, the agents, several of whom spoke French fluently and admitted to being from France, presented the villagers with a list showing the names of those in Bourcy who were said to have been involved with the resistance. Tiring of the villagers' shoulder shrugs and evasive answers, the Gestapo finally decided to round up all the men they could find. The interrogation of some thirty suspects soon left the agents thirsty. A couple of them decided to accompany Marcel Roland to his cellar to fetch some wine. In their search for Mr. Roland's best bottles, they happened to uncover an American flag that the Rolands had stitched together from pieces of dyed cloth to welcome their liberators in September. The fuming agents returned to the house where they kept the prisoners. They arrived with Mr. Roland, the wine, and the American flag. They led the unfortunate villager into a separate room. There they beat him so badly that his screams reverberated throughout the house. A fellow suspect caught a brief glimpse of Mr. Roland's bruised face and blood-stained clothes.

The following day the Gestapo released their prisoners, but Mr. Roland was not among them. Villagers soon discovered his body not far from the gendarmerie. It had been dumped in the mud next to the road to Noville. The Gestapo had apparently dragged Mr. Roland outside after roughing him up and then finished their job by smashing his skull with clubs and hammers. The villagers made some other discoveries. They found Mr. and Mrs. Maquet dead in their bar near the station. Both had been executed. No one in Bourcy could think of a reason why. The couple's son, who had been arrested with the other men on Wednesday, was found dead in a field behind the cemetery. He had bullet wounds in his neck, temple, and stomach. Fernand Maquet had been mentally retarded and totally inoffensive. His death at the hands of the Gestapo remained even more of a mystery than that of the others in Bourcy.[16]

Thick black smoke still hung like a pall when the Gestapo elbowed its way into Noville on Thursday. They immediately arrested twenty-one men who had just come up from the cellars or returned from the surrounding woods to find their village in ruins. The suspects were taken to the municipal building for questioning. Some Gestapo agents maintained they had hidden a transmitter in the church tower. Others upbraided them for having celebrated the arrival of the Americans in September. Although it was clear that they were after members of the resistance, none of the specific accusations made sense. The fruitless interrogation terminated, the agents marched the men to the main road in groups of three. There they made them scoop mud and debris with their hands. After about fifteen minutes of such humiliation, they took the men back to the municipal building. They now told five of the younger men to stand apart from the others. Then they motioned the village priest and schoolteacher to join them. The seven men were marched off with their hands behind their heads. Not much later shots could be heard from behind the ruins of the café Louis. Agonized villagers dared not verify their worst suspicions before the Gestapo had moved out again. When they arrived at the place of the shooting, they found eight bodies, each with a bullet in the neck. The eighth body turned out to be that of Michel Stranen, a young refugee from Luxembourg who had refused to serve in the German army.[17]

2 In the race to Bastogne, two divisions cooperated closely with each other on the 2nd Panzer Division's left flank. As soon as the barrage lifted on Saturday morning, foot soldiers of the 26th Volksgrenadier Division negotiated their way across the Our. The division had been destroyed on the eastern front more than once, but it had been rebuilt for the Ardennes offensive into a considerable force of seventeen thousand men. The Volksgrenadiers were joined by the Panzer Lehr Division late on Saturday afternoon, after a bridge was put in at Gemünd. The armored division was a veteran outfit. It had, however, been badly mauled in Normandy and, while being rebuilt for the counteroffensive, abruptly thrown against the American Third Army to stop the offensive in the Saar region. There had not been enough time to bring it back to full strength for battle in the Ardennes.[18]

Wahlhousen was one of the first villages to be overrun by the left flank of the 47th Panzer Corps. German troops penetrated the small Luxembourg village on Saturday morning, and by the time darkness came several of its farms were no more than glowing heaps of ashes. But Wahlhousen had been lifeless long before the Germans arrived. On October 10, amid skirmishes and artillery exchanges at the West Wall, GIs and militiamen had gone door to door ordering people to evacuate their homes. They had allowed them two hours to pack. The militiamen were Luxembourgers who in most cases had belonged to the resistance. Many were young men who had been in hiding during the German occupation to escape conscription. As soon as the Allies arrived in September 1944 they had volunteered their services. Before long nearly every locality had put together its own *Miliz*. Members helped keep law and order (which included arrests of real and presumed collaborators) and accompanied American troops as scouts on forays into the West Wall zone. At least ten of Wahlhousen's young men had deserted the German army, and most of them after the liberation had joined the village Miliz. As the militiamen were not under the direct command of the Luxembourg gendarmerie or the U.S. military government, misunderstandings were rife. Late in October, for example, a GI had taken Jängy Frieseisen, one of Wahlhousen's militiamen, for an enemy and killed him with a shot in the head. Now, on the opening day of the German counteroffensive, the poorly armed

Wahlhousen militiamen were among the very last to abandon their beloved village.[19]

Some trouble spots notwithstanding, infantry and tanks of the second German prong cut through the thin American defenses just as easily as the 2nd Panzer Division to the north. Siebenaler, some six miles west of the West Wall, fell on Sunday afternoon. There was no end to the horses and wagons passing the village throughout the night. Like most German units thrown into the offensive, troops here suffered from a chronic shortage of motor transport. By Monday morning Siebenaler's farmers would have neither fodder nor horses left. On Sunday evening the Germans captured Drauffelt and its bridge over the Clerve. They herded the few remaining villagers into a single cellar and threatened to shoot them all the following day. After a frightful night, however, the villagers were released. The headlong race to Bastogne continued. Monday morning at nine, nervous GIs urged people in Eschweiler to leave their village immediately. What followed was pandemonium. Within barely an hour, no more than 11 of the 250 inhabitants remained. Less than half an hour later the first shells were rocking Eschweiler. The village had changed hands by mid-afternoon. A little later the Germans were also calling the shots in Knaphoscheid, Brachtenbach, and Derenbach. Of the latter two villages, more than 300 of the 320 inhabitants had taken to the roads in wild confusion. From Niederwampach, the last Luxembourg obstacle on the left flank, another 160 panicking people made a wild dash for the Belgian border. The Germans caught up with the first of them that same night.[20]

Early on Tuesday the 26th Volksgrenadier Division plunged into Belgium on the road through Longvilly, slightly northeast of Bastogne. Shell fire brought down on Longvilly made sixty-year-old Constant Clause one of the outfit's first Belgian victims. From Longvilly the Volksgrenadiers pushed on to Arloncourt, where they were already in control late in the afternoon. Barely twelve years old, Marcel Leonard was particularly fascinated by the tiny four-wheeled, horse-drawn carts loaded with ammunition and food. The soldiers were dying from thirst and demanded water. But they risked drinking it only after making villagers taste it first. Next, the Germans commandeered the houses most to their liking, relegating their occupants to a single room—if they were lucky.[21]

From Arloncourt a secondary road led to Bizory, a village two miles northeast of Bastogne. Volksgrenadiers first penetrated parts of

Bizory after dusk on Tuesday. One group claimed Mrs. Billion's house and asked her how far it was to Antwerp. Mrs. Billion found herself brewing coffee for the Germans until the Americans repulsed them all from the village later that night. But the Volksgrenadiers attacked again before dawn on Wednesday. Mr. and Mrs. Nisen had had enough. They wrapped up their two small children against the biting cold and drove them off in a cart. They dropped them off at Bastogne's Franciscan church and headed straight back to Bizory to watch over their farm. The Germans launched yet another attack after dusk on Wednesday. Again they failed to take Bizory. When it looked to the Nisens as if the Americans were going to hang on to their village after all, they hurried to get their children back. By then, however, unrelenting GIs refused to allow the worried parents access to Bastogne for fear of letting in enemy infiltrators. The Nisens and their children were to live through the siege cruelly separated from each other by two miles of frosty fields.[22]

3 For his blow against Bastogne just south of the 26th Volksgrenadier Division, Fritz Bayerlein, commander of the Panzer Lehr Division, split his column into two. By way of a mud-covered secondary road leading into Belgium from Niederwampach, just south of Longvilly, Bayerlein's right wing on Monday night smashed into Mageret. The village sat on a vital crossroads nearly three miles east of Bastogne. The villagers found the Germans already firmly in control at dawn. Many of Mageret's inhabitants had fled to Bastogne the previous day. Others had stayed, however, and hidden in their cellars between piles of potatoes and beets. When they returned upstairs on Tuesday morning anything useful—clothing, shoes, medicines, food—had gone. The first German who addressed Mr. Koeune in his home was a soldier who wanted to eat bacon.

Throughout Tuesday a combat team of the 10th Armored Division and soldiers of the 501st Parachute Regiment launched counterattack after counterattack to repulse the Germans from Mageret. The villagers took to their cellars again. Each American attack was preceded by ferocious artillery fire. Each clash between troops was accompanied by terribly frightening sounds in the upstairs rooms. People in the cellar of the Nickels farm, its back to the fields from which the Americans launched their first attack, heard soldiers break through the rear windows while the Germans held on to the front rooms. The civilians were forced to listen to shuffles, yells and screams, exploding grenades, and tumbling furniture. Each incursion into the basement caused a wave of panic.

By midnight on Tuesday the Germans were still in control of Mageret and the Americans backed off. Farmers defied danger and cold to rescue what they could in the dark. The roof of their farm badly damaged, Mr. Koeune and his son climbed to the attic to rescue the wheat harvest. They spent hours filling sacks and storing them in drier places. Some farmers wished they had lost only their harvests. A burst from a machine gun into one of Mageret's cellars that Tuesday had killed twenty-two-year-old Oliva Martin. Bullets from the same gun had wounded Mrs. Toussaint so badly she would die a week later.[23]

While Bayerlein's right was stubbornly holding on to its prize, troops on his left in the early afternoon of Tuesday began the battle for Wardin, some one and a half miles south of Mageret. Frantic Luxembourg refugees on bicycles had hurried through the village on Tuesday morning with cries that the Germans were already in Benonchamps, barely a mile from Wardin. The shaken villagers were busy packing when two American reconnaissance officers drew up in a jeep. Besieged by distressed civilians quizzing them about the enemy's exact whereabouts, Lt. John Devereaux jumped onto the hood. A Broadway actor before he became a soldier, the lieutenant used all his powers of persuasion to calm the people down. "Don't be afraid," he assured them in French. "We Americans are here to stay. Keep to your cellars, and don't be afraid." Minutes later the jeep could be seen racing back to Wardin from its eastern edge. The vehicle slowed down long enough for an excited Lieutenant Devereaux to yell: "The Germans are coming. Get back to your cellars!"[24]

The Americans were barely out of sight when machine guns and tanks opened up on Wardin. Some houses and barns caught fire immediately. Léopold Mostade was killed trying to rescue his harvest. The village convulsed with fear. People barricaded doors and windows and fell back to their cellars. Some, too horrified to think, ran for the open fields or tried to become invisible behind banks and inside hollow roads. Only a few handfuls of people, mostly former resistance fighters, managed to flee west and reach Bastogne. There the Americans intercepted some of them and for several days kept them locked up with German POWs until their identities had been verified.[25]

Paratroopers from the 101st Division entered Wardin from the west at about the same time Panzer Lehr hit from the east. Troops rolled back and forth across the village until dusk. Then the Americans pulled back. Field artillery laid powerful concentrations of fire on Wardin to cover their withdrawal. When icy winds at last chased the smoke from Wardin the following morning, they revealed the shell of a village. Still, the rock-solid cellars of the Ardennes had helped most villagers survive the withering storm. Florent Calay, however, lay dead in a stable. And twenty-two-year-old Margareta Schank had been killed by a shell when she tried to escape from the cellar of a farm in flames. She had come all the way from Hüpperdingen in Luxembourg to find refuge in Wardin. Fellow refugees buried the girl beside a road. A week later, the front rumbling not far from Wardin, they unearthed the body and wrapped it in a shroud. An ox laboriously pulled the sledge that took her home.[26]

On Wednesday morning the Germans tried to build on their victory at Wardin by taking Marvie, a hamlet barely a mile southeast of Bastogne. They clashed with paratroopers determined not to let Panzer Lehr get closer to the vital town. For the better part of the day Germans and Americans fought savagely, often man to man. A German tank fired point-blank into the house of Ernest Annet, killing him and his six-year-old daughter, Marie. Desperate villagers bunched together in the strongest cellars. Some twenty people were hiding in the Beauve farm. The cellar of the Rossion farm harbored six families, including a badly wounded man and woman. In the microcosm of war for Marvie each sturdy farm became a fortress in its own right, offering protection against enemy fire as well as the cold. To the warring parties the farms' inhabitants were nothing but a hindrance and a liability. The Delperdange farm was just one of the bulwarks that the Americans commandeered. They quickly turned the farmhouse into an aid station, then chased the cattle into the open and made the stable into a morgue.[27]

The bitter American stand made the civilians' position unbearable. During a lull in the fighting late in the afternoon, paratroopers with the help of Father Vanderweyden, the village priest, let people know that Marvie would be evacuated right away. Some three hundred people hurriedly loaded food and blankets on carts, then pushed off into the dark in different groups. One group wandered into the arms of the Germans and was evacuated to Lutrebois. The others made it to Bastogne. Father Vanderweyden was the last civilian to leave Marvie. Because he was of Dutch origin and spoke English with a

German-like accent the Americans arrested the priest and kept him imprisoned until the next day.[28]

While Panzer Lehr was hitting a brick wall at Marvie, Bayerlein's troops on the right were having no more luck at Neffe. A hamlet slightly southwest of Mageret, Neffe practically leaned against Bastogne's eastern gate. The Joseph farm was the last of Neffe's twenty-odd buildings on the road to Bastogne. It was to be the unfortunate witness to Panzer Lehr's repeated furious attempts to reach beyond Neffe and penetrate the coveted town. On Tuesday morning Mrs. Joseph's eldest sons fled to Bastogne just in time to avoid the Germans. By the time her husband slipped into the garden, however, a violent battle was already raging between German Panthers and Americans holed up in the Vanderesken Château. While burying incriminating papers that he did not want the Germans to find, Mr. Joseph was killed behind his house by American fire. Mrs. Joseph and her two youngest children laid out his body on a mattress in the living room.

German tanks again tried to launch themselves at Bastogne from Neffe after dusk on Wednesday. Again they were stopped, this time by what would be one of the most ferocious American artillery bombardments of the siege. The barrage laid waste to Neffe, setting the Joseph farm ablaze. Mrs. Joseph screamed at her children to hide in the garden. Then she dived into the sea of flames and returned with her husband's corpse. Mother and children spent the freezing night in the garden covered with humid straw and heated by the bodies of their four dogs. The following day they learned that the fire had spared only the stable. They would live in it for almost two weeks together with four cows and a horse. The animals survived on barley. The Josephs kept themselves alive with milk, water from a nearby well, and oatmeal rescued from the fire. All that time the Germans failed to break out from Neffe and get a grip on Bastogne. It did not make much difference to Mrs. Joseph.[29]

4 Stonewalled by armored teams and paratroopers east of Bastogne, Gen. Heinrich von Lüttwitz, commander of the 47th Panzer Corps, ordered a task force of the 26th Volksgrenadier Division to push ahead south of the town. With most of the American defenders concentrated east and northeast of Bastogne, the German task force was able to advance rapidly. Around noon on Tuesday, impatient Volksgrenadiers stepped out of the dense fog and into Bras,

not quite two miles southeast of Wardin. They encountered no opposition because the Americans had withdrawn earlier, but the Germans were nervous and refused to believe that the enemy had gone. Irked by a wooden observation tower on the village's edge, they requisitioned Camille Lambert and her brother Robert to take it down. They told the siblings that if they did not get the job done in half an hour they would be shot. Armed with ax and saw Camille and Robert made the tower collapse in less than the allotted time.

Inside Bras the Volksgrenadiers employed drastic measures to rid the village of any GIs who might have remained to slow them down. They decided to purge Bras with fire. The soldiers went about their business in a systematic fashion, aiming bursts of incendiary ammunition into the hay of barns and lofts. Four of the tiny community's houses and thirteen of its farms were ablaze in no time. The Germans were in no mood to brook opposition of any kind. When Mira, one of the village dogs, barked like mad at the chaos around him, a Volksgrenadier shut him up with a shot from his pistol.[30]

From Bras the German task force pushed on, swiftly skirting Bastogne. At noon on Sunday, inhabitants of Lutrebois, a village three miles south of Bastogne, had gone to town for an update on the situation and drawn comfort from the news that most trains were still running as usual. By noon on Wednesday, Lutrebois's stupefied population suddenly found itself living with the Germans again. In Bras, meanwhile, the Volksgrenadiers settled down for the siege and turned the forge and carpenter's shop into an abattoir. Every day they butchered hogs and cows and distributed the meat among the soldiers in the village. There were no leftovers for the civilians.[31]

More and more Volksgrenadiers poured into the area south of Bastogne. From Lutrebois on Wednesday they pushed westward to Remoifosse, where so many refugees had arrived from the fighting east of Bastogne that farms were housing up to eighty people. In Assenois, about a mile and a half west of Remoifosse, people were holding their breath. The village's power lines had been cut since Sunday night. The able-bodied men had fled Assenois even while families from Bastogne were arriving. Some had placed their children, the sick, and the infirm in the village and had then hurried back to their properties in and around town. As Assenois sat astride a major road leading into Bastogne from the south, the Americans were determined to put up a fight for the village. The first clashes occurred late on Wednesday. Artillery rumbled on all sides. In the basement of Mrs. de Coune's château, refugees repeatedly dipped linen rags in buckets of water so as to be ready to cover their mouths against the smoke and dust that would come with direct hits. Like reciting the rosary, the ritual was more a way of putting one's mind at ease than a meaningful attempt to avert danger. The battle for Assenois would subside no earlier than Friday morning, leaving one civilian dead and many others traumatized.[32]

While the battle for Assenois raged, Volksgrenadiers converged on Sibret. From there they would be able to cut the highway from Neufchâteau, one of the main arteries into Bastogne. A task force built from remnants of the 28th Infantry Division had dug in to defend the village by the evening of Tuesday, December 19. Exhausted and jittery, the GIs arrested four people from Bastogne and nearby villages who passed through Sibret on Wednesday. They put them in the gendarmerie's prison on suspicion of spying. One of them had done no more than wear olive-drab clothing given to him by a GI as a present. The following day, all four civilians would have the strange experience of being liberated by the Germans. Before dawn on Thursday, troops of the 26th Volksgrenadier Division launched a coordinated attack on Sibret. People in the Hankard house somewhere between eight and nine o'clock made the fatal decision of abandoning their cellar to snatch something to eat. A shell crashed into the kitchen killing five people at once, one of them a two-year-old boy. A sixth victim lay in a pool of blood with lacerated arms. She was carried to a nearby store where a civilian doctor and a German surgeon worked side by side to save her left arm. The right one had to be amputated. Two more civilians had died from bullets and shrapnel before the Germans could claim all of Sibret to be theirs around noon on December 21.[33]

That same day, the Volksgrenadiers reached as far as Chenogne, not quite four miles west of Bastogne. American field artillery units in and around the village hastily withdrew as shells began to crash in late morning. Though they managed to extricate most guns, they left behind everything else. Scared villagers hurried to do away with all of the American items that might raise suspicion if the Germans found them in their homes. They destroyed staff carts, ripped out field telephones, hid binoculars. Six of the last of Chenogne's young men jumped on their bicycles and headed west. When darkness came that Thursday their village already belonged to the Germans.[34]

Increasingly, the siege of Bastogne was left to the 26th Volksgrenadier Division. From the outset, Hitler had made clear that reaching the

Meuse, rather than capturing Bastogne, was his top priority. Von Manteuffel therefore ordered the 2nd Panzer Division to disengage from around Noville in the northeast and to resume its advance toward the main target. Likewise, Panzer Lehr on Tuesday night was told to pack up at Bastogne, leave behind one Panzergrenadier regiment in support of the 26th Division, and head for the Meuse straightaway. To steer clear of the boiling cauldron, the armored division swung south of Bastogne in a slightly wider arc than the Volksgrenadiers.

On the second day after having been ordered away from the town's eastern gates, spearheads of the Panzer Lehr Division emerged already deep behind Bastogne. On Thursday, December 21, they captured Tillet, some eight miles west of the crucial crossroads. Slightly farther west, in villages near the Ourthe River, small groups of young men had begun to flee on bicycles on Tuesday. More had followed their example on Wednesday. The withdrawing Americans were exhausted, disoriented, and in a foul mood. Villagers who tried to approach GIs regrouping at Moircy were chased away in a rude and cold-hearted manner. In a kitchen in Jenneville little Marcel Lassence and his sister were dividing their war chest of GI gum and chocolate from the previous weeks when on Thursday a forceful explosion blew in the windows. In their haste to destroy the village's bridge over the Ourthe the Americans had forgotten to warn the Lassences about the explosion. Marcel's frantic father flagged down a GI and entreated him to have a look at his children's bleeding faces. The cuts fortunately turned out to be superficial. The nervous soldier hurriedly dressed the children's wounds. Then he, like his comrades, disappeared behind the Ourthe.[35]

5 With the Panzer Lehr Division at the Ourthe west of the town and the 2nd Panzer Division at the same river northwest of it, Bastogne for all practical purposes was cut off from the outside world. The town appeared to sit amidst the surging German tide like a sandcastle waiting to be washed away. In a sense the market town with its slightly more than four thousand inhabitants was an unlikely place to be suffering a siege. Its medieval towers and walls had been demolished by the French in the late seventeenth century. The only natural defenses were the gently rolling hills marking the plateau on which it was located. At the same time, however, it was Bastogne's central position on that plateau and the knot of major and secondary

roads that had formed around it that made the town of great value to both defender and assailant.[36]

In the rout that had followed the Allied breakout in Normandy, retreating German troops had not bothered to make a stand at Bastogne. Americans of the 28th Infantry Division encountered virtually no opposition when they entered the town on September 10, 1944. A small German rearguard provoked some skirmishes that caused no more than a handful of casualties on both sides. The people of Bastogne hailed the GIs of the 110th Infantry in a state of delirium. Civilians lined the streets applauding; Belgian and American flags fluttered; church bells tolled; bottles of wine passed from hand to hand; and people danced and sang in the streets. Barely more than three months later all these events would appear to have taken place in a beguiling dream.[37]

So cruel was the irony of what was heading Bastogne's way on Saturday, December 16, that it took the inhabitants several days to fathom the severity of the situation. In fact, no one in town that Saturday seemed to be aware that the Germans had launched a major offensive at the German-Luxembourg border, no more than twenty airline miles to the east. The day unfolded in all calm, and in the shops it was business as usual. All through the night, however, the distinct rumble of explosions could be heard in the east. Civilians who wanted to know what was happening the following morning found the GIs reticent and irritable. During Mass at 9:30 A.M. one of Bastogne's Franciscan fathers lambasted parents for the indecencies he believed to have taken place at a ball organized by the Americans. From his pulpit he warned the adults to watch over their children and daughters more closely. He also reminded them of what the Romans had done to Hannibal's troops in Italy after their strength had been sapped by a winter of decadent pleasure at Capua. History tended to repeat itself, he thundered, the sounds of war audible in the distance, and American troops, like the Carthaginians, might be asked to pay for their sins.[38]

Unsubstantiated rumors flew about until, late on Sunday afternoon, the power lines from Malmedy were cut and everyone in Bastogne was thrown into stygian darkness. People lit candles and flocked to the church to get more. American Civil Affairs officers announced a curfew to begin at six o'clock that evening. Although there was neither electricity, nor heat, nor water, on Monday morning the principal of Bastogne's seminary decided to proceed with the first of the Christmas exams as if nothing was wrong. Other schools continued their routine, too. By noon, however, large numbers of haggard refugees from Luxembourg were pouring into town and anxiety spread like a virus. Unrest became outright fear when the first shell hit Bastogne in mid-afternoon. Classes were cancelled and exams broken off. Distraught parents came to fetch their children. Eight-year-old Michel Mazay knew Mr. Mayeresse, the schoolteacher with the dark-rimmed glasses, as a stern and imposing man. But now he returned to his class with news that left him pale and distressed. "Children, school is out," he announced, his voice trembling, "go home immediately, the Germans are at the gates of Bastogne." As they filed out of the door, Mr. Mayeresse shook his pupils' hands one by one.[39]

"At night," wrote Maria Gillet, a student at the boarding school of the Sisters of Notre Dame, "the enormous traffic does not end—the helter-skelter flight of our Americans." "Is it," she asked herself, "that serious then?" On Tuesday the unmistakable noise of battle drifted in from the east and jeeps arrived with soldiers wounded near Neffe and Wardin. More refugees streamed into town. Some panic-stricken parents from outside Bastogne arrived to pick up children from boarding schools. Trams and trains stopped running as the day wore on. By the time night came again, shells were rocking Bastogne in rapidly increasing numbers.[40]

American authorities never ordered a general evacuation of Bastogne. Although they much preferred to fight the battle unhampered by civilians, they also realized that a swift and orderly evacuation of so many people was impossible in the circumstances, especially because transportation was lacking. Still, people began to leave on their own initiative around noon on Monday. The first explosion in town that afternoon caused many others to pack with even greater urgency. As usual, young people and most of the able-bodied men went first. Town officials joined them. Only some refugees were fortunate enough to be given a ride by GIs heading west in trucks. Tuesday morning's chaotic scenes wryly reminded some of the exodus that had followed the German invasion in May 1940. So many people were now streaming out of town that American vehicles could hardly move. But the opportunity for flight was disappearing fast.[41]

Alphonse Dominique and Paul Goosse, students at the seminary, had left on Monday afternoon determined to reach Bourcy, their home northeast of Bastogne. Each holding a heavy suitcase and slowed down by refugees heading into Bastogne and American troops on the march to the town's eastern defenses, it had taken the teenagers two long hours to reach Mageret. The noise of battle at midnight had torn them abruptly from a deep sleep in the house of Alphonse's grandparents. Fooled by a lull in the fighting early on Tuesday morning, the boys decided to continue their way home. They had not gone far when machine guns suddenly opened up. Paul threw himself into a ditch. He tried to catch sight of Alphonse, but even the slightest movement made bullets whine and the dirt jump up around him. Paul yelled at his friend to follow him, darted from the ditch, and disappeared into the woods. Alphonse was nowhere to be seen. Paul assumed his friend had taken a different route and made haste. A little later GIs picked Paul Goosse up, questioned him, and took him back to Bastogne. The body of Alphonse Dominique, riddled with bullets, would be found more than a month later beside two suitcases in a ditch.[42]

On Tuesday GIs and gendarmes began manning checkpoints on roads leading out of Bastogne. They were under orders to turn back people who wanted to flee. Father Musty, a teacher at the seminary, took it upon himself to guide the forty remaining students safely out of town. First they tried the main road leading west. American MPs checked their papers and let them pass, but a little farther on Belgian gendarmes refused to let them through. They tried a smaller road, but again were turned back. On Wednesday morning teachers and students were still trapped in Bastogne and time was pressing. Father Musty accosted several American officers in the hope of obtaining a letter of safe-conduct. But the soldiers had other things to worry about and no time to draw up official papers. Father Musty and three of his colleagues therefore decided again to try and hurry their flock out of town without an official permit. The last gendarmes had now fled, too, and this time no one stopped the group from leaving Bastogne, though shell fire from time to time forced them to hit the ground hard. At a crossroads just west of town, the group split into three. Seven of the youngest boys were taken to the château Greindl in Isle-la-Hesse, a hamlet close to Bastogne. The others struck out along the main road leading northwest to Marche. One group, accompanied by Fathers Mottet and Zeler, halted at the monastery of the Redemptorists in Beauplateau. Father Musty, however, decided to push still farther so as to leave the Ourthe between him and the Germans. He took eight boys with him. Little did he realize that half his small band of travelers would be dead before Christmas.[43]

The teachers and students from the seminary were among the last to break free from the beleaguered town. By the end of Wednesday, December 20, the German noose had tightened to the point where it prevented civilians from escaping from the greater Bastogne area. The townspeople could now get no farther than the villages and hamlets located inside the immediate perimeter. And since these were the places on which the Americans were anchoring the town's defenses, they threatened to be even worse deathtraps. Three thousand civilians inside Bastogne braced themselves against the inevitable siege.[44]

With most town officials gone, the American Civil Affairs detachments urgently needed a civilian authority to help them organize the defenses and look after the needs of the population. They found the ideal person in fifty-year-old Léon Jacqmin, a respected businessman and veteran of the Great War. Mr. Jacqmin knew how to take charge and, in his capacity as acting mayor, immediately set to work to deal with a variety of pressing issues: the appointment of auxiliary policemen, the procurement of flour and meat, the distribution of foodstuffs, the care for the sick, the transport and burial of the dead.[45]

Bastogne's remaining inhabitants scurried to the places they hoped would help them survive the siege. Some people prepared their own cellars for an underground existence whose length they could only guess at. Others sought out sturdier cellars and the comfort of neighbors. In the strongest of the private cellars civilians were often packed together in groups of 20, 30, and 40. In some streets holes were made in the cellar walls to allow people to move from one house to another without having to step outside. Close to one-third of the population packed some clothing and blankets and moved to one of three collective shelters. No less than 600 people, including 100 schoolgirls, thronged the underground corridors of the Institute of the Sisters of Notre Dame. The Franciscan fathers welcomed some 150 people into a shelter beneath their church. The Récollets offered enough room for another 100 civilians in the vaulted cellars of their seventeenth-century monastery. On Wednesday the Franciscan sisters evacuated the home for the elderly. They settled down with them in the seminary's cellars where they tried to make the old people as comfortable as possible.[46]

The Americans, meanwhile, had their hands full with security. Rumors persisted of German agents inside the town gathering intelligence and directing artillery fire on prime targets. That problem was made worse by hundreds of refugees who had become mixed up with the locals. Several had come from Liège, a city the Germans were terrorizing continually with V1s and V2s. Many more had poured into town while battle was flaring up in village after village in the surrounding area. In the swelling chaos it was hard to determine who was who. Already on Sunday GIs had been scrutinizing closely the papers of people entering town on foot and in trams. In the tense days that followed suspicious Americans arrested many civilians, taking them to the hôtel Lebrun for questioning. Most suspects were released within hours. Even Charles Govaerts, one of the town's well-known doctors, was shoved into a jeep during one of his rounds and kept in a cellar for interrogation until his identity was at last confirmed.[47]

Nothing heightened the nervous mood inside Bastogne more, however, than the ever deadlier German artillery. Shell fire on Tuesday wounded several civilians while claiming the lives of at least eight American soldiers. Shortly after noon on Wednesday an explosion rocked a wing of the Institute of Notre Dame. A shell had burst next to the window of a makeshift chapel in the cellar. Several nuns had been praying inside the small room, and in the dust and smoke Sister Céline could be heard crying for help. Sister Augusta, the convent's nurse, rushed to her aid. The victim's left leg was too badly mangled, however, for a nurse to be of much help. American medics put the nun on a stretcher and quickly took her away. Then, suddenly, someone noticed a lifeless figure beneath the tabernacle. It was Sister Emmanuel, the convent's mother superior. A fragment had pierced tabernacle and chalice and buried itself in her chest. She was bleeding profusely. Sister Marie-Paul bent over her just in time to hear her gasp, "Don't you recognize me?" The words appeared not to be spoken for anyone in the room. Minutes later Sister Emmanuel was dead. The news spread fast and an atmosphere of dark foreboding descended on the town.[48]

Another shell pierced a wall of the Cornet home moments before midnight that same day. The explosion at once decimated three generations of the same family: sixty-year-old Nicolas Mahnen, two of his daughters, and Nicole, his eleven-year-old granddaughter, were killed instantly by the searing blast. Catherine Merken, one of the refugees from Liège, lay dead, too. Mrs. Mahnen survived. When she came to, she found their other granddaughter, four-year-old Jacqueline, under the rubble in a corner, her arm severed. The frenzied grandmother picked her up and rushed her to a nearby house. The child had bled to death before she got there. Maddened by the loss, Mrs. Mahnen somehow broke through both the American and the German lines, got onto the main road to Arlon, and did not stop walking until her bleeding feet made her halt at a farm at Malmaison, eight miles from Bastogne.[49]

The following morning, Thursday, December 21, hundreds of refugees in the cellars of the Institute of Notre Dame pressed against each other. They were jumpy and irritable, and the death of mother superior had left them more frightened than ever. Tanks could be heard battling each other not very far from town. About an hour after dawn, another shell hit the institute, shaking its walls. The boarding-school girls threw themselves to the floor, some hiding their heads beneath blankets. American soldiers asked the institute's chaplain to celebrate Mass. The chaplain administered Communion to as many soldiers and civilians as he possibly could. Then he dispensed general absolution to the crowd. Fearing the effects of another direct hit, GIs urged the refugees to form teams with shovels and pickaxes so that they could dig their way out of the rubble if necessary. People began to chant the Ave Maria. "My friends," Father Dethienne spoke up, "the Americans do not hide the danger. The Germans can enter the town any moment now. Let's make certain not a single light can be seen."[50]

Chapter 5

The Houffalize Corridor

"Cutting off a leg or something else, it is still only meat."

1 On Monday, December 18, Rettigny woke to biting cold weather. The tiny village lay tucked in the forests midway between Houffalize to the southwest and Gouvy to the northeast. Henri Collette had risen long before the feeble sun. As dawn gathered its courage, it found the teenager, his boss, and other farmers on the village fringes, busily gathering bundles of twigs. The heavy logs that made fireplaces crackle and roar had been sawn and stocked in dry places weeks earlier. The twigs were meant to stoke the ovens that would transform carefully kneaded balls of dough into the large, crusty breads for which the Ardennes are known.

By nine o'clock, Henri had tired of his work somewhat and was very hungry. Continuing his task mechanically, he allowed his mind to wander. It drifted back to how fate had brought him to this place. More than four years ago, Hitler's Germany had invaded Belgium. As the occupation of his hometown, Chaudfontaine, some six miles southeast of Liège, dragged on, food had become ever scarcer. Together with a friend, he had roamed the countryside to the south on his bike, in search of the butter, eggs, and meat that war had made difficult to find in urban areas. He had eventually ended up in Rettigny, not quite thirty-five miles southeast of his home as the crow flies. One of the village's farmers, his present boss, had asked if he cared to stay on as a temporary laborer. Henri had not needed much prodding. Now, many months later, despite the nagging separation from his family, Henri felt warm and happy inside. The war was over at last. In barely a few weeks he would be sixteen and, as far as he could tell, an adult. Next spring he would go home and start a new life in a brave new world of peace.

Peace had suddenly come to Rettigny on a Saturday last September. Henri smiled as he made the scenes of that exhilarating day replay in his mind's eye once again. Haggard German troops had passed through Rettigny in disorder for days on end. Most had been on foot, pushing carriages or wheelbarrows in which they carried guns and bags. Vehicles in the trudging columns had looked like moving beehives with soldiers clinging to all sides for dear life. One lone tank had lumbered by with its front wheel missing. In the wake of the retreating columns had followed total silence. It was, almost irreverently, pierced by the unfamiliar sound of an American jeep. Then the villagers had spotted their first GIs, walking single file on each side of the road leading to Gouvy. Henri's boss had thrust a bottle and two glasses into his hand and dispatched him to the road. There he had served drinks to a seemingly endless stream of thirsty soldiers. Henri's only regret was that the Americans had not deemed Rettigny worthy of a prolonged stay and that, as a consequence, he had tasted little of the chewing gum and chocolate he knew they had been handing out freely in the bigger towns where they were billeted.

The hollow rumble of wooden wheels on frozen soil awoke Henri from his reveries. Peering out of the woods to catch a glimpse of the passersby, his heart experienced a sharp jolt. Heading in the opposite direction of the beaten Germans he had just recalled was a snakelike column of wagons pulled by horses and oxen. They were piled high with furniture and mattresses hemming in children and old folks covered in blankets. Ashen-faced men and women walked between and alongside the wagons, some driving cattle before them. The scene immediately reminded Henri of the exodus of Belgian civilians that had followed the German invasion of May 1940. Eager to learn what was going on, Henri and the other men stepped out of the forest, lining the road to question the refugees. The frightened people, whose accents instantly made clear they were from the Grand Duchy of Luxembourg, warned the astonished farmers that the Germans were coming. The enemy had crossed the German border again, they claimed, was ripping through Luxembourg's northern tip, and was now already as close to Belgium as Bas-Bellain and Haut-Bellain, the very villages they had left in such a hurry not long ago.

Lacking time even to digest the news, the farmers rushed to their homes. Henri felt a nauseating knot in his stomach. They had been hearing the rumble of artillery from the West Wall for some time, but that was nothing new and no one had given it another thought. What to do now? His boss never wavered: he, like the majority of Rettigny's farmers, was going to stay put. Jean, on the other hand, his boss's brother-in-law, decided to make a run for it. In a split second he could be seen furiously pedaling his way west. Minutes after Jean had disappeared from sight, two German behemoths were already clanking past the farm of Henri's employer. Somehow Jean on his rickety bike would manage to evade the German panzers all the way to safety. Two or three other young men from his village, however, were to ride to their deaths on one of the roads leading west.

The following morning more than a dozen enemy tanks could be seen sitting on a nearby hill, pointing their guns in the direction of Montleban and Cherain. These fat German targets finally taunted the American artillery into action later that day. As the first salvos came crashing down in and around Rettigny, the electricity was abruptly cut off and the village was thrown into darkness. It was the beginning of a night that seemed without end. Rettigny's inhabitants raced into the cellars, bunching together in those deemed most solid. In the vaulted cellar where Henri was hiding, three neighboring families soon joined his employer's family. One of the villagers arrived wounded, a piece of wood sheared off by an explosion having ripped open his brow. There was nothing to treat the wound with and no one dared leave the cellar to get what was needed. A single candle faintly lit the catacomb for a while and then died down. The inky gloom was broken only by flares from the explosions occasionally flashing through the hatch's cracks; women sought solace in an interminable recital of the rosary.

Toward morning the barrage lifted as suddenly as it had begun. People let the awkward silence sink in for a few minutes. Then someone nervously suggested, "What if we have a look?" The hatch was pushed away. As the villagers shuffled into the farm's courtyard, their eyes met nothing but half-tracks, ambulances, and German soldiers. Distressed families quickly peeled away from the group to check on their own homes. Henri's home had already been taken over by enemy troops. He and his host family had no alternative but to retire to the stables, where they were glad to share in the cattle's warmth.[1]

Unbeknownst to the villagers, the German troops who had taken hold of Rettigny so brusquely belonged to the 116th Panzer Division. That elite division, nicknamed the Windhund, or Greyhound Division, had fought hard all the way from Normandy to the Hürtgen Forest. The armored outfit had been completely refitted for the

Ardennes offensive. It had been brought back almost to full strength in men and had started the first day of the offensive with close to one hundred tanks and assault guns.[2]

Together with the 560th Volksgrenadier Division the 116th Panzer Division made up General Krüger's 58th Panzer Corps. Krüger's force had launched its attack on the morning of December 16 in an area just below the Schnee Eifel. Contrary to expectations, it had taken both divisions two long days to seize the Our bridges and break through two heavily outnumbered regiments of the 28th U.S. Infantry Division dug in on the other side in the northern tip of Luxembourg. The understrength 560th Volksgrenadier Division, running mate and flanking force of the 116th Panzer Division, proved the weak link in the corps. The infantry division had been scraped together from occupation troops in Norway and Denmark. Its men, many rather old for soldiers and in poor physical condition, had not seen combat and had received little training.[3]

Once the 58th Panzer Corps had finally broken through the defenses of the 28th Infantry Division, however, it had gained more speed while racing through the northern part of Luxembourg and into Belgium virtually unopposed. As American troops began to coalesce around the St. Vith salient in the north and the Bastogne stronghold to the south, a gaping corridor of some thirteen miles was opening up between them. Into this gap poured the 116th Panzer and 560th Volksgrenadier Divisions like a river that had burst its dam. Like water flowing rapidly to the point of least resistance, so the 116th Panzer Division now rolled headlong through village after undefended village between the larger communities of Gouvy and Houffalize. Rettigny was just one of many farming settlements in the area overtaken by German troops before the inhabitants even had time to contemplate what was happening.[4]

2 Things were different in Gouvy. Situated some three miles northeast of Rettigny, a railroad connecting the Grand Duchy of Luxembourg with Belgium's eastern provinces brushed past the small town. The Americans had transformed it into a vehicle park with earth-moving machinery and a supply dump that held, among other things, eighty thousand rations. Moreover, Gouvy's small number of depot guards and MPs were watching over 350 German POWs. On the same day that its first tanks entered Rettigny, the 116th Panzer Division began reconnoitering in the direction of Gouvy on its right

flank. At the sight of the first German tanks, the handful of Americans in the town instantly set fire to the store of rations. Just as the smoke began to rise, however, a detachment of the 440th Antiaircraft Battalion arrived. It was one of several detachments sent south by the commander of the St. Vith defense force to block key road junctions on its right flank and provide advance warning of German attacks building in that direction.

Col. Robert Stone, commander of the antiaircraft battalion, was ordered to hang on to Gouvy for as long as he could. The fire was put out and fifty thousand rations were rushed to the forces in St. Vith who badly needed them. Later that day Colonel Stone received a platoon of light tanks as reinforcement. A nearby battery of 155mm howitzers trained its guns on the approaches to Gouvy in support.[5]

As German troops inched closer, Colonel Stone worried not only about the large group of German prisoners in their midst, but also about possible infiltrators. Having fled before the new German onslaught, many young Luxembourgers were hiding in Gouvy for fear of being forced into the German army. Colonel Stone called on the local Belgian gendarmes to help verify the identity of suspect men in civilian clothing. Three gendarmes who had stayed put volunteered for the task. They had barely entered the American lines, however, when gendarme Schröder was hit by what appeared to be a German dumdum bullet. It cut through the flesh of his right leg and then ripped into his left leg, where it exploded against the thighbone. His comrades hurriedly dragged the badly wounded man into a ditch.

When an American medic arrived at the scene, he found the bone shattered over a length of four inches and the arteries severed. In a hail of fire GIs and gendarmes transported the thirty-one-year-old Schröder to a dentist's office. There, in the company of the wounded man's wife, they succeeded in stemming the bleeding a little. It was the closest Schröder would come to medical treatment for several days. Troops of the 560th Volksgrenadier Division stormed Gouvy, were thrown out, then took it again and held on. On the night of December 21, a German officer with three bullets in his stomach was placed next to the gendarme. He was left there to die.

It looked as if the same fate would befall Gendarme Schröder. Gouvy's local doctor, Mr. Charles, could not get to him because he had been requisitioned by the Germans to take care of their wounded. He barely had time to slip into his own cellar now and then to check on his family and take a quick sip from a carefully hidden bottle of calvados. When he finally did manage to reach his townsman, the casualty's left leg had become so seriously infected that Dr. Charles could see no solution other than amputation.

Even that was easier said than done. The doctor had little if any surgical experience and lacked even the most basic instruments for such a risky operation. German medical personnel at that point in the battle needed more help than they could give. Realizing that the gendarme would certainly die if nothing was done, Raymond Laloux, noticing the doctor's hesitation, offered to perform the operation himself. Laloux was the town's butcher. "Cutting off a leg or something else," he tried to convince the others as well as himself, "it is still only meat. We're going to do it."

By the time Laloux returned with saw, knife, and cleaver, the dentist's office had been readied as operating room. Blood, plasma, and a few medicines were recovered from a bag the Americans had made sure to leave with the gendarme. Schröder was anesthetized with the help of alcohol and a whiff of ether that someone had turned up. The casualty was strapped to a stretcher, with Mr. Robert, the dentist, and Miss Calbuche, the midwife, each firmly holding on to an arm.

Several hours later, butcher Laloux, his face drawn, stepped out of the operating room to announce that, should no complications set in, Schröder was saved. But the doctor worried that complications would be difficult to avoid. Because the pharmacy was in ruins, he decided to draw up a list of useful medicines and have it circulate among the inhabitants hiding in their cellars. With the battle not yet decided and shooting continuing from all sides, Schröder's despairing wife rushed from door to door to collect what she could. Together, the people of Gouvy would somehow manage to keep Gendarme Schröder alive until the long-awaited return of the Americans in January.[6]

3 Houffalize, with slightly more than 1,300 souls, was located more than four miles southwest of Rettigny. In its drive toward the Ourthe River, the last important natural barrier before the Meuse, Houffalize was the first town of some size that the 58th Panzer Corps encountered in the undefended gap between St. Vith and Bastogne. The town and surrounding villages had been liberated by the 4th U.S. Infantry Division on and around September 10, 1944. If the invasion of Normandy on June 6 had brought "the end of the tunnel" in sight, then for Gabrielle Kauffmann in Mont, a town just northwest of Houffalize, the arrival of American troops in her own village three months later meant the definite close of "a long nightmare." "It is euphoria," she wrote, "another life is being born; at last, the hope of freedom!"[7]

The inhabitants of Houffalize itself were no less euphoric. They were not content hailing the Americans of the 22nd Infantry with flowers, fruit, cakes, and their best wines. By the time the regiment's engineer units caught up with the spearheads, the Houffalois had cleared away the trees that the Germans had blown up across the roads, and in only forty-five minutes, the town's artisans had replaced one of the three bridges over the Ourthe that had been blown up by the enemy while retreating. This wooden bridge succeeded in carrying even the heaviest equipment until the Americans themselves were able to build a new one three days later. The men of the 22nd Infantry had seen nothing like it since Normandy.[8]

Even after the euphoria had exhausted itself, relations between the population and American troops remained warm. Though few, if any, GIs were stationed in the surrounding villages, Gabrielle Kauffmann was fortunate to live next to the road in Mont that fed into the main north-south artery connecting Houffalize with Bastogne. Before long, she could hardly keep up with the American demand for butter and eggs while also taking care of the GIs' laundry. In return, soldiers rewarded her handsomely with canned goods and the soap she had craved for so long. Any children around could count on being spoiled. Meanwhile, the fair share of American troops billeted in Houffalize (as a tourist spot the town boasted no less than fifteen hotels) easily succeeded in punctuating the gloomy onset of autumn. Most of them belonged to the 59th Signal and 518th Military Police Battalions. They organized movie shows that were open to the excited civilians and dances that were designed to attract any inhabitant of the female sex. In the loaded atmosphere of a war that was dying but not yet dead, intercultural friendship and romance flourished. At least one Houffalize girl would later marry the American soldier of her dreams.[9]

Though liberated and terribly relieved, the Houffalois continued to live in the shadow of war. The heavy military traffic droning through their town in endless procession inevitably took its toll. On September 19 an American vehicle killed Louis Nicolay, a fifty-eight-year-old farmer. Americans not much later had to rush bailiff Emile Dubru to their hospital in Clervaux. His motorcycle had been swept from under him by a jeep racing down from Bastogne. He was diagnosed with a badly fractured skull. A large truck that was transporting a tank failed to negotiate a turn in a narrow street in the town's center and smashed into the facade of the Jacqmin home, but this time there were no victims. Fate struck again, however, at the end of October when an explosive device blew up in the hands of two children who were examining it. A couple of days later one of the boys had died; he was ten.[10]

All that time Gabrielle Kauffmann had been unable to savor her newly gained freedom the way she had envisaged. For too many nights she had been reminded by the faint rumbling of explosions that war had stalled not much farther than the border with Germany, barely a few dozen miles from where she lived. Not even the hustle and bustle of the happy-go-lucky GIs in and around her home had prevented the unfinished war from keeping her jittery. When on December 16 rumors started to circulate in Mont about a major German offensive in Luxembourg, Mrs. Kauffmann instantly sensed that something was wrong. Her fears were rudely confirmed late that evening when a man claiming to be the mayor of the Luxembourg town of Troisvierges asked if he and his wife could stay for the night. Fearing a German breakthrough, they had not hesitated to flee on their bicycles.[11]

The next day, while more and more people from Luxembourg poured into the villages around Houffalize on foot, on bicycles, and in wagons, refugees from St. Vith and the surrounding area began arriving in the town loaded on American trucks. That the Americans themselves were showing increasing signs of nervousness and tension worried the Houffalois more than anything else. The Houffalize mayor, Joseph Maréchal, begged the American commander to take care of his people, too, should the Germans threaten their town. The officer evasively replied that all everyone needed to do was stay calm and that, in the worst case, the people would be warned in time. Meanwhile, however, he imposed a curfew, set to begin at dark, around five o'clock in the afternoon. American patrols would shoot without warning at anyone outside their homes after that time. That same Sunday, in Tavigny, a village to the southeast, scared people crowded together in the church. They formed a procession, feverishly chanting the names of all the saints they could remember for protection.[12]

As day broke on Monday, December 18, the Houffalois watched in astonishment as the mighty American military began to pull out of their town without official warning, leaving behind only a rearguard force. A handful of former resistance fighters from the *Armée Secrète* called on the commanding officer of this token force, volunteering their help in whatever way possible. Thanking them, the American politely declined their offer. He knew there was not going to be even as much as a delaying action to prevent Houffalize from falling into German hands.[13]

Distraught inhabitants now had to make tough decisions at a moment's notice. Should they stay or flee? What should they take? Should they leave someone behind to guard property and possessions? For those who had belonged to the resistance as well as for most young people (afraid of being sent to Germany as forced laborers) there was not much of a dilemma: they could be seen heading west on the heels of the withdrawing Americans. Families needed more time to decide and get organized. Many began a doomed race against time on foot or on bicycles. Others took to the roads in animal-drawn wagons. A few fortunates hitched a ride with the Americans or managed to secure a place on the handful of trucks owned by the more privileged of Houffalize, such as the brewer and the lumber merchant. Jostled along by refugees from the East Cantons and Luxembourg, most Houffalois decided to go no farther than the surrounding countryside. There they found temporary shelter in presbyteries, convents, schools, and the homes of friends and relatives. Some, however, barely stopped moving until they had reached as far as the provinces of Namur, Hainaut, and Brabant. By nightfall on the day that the American troops had begun abandoning it, half the population had hemorrhaged from Houffalize.[14]

Those civilians who had decided not to leave almost instinctively sought strength in numbers. Many joined three large groups taking refuge in the most spacious and reliable cellars in town, two of which ran under the presbytery and the tannery. The first German shell hit the town Monday evening, blowing up a cross in the old cemetery and shattering the church windows. With power cut off even before the first explosion, darkness and uncertainty descended on the town together with a heavy fog.[15]

While only a small outpost of the 7th U.S. Armored Division remained at Houffalize on Tuesday, December 19, General von Waldenburg, logically expecting a strong American force to be holed up there, ordered the reconnaissance troops of his 116th Panzer Division at dawn to bypass the town and scout for a bridge across the west branch of the Ourthe. Later that day, however, von Waldenburg's corps commander decided to have the division backtrack to Houffalize—which patrols had meanwhile established to be nearly empty of the enemy—and continue the advance on the other side of the Ourthe River's main arm. Farther west than any other German troops in the Ardennes, the 116th Panzer Division began rolling toward Houffalize in full force.[16]

In the dead of night, Gabrielle Kauffmann was rudely awakened by loud banging on her door. While holding her breath, she could hear gruff voices arguing on the sidewalk. The banging on her door resumed, more impatiently now. Then, suddenly, a projectile shattered an upstairs window. Gathering all her courage, Mrs. Kauffmann tiptoed down the stairs and slowly opened the door. She stared into the faces of German soldiers demanding food. They took the bread she came back with from the kitchen and hurried away. Mrs. Kauffmann did not go back to bed that night.[17]

People in the town of Houffalize, meanwhile, had bedded down not knowing what to expect in the next hours. Behind the tightly drawn blackout curtains simmered a nervous tension. With the power lines cut, the radios could not be turned to for news. The last departing GIs had been unwilling or unable to tell the inhabitants the latest developments. As they pulled out, they had, in fact, not even bothered to blow up the two bridges now spanning the Ourthe. There was nothing for people to do but wait and listen.[18]

Sometime between two and three o'clock in the morning of Wednesday, December 20, the Houffalois froze as they caught the unmistakable noises of an army passing through. Nelly Simon was startled to hear boots stamp on the floor above the cellar she was hiding in with family and neighbors. The cellar door was thrown open within minutes. German soldiers, in search of Americans, descended, shining their lamps on the pallid faces of the hideaways. Gaby Dislaire watched how Germans forced their way into her family's café and with their guns motioned her father to accompany them into the cellar. With an eye on Christmas and the many Americans around, Gaby's father had the cellar well stocked with beer and liquor. The Germans took all they could carry. Marie-Thérèse and Elisabeth Otto, having dozed off in their upstairs bedroom, were awakened by the commotion around three o'clock. They sneaked to the front window, opened it as far as they dared, and peeked into the street. They stared down on a tank so big it seemed they could reach down and touch the turret. As German soldiers bawled at them, they slammed the window shut again. The two women needed to think quickly. They were not alone in the house: they had put up two GIs downstairs who had not yet managed to get out of Houffalize. Only now did they realize what the consequences would be for civilians caught hiding enemy soldiers. They rushed the drowsy men to the back of the house and into the garden where they opened a gate leading onto a road. They had barely closed their backdoor when they heard shots ring from the escape route they had urged the GIs to take.[19]

Houffalize was firmly back in the hands of German forces even before dawn had a chance to break. While enemy troops continued to rush past on their way west, others began to settle down. The marketplace teemed not only with tanks and trucks, but also with restless horses. Perceptive Houffalois noticed the German car park to be rather a ramshackle hodgepodge. Some of the vehicles moving out again had to be stopped now and then to allow bolts to be tightened. In no time German troops could be seen plundering stocks left behind by the Americans. This did nothing to dampen their arrogance toward the Belgians. At first light enemy soldiers were barging into houses all over town, demanding fires to be stoked and hot coffee to be served.[20]

None of the saints invoked by the people in Tavigny on Sunday night proved powerful enough to force German armor to bypass their village. A small and isolated American unit in the vicinity, caught by surprise, could hardly have been expected to do better. When the civilians finally dared to come out of their cellars, haystacks and barns were roaring balls of fire, although their homes, as if by belated miracle, had been spared. The Americans, however, had been annihilated. Five wrecked tanks littered the village; two twisted hulks rested in the surrounding meadows. Roads were strewn with American clothing, equipment, and numerous bodies. Marie Crémer, having hidden in a shelter on the edge of the village during the battle, returned to her home to find all the windows shattered and the linen in two bedrooms ripped up and soaked with blood. She would never forget the sight of a dead American spread out in the gutter amidst broken gramophone records. The Germans had been confident enough to comb through the inhabitants' possessions before moving on. Only after a painstaking search did Ghislaine Collette discover her smudged identity card on a stack of wood outside her house. She never located the beautiful gold ring her mother had given her.[21]

On the streets of Mabompré, a village southwest of Houffalize, victorious Germans taunted the villagers they knew were hiding inside their homes. "Chocolat! Cigarettes! Mademoiselle!" they whined, mocking the GIs who had called themselves liberators too soon.[22]

4 Because the Germans carved through the Houffalize corridor like a hot knife through butter, civilians escaped much of the death and destruction that clashing armies were wreaking north and south of them. They did not, however, suffer less from occupation. Reduced to pawns in the clutches of a superior force, the nature of the occupation the civilians had to endure depended largely on the kind of troops that were sent their way. As German forces were constantly being reconfigured in response to the changing circumstances of the offensive, civilians were forced to put up with living conditions that could change rapidly and sharply.

In Rettigny, Henri Collette and his employer's family were destined to continue sharing the stables with the animals for the remainder of the occupation. They were to live jammed together, subjected to chronic cold and damp, unable to change their clothes, barely able to wash until the Americans again liberated the village about a month later. Their house had been earmarked as a field hospital as soon as the first troops of the 116th Panzer Division had arrived on December 18. The wounded were given first aid in the farmhouse's numerous rooms, then they were loaded into large ambulances heading for the rear. After a few days, because her children were growing ever more hungry, the wife of Henri's boss decided to have Henri fetch food in the main house. Slipping past the guard unnoticed in the morning, treading his way through rooms full of stretchers displaying dead and dying, Henri, stomach tightening with each step, finally reached the kitchen. Nothing could have prepared even an adult for the scene in what was now the operating room. Henri experienced such a rude jolt that he thought his heart had jumped from his chest. Blood was the one element keeping together the blurred picture before his eyes. It stuck to the surgeon's arms and clothes, to the table and its heaps of bandages, to the floor. Henri, nauseated by the rank smell of so much blood, and still unnoticed, groped through the cupboards, grabbing bread as fast as possible, gathering in his arms anything for his boss's family that their stomachs might accept.

Then, as he was about to burst from the house, the guard suddenly blocked the way out. A trembling Henri was made to look at a photograph of a young man wearing a beret, white overalls, and tri-color armband. He was posing with a gun. The man was Eudore, nephew of the boss and resistance fighter who in the days of the liberation had proudly given his uncle a picture of himself. The picture had been forgotten on the mantelpiece when the Germans barged into Rettigny. "Terrorist," the German barked, waving the picture. "Nein, nein, nicht terrorist," Henri denied, groping for German words. He rushed back to the stable with the food. Minutes later, an officer, flanked by two guards, stamped into the stable demanding an explanation from Henri's boss for the photograph. The farmer tried to argue that his nephew was a gendarme, but that he had been forced to don a resistance outfit for lack of a regular uniform. The irate officer stormed away unsatisfied, leaving his escort behind to guard the stable.

Sick from fear, Henri and the boss's family spent the rest of the day expecting the worst. Then, in the evening, amidst great commotion, the panzer troops suddenly moved out of Rettigny as swiftly as they had captured it. In their wake followed troops who looked much less impressive. They were made up of soldiers of wildly varying ages. The pallid cheeks of boys no more than Henri's age sharply contrasted with the dark stubble marking those old enough to be grandfathers. Rest and meals were their main concerns. They took possession of the former field hospital, spread straw on the floors, and collapsed onto it. A tug-of-war soon ensued between Volksgrenadiers and civilians over food. The Germans scoured the farm for anything edible. The farmer's wife did everything she could to quiet the hogs and on one occasion even had the audacity to chase after a soldier who had stolen a chicken. Having to make do without a source of heat in the stable, Henri was sent to the boss's brother's home on the other end of the village every day with a bucket of sloppy liquid made of milk, flour, and an occasional egg the soldiers had overlooked. There it was baked into pancakes that Henri hurried back to the stable, stearing clear of any soldiers for fear the heavenly smell would attract their attention.

Within days, however, the mood changed again, turning grimmer than ever when SS troops began pouring into the Houffalize Gap. Having run into a brick wall on the northern shoulder, they were now ordered to help exploit the breakthrough in the center forced by von Manteuffel's Fifth Panzer Army. As early as the evening of Thursday, December 21, units of the 2nd SS Panzer Division poured into the gap, their sights set on the vital Baraque de Fraiture crossroads. In their wake more SS divisions were soon cutting through the corridor to help strengthen the attack against Bastogne from the north and northeast. Impatient troops dressed in the ominously black uniforms of SS tankers began to harass the civilians day and night in the stable that Henri had begun to call home. Officers, hunched over maps on the kitchen table lit by faint petrol lamps, repeatedly summoned them from the stable, demanding to know the shortest route to this or that destination, heatedly discussing alternative routes among each other. One night they sent for the boss's wife. Henri, chaperoning the frightened woman, watched with a watering mouth as she hurriedly fried huge steaks cut from a slab of beef slammed down before her.

A few days later it was Henri's turn to be terrorized. He was just crossing the courtyard when a group of five or six soldiers marched past. Their leader pulled him over and in a metallic accent snapped at him: "Toutrou." Henri gave the German an astonished look. He had no idea what he was talking about. The soldier repeated, bellowing this time: "Toutrou!" "Ich kenne nicht," Henri stumbled in German. In a flash, the annoyed soldier grabbed Henri by the throat, his pistol at the boy's temple. Dragged along the road, Henri, terrified, his mind threatening to go blank, screamed for a neighbor he knew spoke German. The farmer quickly learned that the testy SS troopers were to be billeted in the house of the "Dutroux" family. He hurriedly pointed them in the right direction. Only then was a pale-looking Henri released.[23]

Like other communities in the corridor between St. Vith and Bastogne, Houffalize was soon making the painful adjustment to renewed occupation. Civilians who had fled no farther than the neighboring villages and had seen the tanks roar by, trickled back into town to watch over their homes. On the roads leading into Houffalize, German soldiers jeered at the returning civilians whom they knew had hoped to be rid of them forever. Madeleine Simon returned to her house to find that it was not quite hers anymore and that the Germans had thought nothing of eating most of the hog her family had slaughtered just days earlier.[24]

In a matter of days the Germans wiped away all memories of the giddy times of liberation. They reinstalled the loathed *Feldkommandantur*. They set up flak batteries at key points across town. The mayor was summoned to the town hall, where an officer coldly told him: "In September you covered the Americans with flowers, these German soldiers you will cover with stones." The first occupiers made themselves comfortable in the hotels and abandoned houses of Houffalize; those who followed took up residence with families. To have hardened oneself against occupation once had been difficult. To have to begin the process over again, after having been allowed to taste freedom, however briefly, was too much for some. Gaby Dislaire's mother, her café having been plundered only hours earlier, could not bear the thought of having to put up with the group of cocky Germans who had been ordered to her doorstep. A heart patient, she suffered an attack so severe that a German army doctor had to come to her aid.[25]

In nearby villages, people who, to their acute disappointment, had seen relatively few liberators stationed in their homes, were now struggling to find enough room for hordes of enemy soldiers—and even more horses. For nearly three hours Marie Crémer's father made the rounds of Tavigny with some Germans to procure enough room for their animals in the village's stables. Some had to be wedged between the cows. His task finally completed, the soldiers returned the favor by commandeering his house, leaving his family to fend for themselves in the cellar, where they settled down on some straw and a few blankets. Unable to change their clothes or wash, they would live there until again liberated on January 18.[26]

Cut off from newspapers and radio, some desperately sought solace in rumors. On Friday, December 22, almost a week after the offensive had begun, people in Houffalize began whispering that the Germans were withdrawing. However, the disheveled and numbed soldiers who arrived later that day were not retreating Germans but captured Americans. Jolts of disappointment mixed with pangs of pity for the soldiers they had come to associate with freedom and good times. Women flocked to the schools where the GIs were being herded into the playgrounds. The Germans robbed them of their wallets, watches, and anything else they thought useful. Some GIs were forced to hand over coats and jackets. Seeing that the Americans were starving, the women swung into action, inspired by charity as much as by a chance to thumb their noses at the enemy one more time. Despite the fact that the occupation had brought tightened rationing again and that queues for milk and bread had reappeared, they rushed home to return with whatever they had been able to scrounge from their meager stocks. They even organized a soup kitchen, passing out bowls of hot broth among the GIs under the watchful and disapproving stare of the German guards. Enemy supervision could not prevent Renée Wathelet from slipping notes from four prisoners into her shoes. They contained the names and addresses of their families. Beneath an address somewhere in Kansas, one GI had scribbled, "I am prisoner but O.K." As soon as the Germans were pushed out of Belgium again and the postal system was up and running, Renée would dutifully inform the men's families of her encounter with them. Meanwhile, because there was not enough food in the town to provision all of the prisoners, German soldiers turned to the countryside for bread, butter, and other foodstuffs. Though they insisted it was for the prisoners, much never made its way to the stockades in Houffalize. Farmers in the nearby village of Mont made sure to put their food directly into the hands of the American prisoners who had been crowded into their church. In an ironic reversal of roles, it was now their turn to spoil their onetime liberators with apples, sandwiches, cookies, and buckets filled with milk—until the guards put and end to it all and started the POWs on their long way to Germany.[27]

As the GIs disappeared from sight, Christmas drew near. The Germans were determined to make themselves feel at home again in the territory wrested back from the Americans. A baffled Anne Marie Dubru opened her door in Houffalize to find the local constable and a German soldier on her doorstep. The constable, visibly embarrassed by the task assigned to him, explained to her that they were requisitioning her to work for the Germans at the hôtel Vieille Auberge. Understandably worried, the young girl tried excuses, then protests, but to no avail. Two other girls, familiar to Anne Marie, were already waiting at the hotel. There they were made to fix meals, wash dishes, and clean the soldiers' rooms. The indignity of having to work as the enemy's chambermaids was made bearable only by the immense relief of being treated correctly.

In preparation for the feast of nativity, German soldiers were requisitioning, extorting, and stealing food wherever they could find it. Many families on Christmas Eve experienced the humiliation of having to prepare sumptuous meals for enemy soldiers who had taken up residence in their best rooms. In one home they sent the owner out into the snow under orders to return with a fine Christmas tree; they told his wife to go to the kitchen and prepare a special treat with stolen beef and poultry. They did have the courtesy, however, after having decorated the tree and engaged in boisterous sing-alongs, of offering the chilled owner a cigar. In the café owned by Gaby Dislaire's parents, celebrating Germans felt generous enough that same night to offer the family beer drawn from their own tap. In Mont, meanwhile,

Mrs. Kauffmann was trying to get her children to sleep, at last. For several hours the Germans in her house had been drinking, singing, and cracking jokes around a fir tree decorated with candles. A soldier would occasionally hurry through the cold to keep tabs on the owner and her numbed children. For some time now the family had been living in the stable.[28]

If the Germans' facade of haughty merriment was meant to obscure the fact that theirs was not the glorious army of 1940 anymore, they failed to fool the civilians. To be sure, elite Wehrmacht units still contained cores of experienced soldiers willing to abide by certain codes of military behavior. In Tavigny, for example, German soldiers, belonging almost certainly to the veteran 116th Panzer Division, requisitioned a civilian for the purpose of providing a GI killed in a nearby field with a proper burial. When they noticed the man tug the corpse with a rope he had wrapped around its neck, the soldiers were incensed by the civilian's disrespect for the fallen soldier. They gave him a violent kick in the rear, making him start all over again at gunpoint. The cowed villager tried again, this time gently dragging the soldier to his grave by the arms.

But the worn German ranks had been patched up with too many replacements for whom professionalism and military codes had little if any meaning. Three soldiers billeted in Marie Dubru's home in Houffalize, for instance, were no more than sixteen years old. They professed a holy fear of being sent into battle. One of them actually forgot his rifle when they moved out, and Marie's father had to call him back and hand it to him. Discipline slipped as it became clear that the offensive was running out of steam. Civilians soon came to prefer the Germans haughty and derisive rather than unpredictable. Two drunken soldiers burst into the Raveau home one evening and demanded meat. Mr. Raveau explained there was none, showing them around to have his claim verified. Next the Germans demanded hot coffee, elbowing themselves in between Mrs. Raveau and her two young daughters and grabbing food from the table that had just been set for dinner. They left when they were full. But they returned a half an hour later and this time their demand was less innocent: they wanted the young girls. A horrified Mrs. Raveau slipped away, locking the door of the bedroom to which her daughters had just retired. When she returned, she learned that the Germans had gone into the cellar, apparently in search of yet more food and drink. She rushed back upstairs, grabbed the girls, and this time hid them behind a false wall in the attic. After a superficial search of the house, the drunken soldiers, irate at having their sordid plans thwarted, finally disappeared into the dark. Before they did, however, they made sure to shoot the dog that had been barking madly at the foreign intruders.[29]

5 Special SS security forces followed the trails of the spearheading Panthers and Tigers like jackals on the prowl. Civilians were being scrutinized, of course, from the very moment enemy soldiers set foot in their communities again. Germans in Houffalize were already searching the home of Marie-Thérèse and Elisabeth Otto from top to bottom on the first day of occupation. They had captured two GIs in a street just behind where they lived and they suspected the women of having harbored them. The women escaped serious harm only because the soldiers could find not the least shred of evidence against them.

Others were in trouble, too. When the Dubru family set off to return to Houffalize from the village they had fled to before the arrival of the Germans, acquaintances warned them to stay away. It was rumored that the enemy had found incriminating papers in their home and was looking for them. Renée Dubru could not understand what had happened. She knew her father had never been involved in the resistance. But then she remembered the letter she had been writing to a school friend when her parents had suddenly decided to pack and leave town. In it she had made a number of unflattering comments about the Germans, blurting out on at least one occasion, "We have at last been delivered from the dirty Boches." Whatever the exact reason for having incurred the wrath of the occupier, the Dubru family turned on their heels and did not return to their home in Houffalize until the Germans had been pushed out.

The occupier was all too well aware that the Houffalois had welcomed the Americans with open arms. The most glaring proof of this was a letter written by Colonel Lanham, commander of the liberating 22nd Infantry. Still posted publicly in various places when the Germans returned, it thanked the citizens of Houffalize for their "magnificent work in aiding our advance," calling their town "a living symbol of the Belgium that all Americans respect and admire." No town, the commander made sure to emphasize, had "helped us as much and as intelligently as Houffalize." Before long, having been threatened by the Germans several times, the mayor went into hiding, one of the aldermen taking over his post for the duration of the occupation.[30]

The Wehrmacht's punishment of civilians could be harsh and summary. When toward the end of December soldiers at Houffalize's Randoux farm discovered that one of their pistols was missing, they announced that everyone on the farm would be shot unless the weapon was returned by noon. The culprit finally decided to own up to avoid a bloodbath. Despite emotional pleas from family and neighbors, he was mowed down with a short burst from a submachine gun. Unlike the regular military units, however, the SS *Sonderkommandos* hastened into the area with the express purpose of keeping tabs on the population and rooting out all opposition. And they went about their business in a coldly systematic and clinical fashion. Even before Christmas, *Einsatzgruppe L* had descended on Houffalize and begun combing through official and personal papers. They were not interested in who had been throwing flowers and kisses at American liberators. What they were eager to know was who had belonged to the resistance movements responsible for the sometimes deadly actions against German forces. In a matter of days they had sniffed out lists, letters, and liberation-era newspapers revealing the names of scores of local resistance fighters. The repercussions of the finds soon rippled beyond the confines of Houffalize proper.[31]

Marie-Thérèse Urbin Choffray had just returned home from Mass early on Saturday morning, December 23, when three SS men showed up to arrest her. When asked if she knew German, she pretended not to understand. She was taken to the town hall where she was placed under guard in the courtroom. Despite temperatures far below freezing, all the room's windows were open, and Marie-Thérèse could see the vapor of her breath. She was not alone. A few men, pale as death, sat in stony silence. She tried to inch closer to find out who they were but was ordered back to her chair. Meanwhile, the news of her arrest had spread. An acquaintance rushed to the Feldkommandantur where he knew an interpreter who had been assigned a room in his home. In the presence of the commander, the interpreter, and other soldiers, the man pleaded Marie-Thérèse's cause. While the soldiers fetched her mother and tried to calm her as much as possible, the interpreter was told to go to the courtroom to see what was going on.

Marie-Thérèse was made to wait until early afternoon for the interrogation to begin. She was taken to a separate office where several Germans were waiting for her. They shoved a paper in her face. The document, the men claimed, had been found at the gendarmerie. Marie-Thérèse was staring at the complete list of the members of *Groupe G*, a local resistance group specializing in sabotage, to which she herself had belonged. Though her name jumped out at her as the second one from the top, Marie-Thérèse somehow managed to summon up an icy calm. She insisted that she was on that list for no other reason than that she had provided financial aid to the families of those forced to work in Germany. One of the interrogators flew into a rage, slamming the desk with his fist, warning her to stop lying. "Where did you get that money?" the others demanded. "What does your father do?" She replied that he was a notary. The interpreter from the Feldkomman-dantur had been present all along. He not only intervened from time to time with what seemed words in her favor, but also with his eyes appeared to be goading her on to continue the lie she had spun. The interrogation lasted about an hour and a half. It took until evening for the verdict to be handed down at last. A piece of paper was brought to an elderly guard. He glanced at it. "*Raus!*" (Get out!), he suddenly yelled at Marie-Thérèse, as if talking to a dog.[32]

The men Marie-Thérèse had glimpsed in the courtroom that day belonged to a group of six who would be less fortunate than she. The day before, Eudore Weinquin had been arrested in the village of Nadrin, about halfway between Houffalize and La Roche. Weinquin had belonged to the *Mouvement National Belge* (MNB), and the SS men, speaking impeccable French, appeared to know everything about him and the organization's local resistance network. Threatening to burn down his family's home if he resisted, they took Weinquin to a command post, a pistol in his back. At the post he was made to face the wall with his hands above his head for close to two hours. As he stood there, two other members of the MNB, Léon Dethor and Emile Remy, were brought in. In the evening all three were driven to Houffalize where they met up with fellow resistance fighter Sylvain Martin, who had been arrested in Wibrin, a village not far from Nadrin. The following morning they were herded into the courtroom where Marie-Thérèse was soon to await her fate, too. The four men were almost immediately joined by two MNB members from Houffalize, Antoine Bollet and Jean Nadin. The twenty-four-year-old Nadin had been shot in the leg while trying to outrun the German spearheads. He had to be carried up the stairs by his father and aunt. They walked away not knowing if they would ever see him again.

Questioning continued throughout most of the day in separate offices. The SS interrogators turned out to have a list with more than fifty names of local MNB members. Six of the names were theirs, and they were accused of sabotage. Denials drew heavy beatings accompanied by the dry tapping of typewriters recording their words. As the day came to an end, the SS men fleeced the accused of all their belongings: money, cigarettes, watches, even the religious medals pinned inside Léon Dethor's vest.

The six men under cover of darkness were loaded onto a truck together with ten armed guards. The vehicle wound its way out of town and into a pine forest between Houffalize and Mont. On a rutted track the men were pulled from the truck and led to an old anti-tank trench. The guards had to carry the wounded Nadin. Mr. Remy, father of six children, sensed what was about to happen. He tore himself loose from his guard. He did not get far and was shot on the spot. The others were now quickly lined up along the trench, faces toward the abyss. One by one, the SS men seized the victims by the left collar, put a pistol to the neck or behind the ear, and pulled the trigger. Nadin tumbled into his grave, followed by Martin, then by Bollet.

Weinquin was next. He felt the cold steel in his neck, then heard a dry click. In a flash, Weinquin, who had already reconciled himself to death, understood that the gun had jammed. He pushed his executioner away with all his might and made a run for it. Bullets whizzed among the trees, one gashing his jaw, but after about a mile on his stockinged feet he knew he had shaken off the SS men. Weinquin eventually managed to reach Engreux, where villagers took care of him, hiding him from the Germans until the second liberation. It was only when he returned to Houffalize at the end of January that people would learn what had happened to the men interrogated in the town hall that Saturday in December. Accompanied by an American officer, villagers located the antitank trench from which they dug up five bodies on February 2, 1945. Léon Dethor, whom Weinquin thought had also been able to escape, was among the victims.[33]

On Christmas Eve, the day after the first killings, Einsatzgruppe L struck with renewed vigor. This time they arrested Albert Huberty and Armand Bastin, the former a teacher, the other a farmer. Both were from Wibrin; both were accused of belonging to the MNB. On Christmas Day an anxious Bernadette Bastin learned through the grapevine that her brother and Albert Huberty were thought to be held at the hôtel Vieille Auberge in Houffalize and were permitted to have visitors. She had a friend accompany her and immediately started down the long road to town with food and clothing. As they neared Houffalize, they were overtaken by a column of American prisoners. A little further, Germans manning the town's antiaircraft batteries jeered at the women, asking them in plaintive voices if they were going to see the "English."

The Vieille Auberge was a total mess. German soldiers had been celebrating Christmas Eve, and there were bottles and glasses everywhere. The women went from one soldier to another to see what they knew about the men who had been arrested at Wibrin the other day. "Ah! Gone!" a bear of a soldier finally told them mockingly. "Gone where?" Bernadette begged to know. "Gone to work in Germany," the German said. Bernadette burst into tears. "How am I going to break that news to my parents," she sobbed, "I already have two brothers as prisoners in Germany." The women left the hotel. They hurried back along the same road they had come, hoping to regain their village before dark. For the second time that day they passed not far from where Bernadette's brother and Albert Huberty lay buried. They had been shot on the evening of the very day they had been arrested, both with a bullet in the back of the head. Their families would not learn their true fate until the end of April 1945.[34]

In numbing repetition, the day after Christmas again brought terror to the Houffalize region. Fearing reprisals, three former members of the Armée Secrète, Léonard Berscheid and Michel Crémer from Cherain and Joseph Pondant from Limerlé, had fled in the direction of Wibrin before the arrival of the Germans. Once their villages were firmly in German hands, however, they decided to retrace their steps, no longer able to bear the thought of their wives alone with the enemy. They paid for the decision with their lives. Arrested and taken away on Tuesday, December 26, their mutilated corpses were eventually found in the Cedrogne wood just north of Mont.[35]

On the next to last day of 1944, a German military doctor informed the Red Cross of Houffalize that the body of a civilian had been found in a wood near Fontenaille, just north of Cedrogne. Investigation by local authorities revealed the remains to be those of Jules Dubru, a forty-eight-year-old tanner, married to Louise Lammers, father of a daughter called Jeanine. But Jules Dubru had also been the leader of a local MNB group. He had been arrested on December 22, never again to be seen alive. He had died alone with his tormentors, his face roughed up, his body sprawling at the foot of a tree that alone had witnessed the crime.[36]

6 What made the irony of Christmas still more painful for the people in and around Houffalize was that, with the clearing of the skies over the Ardennes, the Allies began sowing more death and destruction than the Wehrmacht and SS combined. Tactical air commands, frustrated by the long wait, feverishly sprang into action. Scores of fighters and fighter-bombers appeared out of the blue, hovering overhead like birds of prey, attentive to the least movement, pouncing upon any tanks, trucks, dumps, or troops caught in the open. As soldiers and vehicles fanned out to buildings for safety and supplies were hidden under roofs, not even the tiniest village could hope to escape the scars of air war.[37]

Montleban, for example, a mere pinprick on the map northeast of Houffalize, would suffer three separate days of bombing even before the year was out. In Vissoule, a hamlet still smaller than Montleban, a bomb on Christmas Eve destroyed the community's most impressive building, the church. People in Tavigny were readying themselves for Mass on Christmas Day when fighter-bombers let them have it. The home of the Liégeois family was instantly ablaze, villagers dashing in and out to rescue furniture, chains of people rushing water in buckets to the flames. Alphonse Antoine, his stables on fire, burst into tears, demanding to know why, as he had never done anyone harm. The day after, the unrepentant planes were back and set the Kettels home on fire.[38]

Rettigny might have remained as inconspicuous a village as ever, had it not been for the German vehicles drawing attention to its crossroads in the days following Christmas. The air raid was over in a flash, but when Henri Collette emerged from the cellar, greasy plumes billowed from a number of enemy vehicles. An agitated German plucked Henri from a chain of civilians forming in front of a house in flames near the crossroads. The soldier shoved a wooden pole into the boy's hands, pushed him toward a sea of flames, and motioned him to try and rake aside the burning debris threatening to ignite the remaining vehicles. Henri struggled in the searing heat until something suddenly distracted the German. Without a second thought Henri dropped the pole and dashed to his boss's house. He thought it wiser not to leave the stable for the rest of the day.[39]

If villages like Rettigny failed to escape brushes with the Allied air forces, Houffalize was bound to attract their full wrath. Though made up of barely 350 houses, the town sat on a crucial road junction, with two bridges across the Ourthe still intact, in the equally crucial corridor between St. Vith and Bastogne that ran more or less through the middle of the German bulge. The first Allied planes appeared over Houffalize around nine o'clock in the morning of Sunday, December 24. Daringly swooping down on the antiaircraft guns, they challenged the flak batteries to bitter duels lasting the better part of the day. Civilians dropped preparations for Christmas Eve, thinking it safer to retreat into their cellars. Cinette Urbin Choffray, overjoyed that her sister Marie-Thérèse had recently been released by the Germans, dashed upstairs from time to time to gape at the planes through the broken windows of their home. "We dare not go outside anymore," she noted in her diary.[40]

Much the same happened on Christmas Day, but this time Allied planes claimed the lives of two civilians. One of them was hotelkeeper Charles Cawet. Having been badly wounded around ten o'clock that morning, Mr. Cawet was transported to the cellar of Dr. Verheggen. There was, however, nothing the doctor could do about the mangled leg from his cellar. An alerted military surgeon at last managed to join Dr. Verheggen around five o'clock in the afternoon. By the time the German had amputated the leg, Mr. Cawet had died from the loss of blood.[41]

With many of the flak batteries silenced, the town itself now became the target as Allied planners wanted to paralyze all German movement by bombing Houffalize into what they called a "choking point." The first serious bombing raids shook the town on December 26. Allied medium bombers appeared in waves between mid-morning and late afternoon, hitting more flak installations, the station, and several sections of town. Inhabitants from St. Roch, a neighborhood close to one of the flak spots, emerged dazed from the rubble after one of the first attacks. Men rushed Marie-Louise Renard, her leg mauled, to the nearest safe haven, using a door for a stretcher. They saw how German soldiers jumped from the windows of a blazing hotel. Wave followed upon wave, aircraft now also pouring incendiaries into the cauldron, causing the dust to be chased by licking flames and acrid smoke. The phosphorus fires created a panic. Even the Ourthe River could be seen burning. Those who could stampeded to the roads leading out of Houffalize. Some poured into the surrounding villages. Many others let themselves be gobbled up by the nearest forests.[42]

"Damage everywhere," Cinette wrote that night. "Dead, wounded. Houses burning. What a mess." For the havoc wrought on the Germans on December 26, Houffalize paid with the lives of at least twenty-eight of its citizens. One of the families worst hit that day were the Wuillemottes. Gisèle and her brother, Robert, spotted the bombers through the kitchen window shortly before noon. They had barely wriggled into the cellar with the others when a bomb squarely punched through the roof. The dust inside the cellar made breathing near impossible. Gisèle cried out. "Save yourself," her mother groaned from somewhere in the dark. Gisèle looked up to see a ray of light. The day before, her father had made a small hole in the ceiling with the intention of leading a stovepipe through it. She climbed the rubble and hoisted herself into the open. A German tank was ablaze in the street. Gisèle noticed she was bleeding from a wound she did not even know she had. A German soldier caught sight of the dazed girl and whisked her off to one of the neighbors. During a lull people rushed to the fateful scene to find seven of the family's eleven dead. They included the girl's grandmother, father, three brothers, sister, and sister-in-law. Gisèle's mother was pulled from the rubble with fractured legs and wounds to the head. By a strange twist of fate, the only person to emerge from the cellar unscathed was Gisèle's six-week-old niece. The infant had to be pried from the arms of her dead mother.[43]

Gisèle learned only a day later that her mother had been taken to a German military hospital in a château just outside Houffalize. When she arrived there with her baby niece, she found her mother on a stretcher surrounded by wounded soldiers. Mrs. Wuillemotte had only the company of a young girl from the village of Fraiture. The girl's feet had been ripped off by an explosion; her brother had brought her to the hospital in a wheelbarrow. Overworked German medics allowed Gisèle to take care of her mother and her civilian neighbor with warm water that she begged from a farmer's wife. It was only when a German ambulance transported her mother to Luxembourg in the afternoon that Gisèle was able to give the baby a long-needed bath. The farmer's wife parted with towels and a small shirt. One German soldier contributed some talcum powder, another a snippet of soap. Gisèle fed the infant with spoonfuls of German soup and a pinch of sugar drawn from her handkerchief and wetted with saliva. Her mother would die in a hospital in Marche a month after the war in Europe had ended.[44]

Even while Gisèle was tending to her mother and niece at the château, the bombers again returned to Houffalize. One of the local priests on Wednesday morning, December 27, had barely made the rounds of the shelters when bombs began killing those he had just comforted and given general absolution. One of the explosives leveled the Gottal garage, claiming five victims. Another one wiped away the Daulne home, somehow leaving the cellar intact and sparing the twenty-six people inside. Dust threatened to suffocate the survivors. There was no water, so someone yelled to grab some bottles and daub their handkerchiefs in wine to protect mouths and noses. As soon as the mayhem began to die down, neighbors rushed to their aid, one by one pulling them from under the rubble via the cellar window. They struggled to free six nuns whose bulging habits made them get stuck in the exit, a man nervously yelling at them to remove their clothes. The last survivor to try and escape through the window was Mrs. Bastin. She weighed more than two hundred pounds, however, and the window refused to let her pass. Only after Dr. Verheggen arrived with tools to enlarge the hole did the woman finally manage to break free.

Crazed with fear, the survivors spilled into the street, desperately looking for safety. Some quickly jammed themselves into already packed cellars nearby. Eva Dubru was still climbing the road when bombs started whistling again. Panting, her shoes lost in the cellar's pandemonium, she dragged both her children after her. Germans hiding in the doorways wanted to help her. She just snarled at them, not even slowing down. Mrs. Dubru finally found refuge in her godmother's home. The bombardment had so traumatized her that even the distant sound of an aircraft sufficed to throw her into a fit. Germans sharing the house took such pity on the young mother that they posted a guard for the specific purpose of warning her in case of real danger. Others who had survived with Mrs. Dubru kept running that Wednesday until they reached the woods. German soldiers hiding in the Bois des Moines offered to help a pregnant Mrs. Desset when she arrived exhausted. She went into a rage, warning them to stay away from her, blaming them for the death of one of her children, lost in the bombardment the previous day.

As if that Wednesday had not already been unsettling enough, in the evening the home for the elderly caught fire. People tried to rush as many as possible to safety on their backs, but before midnight flames had also devoured two of Houffalize's eldest citizens.[45]

Increasing numbers of Houffalois, obeying an "old ancestral reflex," tried to escape the danger by taking to the dense forests. Many thought it safer to remain there. The bombardment of December 30, claiming at least seven more lives, and that which followed on its heels on New Year's Eve, killing another two and bringing the total number of bombing victims to forty-two, swelled their numbers further. A foot and a half of snow had piled up and cold bit to the bone, but the refugees preferred these conditions to the maddening shock waves and phosphorus that came with bombing.

Civilians on their way to the woods in the moonlit night of December 31 brushed past German soldiers who yelled, "Houffalize! Stalingrad!" as if they were deriving perverse pleasure from the ruin of their town. Among the refugees that night, Mrs. Fux and her son Léon had special reason to ponder the cruel vagaries of fate. They had avoided deportation with the rest of their Jewish family in Antwerp in 1942 only by staying invisible in their attic. Later they had gone into hiding in faraway Houffalize. No sooner had they returned to Antwerp after the liberation than Hitler's V1s and V2s had begun threatening their lives all over again. Once more Mrs. Fux had thought it safer for her and her son to sit out the war in the quiet Ardennes.[46]

Nelly Simon's family had arrived in the forest four days earlier. They had joined a number of other families in building four cabins, theirs housing no fewer than twenty-seven people. Every day made the hunger gnaw more. Two of the men went as far as Engreux to look for food. But when they begged the Germans there for bread, they were kicked out. By the turn of the year, enemy soldiers in and around Houffalize were getting as desperate for safety and food as the civilians. The Houffalois had to abandon some of the sturdiest cellars because the Germans were claiming the shelters for themselves. While the Urbin Choffrays stuck to their cellar, Germans hid behind the thick walls upstairs. "They steal a kilogram of butter," Cinette jotted in her diary on January 1. "Have no more doors that close. . . . At night they steal five rabbits and kill them with their guns."[47]

After nine days and nights miserable with cold, one of the forest cabins of Nelly Simon's group was set ablaze on January 5 when someone inside tried to build a fire that would not attract aircraft. It was the signal for the entire group to return to Houffalize. Little did they know that the worst bombardment of their badly battered town was still to come.[48]

Chapter 6

The Southern Shoulder

"If you won't let us through, you'll have to shoot us."

Of the three armies that Hitler lined up for his surprise offensive, the Seventh Army was in every regard by far the weakest. Closer scrutiny of its troops and equipment in fact revealed it to be "more a reinforced corps than a field army." Its commander, Gen. Erich Brandenberger— a potbellied, balding man wearing glasses—could count on no more than one parachute division and three Volksgrenadier divisions. Compared to the two panzer armies to his north, he had a meager 427 artillery pieces and rocket launchers at his disposal, some 30 assault guns, and no tanks. His army relied almost entirely on horse-drawn transport. All this was in large measure a reflection of its less heroic task, for the Seventh Army was designed to operate not as a fist, but as a shield. Brandenberger's orders were to have his troops form a barrier against the counterattack everyone knew Patton would eventually launch from the south with his formidable Third Army.[1]

When the guns opened up along a seventeen-mile stretch of border between Germany and the Grand Duchy of Luxembourg before dawn on Saturday, December 16, none of the weakness of the Seventh Army on paper was apparent to the American troops facing the Germans in the field. Spread thin and yearning for rest, the battered 4th and 28th Infantry Divisions, separated by the 9th Armored Division, were taken completely by surprise and, heavily outnumbered and outgunned, came under tremendous pressure from day one.

Two-thirds of the shells and rockets that first morning pounded troops of the 28th Infantry Division in front of Brandenberger's 85th Corps. Its two divisions were to cover the Seventh Army's sector closest to von Manteuffel's armored spearheads. The most ambitious task was assigned to the 5th Parachute Division. As Brandenberger's northernmost division, it was to push west alongside Panzer Lehr, bypass American-held towns and villages wherever possible, and rush to a blocking position south of Bastogne.[2]

The division's southern prong reached Vianden early on Saturday morning. Already by noon, paratroopers were in control of the town's nine hundred houses and its medieval castle perched on a majestic rock. They discovered the town to be all but empty. American troops had liberated Vianden on September 12. Mad with joy, people had draped the town with their nation's flags and smashed all the Hitler busts in sight. But then the Allies had run up against determined resistance at the German border. Vianden turned out to be too close to the West Wall for comfort. Enemy artillery repeatedly forced the inhabitants into their cellars while sizeable German patrols in search of food and information made the area still less safe. Before long, only a minimum of American troops remained in Vianden and, as in many other Luxembourg border towns and villages, they ordered the civilians to evacuate. By the end of October, no more than 120 of Vianden's inhabitants still lived in what had effectively become no-man's-land. Some 30 of them belonged to the Miliz. One of many local militia that had sprung up in Luxembourg immediately after the liberation in September, Vianden's Miliz—mostly young men who during the occupation had dodged German conscription or deserted—gladly offered its services to the Americans for such tasks as guarding bridges, escorting patrols, and gathering intelligence. They were also keen to prove their mettle in denying access to German patrols. On November 19 this led to a fierce fight inside Vianden that left one militiaman dead as well as a civilian bystander (a woman killed by a hand grenade in her home); four militiamen ended up gravely wounded. The incident had caused still more civilians to pack their bags and abandon their beloved town. Now, less than a month later, Vianden's no-man's-land was unquestionably German again.[3]

Civilians in villages far enough from the West Wall to have escaped American evacuation described the paratroopers filing past as "starving, bedraggled, dirty, and ill-equipped." They were clearly a far cry from what had once been Hitler's elite troops. The 5th Parachute Division, after having been virtually destroyed in Normandy, had been put together again with troops combed mostly from Luftwaffe ground personnel. Under twenty years old on average and in good shape physically, the new soldiers had never gone through paratrooper training and had not the least experience in infantry combat. Moreover, they had been thrown into battle lacking everything from radios to optical devices and, above all, winter clothing. This, combined with logistical difficulties as American artillery hampered bridge-building at the Our and Sûre, gave rise to what an inhabitant in Bourscheid called "organized plunder." Pistols drawn, the paratroopers searched every house and room and "stole bacon and hams, butter and eggs, wine and liquor, typewriters and bicycles, clocks and watches, cans and chickens." They loaded the loot onto carts and then moved on. The scene was to be repeated time and again.[4]

Still further west, in Esch-sur-Sûre, the bells were tolling violently long before dawn on Tuesday. It was the agreed signal for the inhabitants to pack up and flee. Several hours later the village priest arrived in Lultzhausen with the first refugees of his flock. He quickly assembled them to administer Communion. Then he hurried back to get the others who were still packing. In the afternoon he returned with close to three hundred people in a convoy composed of horse-drawn wagons and some rickety automobiles. Lultzhausen's compassionate inhabitants rushed to their aid with pitchers of hot frothy milk.

When the paratroopers took control of Esch-sur-Sûre that same afternoon, fewer than eighty inhabitants remained. They forced one of them, Franz Nicolai, to climb onto a scout car and point them the way to Bavigne. The fifty-three-year-old man never returned. Friends found his lifeless body next to the road some time later. From the back they could see a gaping hole where once his heart had been.[5]

The division's northern prong as well as the paratroopers in the center were making good progress, too. By Monday, December 18, Wiltz, a town with a population of about four thousand, had little military value left as the Germans were already in control of the roads north of it leading to Bastogne. The American troops in Wiltz nevertheless received orders to fight a delaying action. The 44th Engineer Combat Battalion and a provisional battalion of the 28th Infantry Division (composed of headquarters personnel, postal clerks, bandsmen, drivers, and MPs) dug in on the town's outskirts. Fire support was limited and for the best part had to come from the 687th Field Artillery Battalion. Colonel Heilmann, commander of the German parachute division, did not want his men to fight for Wiltz and waste precious time. But the ill-equipped soldiers were inexorably drawn to the town in search of warmth and loot. Their officers, inexperienced in battle and loathe to risk their lives in a war that appeared to be nearing its end, did little to stop them. The paratroopers, against the wishes of their commander, were heading straight for Wiltz.[6]

On Sunday the Americans had done what they could to prevent Wiltz's inhabitants from fleeing and blocking the roads. At their urging Mayor Joseph Simon had crisscrossed the town, driving home the message that there was no reason for panic. On Monday, however, when the first skirmishes erupted as German troops brushed past Wiltz on their way to Bastogne, the civilians could no longer be held back, and despite orders to the contrary, refugees began slipping away. Fearing that the Germans might retaliate against the mayor for having cooperated with the enemy, the Americans agreed to provide Mr. Simon with a pass that would allow him to travel as far back as Brussels without much hassle at security checks.[7]

The 28th Infantry Division's headquarters as well as personnel from the 42nd Field Hospital were told to pull out of Wiltz before dawn on Tuesday, December 19. The Americans now also ordered the civilian population to get ready to leave their town. They let it be known, however, that the only road still available to them was the one leading southwest to Bavigne. People did not need prodding and were assembling in no time. Many were on foot, pushing wheelbarrows and carts or carrying bundles on their backs. Others were balancing suitcases on bicycles. Some had heaped possessions onto horse-drawn wagons or into one of the few cars still running. Around noon the column of several thousand distraught refugees started moving in the damp and foggy weather. Many got as far as Baschleiden, only to be overtaken by the Germans hours later. Their mayor, meanwhile, never made it to Brussels. The Germans halted him at Doncols, barely four miles west of Wiltz. They instantly sent him back to where he had come from.[8]

The defending American troops tried to withdraw from Wiltz on Tuesday night. Having failed to secure their escape routes, however, most of the units were largely destroyed by the onrushing paratroopers. Enemy troops were pouring into Wiltz from all sides by noon on Wednesday. They were rewarded not only with empty homes, but with huge amounts of American supplies, too. For the remainder of the offensive, even Germans from the surrounding villages would come down to Wiltz to stock up on necessities like clothing and luxuries like sugar, coffee, and wine.[9]

Most of the people who had fled from Wiltz and the surrounding area hastily returned in the next few days hoping to keep their homes and animals safe. Through snow that had begun to fall on Monday, farmers from Schlindermanderscheid, for example, some with their cows, gradually trickled back to their village. One of them was Nicolaas Kneip. Because of the bad weather, he had left his wife, four children, and mother behind in Bourscheid. At the end of the week a German driver finally agreed to give his family a lift. The truck stopped on several occasions to pick up wounded soldiers, and the ride in the bone-chilling cold took hours. By the time Mr. Kneip's family arrived in Schlindermanderscheid they were blue with cold. It was too much for Nicolaas Kneip's aged mother who would not live to see the village's second liberation.[10]

Wiltz's inhabitants, meanwhile, proved powerless to stop the paratroopers from plundering their town. To make matters worse, many had to accept the ultimate humiliation of having the enemy billeted on them. Still, in the long month of reoccupation that was to follow, some succeeded in defying the Germans in a manner that could easily have cost them their lives. In attics and basements, civilians hid at least three GIs who had failed to make it to the rear, two of whom were badly wounded. To the women and men involved, the act was one of resistance as much as humaneness.[11]

2 Teamed up with the 5th Parachute Division in General Brandenberger's 85th Corps was the 352nd Volksgrenadier Division. Mainly put together with troops taken from the Luftwaffe and the navy, most of its soldiers, like the paratroopers on their right flank, lacked frontline experience. They were to stab through the American defenses in the direction of Diekirch and then to punch their way to Ettelbrück. The latter town sits at the confluence of the Sûre and Alzette and controls the main road leading straight south to Luxembourg City, the grand duchy's capital.[12]

The Volksgrenadiers, too, were facing Americans of the 28th Infantry Division. Civilians in this sector had been astonished by the appearance of "the smoke-blackened, unshaven, exhausted, ragged and totally worn-out soldiers" when late in November the GIs heaved themselves from the trucks that had brought them straight from combat hell in the Hürtgen Forest to the peaceful Ardennes.[13]

People in Longsdorf, a hamlet of no more than nine houses situated on the Volksgrenadiers' right flank, had seen little of the American newcomers. The GIs had traded rations for homemade food and brandy, but had generally preferred to keep to themselves. Despite its proximity to the West Wall, Longsdorf had somehow escaped evacuation by the Americans. Still, unnerved by enemy patrolling and the constant sound of artillery, three families had left of their own accord. Now, before daylight on December 16, their neighbors were wishing they had joined them when they could. The bark of cannon and howling of Nebelwerfers lasted more than two hours. Then things quieted down and Volksgrenadiers swarmed into the hamlet. They forced the Sinner family to come out of their cellar. While the Germans searched their home, the Sinners stood in the paved yard with their hands in the air. "The Faust family next door was already out in the street under guard," fourteen-year-old Joseph Sinner noted. "We looked at each other in despair. Nobody dared say a word." All they could do was watch as the Germans led away the handful of Longsdorf's American defenders.[14]

The following day Germans and Americans battled for Tandel, a collection of some fifteen houses, a school, and a church about a mile west of Longsdorf. Tracing American telephone wire to the windows of a farm owned by yet another Sinner family, Volksgrenadiers wrongly assumed that the enemy was still holed up inside. They lobbed grenades through the window and into the hallway; then burst into the house with their machine guns blazing. In the solid cellar of the century-old farm, more than forty civilians began screaming as they heard the blasts upstairs. The door to the cellar was kicked in, and barking German voices chased the frightened people from their hiding place. They waded through the acrid smoke that filled the hallway. On the floor, in an oily pool of blood, lay the lifeless body of Marie Duszynska, a Polish girl and forced laborer whom the German authorities had put to work on the Sinner farm in the summer of 1944. Outside, the Volksgrenadiers ordered the civilians to line up against the wall with their faces to the yard and their hands in the air. The roof of the cow barn was on fire. Animals bellowed with pain. Peter Ney tried to escape to the road but was shot almost instantly. In the turmoil that erupted Peter Winter tried to get away, too. A bullet stopped him before he even made it to the brick bakery house. As heavy shelling resumed, the soldiers herded the villagers into a flimsy wooden shed and disappeared from sight. By the time Tandel was firmly in German hands on December 18, shrapnel had claimed the lives of two more civilians.[15]

The two men the Germans shot in Tandel on Sunday were, in fact, from Fouhren, a village of some forty-three families, located a couple of miles north of Tandel. Wedged between paratroopers passing to the north and Volksgrenadiers to the south, the village had become isolated, with Company E of the American 109th Infantry determined to hold out. Though Fouhren was not much more than a mile away from the West Wall, the Americans had not forced its inhabitants to evacuate. Even when German shells had started falling on September 27 and continued to do so at regular intervals, the villagers had stubbornly stuck to their land. Disaster had struck late in the afternoon of November 18, when a shell exploded in the midst of people harvesting potatoes. Smoke and dust had cleared to reveal two young men dead and several people horribly mutilated. Two girls had died from their wounds soon after. Still, no more than five families had abandoned Fouhren by the time fate cruelly struck again early on December 16. With the din of battle closing in fast, six families had immediately left in the direction of Bastendorf. A couple of hours later, another fourteen families had fled as far as Tandel, where most of them had found shelter in the ill-fated Sinner farm. By the time the remaining villagers had wanted to escape, the GIs had deemed it too dangerous and had driven them back to their cellars. The fight for Fouhren lasted until the stubborn American company surrendered on the evening of December 18.[16]

Further south, on the 352nd Division's left flank, Volksgrenadiers were fighting their way through the Sûre Valley in the direction of Diekirch. A town of about 4,000 people, Diekirch had already been dealt its share of the war's burdens. Some 160 of the town's young men had been made to join Germany's armed forces. By the summer of 1944, close to 30 of them were known to be dead or missing. Dozens of townspeople, many of them deserters, had joined resistance groups. Several members had been caught and incarcerated in prisons and concentration camps. It was no surprise then that when the Americans liberated the Diekirch area on September 10 and 11, 1944, the elated people barely knew how to express their joy. Within weeks, Diekirch's populace, especially its girls, was merrily singing the praise of "the sugar boy from America" to the melody of a well-known Boy Scout ditty.[17]

With German forces gone and Luxembourg civilian authorities in disarray, the U.S. military quickly filled the vacuum by setting up a government of its own. American Civil Affairs personnel were soon running much of the town. Since Diekirch was only five miles away from the West Wall, many aspects of life remained on a war footing. The Americans strictly enforced blackout measures, imposed a curfew, and prohibited civilians from driving a car or leaving town without the appropriate papers. In time, however, the GIs also restored a much-needed sense of normalcy. They made sure a steady supply of foodstuffs reached the town. To prevent crime and, more particularly, violent acts against collaborators, all civilians not officially registered as belonging to the police force or its auxiliaries were disarmed. German place and street names were replaced by the French signs that had been there before the occupation. The sole movie theater in town received permission to show movies again on weekends. On October 7 Diekirch's schools reopened. On November 5 the local soccer team beat the U.S. Army's team 9 to 3. As far as Diekirch's inhabitants were concerned, the war was over. A week before the German counteroffensive was to be unleashed, U.S. Army posters in Ettelbrück and Diekirch announced a huge ball open to soldiers and civilians. The date for the big event was Saturday, December 16.[18]

Long before dawn that Saturday, in a street north of Diekirch, Mr. Zeyen woke up to a jumble of noise. The sounds had nothing to do with the military band they were expecting that day. There was a strange whistling in the air followed by rumblings inside the town. American batteries were opening up in reply. Then, suddenly, there was a rapidly swelling hiss, followed by an immense explosion nearby. Mr. Zeyen heard the windows crash into his home and in a split second was out of bed. An American soldier darted into the house. While yelling at the Zeyens to seek shelter in the cellar, he plucked their baby boy, Albert, from his bed, rushing him to safety.[19]

The heavy predawn barrage lasted until eight o'clock. A welcome lull held until eleven o'clock. Then the shelling resumed without much let up for the rest of the day. A terrifying blast in the Rue Clairefontaine early in the afternoon caused horrific injuries to six GIs and seven civilians. Gendarme Gillen at the Nitrolux Shoe Cream factory witnessed scenes of carnage: wounded soldiers and civilians splayed in the street; others stumbling around blindly; a dazed man slumped onto the sidewalk, his lower arm virtually severed; fearless medics darting to casualties who appeared beyond help. So precise and devastating was the shelling that the Americans figured observers must be directing the fire from within Diekirch. Orders immediately went out to the troops to keep an eye out for German infiltrators or civilian spies. To add to the chaos, bedraggled civilians from villages near the West Wall began pouring into Diekirch, bringing news of a major German offensive. This worried Diekirch's inhabitants even more than the shelling, and soon the first families were heading out with packed wagons and carts. They did not get far. To prevent the supply routes for the 109th Infantry from getting jammed, MPs, gendarmes, and militiamen had quickly been posted on all of Diekirch's exit routes. Under strict orders to let none of the civilians through, stone-faced guards turned the pleading people back to a town that now looked more like a trap.[20]

German artillery continued to pound Diekirch day and night with only an occasional pause. By the end of the second day, some sixty wounded civilians had been hustled to Ettelbrück and then driven to hospitals in Luxembourg City. A number of the town's blocks and sections were reduced to rubble. Many more buildings were damaged. Fires were raging everywhere, and several fully equipped fire engines arrived from the Luxembourg capital to help prevent a catastrophe. A group of German prisoners that was marched through the smoke-filled town that Sunday had their American guards to thank for escaping a lynching at the hands of outraged mobs.[21]

Gilsdorf, a village less than a mile east of Diekirch, but located south of the Sûre, fell prey to the fury of German cannon on Monday morning. Sizzling shrapnel mowed down Mrs. Thielen and her ten-year-old daughter, Therese. Americans rushed the victims to the nearest hospital, where Mrs. Thielen lost one of her legs, and her child had a foot amputated. In the afternoon, news of the sighting of the first Germans on the edge of Gilsdorf quickly drove the harried villagers into the cold and onto the road to Diekirch. The refugees succeeded in entering the town, but failed to get out of it again. American guards and their auxiliaries remained under orders to stop civilians from pouring out of Diekirch. All of the more than one hundred men, women, and children, who around noon had managed to escape in the direction of Ettelbrück over a dirt road, were back in Diekirch in less than two hours. They were briskly escorted back to their homes by GIs and militiamen with rifles at the ready.[22]

With the enemy clearly at Diekirch's gates on Tuesday, American appeals for calm were falling on increasingly deaf ears. The previous day, the exhausted Sinner family had arrived in Diekirch from Tandel, where on Saturday they had been fortunate to survive the bloody German attack on their farm. Now, as dawn broke, militiamen were telling the traumatized people they were not allowed to leave Diekirch for a safe haven still farther west. Twenty-year-old Marianne Sinner was beside herself with fear and rage. "If you won't let us through," she threatened, "you'll have to shoot us." The guards dropped their stone masks and stepped aside.[23]

Panic soared later that day when unmistakable signs told the stunned inhabitants that the GIs themselves were preparing to abandon Diekirch. American officers had indeed quietly informed town officials that their troops would commence a phased withdrawal as of eight o'clock that evening. At the same time they had told them that evacuation of the civilians would be out of the question. It would alert the Germans to the withdrawal, lead to road congestion, and invite enemy infiltration. Horror-stricken, the town officials argued and pleaded with the Americans until those in command at last did agree to allow the population to get away. But they set strict conditions. The evacuation was not to start before midnight, by which time most of the troops would have gone. Moreover, with the vital Diekirch-Ettelbrück road reserved for American troops and the northern roads threatened by the Germans, people would have to cross the small railway bridge over the Sûre and flee southward to Stegen. They could take no lights and there was to be as little noise as possible.[24]

Gendarmes, militiamen, and firefighters immediately fanned out to inform people in their cellars of what had been agreed with the Americans. As darkness closed its grip, however, plans for the orderly withdrawal soon unraveled. Hours before the agreed departure time, MPs were forcefully removing groups of anxious civilians trying to slip out of town with the American convoys. Already by ten o'clock, hundreds of fearful inhabitants were assembling at the railway bridge. Not enough guards were present to restrain the crowd because, at the urging of the Americans, most gendarmes and militiamen had fled Diekirch before the civilians. The stampede for the narrow bridge began before midnight. A jumble of people elbowed their way across. Bicycles got tangled up, packed wheelbarrows and carts obstructed free passage, horse-drawn wagons and even some cars attempted to negotiate the steel tracks and force their way through. Enemy shelling sent ripples of fear through the surging mass. Then a deafening explosion rocked the bridge. A mine that the Americans had neglected to remove had gone off, tearing a hole in the steel plating, maiming several people and killing a horse. Similar scenes of confusion were taking place on the wooden bridge over the Alzette as the Ettelbrück populace, two miles southwest of Diekirch, had been given the green light for evacuation, too. Amid the pushing and shoving in the dark, Mrs. Goergen fell off the bridge and into the swollen river. It was March 1945 before her body was discovered somewhere downstream.[25]

The following morning American troops of the 10th Armored Division, rushed in from the south as reinforcements, were blocked in the roads by endless throngs of refugees, several of them so old, ill, or injured they had been loaded onto carts and wheelbarrows. Some three thousand civilians were swarming down from Diekirch, their ranks swelled by inhabitants from Ettelbrück, including dozens of mental patients from the town's sanatorium. Medical units and service companies fell out to provide aid and helped to remove the unfortunates from the danger zone in trucks.[26]

The Volksgrenadiers, meanwhile, made their way into Diekirch and Ettelbrück unopposed. Between three and four hundred of Diekirch's inhabitants had remained behind. Many of them were elderly who had refused to leave their homes. Others had failed to receive the news of the evacuation and awoke startled to find their town suddenly deserted. As the Germans stalked Diekirch's ghostly streets, the shadowy presence of civilians made them jittery. They kicked in doors, checked identities, and eventually were herding along fifty to sixty men and women. The terribly frightened people were locked up in the town church and placed under armed guard. Their identities were checked again; they were questioned; there were hints and accusations of partisan activity, of franc-tireurs taking pot shots, of civilians cutting telephone cables. By evening, however, the women were told they could leave. The following morning the men, too, were released.[27]

The soldiers' focus quickly shifted from the civilians to plunder. By noon on Wednesday, December 20, more than a hundred bicycles were lined up in front of the Diekirch post office. Stables were emptied of their horses. Germans roared by on stolen motorcycles and in the cars of local doctors and businessmen. The town's shoe stores were broken into and emptied. Bedding and mattresses, even razors, combs, and hairbrushes disappeared from people's homes. Above all, however, the Volksgrenadiers needed food. From Ettelbrück all the way back to the West Wall, German troops were scouring stores and farms to supplement the meager rations that were only sporadically reaching them. By the time the Volksgrenadiers captured Diekirch and Ettelbrück, for example, nothing much remained for the people to eat in Longsdorf, the village that had been occupied early in the morning of December 16. Cows and beef cattle had disappeared. All of the pigs had been slaughtered. There was no more cackling of chickens. In the Faust farm, the Germans had even laid hands on the mashed pears and set to work distilling them into brandy. For the remainder of the occupation, the Faust family had practically nothing left to eat but a kind of "mush," cooked from wheat flour and sugar.[28]

3 While General Brandenberger's northern divisions were clawing their way to Wiltz and Ettelbrück, his southern wing, formed by the 80th Corps, crossed the Sûre under orders to capture the high ground to the southwest and form a blocking position in the direction of the Luxembourg capital. Volksgrenadiers of the 276th Division jumped off from an area roughly between Wallendorf and Bollendorf. The outfit had been destroyed in Normandy and had just arrived from Poland where it had hurriedly been rebuilt. Its soldiers were young and, like many of Brandenberger's troops, they lacked any experience in combat.[29]

In the 276th Division's assault sector, too, most of the villages closest to the West Wall had long been evacuated. In Eppeldorf, however, a village located no more than three miles from the German defense line, the Americans after their arrival in September had granted the inhabitants permission to stay. At the time the villagers had felt incredibly fortunate. On Saturday, December 16, as German shells shattered the village windows, battered the church, and ripped apart the Reuter home, they cursed their bad luck. They did even more so on Sunday morning when one of the villagers hurried through Eppeldorf with the stunning cry that the Germans were back and digging in nearby. The news sent a shock wave through the village. Young people hopped on bicycles and sped away, pedaling for their lives without looking back. Families rushed to fetch horses and load wagons. By the end of the day, Eppeldorf had emptied of all but eighty of its inhabitants, many of them elderly. It took the Volksgrenadiers another day to wrest the village from the outnumbered Americans. At sundown on Monday, hundreds of German soldiers were scouring Eppeldorf for food, clothing, and alcohol. American artillery did not leave them alone for long. Around six o'clock that evening the large Koenig barn was ablaze and flames threatened to leap to adjacent buildings. Handfuls of able-bodied men and women, helped by the village priest, tried to prevent the fire from spreading. Some German soldiers were decent enough to pitch in. Others took full advantage of the chaos and went about emptying the local grocery store of food, sugar, and tobacco.[30]

On the fourth day of the offensive, the Volksgrenadiers of the 276th Division had gone as far as they could and began preparing defensive positions. American troops of the 9th Armored Division facing the Germans were happy to do the same and wait for Patton's Third Army reinforcements to arrive.

The 212th Volksgrenadier Division, the second outfit in the 80th Corps, was the Seventh Army's best. That is why General Brandenberger chose its experienced officers and youthful Bavarian soldiers to perform the crucial task of anchoring the army's flank in the area around Echternach, the southernmost point of Hitler's counteroffensive. Under cover of fog and darkness, the Volksgrenadiers on December 16 crossed the Sûre on both sides of Echternach, leaving a small American outpost trapped in the town. The forward unit was Company E of the 12th Infantry, a regiment of the 4th Infantry Division that had arrived battered from the Hürtgen Forest earlier that month. The exhausted men of Company E until that fateful December 16 had enjoyed every day in Echternach. Not only was the medieval, abbatial town picturesque and one of Luxembourg's prime tourist attractions in peacetime, the soldiers were also free to sleep in whatever bed they fancied and plunder all the wine, canned foods, and potatoes they could eat. Echternach, in fact, was a ghost town, for on October 6 all of its five thousand inhabitants had been forced to leave their homes.[31]

The evacuation had been a traumatic experience for the inhabitants. In the shadow of the West Wall, the Germans in September had held their grip on Echternach as a bridgehead on the right bank of the Sûre even while abandoning the surrounding villages. The Americans were still pounding the town early in October and causing increasing numbers of civilian casualties despite the fact that most people had been living in the basements continuously since mid-September. In the early hours of October 6 the Germans decided that it was time for the inhabitants to go. They sent a civilian delegation with a white flag to the American lines and managed to obtain a cease-fire for the next few hours. Church bells and town criers signaled the start of the evacuation. Mayhem erupted when shortly before noon a misunderstanding caused American artillery to fire into the assembling crowds, killing and maiming several people, horses, and oxen. When order and calm returned at last, a two-mile-long caravan of wagons and carts piled high with possessions pushed off, slowly winding its way to the American lines at Herborn and Berbourg. There, however, the GIs wanted the evacuees off the roads as soon as possible, sending them on to Bech, a village where gendarmes and militiamen soon failed to cope with the civilian deluge, and people ended up sleeping even among the animals in the stables. Meanwhile, civilian volunteers rushed a fire truck back and forth between the American lines and the Echternach hospital four times, carrying off half of its one hundred patients. The next day, the Americans attacked Echternach, leaving parts of the town ablaze. Troops created artificial fog to shield the doctors and militiamen who, while the battle raged, continued to rescue patients from the hospital in the beat-up fire truck. Even during the mop-up in the days that followed, American soldiers had discovered civilians determined to cling to their homes. The GIs had remained deaf to their pleas and forced them all to evacuate.[32]

Traumatic as September and October had been for the people of Echternach, on December 16 they soon came to realize they had escaped much greater harm because of the evacuation. In the town's deserted streets, Company E managed to hold out against the Volksgrenadiers for five days. Then it was all over and the Germans were master again of the town minus its inhabitants. That same day the Germans also captured Berdorf, located northwest of Echternach, and Lauterborn, a village just over a mile behind Echternach. It was the signal for the GIs of the 12th Infantry to fall back to a second line of defense anchored at Consdorf. Only in Osweiler and Dickweiler, villages southwest of Echternach and at the extreme base of the German southern flank, two surrounded forward companies of GIs refused to budge until reinforcements eventually arrived.

Consdorf lay just outside the zone marked by the Americans for evacuation in September and October. By November, the village, inhabited by some five hundred people in peacetime, had been bursting at the seams as it tried to absorb most of Berdorf's evacuees and their livestock. Animal feed became so short in supply that on December 15 the mayor and American Civil Affairs officers decided to organize a caravan of fifteen wagons and forty-five farmers (all of them subjected to thorough security checks) to gather whatever fodder could still be found at Berdorf.[33]

A second trip, planned for the morning of December 16, never took place. The village mayor and priest did manage to complete the marriage ceremony for two of Consdorf's couples that Saturday morning, but gendarmes had to disperse the curious crowd when shells began to fall close enough to shatter nearby windows. Enemy pressure on Consdorf three days later was serious enough for the Americans to order the evacuation of the village. At noon a Civil Affairs detachment of the 4th Infantry Division was planning the evacuation in close cooperation with the mayor and priest. A bus sped away to Junglinster with most of the elderly and infirm on board. The villagers in less than an hour had loaded wagons and carts and were assembling near the church. Of the many roads radiating from Consdorf only one remained open to the evacuees as all others were reserved strictly for military traffic. To avoid congestion, groups were to leave at five-minute intervals. From a distance, however, German artillery was unable to distinguish between American convoys and civilian caravans. By late afternoon, four of Consdorf's evacuees, one of them the mayor's wife, lay dead beside the road.[34]

When the retreating troops of the 12th Infantry took up positions in Consdorf on December 21, they found that village empty, too. Only a few farmers, all of whom were carefully screened, had been allowed to stay behind and care for the animals. The courageous volunteers were to experience frightening days. But they would also taste the sweet satisfaction of seeing the Americans deny the enemy access to Consdorf and their beloved land beyond.[35]

5 For those in Luxembourg trapped on the wrong side of the front line, the nightmare of life in a police state resumed almost as soon as German troops regained control. A variety of security forces descended on the grand duchy even before von Manteuffel had brought his full strength to bear against Bastogne from the north and Brandenberger had run out of steam in the assault sector to the south. A *Kommando* of Einsatzgruppe L, the same outfit responsible for a wave of terror between Houffalize and Bastogne, settled down in Clervaux while the town still smoldered. Its agents were led by an SS officer who had earned himself a reputation for the role he had played in putting down the Warsaw ghetto rising. Although he and his men in the Ardennes operated under direct orders from Berlin, they soon

found themselves competing with four Kommandos of the Gestapo that were being led from Trier. To complicate the repression, the Sicherheitsdienst in Koblenz sent some of its agents, too, though they were to prove less active. On top of that, the *Feldgendarmerie*, the military police, could also be counted on to arrest civilians and, if warranted, hand them over to the party's watchdogs. Together, the various security forces were responsible for protecting the troops, emasculating the resistance and militia, and hunting down Luxembourgers who had escaped conscription or forced labor.[36]

Having been handed the unexpected opportunity to avenge the humiliation of September 1944, the security forces set to work with relish. Many of the men in the Gestapo Kommandos, for example, had been active in Luxembourg during the first occupation and were now itching to settle the score. A series of arrests took place across occupied territory as early as Tuesday, December 19. In Clervaux, Theodore Knauf and Henri Fischbach were captured and transported to Germany. Mr. Knauf never learned exactly what it was they accused him of, but he was fortunate enough to be liberated by American troops early in April 1945 while on a forced march to Buchenwald. Henri Fischbach paid the ultimate price for having deserted from the German army: all trace of him vanished somewhere between the concentration camps of Buchenwald and Neuengamme late in March 1945. More arrests followed that Tuesday among young Luxembourgers, many of them deserters, who were fleeing to the Belgian border. Three men from Bettendorf and one from Reisdorf were collared in Sëlz and whisked away to Germany. All of them returned home at the end of the war, though Joseph Wagner did so without his lower right arm. Around that time, three more men—two from Eselborn, one from Clervaux—were apprehended at Moinet, just inside Belgium. No one ever heard of them again.[37]

On Wednesday, December 20, a Kommando of the Gestapo descended on Tandel. They drove all men between the ages of seventeen and sixty-five into a large cellar. These included refugees from Fouhren and Vianden and villagers brought in from Longsdorf. All of them were subjected to long and tense questioning about the resistance and Miliz. The prisoners were released the following day, but not before having been made to bury dead soldiers and cattle even while American shells rocked the village. Still, the men were glad to be let off the hook so easily. Not all victims of the Gestapo that Wednesday were as lucky as the men in Tandel. In Troisvierges, about a dozen men were hauled in for interrogation, seven of whom were put on a transport to Germany. Three of them would die on enemy soil. Leo Despeler, for example, accused of evading forced labor and having mistreated a Luxembourg collaborator in September 1944, is believed to have perished at Buchenwald. Matherne Geib was badly wounded during an Allied air attack on a camp near Hinzert and died in a hospital at Hermeskeil in February 1945. He was guilty of nothing more than having returned to his hometown unauthorized from forced labor on the German railroads. Though the reoccupation was to be short-lived, Mr. Geib and the others were only the first of a long list of Luxembourgers to fall victim to Nazi executioners eager to participate in extending the Reich's reach once again.[38]

Part II
Islands and Dams

Chapter 7

The Fall of St. Vith

"They screamed like an army of Redskins."

So many soldiers of the 18th Volksgrenadier Division converged on Wallerode for the final push against St. Vith that the villagers themselves threatened to be squeezed out. Josef Theissen, the fifteen-year-old who had seen the Germans arrive on Sunday, December 17, watched the soldiers' every move with the fascination for things military characteristic of boys his age. He was brusquely torn from his reveries, however, when German soldiers suddenly ordered him and his family out into the street: their home had been chosen to serve as a command post. Only the vehement protests and emotional pleas by Josef's father made the Germans finally change their minds. Josef breathed a sigh of relief—for a moment the reality of war had come uncomfortably close.[1]

In Eiterbach, a hamlet not far from Wallerode and a touch closer to St. Vith, the Backes family was less fortunate than the Theissens. On Tuesday German officers commandeered their home in the name of no one less than General von Manteuffel. To argue with his high-ranking staff would have been a waste of breath: the Backes family meekly packed their suitcases and disappeared in the direction of Wallerode. When a little later Mr. Backes sneaked back to check on his house, he learned that even Walter Model, field marshal and von Manteuffel's superior, had spent some time in his living room. Mr. Backes remained unimpressed, however, and insisted on expressing his displeasure at the situation. But a German officer merely quipped: "You have now had von Manteuffel and Model over, the next one to show up will be the Führer." Mr. Backes failed to smile.[2]

1 Model and von Manteuffel had not been given to smiling either lately. Von Manteuffel had thought it possible to capture St. Vith by the end of the first day of the offensive. On Tuesday, however, the fourth day of the operation, German troops were still probing the town's defenses without much success. If Model sat in Mr. Backes's living room that day, it was to urge von Manteuffel on while promising reinforcements.[3]

Inside besieged St. Vith, GIs and civilians tried to continue life with at least a semblance of normality. With the mayor, aldermen, and police forces gone since Sunday, Americans hastily appointed Paul Freches mayor ad interim. Mr. Freches was a prominent citizen in good standing with the Allies. He immediately donned a white armband as token of his new position, then rushed off to deal with the mounting problems facing the civilian population. The most urgent one was food. Milk was almost impossible to get. Many people were eating nothing but potatoes, heaps of which fortunately had been stored in their basements before the onslaught of winter. All the GIs could do was pitch in with manpower, fuel, and flour to help local bakeries produce more bread.[4]

The situation gradually grew more desperate. On Wednesday, tanks and infantry of the newly committed *Führer Begleit Brigade* tried to get into St. Vith from Wallerode. The attack was beaten off. The morning after, however, Americans dug in around St. Vith reported signs that told them an all-out offensive could be expected at any moment. Tension inside the town rose to a feverish pitch. Erna Endres briefly left the safety of her home to get some bread early on Thursday. GIs promptly halted her and asked for her papers. Miss Endres had forgotten them. The soldiers in a jeep rushed her to the Schiltz pharmacy for interrogation by the senior officers assembled there. A bewildered Miss Endres watched how Mr. Esselen, too, was brought in. Both were hugely relieved to find Miss Jamar in the presence of the GIs. Mr. Esselen threw his arms round her neck crying. Lia Jamar had served as an interpreter for the Americans ever since the liberation. She knew the two civilians well. She convinced the soldiers that these people were not spies.[5]

Margaret Doepgen also ventured out that day to run some errands. In the Heckingstrasse she suddenly bumped into American soldiers. They stood alongside some trucks ready to transport more civilians out of town. One of the GIs urged Mrs. Doepgen to get in. A cold fear seized her. She had left her mother and two children behind. She could not risk being taken away without them. Margaret Doepgen turned and bolted. She heard the soldier yell behind her but refused to stop for explanations. A couple of shots rang out. Mrs. Doepgen disappeared into an alleyway and ran for her life. Some Americans clearly thought the enemy was already in St. Vith.[6]

Mrs. Münster and her family would have been glad to accept a ride in an American truck had they known about the convoy. Maria Münster had come to live with her cousin in St. Vith to escape the fierce bombing of her German hometown, Cologne. Her cousin had first considered escaping to Galhausen, a hamlet barely a mile south of St. Vith. But Mrs. Münster had so much difficulty walking that it was clear she would not even make it that far. If she had to be left behind, the family decided firmly, they would all stay. They packed some belongings and sought refuge in the nearby convent and town landmark, St. Josef's Kloster.[7]

All the while the shelling steadily increased. German artillery had caused significant damage during the first days of the offensive but had never turned into a barrage. On Wednesday, however, the explosions grew so intense that even Father Goffart decided to join the refugees in the cellar of the St. Josef's Kloster. He took a chalice and wafers with him and built a small altar in one of the subterranean storage rooms. St. Vith's streets were littered with glass, the slaughterhouse was burning, and frightened cattle were roaming the streets. The number of refugees in the huge vaulted cellars beneath the convent now swelled to the point that they could barely be counted. By Thursday morning there was simply no more room for some of the desperate new arrivals. The chaos worsened by the hour as more and more wounded GIs from the front lines poured into the cellars. The Americans finally told the civilians to make room and move to the basement of the convent's chapel.[8]

Mrs. Doepgen was one of many people who had traded the small basement of a private home for the sturdier construction of the convent's cellars and their comforting feeling of community. But she noticed right away that the vaults in the chapel's cellar were flimsy compared with the others and thus more likely to collapse under the weight of direct hits. She grabbed her two small children by the arm and dragged them into the street. With nine-month-old Heinz in a baby carriage, hidden beneath blankets and suitcases, and her three-year-old daughter on one arm, she zigzagged through St. Vith and a hail of shells until she reached her aunt's house.[9]

German troops reached their jump-off positions for the final attack against St. Vith around noon on Thursday. At three o'clock their artillery unleashed the preliminary bombardment on the American lines. So ferocious was the barrage that even veteran GIs swore they had never experienced anything like it. At around four o'clock, as dusk approached, the shelling was redirected and began blasting the rear of the lines and the town itself. It was the signal for Volksgrenadiers all along the line to hurl themselves forward at St. Vith.[10]

The battered American defenses east of St. Vith were crumbling before midnight. A heavy snowstorm raged while a motley collection of GIs and vehicles streamed through town heading west. Fires soaring from buildings burned orange holes in the gloomy night. The glow revealed German flags on houses where not even a week ago had fluttered Belgian and American ones. Glimpses could be seen in the upper windows of men in civilian clothing holding rifles: they were sniping at the retreating GIs.[11]

By the early morning hours of Friday, December 22, American troops had withdrawn from their defenses in front of St. Vith to a more or less stable line behind it. The town now lay wide open to the Germans. In the house of her aunt in the Rathausstrasse, Mrs. Doepgen knew that St. Vith had changed hands that night when she heard the noise of hobnailed boots in the street and the rooms over their basement. The metallic, grating sound was unmistakably German, for most GIs in the past three months had trod softly with quiet rubber soles.[12]

Frozen to the bone after almost six days of uninterrupted fighting in windswept fields and forests, German soldiers were determined to enjoy the warmth of St. Vith's houses as soon as possible. Soldiers of the 18th Volksgrenadier Division as well as a regiment of the 62nd Volksgrenadier Division stampeded into town all at once. Service troops followed close on their heels. Even some SS units of the Sixth Panzer Army elbowed their way into town in an attempt to bypass the stalled traffic in the Losheim Gap. The modest town in no time turned into a bottleneck of such massive proportions that German traffic came to a complete standstill.[13]

Utter confusion reigned. Large parts of St. Vith had been badly damaged by German artillery fire. Streets were filled with rubble, glass, and plaster. Buildings were burning or smoldering. Acrid smoke filled the air. The town was a jumble of civilians, soldiers, and prisoners crisscrossing the streets, plowing their way through traffic jams, swarming in all directions. German soldiers everywhere were claiming abandoned houses. Veterans dragged mattresses from the bedrooms into the safer rooms downstairs. While some Germans hurried to stoke kitchen stoves and ovens with whatever would burn, others feverishly scavenged for food. They plundered American stocks and scoured cellars for preserving jars holding anything from blueberries to blood sausage. The main problem turned out to be the water supply. Their own army's shells had done so much damage to the town's mains that finding even enough fresh water to drink proved difficult.[14]

Yet, even amid the chaos of the occupation's first days, the newly installed *Stadtkommandantur* deftly went about the business of reestablishing political control over the civilian population. St. Vith had barely fallen to the Germans when Paul Freches was arrested. He was accused of collaboration with the enemy for having agreed to serve as the town's mayor for exactly four days. His case was further aggravated by the fact that his son had failed to return to his German unit in September. Several other civilians were rounded up for no other reason than that they had worked as police auxiliaries under Freches in the days of the siege. Some of St. Vith's notables pleaded their case with the Germans, however, and within days managed to secure their release from the town's prison.[15]

American artillery was quickly adding to the confusion paralyzing St. Vith. As soon as they had taken up new positions behind the town, guns began blasting buildings and streets with all their might, hoping to delay the enemy's advance as long as possible. During the German barrage Elly Meurer and her son Erich had found refuge in the *Hotel zur Post* that was owned by her sister. There were forty people in the basement, mostly neighbors and refugees from the German town of Bleialf. With the town firmly in the hands of the Germans again on Friday, many had clambered out of the hotel's basement to scrounge something to eat. Mrs. Meurer stayed below with the children. The adults had barely gone when she heard shells crash with a deafening roar into the kitchen and adjoining rooms. A terrible panic erupted both upstairs and downstairs. Mrs. Klein was the first to stagger down the stairs. "Mrs. Meurer," she whispered, "I think we can go back now." "My God," Mrs. Meurer cried, "Mrs. Klein, your arm!" Mrs. Klein stared at her; then she fainted on the stairs. Her left arm flopped beside her body, held by the merest thread of flesh. Blood gushed from the wound, coloring the steps a dark red. Soldiers and civilians carried more injured into the basement one by one until the space was crammed with people crying and screaming. A German medic and a civilian placed Mrs. Klein on a stretcher. All they could do for her was recite a prayer.

It is not clear how many civilian victims the battle for St. Vith claimed. But Mrs. Meurer had seen enough that Friday to want to leave the town as far behind as possible. At night she and her son arrived in Galhausen. She had to go from house to house to find shelter. German troops in Galhausen had claimed not only the stables for their horses, but also some of the living rooms. Mrs. Meurer finally succeeded in finding accommodation in the home of the Schraubers, a privilege she had to share with between twenty and thirty other people from St. Vith.[16]

2 While German commanders attempted to disentangle their troops inside St. Vith, other units battered their way west circling the town. The Führer Begleit Brigade had its origins in Hitler's headquarters guard. It was made up of a tank battalion and some infantry from the famed *Gross Deutschland* Panzer Division, which remained on the eastern front. Field Marshall Model had ordered von Manteuffel at the end of the offensive's first day to use the brigade, part of the general's reserve, to force a breakthrough at St. Vith. The unit took part in failed probes toward St. Vith from Wallerode on the morning of December 20. Its efforts were halfhearted because its commander, Otto Remer, cherished more ambitious designs. Without consulting von Manteuffel, Remer around noon the same day sent part of his brigade to the village of Rodt, just northwest of St. Vith. If his tanks could capture this crossroads, they could roll straight to the Salm River, cross it at Salmchâteau and Vielsalm, and begin the drive to the Meuse, a far more glorious goal than provincial St. Vith.[17]

Rodt was unremarkable in every way, except that it happened to lay where roads from the north fed into the main road connecting St. Vith with Poteau and Vielsalm. It was reason enough for the village to become embroiled in some of the heaviest fighting north of St. Vith. On Thursday evening, December 21, ten-year-old Peter Flemings was having dinner with his family when deafening shell bursts smashed the farm windows. The inhabitants left the food on the table and hurried to the much larger and stronger cellar of their neighbors. The village was only weakly defended by armored infantry. Still, with the support of an artillery battalion, the Americans managed to hold off the Führer Begleit Brigade's tanks for a while. Furious duels kept the

Flemings and their neighbors in the cellar throughout the night. At dawn horrific explosions shook the cellar walls as an American armored vehicle caught fire and the ammunition inside blew up.

The danger was not enough to stop Mr. Flemings and his neighbor that Friday morning from making a dash for their stables in an attempt to feed their livestock. Peter heard the angry snaps of bullets as he ran after his father. An upset Mr. Flemings scolded his son and made him stay inside the stable while he climbed the ladder to the hayloft. Stooping and crouching, the farmer hurriedly scooped hay and dumped it down the ladder. He listened to the bullets rattle against the roof like thick hail. American machine guns angrily barked back from buildings nearby. Their heads low, Mr. Flemings and his son ran back to the house. Through a shattered window, they saw a tank with a big black cross roar across their meadow. The colossus flattened hedges, fences, and fruit trees. The American machine guns fell silent.

There was loud banging on the door. Two German soldiers entered the room shouting, "Heil Hitler!" The inhabitants returned the salute. "German troops have already captured Liège," one of the soldiers falsely announced, "and they are close to taking Antwerp." Then they proceeded to search the house for American soldiers, grabbed a couple of jars with preserved meats, and left again. Peter followed the Germans to the door. A scout car was parked in the street. A soldier in the vehicle beckoned him to come closer. "Are you a German boy, too?" the soldier asked. "Yes," Peter beamed. "Good," the German smiled, "then quickly find me some matches." Peter returned not only with matches but with a *Hitlerjugend* cap on his head. He had gotten it from an older boy in the village years ago. When the Americans arrived in September, his father had ordered him to throw it into the fire. But Peter had hidden it in the drawer with the matches. The German soldier laughed approvingly. "Heil Hitler," he greeted. Peter raised his right arm in reply. The soldier shook his hand. "You are a brave boy," he said.[18]

3 With the exception of one of its three regiments, earmarked to capture the town itself, the 62nd Volksgrenadier Division fought its way to the Salm River through territory south of St. Vith. The division's southernmost troops encountered only weak resistance from the inexperienced 424th Infantry and a badly mauled 112th Infantry as both American regiments scrambled to get to the new line behind St. Vith on December 21. Still, the Volksgrenadiers pouring through

Burg Reuland struck the civilians as anything but impressive. Retreating American troops in Auel had failed to destroy the temporary bridge over the Our. Fearing it had been mined, German soldiers forced a local woman to cross the bridge first. Only when she safely made it to the other side did the soldiers have the nerve to follow. They went on to empty Auel's houses of all the linen and food they could find, then requisitioned horses and wagons to haul the loot away. Troops who marched through Reuland on their way to Alster looked tired and weary. Onlookers noticed that all they had to eat were canned goods scavenged from abandoned American stocks. The first items that Volksgrenadiers in Lascheid coaxed out of the civilians were American cigarettes and soap. Cattle disappeared from the stables at an alarming rate and carcasses could be seen tied to vehicles passing through. By the end of December, an estimated two thousand soldiers belonging to service and flak units were stationed in and around the tiny village of Lascheid alone. As the cold got worse during the last days of 1944, German troops in Burg Reuland abandoned dugouts and barns. Some were content to move to the warmth of the cow stables. The civilians had to put up with most other soldiers in their homes.[19]

In the wake of the drained Volksgrenadiers followed the hard-bitten Gestapo. During the American occupation its agents had infiltrated the former German Kreise in Belgium's East Cantons not only to gather news on troop formations and the civilian mood, but they had been under orders also to register the names and functions of those guilty of collaboration with the Allied forces. Instructions to the Frontläufer urged them to take this task to heart so as to make sure that, as one document from the Gestapo in Cologne put it, these people "during a recapture of the territory could be severely punished by us." The Frontläufer appeared to have carried out their instructions well, not only in St. Vith but also in the surrounding countryside. Reuland had barely been retaken by German troops when two Gestapo agents appeared in the village to arrest Mr. Houscheid. In Thommen that same day they also took away Mr. Neissen. Both had served as mayors of their villages during the three-month-long American occupation. The Gestapo subjected the men to harsh interrogations in the Houscheid home. Perhaps the fact that they had decided not to flee lessened their suspicion in the eyes of the agents. Whatever the case, the villagers breathed a sigh of relief when both men were eventually released.[20]

In Reuland, Fritz Oestges was at least as relieved when his family received a bundle of letters bringing long-awaited news from his father on the eastern front. They had been piling up somewhere in Germany ever since the Americans had arrived and cut off communications with the Reich. Renewed contact with fathers, husbands, and sons fighting for Hitler on faraway fronts was for many by far the best improvement that came with the return of Germans troops to the Ostkantone.[21]

If the 62nd Volksgrenadier Division recaptured the area around Burg Reuland and Thommen without much of a fight, its troops encountered more stubborn resistance immediately south of St. Vith, for here the 9th Armored Division stood in the way. German troops on Friday, December 22, concentrated their attacks on Crombach. Comparable in importance to Rodt in the north, the village was a juncture of roads fanning out to the Salm River. The furious battle lasted until daylight on Saturday. Crombach's inhabitants tried to put out the raging fires, but it was too late. Some searched the badly damaged church. They pulled the tabernacle from the rubble and carried it to the sacristy. It was one of very few things the villagers were able to save that morning.[22]

Four days later, when the front had moved far enough west, a German officer assigned Franz Rätz the task of collecting and burying the Volksgrenadiers who had fallen near his farm during the battle for Neidingen. The villager obediently buried two soldiers in a meadow beside his house. As he made his way to a third corpse, however, Franz Rätz stepped on a mine. The Germans rushed the civilian to a hospital in Bleialf. From there he was sent deeper into Germany. Franz Rätz's mangled leg was amputated at Bad Godesberg early in January.[23]

4 Some ten miles to the rear of St. Vith, in the French-speaking part of Belgium, meandered the Salm. North of Vielsalm, about three miles downstream from the town, Grand-Halleux straddled the small, swift river. In the weeks following its liberation on Monday, September 11, the First U.S. Army had installed a hospital in the village's most imposing building, a three-floor boarding school, while GIs of the 291st Engineer Battalion had tried to make themselves comfortable in the parish hall. Though the GIs intrigued the locals as much as they reassured them, life in Grand-Halleux after the initial stir had quickly returned to its normal, quiet self.[24]

In the course of Saturday, December 16, however, the villagers sensed that something was wrong. GIs hurried in and out of buildings, talking nervously, and smoking even more than before. Rumors of a big German push swirled about, but radio newscasters remained tight-lipped and it was hard to find out what was really going on. That evening, like every evening before, Paul Dropsy, one of the village's altar boys, dropped by the parish hall to stare at the engineers and try his English on them. But this time the Americans barely noticed him. They were all busy packing. Some were dusting off their gas masks. One of the engineers finally turned to the puzzled boy. "The Germans are on the way back," he explained mischievously, "and they will massacre everyone, children included." He slowly slit a finger across his throat. Paul stumbled out of the hall and ran all the way to the church. Inside he fell on his knees and fired prayer after prayer at the saints looking down on him with tortured faces.[25]

On Sunday, after morning Mass, American jeeps, trucks, halftracks, and tanks began rumbling through Grand-Halleux in a never-ending column. Unlike other GIs the villagers had seen, these soldiers were silent, cold, and morose. They were on their way to help defend St. Vith, and the last vehicles of the 7th Armored Division did not pass the village until after dawn the next day. Several hours later that Monday, the engineers of the 291st piled bags and equipment onto trucks and hurried westward. The wounded were evacuated from the boarding school late in the afternoon. Jeeps buzzed through the streets, tense GIs in the back hugging their machine guns, fingers on the trigger.[26]

The villagers were getting agitated. Groups assembled to discuss what should be done. On Tuesday the rumble of artillery drifted in from Trois-Ponts to the northwest, and that night bright flashes and tracer fire could be seen at Wanne to the north. It was the signal for most of Grand-Halleux's able-bodied men to take to the roads.[27]

Also on Tuesday the Americans identified a strong new force in the vicinity of Recht: the 9th SS Panzer Division. Known also as the *Hohenstaufen* division, it had been rebuilt after heavy fighting in Normandy and Holland. General Dietrich had ordered it to cross the Salm and join the race to the west. In doing so, he hoped the division would also be able to rescue Kampfgruppe Peiper. The Allies were in the dark about Hohenstaufen's exact plans. All they knew for sure was that if this SS armored division made it to the Salm at Grand-Halleux, captured its bridge, and then plunged southward along its banks, it might cut off all American troops involved in the defense of St. Vith east of the river.[28]

In the course of Wednesday, haggard refugees from Wanne began telling hair-raising stories of SS atrocities against civilians. Panic now gripped the entire village. People assembled in front of the church with their village priest. He urged the remaining men to flee immediately. But before he sent them off, the priest hastened inside to get a chalice, and from the steps of his church handed each a consecrated wafer.[29]

Meanwhile, fresh American troops had been making their appearance in the Salm Valley. They were men of the 82nd Airborne Division who had been ordered to protect the rear of the defenders at St. Vith. The first paratroopers had arrived in Grand-Halleux on Tuesday. They were part of the proud 505th Regiment and belonged to its 3rd Battalion, the outfit that had seen combat at Ste.-Mère-Eglise on D-Day. As early as Thursday SS troops launched a first attack in the direction of Grand-Halleux. It was just one of many attempts in several places that day by the 1st SS Panzer Division to reach the ill-fated Kampfgruppe Peiper. Like all others, it failed. The paratroopers at Grand-Halleux held them off long enough to blow the bridge at the nearby hamlet of Rochelinval.[30]

But the paratroopers in the village had felt enough of the hot breath of the SS to be alarmed. They strengthened the roadblocks and placed rows of mines in front of the church and along Grand-Halleux's main street. Sensing that their village was about to become a battlefield, still more villagers decided to pack and leave. Some went no farther than the hamlets located just across the river. Others continued for another two miles to join hundreds of civilians from the vicinity who were finding refuge in the Farnières château. Many farmers and elderly refused to leave. They and the paratroopers prepared for the clash that was to come.[31]

A group of about ten paratroopers from G Company manned an outpost in a house next to the Jeanpierre farm on the road to Wanne. They had settled in on Thursday, and Mrs. Jeanpierre made a point of keeping a pot of coffee warm for whenever the numbed soldiers returned from patrols. Machine-gun bursts on Friday evening suddenly tore apart the awkward silence that had hung over Grand-Halleux all day. Mr. Jeanpierre was given just enough time to herd his family into a corner of the kitchen under the staircase. Seconds later the door was kicked open and a hand grenade exploded in the middle of the room. From his hiding place thirteen-year-old Marcel Jeanpierre caught glimpses of smoke, an oil lamp hurled to the floor, a chair landing on the stove and catching fire. His mother and grandmother were bleeding. More grenades exploded. The blood-curdling sound of German soldiers howling each other's first names reverberated, "Johann! Manfred! Hans!" Then the attackers disappeared as fast as they had arrived.[32]

The assault on the outpost over, SS troopers of the Hohenstaufen division rushed down the hill to Grand-Halleux. After the failure of their comrades from the 1st SS Panzer Division to get across the Salm the previous day, it was their turn now. According to one villager, they yelled and screamed "like an army of Redskins." One team forced open the door of a house with an axe, stuck a machine gun through the rear window, and fired angry bursts at paratroopers pulling back to the river. In the cellar beneath the German gunners some twenty civilians were holding on to each other for dear life. Several houses were burning out of control in no time. In one of them the Lemaires found themselves trapped in the basement. They managed to wriggle themselves into the garden through a small window. An SS man tore a hole in the hedge so they could get out and hide in another cellar. By midnight Grand-Halleux was firmly in the hands of the 19th SS Panzergrenadier Regiment. A loud explosion announced that the Americans had blown the bridge behind them. The villagers were on their own.[33]

Three SS troopers searched the farm on the road entering Grand-Halleux from Wanne. By the light of a candle they made out Mr. Jeanpierre, two children, and two women on mattresses. "They are wounded," explained Mr. Jeanpierre. "Let me see!" barked the NCO. "It is nothing serious," he concluded after a perfunctory check. "There are many partisans in the area," he changed the subject, looking at Mr. Jeanpierre intently. "I wouldn't know," the farmer replied. "Yes, there were some in the other village," the NCO clarified. "We had to kill them." Then he and his troopers stepped back into the dark.[34]

The following morning, December 23, the first of the close to twenty thousand American troops defending St. Vith began withdrawing behind the Salm River. Twenty-four harrowing hours later most of them had made it across. The bridges at Vielsalm and Salmchâteau were blown in the faces of Volksgrenadiers and SS troopers converging on the towns from various sides. To allow troops to reorganize and establish a more orderly defensive line behind the river, the 82nd Airborne Division from the Salm's left bank tried to keep pressure on the Germans on the other side as long as possible. In and around

Grand-Halleux paratroopers used mortars and light artillery to harass the Germans day and night. The civilians were made to share the fate of their occupiers. Burst after burst damaged more and more of their homes. On Saturday, December 23, in the hamlet of Ennal, an elderly farmer was killed by a shell while feeding his horse in the courtyard. Inside Grand-Halleux, the bakery caught fire, the café Servais was set ablaze, and flames destroyed the Sevrin farm. The Germans finally ordered the civilians to evacuate the village center at dusk on Sunday. A group of about seven women and more than a dozen children set off to a farm to the rear. Anna Rouche never made it. An American bullet or shell fragment killed her in the street. Her neighbors and her eight children ran the rest of the way without looking back. Mrs. Rouche's body remained in the street until the next day.[35]

American mines were claiming even more victims. The moment they had captured the village, the SS had forced seventy-four-year-old Alfred Lekeux at gunpoint to remove the mines from the main street. Without the knowledge of the civilians, however, the paratroopers had planted more mines on the road leading into Grand-Halleux from the hamlet of Hourt. On Saturday one of those mines killed forty-one-year-old farmer Jean Klein. The same device wounded another person and so horribly maimed fourteen-year-old Henri Moutschen that the boy would die in a nearby hospital a little later. Also on Saturday, another vicious mine at Hourt took the lives of Mrs. Bouharmont and her six-year-old granddaughter.[36]

On Sunday the paratroopers received orders to pull back that night to a more stable defensive line slightly to the northwest. The Belgian resistance had officially been demobilized in mid-October. A handful of members from Vielsalm's notoriously active Armée Secrète had nonetheless offered their services as soon as the 82nd Airborne Division had arrived in the valley. Brave as the maquisards were, however, the paratroopers had not known how to use them and in the nervous days that followed had even taken some for enemy agents and arrested them. Now the paratroopers entrusted the Belgian maquisards with the sorry task of informing the inhabitants on the Salm's left bank of the coming withdrawal. They were also to aid the civilians in their evacuation to the château at Farnières. German troops greedily poured into the void the following day, now quickly taking control of that part of Grand-Halleux located on the Salm's far side. Once they had made it to their new positions, however, the paratroopers barely budged another inch. For the next two weeks, until the start of the Allied counterpunch, the inhabitants of Grand-Halleux would suffer the humiliation of renewed Nazi occupation while separated from the Americans by no more than a few dark forests of no-man's-land.[37]

Ironically, in those two weeks, the villagers were to suffer even more from the terror rained down by Allied planes trying to rid them of the Germans. On Christmas Eve aircraft set the Pafflard mill on fire. On Christmas Day they strafed the village center and the day after targeted even a funeral procession. On Wednesday, December 27, exasperated Germans in the hamlet of Mont at gunpoint forced a group of twenty male inhabitants to dig trenches. American planes bombed Mont two days later. On January 2 more bombs ravaged houses in Grand-Halleux, Mont, and a string of other hamlets in the area. For Mrs. Pirotte, however, death did not come from the air. She stepped on a mine on the first day of the new year. The explosion ripped off both her legs. Though German medics did all they could to save her, Anna Pirotte died in the presence of Father Jacquemart, who could do no more than comfort her with the last rites.[38]

5 The sudden increase in Allied air strikes in the Salm Valley after December 22 was part of a larger pattern in the Battle of the Bulge. Thick low clouds had severely limited air activity during much of the first week of the German offensive. But in the night of December 22 a so-called Russian High abruptly moved westward. The high-pressure area from the east brought icy temperatures and stinging winds, but it also colored the skies a magnificent blue. The Allies hailed it as "victory weather." German troops called it *"Jabowetter"*: they knew that from the azure heavens *Jagdbommenwerfers*—the dreaded fighter-bombers—would follow their every move and make life on the ground hell.

Much of the focus of the Allied air forces in the next five days of superb flying weather was on the area in and around St. Vith. With German troops already stuck in the town's huge bottleneck, Allied pilots were determined to make things much worse. This would slow the enemy even further in what had become his main axis of advance. Allied aircraft barely touched the town itself during the first two days of the Russian High. Pilots instead scoured the surrounding countryside as if hawkeyed. South of St. Vith, for example, in the Burg Reuland area, the Volksgrenadiers had immediately been followed by units of the 19th Flak Brigade that had aimed their guns skyward from meadows and streets. But flak batteries were prime targets for fighter-bombers, and the aircraft were soon swooping down on the guns in run after run. Father Nols was shepherd of flocks in Steffeshausen and Auel. So dangerous were Allied aircraft soon making the area, however, that Auel's faithful stopped making the one-mile trip to the church in Steffeshausen. Determined to continue tending to their spiritual needs, each dawn Father Nols risked his life traveling to Auel to read morning Mass in the village's tiny chapel. It was in a meadow near that same chapel, rather than in Steffeshausen's church cemetery as was the custom, that Father Nols decided to bury Josef Lentz, a teenager killed by American shell fire on December 21. Even hawkeyes could not always be counted on to see the difference from up high between a funeral procession and an enemy convoy.[39]

Aircraft even more furiously lashed out at key villages and crossroads north of St. Vith on December 23 and 24. On Saturday they bombed Wallerode, destroying a number of buildings and wounding at least one person. When the dust settled over the village, several families grabbed blankets and food and went to live in the surrounding forests. Recht was bombed twice on Sunday. Shortly after noon, a string of bombs ravaged several houses around the village's Great War monument. Bomb shards wounded a farmer who had been made to haul ammunition for the Germans with his horse and wagon. A much heavier attack followed a couple of hours later. At least eighteen aircraft bombed and strafed the convoys and munition depots in and around Recht. Desperate civilians tried to reach the slate quarries even while the attack was going on. When the planes finally pulled away, German corpses in some streets lay piled on top of each other. The villagers had not been spared either: some twelve houses were on fire and six civilians were dead—two of them brothers aged eight and sixteen. Farmer Eligius Mettlen alone lost thirty heads of cattle and three horses. At dusk that same day Allied planes continued their killing spree by gutting Born. They needed no more than ten minutes to kill one man, three women, and a child. The survivors packed a few belongings and hid in a tunnel under the Born-Montenau railroad.[40]

Bombs also shook the village of Herresbach on Christmas Eve. They damaged three homes and completely laid waste to the local milk plant. A single bomb fragment sufficed to cut short the life of twelve-year-old Michel Held. An SS trooper told his grieving mother that where he came from it was the custom to surround the dead with candles before burial. Before long he returned with a stack of them. The following day, each time he passed the boy's corpse laid out in the circle of light, the German soldier halted a few moments, lost in thought.[41]

The civilians inside St. Vith remained relatively safe from the violence hovering over their heads until Christmas Day. Little did they know that the Allied air force was merely tightening the noose around their town. On the night of December 23 fighters strafed the town's railhead. On Christmas Eve a string of bombs, seemingly without clear purpose, ravaged some buildings in a single street, killing an elderly couple. The freak incident was a portent of much more horrid things to come. Shortly after noon on Christmas Day, three American B-26 bomber groups of the Ninth Air Force took off from airfields in France. Their destination was St. Vith. A number of problems made the 394th Bomber Group turn back to base before reaching the town. Navigation and identification failures caused four bombers of the 387th Bomber Group to mistake Malmedy for St. Vith. Still, late in the afternoon, twenty-six of the group's thirty-six B-26s managed to drop 426 250-pound bombs right on target. Forty aircraft of the 323rd Bomber Group proved to be even more deadly, releasing 148 100-pound bombs over St. Vith as well as 533 explosives of 250 pounds each.[42]

Refugees in Galhausen, just south of St. Vith, had been alerted by the monotonous droning of the bombers. The house in which Mrs. Meurer had found shelter a couple of days earlier did not have a cellar, however, so she and a group of other people hurried to a nearby stable, naively assuming that the thick hay overhead might act as a shield. As soon as the bombs from the B-26s hit St. Vith, shock waves rocked the people inside the stable with such force that one of the women lost her grip on an eight-month-old girl and dropped her to the floor. Another woman fainted. The others barely found sufficient breath to pray.[43]

Most of the deadly bomb loads fell on the southern part of St. Vith. Within minutes several blocks were ablaze. Extinguishing the walls of fire proved an impossible task for the town's modest fire brigade and its outdated equipment. All of St. Vith was veiled in dust and smoke. Everywhere children and adults were crying and screaming for help. Surreal scenes of shock could be discerned through the wounded city's haze. When Willy Mathey, a soldier from the 18th Volksgrenadier Division, emerged from his cellar, he caught a glimpse of a woman pushing a baby carriage and calmly picking her way through a store's shattered display window and into the street. A little farther down the road, the Volksgrenadier helped a woman carry a heavy suitcase. He pretended not to see that on top of her head were piled at least seven different hats. The women and a stream of other refugees poured onto the main road leading to Galhausen and Lommersweiler.[44]

Thinking that St. Vith's fate could hardly get worse now, many people in those parts of town that had escaped destruction grimly stuck to their cellars. They badly miscalculated the odds. The fires of the previous day were still smoldering when on December 26 close to three hundred four-engine Lancaster and Halifax giants fixed St. Vith in their bombsights. On what remained of the small Eifel town, English, French, Australian and New Zealand formations of RAF Bomber Command, between three o'clock and four o'clock in the afternoon, released more than one thousand tons of explosives and incendiaries—almost ten times the bomb load of Christmas Day.[45]

The very moment the bombs started ripping St. Vith apart, Mrs. Doepgen dragged her two children into the basement room with the strongest walls and ceiling. In the tiny, bunker-like space they and some twenty other civilians anxiously awaited their fate, pressed together so closely that they could neither sit nor move. Each new explosion made the bunch of people sway back and forth. Shock waves slammed doors open and shut. Adults and children alternately cried and prayed. Then, suddenly, there was an explosion so violent it appeared to rip out their lungs and hearts. The house above them folded, the room's ceiling and chimney collapsed, the stove exploded. People were struggling against the asphyxiating smoke and soot when another bomb blew a hole in the cellar wall that made them catch their breaths again. Before long, however, burning phosphorus was seeping into the cellar. The malicious substance released poisonous fumes and in the larger rooms set mattresses on fire. With the help of German soldiers, the panic-stricken civilians clawed their way through the hole and into the pulverized street.[46]

For the innumerable refugees in St. Josef's Kloster the bombardment brought the most apocalyptic of scenes. The chapel collapsed and, as Mrs. Doepgen had feared several days earlier, the mass of stone and beams fell through the weak cellar ceiling, crushing everyone beneath it. Phosphorus set both rubble and buildings on fire. Many of St. Vith's elderly and infirm were housed in the convent's upstairs rooms and were unable to get to the cellars in time. Most of them were burned alive. Like a more liquid form of lava, hissing phosphorus poured into the cellars that remained standing. People with horrible burns, broken bones, and blown minds were pulled out through the few unobstructed air shafts. Among the last to leave the inferno were the convent's sisters, blankets tightly drawn over their heads and shoulders.[47]

In the Neundorfer Strasse, Heinrich Peters in a futile gesture had tried to ward off destruction by pressing a piece of canvas against the tiny cellar window. When the maddening explosions halted, they could hear the angry roar of flames upstairs. In the adjoining cellar the ceiling had come down and buried Mr. Peters's brother-in-law. Frantic neighbors dragged him from the rubble alive but wounded. The man's brother was dead. People struggled to free themselves in a daze pierced only by the intermittent screams of the Kohnenmergen children whose feet and legs had been badly burned. The survivors dragged themselves into the street one by one. St. Vith was a sea of flames. Smoke blackened the sky as if in a violent thunderstorm. Mr. Peters and his family were pushed into a Wehrmacht vehicle rushing them to Ober-Emmels, just north of St. Vith. There people they had never seen before kindly offered them shelter. They would stay with them for the better part of a year.[48]

Mrs. Doepgen desperately tried to find a way out of St. Vith's inferno from the Rathausstrasse. Covered in blankets, she and her children plunged into street after street in the searing heat. Stumbling and falling they reached the Aachener Strasse, where a military ambulance was collecting wounded. Because of her small children the driver agreed to take her to Wallerode. Refugees and German troops filled that village to overflowing, however, and the only place that had room for Mrs. Doepgen lacked a cellar. Taking pity on mother and children, German soldiers told them they could join them on a convoy to Germany that night. By the time she awoke from the St. Vith nightmare, Mrs. Doepgen found herself in the vicinity of Bonn. There she was made to fend for herself, uprooted, responsible for two sick children (one had caught pneumonia, the other suffered from a bad ear infection), and with no possessions left but the clothing on their backs.[49]

Like Heinrich Peters, Margaret Doepgen belonged to St. Vith's fortunate ones. Many others never made it out of St. Vith. That was true, for example, of the Terren family. Their fate was probably one of the most gruesome. After the first bombardment on Christmas Day, they decided to hide in the imposing tower that remained of the town's medieval wall. But ancient defenses proved no match for modern firepower. The heaving explosions of December 26 blocked the tower's exit with a massive wall of earth and debris. The Terrens were buried alive. It was not until many months later that the bodies of both parents and their four children were discovered. They had died a torturously slow death either from suffocation or starvation.[50]

No one will ever know exactly how many soldiers and civilians perished in the bombardments of December 25 and 26. St. Vith's population had been swelled by hundreds of refugees after September 1944 but had been emptied by the countless people fleeing in the days following December 16. The town's population records were destroyed. Many bodies were never recovered from the rubble and ashes. Today's most cautious estimates put the total number of civilian casualties for both bombardments at no fewer than 250.[51]

People in the villages surrounding St. Vith witnessed the town's annihilation with as much horror as disbelief. The bombardment of December 26 shook Wallerode so violently that for a while its inhabitants believed it was they who were under attack. Shock waves blew open doors and windows as far away as Rodt, almost three miles northwest of St. Vith. Even the houses in Lascheid, some seven miles to the south, shook to their foundations as Allied planes dumped their deadly loads on the fated town.[52]

Within an hour of the second bombardment, pitiful survivors came flooding into the neighboring villages. Many came down the road to Winterspelt, their faces and clothing caked with dust and soot, their lungs aching from poisonous fumes. Some went as far as Lommersweiler, determined to hide in the village's solid railroad tunnel. Most collapsed as soon as they had reached Galhausen. The hamlet was soon taking care of no fewer than three hundred refugees. Undaunted, its inhabitants immediately set to work in a fine spirit of solidarity, baking breads at production-line speed, slaughtering both a fat pig and a fine cow.[53]

Adele Heinz found the people in Bracht equally caring. The exhausted sixteen-year-old girl stumbled through the village late in the afternoon of December 26. Crazed with fear, she had bolted from the cellar in the middle of the Allied bombardment leaving her mother and seven sisters behind. Oblivious to swooping fighter-bombers and barking flak responses, Adele had covered almost six miles in less than an hour and a half. The dazed girl would have gone on walking had Bracht's inhabitants not stopped her and taken her in.[54]

In two days St. Vith had changed from a town into a giant heap of rubble. There was no time for German engineers to clear the roads. Instead, they simply cordoned off the dead town, rerouting traffic over narrow roads through rural neighborhoods. Heavy military traffic was soon adding to the chaos in small communities already flooded with soldiers and refugees. German engineers descended on Galhausen, for example, where they threw themselves into enlarging roads and succeeded even in turning a dirt trail into a thoroughfare. To help vehicles negotiate the steep incline near the hamlet's church, the Germans impatiently requisitioned Peter Colles's only horse. They probably worked the poor creature to death for the farmer never saw his animal again.[55]

Gazing down on the anthills springing up around St. Vith, Allied pilots worked their aircraft hard in a feverish race to shoot up as many enemy vehicles and troops as possible. Unfortunately, adrenaline as much as distance and speed tended to blur the distinction between combatants and civilians. On December 27, for example, a bomb in one home in Braunlauf killed seven people, three of them children under the age of ten. Although deteriorating weather brought a gradual decline in the number of sorties after December 27, harassment from the air continued almost unabated. On the first day of the new year, a fighter-bomber pounced on a German vehicle racing down the street in Breitfeld, not a mile from Galhausen. One of its bombs hit the house of the Wiesens. Mrs. Wiesen and her youngest son, Joseph, lay buried beneath the rubble. Soldiers hurried to the spot and pulled them out alive. Not far from the house sprawled the lifeless body of Heinz. He was not a German soldier but Mrs. Wiesen's other son. The boy had barely turned twelve years old.[56]

Like the congested traffic knots immediately outside St. Vith, all roads radiating from the town were relentlessly attacked. The Lützkampen-Reuland road was one such target, and the supply convoys that dared use it were sure to draw Allied aircraft like vultures. Villages paid a high price simply for being too close to the road. On December 26 Bracht's inhabitants spent the better part of the afternoon putting out fires ignited by tracer fire. The day after, some six or eight fighter-bombers hurled from the sky over Weweler and let a number of German vehicles have it near the village mill. They left behind smoldering steel, wounded Germans, and an evacuated farmer bleeding to death from a gash in his neck. So unforgiving were the enemy aircraft that German troops increasingly stayed off the roads during the day, switching to nighttime travel whenever possible. During the daytime, people in Steffeshausen found themselves shrouded in an eerie fog. It was caused by smoke pots the Germans used in a desperate attempt to get respite from *Jabos* in the Our Valley.[57]

East of St. Vith, on the even more vital road winding in from Schönberg, life for soldiers and civilians alike became unbearable. Fighter-bombers raked the road near Atzerath immediately after Mass on Christmas Day, injuring at least one woman. After that not a day passed without new attacks, a particularly nasty one hitting the village with bombs on January 1 and destroying several homes. The merest glimpse of an airplane soon sufficed to send everyone in Atzerath scurrying to their cellars. Village masses were canceled altogether.[58]

High altitudes and breakneck speeds prevented Allied pilots from having more than an abstract notion of the suffering they wrought on innocent civilians. They might well have wished it to remain so. On Christmas Eve eight RAF Typhoons of the 137th Squadron responded to an urgent request. A crucial German tanker convoy had been spotted snaking its way to Schönberg: the fuel was not to reach the enemy's armor. By the time the Typhoons identified them, the tankers were nosing into Schönberg. Just as Herb Copeman, an Australian pilot, swooped down on the first of the long line of tankers and fired his cannons, he noticed some thirty people dashing from the church and hurling themselves in a ditch alongside the road. He continued to fire. When he finally pulled up again and banked away, another pilot reported to him over the radio that a massive explosion from one of the tankers had sent a fire-ball roaring down the gutter beside the road. The Australian had no way of knowing for sure, but he realized that quite possibly he had just incinerated thirty innocent people in the blink of an eye. Herb Copeman returned from the war with a terrible stain on his soul for the rest of his life.[59]

Chapter 8

The Siege of Bastogne

"I begin to hate all the armies of the world."

German troops lost the race for Bastogne to the 101st Airborne Division. Before they managed to surround the greater Bastogne area on December 21, some ten thousand paratroopers of the veteran American outfit had poured into the town and nearby villages. These men formed the main core of the defensive force, shoring up a battered combat command of the 10th Armored Division and one from the 9th Armored Division that had been whittled down almost completely. Stragglers, many from the 28th Infantry Division, were organized into a makeshift team. With eleven artillery battalions—about 130 pieces—the Americans were strong in firepower. In all, some eighteen thousand American soldiers stood shoulder to shoulder determined to deny the enemy access to Bastogne.[1]

For the three thousand civilians huddled together in the town's cellars the thought of what lay in store for them was paralyzing. The liberation in September had miraculously been free of bloodshed. But the inhabitants were under no illusion about what the looming battle threatened to bring this time. Fourteen names had been chiseled into Bastogne's Great War memorial; another fourteen of the town's soldiers had lost their lives in the second war against the Germans. The Bastognards also knew what renewed Nazi rule would mean. Six of their fellow citizens had already paid with their lives for opposing the regime; two others were wasting away in concentration camps. People shuddered at the thought of a second occupation.[2]

They had no choice, however, but to make the best of a bad situation, get organized, and cooperate with the American defenders as fully as possible. There were enough capable leaders to help them do that. Apart from acting mayor Léon Jacqmin, several others derived instantaneous authority from the position they held in the community. Two physicians, for example, Doctors Heinz and Govaerts, had remained behind to look after the population's medical needs. Moreover, because of Bastogne's many clergy-staffed schools, the townspeople were relieved to be able to look to several dozen priests and nuns for much-needed spiritual support.[3]

Housing the American forces inside Bastogne did not pose much of a problem. Most troops, of course, took up positions in the town's perimeter, where they lived in foxholes, dugouts, and village farms. The town itself housed mainly command posts or medical personnel and other support troops. The command post of General McAuliffe, acting commander of the 101st Airborne Division and overall commander of Bastogne's defense force, was housed in the Heintz army barracks while the 10th Armored Division's combat command took over the hôtel Lebrun. Troops also found plenty of accommodation in the houses of people who had fled so that civilians only occasionally had to be asked to make room for soldiers by abandoning their homes for that of a neighbor or for one of the public shelters.[4]

As with any siege, the biggest and most pressing problem facing soldiers and civilians alike was food. Mayor Jacqmin immediately called for volunteers to scour the town and report back on the available stocks. They turned up more than seven tons of flour and two tons of tinned biscuits. Valuable foodstuffs such as vegetable oil were found in reasonably large quantities in the Courthéoux store. Mr. Jacqmin decided to have most of the food brought together in one central location where it could be monitored and distributed fairly. The seminary was selected for this purpose and would remain the provisioning center throughout the siege. Bakers and volunteers were put to work in the seminary with the purpose of producing as much bread as possible, a laborious chore as the dough had to be kneaded manually for lack of electricity. Bastogne's butchers set up a central abattoir where they slaughtered all the pigs and cattle that they and teams of volunteers could lay their hands on; questions of ownership had become irrelevant. Once the meat was dressed, it too was transported to the seminary for immediate distribution.[5]

The American defenders found themselves in much more dire straits than the civilians where food was concerned. The 101st Airborne had been rushed to Bastogne from France with much smaller supply trains than those normally found with infantry and armored divisions. The airborne division threatened to run out of rations fairly soon. Its supply officers therefore lost no time in seizing the stocks left behind by the VIII Corps. One depot revealed a large amount of flour for doughnuts, a find that would force paratroopers to eat pancakes for several days. In another corps warehouse, Americans found 450 pounds of coffee, 600 pounds of sugar, and a large amount of Ovaltine, all of which were set aside for the wounded. Inevitably, however, scrounging troops also began to add civilian stores to their stocks. From one of the town's warehouses, for example, they took away margarine, jam, and more flour. Moreover, poultry, hogs, and cattle became fair game for any soldier with a gun. In the war for filled stomachs, the line between cooperation and competition was to remain a fragile one throughout the siege.[6]

Still, soldiers and civilians inside Bastogne realized that, for better or for worse, they were stuck with each other for the remainder of the ordeal. People who attempted to escape town after December 20 learned not only that it was impossible, but that conditions in the perimeter's villages were much more dangerous. Young André Meurisse, for example, on Monday, December 18, had been sent home from school to find his mother next door praying and crying with the neighbors. Only on Friday, December 22, however, did his parents decide to abandon Bastogne and escape the increased shelling. They got no farther than Hemroulle, about a mile northwest of town, before being caught in the cross fire of machine guns. They remained unharmed and waited for the noise to die down before pushing on to Champs. There sudden artillery fire prevented them from getting farther than the first farms. They now hurried southwest and stumbled into the village of Mande-St.-Etienne. But battle raged just outside the village, and they were violently pushed back to the Cawet farm. The farmhouse was made of sturdy stone walls, but it lacked a cellar. More than twenty scared people bunched together under its roof.[7]

Toward evening farmer and guests filled pails with warm creamy milk from cows in the nearby stable. The foam-topped milk had just been brought to the house for distribution when suddenly the door was kicked in. German soldiers stepped inside and gazed at the civilians. Two apparently drunk soldiers noticed the milk, leaned over the pails with sinister grins, and urinated into the contents of each of them. People gritted their teeth and clenched their fists, but there was nothing they could do. The following morning American fighter-bombers swept down on the Germans in Mande-St.-Etienne as soon as the sky cleared. The Cawet farm trembled to its foundations. People dashed to the stables, which had vaulted ceilings of reinforced concrete and promised to be more robust. The earth heaved violently now and part of the farmhouse collapsed. Then suddenly it was over. Villagers and strangers looked each other over to see if everyone was all right. Astonishingly, no one was hurt.[8]

That was what it looked like initially at least. Later that morning, André Meurisse complained of a slight pain in his shoulder. His father slowly peeled off the many layers of clothing. He laid bare a small bloody puncture caused by shrapnel. Mr. Meurisse tenderly moved his son's arm in various directions. Nothing vital seemed to have been hit, but Mr. Meurisse knew that if the wound was left untreated, infection would set in soon. His face drawn, the anxious father said he would get help. The Americans meanwhile had retaken Mande-St.-Etienne, and Mr. Meurisse finally returned with a medic. The GI agreed to take the boy back to Bastogne for treatment—but without his parents. Mr. Meurisse knew all too well how dangerous that road was and pleaded with the American to allow them to accompany their son. The GI reluctantly agreed to take the father with him, but he was adamant that the boy's mother should stay behind. There was not much time to decide. With heavy hearts, André's parents agreed. They said a tearful goodbye. Hours later, André and his father were back in Bastogne. Their ordeal made it clear that for a long time no one would be able either to leave or enter the town. It would, in fact, take almost four weeks for the Meurisse family to be reunited, long weeks of anguish in which neither side had the faintest idea of what was happening to the other in Bastogne's cauldron.[9]

2 As the Meurisses had found out, civilians stuck in Bastogne's perimeter had a much harder time even than those imprisoned inside the beleaguered town. American troops had anchored their defenses on the concentric circles of farm villages around Bastogne and it was there, amidst the sturdy brick and stone buildings, that the battles would be fought to decide the town's fate. In the cruel, cold December weather, the solid buildings themselves were a valuable prize for soldiers of both sides. GIs in Neffe judged the Baisling farm to be located in a crucial spot and moved into it in full force; they left the sick farmer, his wife, and their five daughters only one unheated room. Paratroopers in Longchamps requisitioned the Spoiden farm and advised family and refugees to hide in the more secure stable. As the cold worsened, the eighteen banished civilians had to take turns warming their chilled bones in the farmhouse kitchen, where the Americans kept a good fire going. In Isle-la-Hesse, troops of the 101st Airborne transformed the local château into a command post; Baroness Greindl and her children retained only the privilege of the kitchen and a handful of other rooms.[10]

German troops, unhampered by the sensitivities of allied relations, had to tread even less carefully. Officers in Arloncourt took over a house forcing its ten inhabitants into the kitchen where adults, elderly, and children were to live for days and sleep on nothing but straw. Volksgrenadiers walked into the Menil farm in Fays and simply ordered the inhabitants out into the cold. People and belongings were loaded onto a wagon, but the farmer's horses failed to climb the icy road. After much imploring, the Germans at last allowed them to stay in a cellar beneath the baking place. There they slept on piles of beets, trying to make life as comfortable as possible for an eighty-five-year-old grandmother and feeding a two-month-old baby cow's milk from a lemonade bottle.[11]

Pleas failed to cause a change of heart among the Germans in Bras and Sonlez. On Christmas Eve new troops arrived en masse, invaded several cellars, and threw the civilians out. Dozens of people fled to cabins in the woods. Some had not even been given time to dress their children properly, and adults could do no more than vigorously rub their bodies to prevent them from freezing. At around the same time, similar scenes occurred in Assenois, where Mrs. de Coune and a string of refugees were expelled from the château's underground corridors. Adults thrust a blanket and some bread into the hands of each child, then struggled to a nearby sand quarry in search of cabins they knew the resistance had once used as hideouts. These turned out to have been torn down after the liberation, however, and nothing remained of them now but holes. The refugees hunkered down in the cavities, pressing together for warmth. Water was taken from a small stream. Someone would occasionally slip into the village and return with some sheep skins or a pail of milk. The ordeal would last until Patton's troops at last lifted the siege from the south.[12]

Most of the forced wanderings ended as soon as refugees could find room in another cellar or vaulted stable. These were the places where almost all of the civilians in Bastogne's perimeter lived throughout the siege, occasionally with exhausted frontline soldiers—German or American—fast asleep at their feet. But the long weeks in dank and drafty shelters were terribly uncomfortable, extremely unhealthy, and dangerous. To begin with, the cold grew worse as December wore on. Stoves were dismantled from upstairs rooms and dragged into shelters, crooked pipes sticking from windows and vents. Those without stoves were irrevocably drawn to the only remaining source of warmth, that of bodies; whether these belonged to people, cows, or horses mattered little.[13]

Moreover, in all of the perimeter's villages electricity had broken down in the first days of the offensive. December days were exceedingly short and what small windows there were in cellars or stables let in little of the sparse light; in fact, some preferred to board up even these narrow slits for fear of shrapnel. In only a few houses were people lucky enough to be living with American troops who had a generator at their disposal. Most civilians had to make do with candles. Candles quickly became a much sought after commodity, and even the stubs were gathered to make new ones. People also grated the wax from American ration boxes, melted the substance in cans, and inserted wicks. Still, wax of any kind soon became so scarce that in many a cellar people lit candles only at supper, spending the rest of the long evenings and nights in stygian darkness.[14]

Meanwhile, people were in the dark about what was going on around them. There was no more mail delivery, of course, nor could any newspapers be had. Without electricity, the telephones were dead and the radios silent. As a result, civilians knew even less of the bigger picture than did the frontline soldiers. They did not have the slightest idea of the scale of the German offensive, of whether and how it was being countered, and—most of all—of when it might end. Perhaps the insecurity of not knowing strained the nerves more than anything else. To counter futile brooding, people tried to occupy themselves with other things, though that was not always easy in the cramped spaces at their disposal. Prayer, whether individually or in group, was undoubtedly the most common pastime. Many also spent the evenings singing or humming Christmas carols. In the long evenings before being chased out of their château in Assenois, Mrs. de Coune and her refugee guests took turns telling stories to pass the time and keep up morale. They tried different versions of the fairytales of Madame de Ségur and even risked funny stories that triggered waves of nervous laughter.[15]

Most of the civilians' time, however, was spent searching for things to eat and drink. Water was by far the most vital commodity, of course. But to get hold of it proved increasingly problematic as shells and bombs ruptured ever more mains while freezing temperatures played havoc with pipes in the unheated rooms. The way to a nearby stream, well, or pump was fraught with danger. Shells and mortar grenades often fell without warning, and jittery soldiers fired at anything that moved. Still, in each village men and women were brave enough to volunteer as water-carriers. Often, they, together with those taking care of the farm animals, were the only ones to venture outside in a course of days. It inevitably made them the eyes and ears of their community, so that when they returned to the shelter everyone made sure to drink up even the last drop of information. With barely enough water to quell thirst, hygiene was an early casualty, and people were soon maddened by fleas, lice, and scabies.[16]

If hauling water was often urgent and dangerous, finding enough food was a nagging concern and preparing it a constant headache. In many homes people had made sure to hide food as soon as it was clear that the Germans were on their way back. Flour, sugar, hams, and various other foodstuffs had been hidden in nooks and crannies or dragged into the cellars. The latter traditionally served as storage rooms anyway, and people consequently lived and slept on piles of potatoes and beets, jammed between shelves holding preserves, jams, salted butter, and eggs. Farm families in particular could have held out much longer had it not been for the many refugees from requisitioned and ruined houses who were soon filling to overflowing the cellars of buildings still intact. Feeding so many mouths became a challenge to even the best-stocked farmer. Moreover, cooking and baking were always dangerous as they had to be done in upstairs kitchens that were vulnerable to anything from rifle to shell fire. In many a farm that problem was solved by preparing food in a *cabouloir*, a pig's trough in which, after careful scrubbing, large amounts of food (often a kind of soup made of milk and potatoes) were cooked over whatever fire was available and then distributed all at once to the ravenous throng in cellar or stable.[17]

When dispensed in such quantities, family food stocks could not last long. Carefully hoarded flour, potatoes, and preserves dwindled at alarming rates. People in the villages closest to Bastogne from time to time succeeded in reaching the seminary for rations of bread, flour, or yeast, though they always risked drawing fire on these treks. For most civilians, however, the best insurance against hunger was their livestock. The animals ensured a constant flow of milk and eggs, and the selective killing of hogs and cows—as well as rabbits and horses—could add precious meat to the cabouloir stews. It is no wonder that farmers regularly risked their lives for their precious animals. Villagers in Michamps continued to go out to the stables each morning to feed the cows, even when shells forced them to crawl through the ditches; German soldiers failed to understand and scolded them for taking needless risks. In Wardin, Jean Hansen miraculously survived when a bomb exploded not far from where he was out gathering food for his pigs. In Senonchamps, however, fifty-two-year-old Louis Bauvir was less fortunate. In the midst of battle, two of his cows broke loose and began drifting in the direction of Villeroux. Mr. Bauvir decided to go after them. He had not gone far when an angry burst from a machine gun fatally wounded him. The list of farmers who gave their lives for their animals is much longer. Still, farmers fought an uphill battle trying to ensure the safety of their livestock. Shells, and even more so bombs, decimated the cattle of dozens of stables. To make matters worse, German troops routinely claimed cow stables for their horses, chasing the precious animals to an almost certain death in the fury outside.[18]

What animals they did not kill unwittingly, soldiers often claimed as food for themselves. Americans holding out against the Germans in Bizory emptied all the preserves they could find, then began killing the chickens and hogs. They did take time to feed the cows, however, occasionally also selecting one of these for slaughter. In Neffe's Baisling farm, starving GIs refused to leave a single pail of milk untouched until morning for the cream to be scooped off. They also killed three of the farm's heifers in a single day without leaving as much as a slice of meat for the farmer. Still, as they shared the same predicament, GIs and civilians were generally accommodating to each other where it concerned food. Ravenous paratroopers in Mont, for example, selected a big hog from one of the hamlet's dozen farms; they insisted, however, on paying for their meat before eating it. Farmers did their part, too, in keeping up good relations. When the American defenders began running out of rations, people voluntarily started baking bread for hungry combat troops in many a village. Mrs. Spoiden in Longchamps was not an exception when she prepared sandwiches with the famous smoked ham of the Ardennes and asked a sergeant to distribute them among his men in the front line.[19]

In their role of occupier, German troops again could take what they wanted with much less compunction. Moreover, as Allied air forces cut ever more of their supply lines, hunger made stealing and plundering food virtually a necessity. "No Germans at our place," Mrs. de Coune wryly wrote about the troops in her château at Assenois on December 22, "but marauders." They demanded wine, and when this was not forthcoming they emptied her cask of mead; the pillaging and looting continued until nothing much remained. In Bertogne German soldiers hauled butchered pigs into the kitchen of the Bleret farm, smacked them onto the table, and forced the farmer's daughters to clean them. A paratrooper in Sainlez burst into the kitchen of the Reyter farm. He demanded marmalade. When Mrs. Reyter handed him the jar they had been eating from, the enraged soldier drew his pistol. Minutes later the German stepped outside with a full jar from the cellar. Mrs. Reyter and her five children were left trembling.[20]

Still, despite the endless repetition of such incidents, the brutality and gnawing hunger never entirely dulled the reflex of decency, even among those in the aggressor's uniform. The numerous refugees in Engreux, for example, were so hungry that they went begging for potatoes in the farms. Alix Gaspard from Rouette even risked asking a German for some food. The soldier refused to take any notice of the boy. Then, in the evening, the same German, making sure that his comrades could not see him, slipped back to Alix. He handed him a loaf of bread, small and hard as a rock.[21]

Enemy and Allied troops were not solely interested in the food that civilians had to offer. When on December 19 the sound of battle had crept closer to Isle-la-Hesse, just west of Bastogne, Baroness Greindl in her château had made sure to hide most of the silver and jewelry. To combat soldiers fighting for their lives, however, such valuables had lost their meaning. What mattered more were the chairs and cupboards and wooden floors, from which decent fires could be built to keep warm. Or, still better, any kind of stove that could be dismantled and dragged into a cellar or dugout. Bedrooms, bathrooms, and drawers were ransacked for sheets, curtains, towels, clothing—any kind of cloth as long as it was white and would allow the men to disappear into the snow. The commander of a battalion of the American 502nd Parachute Infantry Regiment had the mayor of Hemroulle urge the villagers to hand over almost all their sheets. A German four-man delegation halted at the Lefebvre farm in Remoifosse on Friday, December 22. They were about to ask the Americans in Bastogne for their surrender and needed a white flag to make the trip. But the Germans before them had already robbed the Lefebvres of all of their linen and curtains. One of the daughters had an idea, however. Minutes later the delegation stiffly walked to the American lines waving a fringed bedspread. The Germans returned with General McAuliffe's "Nuts!" for an answer.[22]

Meanwhile, German troops in Morhet were in such a pitiful state that they made the men in the village assemble and then told the incredulous villagers to hand over their shoes. German frustration at the deadlock around Bastogne at times gave rise to blind and wanton destruction. In Michamps German soldiers descended on the Girs farm, dragged glasses, crockery, and china outside, and then proceeded to smash it in a fury. Only when there was nothing left to ruin did they calm down.[23]

In the heat of battle any soldier could loose his calm and victimize civilians. In Champs, just northwest of Bastogne, GIs held on despite repeated assaults bringing the enemy inside the village. During one such incursion, German soldiers carried their wounded comrades to the cellar of the Sélecks, where some twenty civilians were hiding. From the vents the unharmed soldiers sprayed the surroundings with their machine guns. When they finally surrendered, enraged Americans disarmed them, chased the wounded Germans into the open without pity, and even sent kicks in the direction of civilians who did not move fast enough for their liking. They found a nearby cellar empty of Germans: one by one the GIs also checked the upstairs rooms, but not before making sure each time that one of the civilians, Fernand Denis, had entered the room first.[24]

Civilians had to tread even more carefully with the occupying forces. People in a cellar in Compogne suffered kicks from a German for no other reason than that the trapdoor of their hiding place had caused the soldier to stumble. German soldiers in the Widart farm in Michamps caught Jacques, one of the servants, stealing small items from them. They summoned Mrs. Widart and Jacques and, their pistols drawn, slapped and beat the culprit to make him confess to what else he had taken. That the man was old and clearly not in possession of all his mental faculties was deemed irrelevant. Soldiers could be still more dangerous when inebriated. One night in Rachamps a drunk German requisitioned the services of Marie-Louise Maréchal and dragged her into a field. The girl managed to stay calm and bide her time, then suddenly she dealt the wobbly soldier a heavy blow, wrestled away his gun, and took off like lightning. She never heard from the soldier again.[25]

But German troops also endangered the lives of civilians in more calculated ways. In Rouette they requisitioned a man and forced him to lay cable throughout the night while battle thundered not far away. Amidst persistent shelling, Germans in Moinet at gunpoint forced twenty-year-old Joseph Piron to help them push a cart loaded with ammunition that two skittish horses were unable to pull up an icy slope. Women in Noville were summoned to the ruins of a house and told to cut meat and peel heaps of potatoes in the biting cold. In Rastadt heavy snowfall caused the Germans to call out the women to help clear roads with brooms. They also requisitioned all of the village's men and made them shovel snow and extricate vehicles and guns; kicks in the rear encouraged them to work harder and ignore the Allied planes overhead.[26]

Of an entirely different caliber than the German troops were the Nazi regime's imperturbable security forces that followed in their wake. Even while soldiers were pouring all their energy into capturing Bastogne, Gestapo agents clinically went about purging the perimeter of political opponents. On Saturday, December 23, they arrested eight men and boys in Givry, northwest of Bastogne. After questions about the resistance and the customary beatings, they released four of the suspects. But Fernand Pierson, Maurice Laforge, Cyrille Wenkin, and teacher Achille Choffray were loaded onto a truck that soon sped away in the direction of Gives. For many long months the people of Givry wanted to believe the men had been deported to Germany. Then, on March 16, 1945, a farmer in Gives came upon the bodies of the four missing villagers. They lay hidden in two shallow graves, their hands still tied together. The youngest of the executed was barely seventeen years old.[27]

On the very day that the men in Givry were rounded up, Allied airmen joined the battle for Bastogne in full force. From skies that the Russian High had at last cleared of clouds, packs of P-47 Thunderbolts and P-38 Lightnings from the Ninth Air Force, supported by British fighter-bombers, pounced upon anything in the perimeter that dared move. On occasion this meant that overzealous pilots mistook even their own for the enemy. Already on the first day of the all-out air offensive, American airmen bombed and strafed Mande-St.-Etienne, not realizing that GIs had just retaken it. Shaken infantrymen scurried to display brightly colored panels to signal the tragic error. Similar scenes occurred in Savy, a hamlet well inside the American defensive ring. In Bizory, too, GIs made sure to distinguish their positions from those of the Germans by means of panels of a flashy orange-red.[28]

Unfortunately, civilians were unable to stave off danger from the air with colored panels or other such agreed upon signals. And Allied pilots had no means of discriminating between soldiers and noncombatants who were hopelessly intermingled in villages and farms. The raw explosive power of bombs was impossible to apply in a surgical manner anyway. The force of the bombs that fell on the Bouzendorff farm in Remoifosse on Christmas Day, for example, catapulted Paula Renquin through a window. One blast propelled her brother, Marcel, from the stable onto a manure pile ten yards away; the next, incredibly, flung him back to where he had come from. Of the farm's owner, François Bouzendorff, not a trace was ever found.[29]

The shock waves of a bombardment at Michamps caused even the biggest trees to bend and break. But it was not that which horrified Mrs. Girs most. She had been out with the cattle when the bombs started falling and from a distance could see the house of her parents, where she had put her four children, ignite into flames almost instantly. Pregnant with a fifth child, Mrs. Girs scaled the ruptured trees and as if by miracle, managed to get everyone out unharmed. Mrs. Girs did not care what kind of bombs had almost made her family burn alive. Neither did people in Bastogne's perimeter pay much attention to what it was that often drizzled from the air in the wake of Allied bombardments, searing tiny holes into their clothing. But napalm, a kind of jelled gasoline increasingly used by the Allies in the war against Germans and Japanese, was certainly not a weapon more likely to spare civilians than high explosives. On Christmas Eve, fighter-bombers dived down from the sky over Cobru, just north of Bastogne. It was all over in a flash, but when the planes pulled up, the Bergh house was in ruins and ablaze. Of the sixteen people inside, many of whom had been lingering in the kitchen, six—from four different families—were dead by the time the neighbors could get near enough to help. Only one of the ten survivors—a ten-month-old child—had remained unharmed. All the others were seriously injured, most of them horribly burned. The wounded were to remain without proper care for nearly three weeks. It proved too long for ten-year-old Charlotte Genon: she died from her burns before help could arrive.[30]

German troops in Givry had barely finished camouflaging their guns and hiding vehicles under the trees that were still standing when fighter-bombers lashed out at them. They shot across the rooftops as fast as lightning. Their deadly incendiary loads exploded with a roar that made the village tremble. Fireballs rose up from woods and farms. From behind the sheets of fire emerged the flabbergasted villagers who had been made to share the punishment. Some wailed hysterically, others looked dazed; all of them stampeded away from the searing heat. A bull with smoldering burns, maddened with pain, furiously kicked about in the teeming crowd. A German pulled his pistol and put the animal down. Norbert Leonard and his mother, brother, and sister did not stop running until two American aircraft made them. They dipped down strafing, tearing up the field while the Leonards manically burrowed into the earth. Young Norbert cried from rage more than fear when the planes pulled away, maliciously flashing their white stars at him. It was to be a defining moment in the boy's life, the day when he started "to hate all the armies of the world."[31]

The Leonards in Givry survived the strafing. Lydie Gaspard in Rouette did not. Until Christmas Day, Rouette, a hamlet northwest of Bastogne, had remained largely free of violence. German soldiers had fired a couple of bursts at the Frères house, but that was only—so they claimed—because one of its inhabitants had dared feed them faulty information. On December 25, however, German troops assembled at Rouette for yet another coordinated attack against Bastogne. Allied fighter-bombers were on top of them by early afternoon. The attack lasted no more than fifteen minutes. When it was over, eight farms and houses—about half of Rouette's buildings—were ablaze. The fire spread so rapidly that the villagers were unable to save anything, not even their cattle, which burned alive in the stables, together with the German horses. Incredibly, Lydie Gaspard was the only one to die that day. The twenty-three-year-old succumbed not to the scorching napalm, but to slugs from an aircraft cannon. Villagers rushed her to an aid station in a blanket drenched in blood. The German surgeon shook his head. The woman died during transport to Bertogne.[32]

Their houses and farms charred and razed, hundreds of civilians in Bastogne's perimeter were cast adrift. In a matter of minutes a wave of aircraft set fire to five farms in Arloncourt, east of Bastogne, on December 26. One of the homes belonged to the Marons. Sensing the heat, they burst from their cellar. By the time they opened the front door, however, flames already leaped at them, singeing Mrs. Maron's hair and burning her daughter's hands. Mr. Maron tried in vain to rescue their two horses from a blazing stable. The family abandoned everything and headed for the nearest shelter. Aircraft strafed everything that moved: soldiers, farmers, cattle. The Marons dug into the snow. Then they got up again and raced to the stable of Ernest Charneux. Already, it harbored more than fifteen people. A German barged into the stable and barked at the occupants to leave the village at once. The Marons and the others now stumbled toward Oubourcy, hurling themselves into the snow each time wailing fighter-bombers peeled off in their direction. But Oubourcy had already been hit with napalm the day before. Few farms remained standing, among them that of the Léonards. Though almost all of Oubourcy's villagers were jammed together in that one stable—some ninety-two people—they quietly made place for the fellow-sufferers from Arloncourt.[33]

Many other victims of the air attacks simply took to the woods and fields. Refugees from Lutrebois and Villers-la-Bonne-Eau hid in old trenches or frantically dug new ones. Inhabitants from Bourcy hitched their horses to carts loaded with rabbits, butter, and bread; they did not emerge from the icy forest again until three weeks later. Hastily gathered provisions did not last long: people in the woods near Lutremange ended up catching hares to stay their hunger and finally even ate their horses.[34]

During the siege of Bastogne, Allied fighter-bombers flew more than 250 sorties each day. Within a mile or two of the perimeter they hit every village and hamlet at least once with explosive bombs or napalm. Before long, fires were burning all around the defensive circle of the Americans. The smoke became so suffocating that it challenged the dense winter fog for dominance.[35]

The Allied air offensive showed little concern for the plight of the civilians. Neither did some of the German troops when faced by the massive death and destruction poured onto their ranks from the sky. Infuriated soldiers at Bourcy forced civilians to help drag their dead and wounded comrades from the ruins. In Lutrebois on Christmas Day they requisitioned the village's mostly elderly men and had them clear rubble from the roads until deep into the night. And yet, despite the escalating violence in the battle for Bastogne, pity for civilians never stopped punctuating the fierceness. As there were neither doctors nor pharmacists in the perimeter's villages, medical personnel from both armies did what they could, when time allowed, to alleviate the suffering of noncombatants. Civilians who begged the soldiers for help were not necessarily battle casualties. Mrs. Paquay in Bras was terribly relieved, for example, when a German medic was willing to part with a few sachets of powder for her son who had fallen ill and was running a fever. Mr. Poncin was no less thankful to the German in Wicourt who made an effort to get painkillers from his aid station for a son who had had an accident and lay suffering on a straw mattress in a cellar.[36]

The soldiers who came to the rescue of civilians were not always medics or surgeons either. Madeleine Barthelemi, a pregnant woman from Bastogne, had found refuge at the Mignon farm in Isle-le-Pré, a hamlet south of town but still within the American defensive positions. GIs had just joined the civilians in the kitchen when a shell exploded close to the farm. Madeleine was found gasping for air. Shrapnel had torn into her left foot, and when they cut away her shoe, several toes turned out to have been ripped off, leaving white tendons visible through the bloody mess. By evening Madeleine had lost much blood and was moaning with pain. Paratrooper Frank Menard, a Cajun from Lafayette, Louisiana, could not stand having to watch her suffer. He ran outside where shells continued to shake the earth, maneuvered a jeep in front of the farm, and carried Madeleine to the back seat. He assured her in French that he would get her to a doctor in Bastogne. The GI got behind the wheel and made the sign of the cross. Then he gunned the engine and ran the gauntlet of enemy shelling all the way to an aid station in the beleaguered town. "It was the only time in the war," a self-effacing Frank Menard recalled much later, "when I was truly brave."[37]

Madeleine Barthelemi's foot was saved and she would give birth to a healthy son about a month later. But civilians were well aware that they could not all count on being so lucky. Many preferred to put their lives in the hands of God and seek strength and comfort in religion. People in a cellar in Sibret on Friday, December 22, knelt down in the company of a priest. One of the faithful recorded the roll call of those enlisted from above for help: "Our patron saints, Saint Brice, all the saints of our parochial church, the guardian saints, the souls of the purgatory, the souls of the parish's deceased are invoked with great insistence. From all of them we ask assistance and protection."[38]

Though trained and armed for war, soldiers were under no illusion that they had more control over their individual lives than had civilians. They, too, were prone in battle to turn to a Greater Being for support. It was in divine worship therefore that soldiers and civilians were able to meet most unreservedly and rediscover the humanity they shared. On Christmas Day, Father Georges was again celebrating Mass in one of Sibret's cellars when a German chaplain dropped by to ask if he, too, might be allowed to perform his duty as a priest in the cavernous space. The refugees not only made room for the German, but even assisted him in celebrating Mass. Before saying goodbye, both priests embraced. Minutes later Sibret was bludgeoned from the air and engulfed in hellish flames.[39]

The feast of the Nativity meant a great deal to the Germans, and despite the ongoing siege, they were determined to mark this special day with celebrations. They decorated trees with figures made from cans and cardboard. They had civilians bake pancakes and pies filled with preserved cherries taken from their cellars. They gathered instruments and gramophones. Troops in Bourcy on Christmas Eve received extra rations of food and wine and sang carols throughout much of the night. In many a village German soldiers hailed the birth of the Savior dead drunk.[40]

The inebriated mood at times turned nasty: in the kitchen of the Lutgens in Arloncourt, German soldiers set the table to perfection, carefully folding the white napkins; the next day, their idea of cleaning up was to sweep it all to the floor, leaving even Mrs. Lutgen's best china shattered. Generally, however, troops looked upon the holy event as an occasion for reflection. Many turned melancholic. At a farm in Neufmoulin seventeen-year-old Denise Crouquet watched soldiers take photographs from their pockets and turn away from her to hide their tears. Seated around a little tree in the home of the Calays in Magery, German soldiers, some of whom had come all the way from the brutal Russian front, wept openly.[41]

Though they had little to eat themselves, soldiers felt compelled to share with the unfortunate civilians at least on this special occasion. In Bras, Col. Heinz Kokott, commander of the 26th Volksgrenadier Division, called over some children, wished them Merry Christmas, and presented them with chocolate and biscuits that his troops had retrieved from parachuted American containers. All around Bastogne, the lower ranks were showing themselves equally generous. Soldiers at Rechimont, their feet wrapped in rags, even shared food from packages that had miraculously reached them from home.[42]

In one of the largest vaulted cellars in Remoiville, villagers and German soldiers sat shoulder to shoulder. A little stove radiated a faint glow. Someone had placed a crib and a candle on a wooden cask. People were reciting the Ave Maria when suddenly one of the soldiers rose to his feet and started humming "Silent Night." A ripple of emotion stirred the crowd. Germans and civilians listened as if in a spell. Then a comrade asked him to stop. The melody died down and anguish revived.[43]

Because of the battle in Bastogne's perimeter, encounters between civilians and soldiers, even Allied ones, could only be fleeting. In Mont an American chaplain on December 23 raised a cross and invited countrymen as well as civilians to follow him for a service. Both at a château near Champs and in a shed in Neffe, Belgian priests on Christmas Eve went out of their way to enable villagers and GIs to attend Mass. But opportunities to get to know each other better remained few. Henri Spoiden reveled in the fact that an airborne sergeant whom he thought larger than life had chosen his older sister to fall in love with. Time and again the American chose to thaw out in their home in Longchamps not far from his dugout. One day when the paratrooper readied himself once again to leave the Spoiden farm, he seemed more hesitant than usual. He gazed at the members of the Spoiden family one by one, stroked the dog long and hard, and gave Henri's sister a scarf. Then he marched back to the front never to return.[44]

3 Though ground combat never spilled over into Bastogne's streets, the siege was also taking its toll inside the town. There would never be a critical shortage of food for the Bastognards. Still, managing the scarce stocks, preparing food for consumption, and most of all, distributing the rations proved to be problems that grew worse with each new day. The seminary developed into the central base from which the population was provisioned. Every day it had modest rations of bread and meat available, and at times it also offered some soup or even a little extra (some margarine or canned salmon) taken from some of the town's stores. The problem was getting there as shelling was a constant hazard. Because the German guns quieted down somewhat at noon, American authorities daily allowed some two hours of circulation around that time. Even then, however, the danger of Ger-

man artillery remained, and from many a cellar a couple of brave ones were sent out with a cart or sledge to fetch food for the entire group.[45]

For the delivery of food or medicines to some of the elderly who insisted on staying in their own homes, Bastogne could count on a special group of volunteers that had been put together on the second day of the offensive. Many of them were no more than boys who itched to see action and were oblivious to any kind of danger. They referred to themselves—jokingly but not without pride—as "the vagabonds." Civilian leaders were happy to call upon these volunteers for a variety of tasks. The vagabonds helped the butchers get water from the Wiltz River after shelling had ruptured the mains, and they assisted in delivering fresh meat to the seminary. They were also the ones undertaking the dangerous transport of the coffined civilian dead to the cemetery's St. Laurent Chapel, where the ceaseless shelling was to prevent burial for several weeks. The Americans also made use of the vagabonds' services. In the early days they served as scouts pointing out tracks and shortcuts in the fields and woods bordering the town. GIs later asked them to lend a hand in the aid stations and with unloading ambulances.[46]

For those who stayed in Bastogne's subterranean shelters, life, though much less dangerous than in the perimeter, was most uncomfortable. Here, too, candles and petrol lamps did a poor job replacing electricity, spreading the faint light from which phantoms spring. Spread out on mattresses and wrapped in blankets people could hope to draw additional warmth only from nearby bodies or an occasional tiny stove. Hygienic conditions were appalling. In most cellars there was not enough water to wash and people could not change clothes. Lice hatched at lightning speed. The air that people had to breathe grew thick and putrid in the cavernous hideouts. Buckets served as toilets. The pungent smoke of tobacco exhaled by nervous soldiers and civilians made the smell still worse. In the seminary's cellars, where many of the elderly had been relocated, disinfectants no longer sufficed to take away the sickening stench of excrements. The elderly were least able to withstand the pressures of the underground existence. Some lost their minds and had to be restrained; several others quietly wasted away, dying almost unnoticed. Many refugees, children in particular, fell ill with bronchitis or bronchopneumonia, while gastrointestinal diseases became rampant. People sat packed together for so long without moving that in some shelters even the legs of young and healthy people swelled to double their normal size.[47]

(*Above*) Wherever possible civilians flock to subterranean caves, here in Neufchateau. Courtesy of the U.S. National Archives & Records Administration. (*Below*) Civilians killed during the capture of Odeigne by the 2nd SS-Panzer Division. Courtesy of the U.S. National Archives & Records Administration.

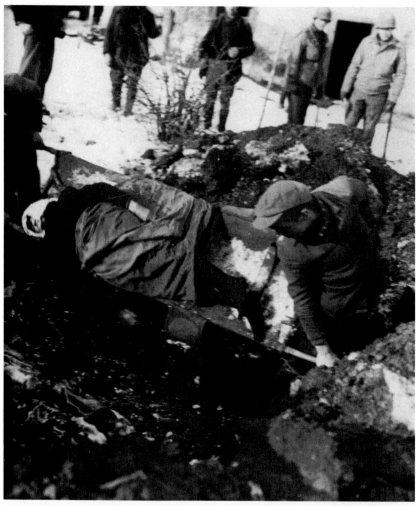

The body of a woman joins that of other civilians killed by American artillery fire in Lutremange. Courtesy of the U.S. National Archives & Records Administration.

(*Above*) Manhay after furious fighting between U.S. and SS armored troops. Courtesy of the U.S. National Archives & Records Administration. (*Below*) The corpses of civilians from the Legaye home, executed by soldiers of the 1st SS-Panzer Division at Stavelot. Courtesy of Centre d'Études et de Documentation Guerre et Sociétés Contemporaines/Studie-en Documentatiecentrum Oorlog en Hedendaagse Maatschappij, Brussels, Belgium.

(*Above*) American soldiers begin evacuating civilians from Malmedy on December 28, 1944. Courtesy of the U.S. National Archives & Records Administration. (*Below*) Inhabitants of a war-ravaged Houffalize begin rebuilding, June 1945. An overturned German tank lies in the Ourthe River. Courtesy of Centre d'Études et de Documentation Guerre et Sociétés Contemporaines/Studie-en Documentatiecentrum Oorlog en Hedendaagse Maatschappij, Brussels, Belgium.

(*Above*) American general Manton S. Eddy tries to comfort an old woman in Diekirch, Luxembourg. Courtesy of the U.S. National Archives & Records Administration. (*Below*) GIs evacuate an old woman from the ruins of Manhay. Courtesy of the U.S. National Archives & Records Administration.

(*Above*) Belgian refugees file through Dochamps, a village north of the vital road from La Roche to Baraque de Fraiture, December 21, 1944. Courtesy of the U.S. National Archives & Records Administration. (*Below*) Civilians in what remained of Malmedy after having been bombed mistakenly by American air forces three days in a row. Courtesy of the U.S. National Archives & Records Administration.

Father Musty takes in the ghastly sight of thirty-four dead young men executed in Bande. Courtesy of the War Crimes Commission, Ministry of Justice, Kingdom of Belgium. *War Crimes Committed during von Rundstedt's Counter-Offensive in the Ardennes, December 1944–January 1945: Bande*. Liege: Georges Thone, 1945.

Civilian victims of war crimes committed by the Waffen-SS in Stavelot find a final resting place in a communal grave. Courtesy of the U.S. National Archives & Records Administration.

Gen. Maxwell D. Taylor, commander of the 101st Airborne Division, meets with officers in Noville after the Belgian village's recapture in January 1945. Courtesy of Centre d'Études et de Documentation Guerre et Sociétés Contemporaines/Studie-en Documentatiecentrum Oorlog en Hedendaagse Maatschappij, Brussels, Belgium.

American soldiers begin evacuating civilians from Malmedy on December 28, 1944. Courtesy of the U.S. National Archives & Records Administration.

(Above) The rebuilding of Stavelot slowly gets started in the summer of 1945. Courtesy of Centre d'Études et de Documentation Guerre et Sociétés Contemporaines/Studie-en Documentatiecentrum Oorlog en Hedendaagse Maatschappij, Brussels, Belgium. *(Below)* American MPs and Belgian gendarmes check the identities of civilians fleeing west in the direction of the Meuse River. Courtesy of the U.S. National Archives & Records Administration.

The gruesome fate of the three policemen from St. Vith after having been arrested by an SS Sonderkommando in La Roche on January 4, 1945. Courtesy of the War Crimes Commission, Ministry of Justice, Kingdom of Belgium. *Les crimes de guerre commis pendant la contre-offensive de von Rundstedt dans les Ardennes, decembre 1944–janvier 1945.* Liege: Georges Thone, 1948.

A Belgian woman tries to salvage some grain from the ashes of a barn.
Courtesy of the U.S. National Archives & Records Administration.

(*Above*) Villagers flee Sart-lez-St. Vith. An ox pulls a sledge heavy with belongings. A white flag is supposed to offer some protection. Courtesy of the U.S. National Archives & Records Administration. (*Below*) Coffins with the victims of the Bande massacre pile up after the village's liberation by British troops. Courtesy of the U.S. National Archives & Records Administration.

Some of the executed young men from Bande after British troops recovered their corpses from the cellar on January 11, 1945. Courtesy of the War Crimes Commission, Ministry of Justice, Kingdom of Belgium. *War Crimes Committed during von Rundstedt's Counter-Offensive in the Ardennes, December 1944–January 1945: Bande.* Liege: Georges Thone, 1945.

(*Above*) Father Musty points out to Allied officers the spot where SS security forces executed the Bande men. Courtesy of the U.S. National Archives & Records Administration. (*Below*) A ruined La Gleize after furious combat with Kampfgruppe Peiper. Courtesy of Centre d'Études et de Documentation Guerre et Sociétés Contemporaines/Studie-en Documentatiecentrum Oorlog en Hedendaagse Maatschappij, Brussels, Belgium.

Cut off from the outside, people in this eerie netherworld lived "in a sort of dream," not knowing how the battle that would determine their fate was going, at times unable even to tell where night ended and day began. And yet, somehow, the small communities in their catacombs managed to hold together. Quite often this was thanks to individuals who revealed themselves to be natural-born leaders. Norbert Nicolay, for example, the town photographer, who with the voice of authority quelled panics and boomed directives through the underground corridors of the Institute of Notre Dame. Julie Bisschoff, who made sure that the hundreds of refugees in this huge shelter complied with Mr. Nicolay's orders. Or Father Fecherolle, who gathered information from the Americans during lulls in the shelling and assuaged fears by spreading upbeat reports.[48]

Pauses in the shelling were few, however, and always tenuous. Refugees in the cellar beneath the Franciscan church in the night from December 21 to 22 alone, for example, registered at least 150 incoming shells. In all, 15 shells would hit the seminary, one piercing the roof and concrete floor before burying itself in the coal room, where it somehow failed to explode. Amazingly, German artillery, while causing injuries, claimed not a single civilian life during the six days of Bastogne's encirclement.[49]

Much more frightening and destructive were the unexpected attacks that the Germans launched against Bastogne from the air. The Luftwaffe, its backbone long since broken, played only a minor role in the Ardennes offensive. But around 8:30 P.M. on Christmas Eve, nervous ears caught the throbbing of unfamiliar engines in the sky over Bastogne. Magnesium flares suddenly caused market square and buildings to stand out as if in an overexposed photograph; then followed the bombs. Several hours later, a pack of aircraft—most of them Junkers 88s—were making yet another run over Bastogne.[50]

The German bombers that night dropped a combined total of two tons of explosives. Though it was much less than the loads usually delivered by Allied bombers, it was enough to wreak terrible havoc on a town the size of Bastogne. Three civilians lay dead in the rubble together with dozens of GIs. The home of the Leperes collapsed on top of their cellar, but the frenzied family escaped suffocation by hacking a way into their neighbors' basement with pickaxes. Many of the houses on the main square were ablaze. In an ironic slight, one of the bombs obliterated the Great War memorial and its fourteen chiseled names, effectively effacing Bastogne's martyrs a second time. People roamed the streets not knowing what to do. Some had lost their minds: one woman tore at her coat's fur collar and screamed that an animal was biting her throat. Others desperately tried to elbow their way into shelters already filled beyond capacity.[51]

Meanwhile, fire obstinately ate its way through the Grand'Rue, threatening the Institute of Notre Dame and the now close to eight hundred people hiding in its bowels. American soldiers blew up one of the street's buildings in the hope that this would halt the fire, but the flames marched on. Despite the continuing danger from shells, GIs, priests, nuns, and refugees swarmed from the shelter. They hastily organized themselves into bucket brigades and somehow managed to keep the roaring fire at bay with valuable water from the convent's cisterns.[52]

Many displaced and frightened people traded the town for some of the nearest hamlets inside the American defenses. A group of close to fifty refugees on Christmas Day made its way into the château of Baroness Greindl at Isle-la-Hesse. When dusk came, however, the paratroopers insisted that they leave what was their command post and return to Bastogne. The Americans trucked the unfortunates back to the dreaded town under cover of darkness. One of them was Mrs. Lizin, who earlier had already fled Liège out of fear for the V1s and V2s raining down on the city. Now she had to beg to be admitted to the Institute of Notre Dame, where she was wedged into the coal cellar with many others. Mrs. Lizin was to stay there for seventeen tortuous days and nights, her two-year-old daughter in her arms, stuck on a chair with barely a chance to move.[53]

Contacts between civilians and defenders inside Bastogne were generally more frequent and intense than those in the fluid and still more dangerous perimeter. American fear of infiltrators and spies in the town remained throughout the siege. Soldiers drove dozens of people from houses near the marketplace into a building opposite the hôtel Lebrun where they were kept for hours while, so the rumor went, the Americans searched their cellars for Germans. At least twenty more people were taken to the hôtel Lebrun on suspicion of having used radio transmitters to contact the enemy. Interrogations and house searches revealed nothing. The spy psychosis became so contagious that the Bastognards themselves on occasion reported refugees they thought questionable.[54]

Civilians on their part had little reason to be distrustful of American soldiers, except perhaps when they were drunk. Marie-Thérèse Kesch, seven months pregnant, held her breath when two inebriated GIs wobbled into the Sevrin cellar at midnight on Christmas Eve. Their guns at the ready, fingers on the trigger, the unsmiling soldiers shuffled from person to person. None of the thirty civilians dared say a word. Everyone feared the worst. Then the soldiers slunk away and stumbled back into the street where the rowdy noise of more inebriated Americans echoed in the dark.[55]

Alcohol inevitably was the favorite spoil for soldiers looking to steady the nerves, boost their courage, or simply drown any thought of what lay ahead. When GIs searched the cellars of the Lejeune building and came upon large caches of wine and cognac, it did not take long for the townspeople to learn of the Americans' discovery. Across town there was a sudden rise in morale and occasionally small groups of GIs actually erupted in heartfelt sing-alongs. Such forms of selective looting were never more than a minor nuisance for the population. GIs tore up bedsheets, curtains, and linen for winter camouflage; they ripped out stoves, and smashed up any kind of furniture they could lay their hands on to keep warm. But the Bastognards hardly minded if that was what would keep their defenders going.[56]

Despite some inevitable suspicion and tension, relations between troops and townspeople were generally warm. The shared experience of life in a besieged town gave rise to a strong sense of solidarity between combatants and noncombatants. Scenes of GIs putting pancakes, gum, chocolate, and even socks into the outstretched hands of civilians reaching through the vents of their underground hideouts were not uncommon. During rests, soldiers often joined civilians in their cellars for company and security, and they reveled in teaching wide-eyed children how to make popcorn from what the Belgians called "maïs."[57]

The Bastognards in turn did what they could to shore up the morale of troops on whom they relied entirely to keep the feared Germans out. Inhabitants of Wiltz road regretted that there was nothing more they could do than speak encouraging words to ashen-faced GIs who were preparing—some of them in tears—to march to the front. In one of the seminary's shelters, Father Godelaine administered the sacrament of baptism to a meek paratrooper about to go to battle. Louise Lamotte, a pupil at the Institute of Notre Dame, fixed her gaze on a soldier on the sidewalk. He knelt, his gun in one hand, a rosary in the other. He was praying feverishly. When he opened his eyes again he stared straight into the girl's compassionate face. Their gazes locked for a brief moment. Then the soldier got up and hurried to where the rumbling came from.[58]

As they began to run out of rations, the Americans in Bastogne had even less to eat than the civilians. People everywhere dug into their reserves to try and give the GIs "a little something." The Genons returned to their cellar with some loaves of bread from the seminary to find the Americans there so hungry they insisted the soldiers take half their supply. But then the skies cleared and between December 23 and 28 more than 1,200 fat C-47 transport planes in wave upon wave dropped more than a thousand tons of supplies. Countless red, yellow, orange, blue, and white parachutes popped open, gently lowering packets of food, ammunition, and other necessities into the hands of the beleaguered troops. The giant resupply operation electrified both soldiers and civilians, showing them that, though they might be isolated, they were far from forgotten. To Louis Massen the gifts were like "celestial manna," and he was moved to see the GIs "happy like big children." "It was magnificent," Marie-Thérèse Kesch concurred even half a century later, "I have never seen anything that beautiful."[59]

The drops by no means allowed a regime of plenty. Still, the arrival of so many unexpected gifts sparked a wave of generous donations further highlighting the solidarity between soldiers and civilians. Within hours GIs with chocolate bars and canned goods from their K rations were repaying the Genons for having shared their bread with them. The first thing Pfc. Bruce Middough did when he opened the packet he had retrieved from a field was to recompense Mrs. Simon, kind host to him and his comrades, with enough food to get by for several days. Similar gestures were repeated again and again across town. The brightly colored silk parachutes themselves became highly coveted among civilians who had not seen or felt such luxurious fabric during years of occupation and want. GIs showered the pupils of the Institute of Notre Dame with pieces of silk the size of scarves. One soldier brought Suzanne Zeller and her friends a parachute of each color. By the dim light of petrol lamps the enthused girls immediately set out cutting, stitching, and embroidering.[60]

The Bastognards again insisted on returning the favors. Volunteer bakers at the seminary stoked the ovens, this time to help broil more than a hundred turkeys that had been dropped for the GIs at the front to celebrate Christmas. Some of the town's girls fabricated silk scarves to help keep the soldiers warm in their foxholes, though they made sure to paint the bright colors black. Mrs. Simon thought Pfc. Middough was too kind for having given her not only food but also the packet's blue parachute. She knew the American had married only recently. From a picture that Bruce had shown her several times, Mrs. Simon guessed the girl's measurements and went to work. Somehow Pfc. Middough eventually managed to send a perfectly fitting blue gown all the way from war-torn Europe to his wife in Los Angeles.[61]

The spectacular air supply lifted the spirits of many, but it failed to alleviate the suffering of the wounded. Though several victims, such as André Meurisse and Madeleine Barthelemi, were civilians, the overwhelming majority were soldiers who kept pouring in from the front lines around Bastogne. Because no one could be evacuated, the aid stations inside the town rapidly swelled into hospitals. Moreover, German troops early in the siege had captured the 101st Airborne Division's hospital with all of its personnel and equipment. In spite of the drops of hospital supplies beginning on December 23 and the arrival of some surgeons by glider, soldiers continued to die from lack of proper medicines and operating facilities. GIs scoured Bastogne's Red Cross building and its pharmacies, houses, and stores for medicines, alcohol, ether, and hydrogen peroxide. They requisitioned all of Doctor Govaerts's surgical instruments, allowing him to keep only his gynecological curettes; fortunately so, for one of the following nights he desperately needed them to save a woman suffering a bad hemorrhage in a dank cellar.[62]

The Institute of Notre Dame was just one of many places in town that the Americans organized into a makeshift hospital. So many casualties continued to arrive at the convent and school that by Sunday, December 24, refugees were ordered to evacuate some of the underground corridors to accommodate them. Meanwhile, civilians at the institute did what they could to help care for the wounded soldiers. Father Fecherolle moved between the patients, speaking words of encouragement and administering last rites. The boarding-school girls shared their shelter with a large group of casualties. The soldiers lay on stretchers and blankets; the pupils sat on chairs arranged in neat, tightly packed rows. A table formed the demarcation between the groups. The girls saw to the needs of the suffering men in myriad small ways and helped keep up morale by singing jazz songs and other ditties they had picked up from American troops. They made

Christmas Eve unforgettable for many of the GIs. A decorated tree was put up on the table that separated them. Each soldier and medic received a little present. Ignoring the chaos caused by the German bombardments later that night, Father Fecherolle transformed the table into an altar and celebrated Mass. When nuns and pupils started singing "Silent Night" in French, deeply moved soldiers weakly joined the sweet female chorus in English and Latin. "The heroism, mutual assistance, and solidarity that we saw around us," one girl observed, "were infectious."[63]

That was also the case in the hospital that had hurriedly been installed in the local Sarma, a large store near the railroad station. Here close to a hundred patients, many seriously wounded, lay crowded together on nothing more than blankets spread across the floor. Two young women from Bastogne, both trained nurses, had volunteered to help the American medical staff. One was Augusta Chiwy, whose father was one of the town's doctors. The other was Renée Lemaire, the dark-eyed daughter of a local businessman. The women's presence was a tremendous comfort to the ailing men who never stopped calling them "Sister." Both women were with the wounded soldiers when German bombers launched their first attack on Christmas Eve. One of the bombs plowed straight into the aid station. It eviscerated the building and set what remained of it on fire. The structure eventually collapsed, burying all those holed up in the cellar. Some thirty people failed to emerge from the ruins. One of them was Renée Lemaire. GIs recovered her badly mutilated body as soon as they could pick their way through the charred rubble. They gently carried it away shrouded in the silk softness of a white parachute.[64]

On Christmas Day news of the dreadful carnage at Sarma and the death of Renée Lemaire was whispered from shelter to shelter. People's morale might have hit rock bottom that day had persistent rumors of relief not followed on the heels of the tidings of doom. American troops were said to be closing in on Bastogne from the south. Some even claimed they were Patton's men. It sounded like a Hollywood western, where cavalry, when all seemed lost, came to the aid of soldiers barricaded behind overturned wagons. It seemed almost too good to be true.

Chapter 9

Between the Salm and the Ourthe

"We are going to die."

On Wednesday, December 20, around 7:30 in the morning, the church bells of Bérismenil, a village four miles east of La Roche, suddenly started chiming wildly without apparent reason. By the time the puzzled village priest arrived at his church to find out what was going on, the bells were silent again and nobody could be seen. The priest firmly locked the doors and made a brief note of the mysterious occurrence in the parish records.[1]

While German troops were being held up at Bastogne and St. Vith, the gap between both vital crossroads had remained wide open. More and more troops of the 58th Panzer Corps had been pulsing through it, thus avoiding the obstacle posed by the Salm River running behind St. Vith. Having bypassed Houffalize as early as dawn on December 19, reconnaissance units of the 116th Panzer Division had that afternoon already been scouting for bridges across the Ourthe, the last important military obstacle in front of the Meuse.

Before the Windhund division was able to locate a bridge across the west branch of the river on Tuesday, General Krüger, the corps commander, had ordered it to backtrack to Houffalize and to try and cross the main course of the Ourthe farther north. As there were an undetermined number of American troops in La Roche, General Krüger at dawn on Wednesday had unleashed the veteran division in the direction of Hotton, a town northwest of La Roche and some nine miles downstream from it.[2]

The impetuous speed of the Windhund division caught the inhabitants of the Ourthe Valley off guard that morning. Little did

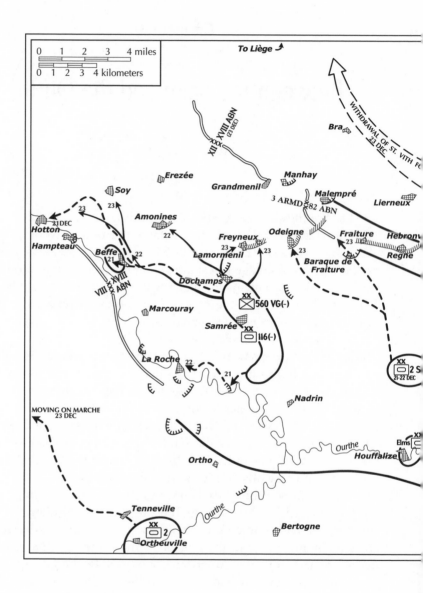

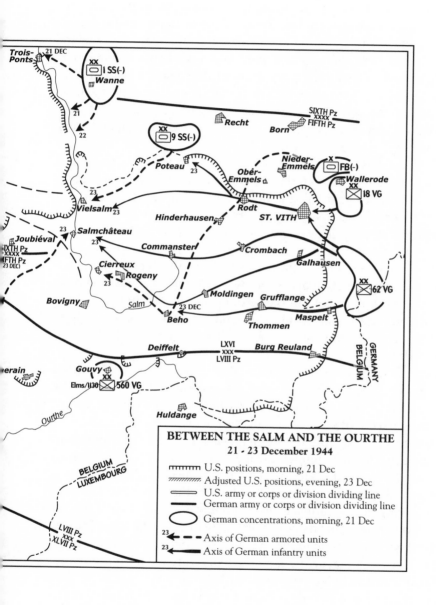

Trois-Ponts
21 DEC
XX
I SS(-)
Wanne

21

22

SIXTH Pz
XXXX
FIFTH Pz

Recht

Born

XX
9 SS(-)

Poteau
23

Nieder-
Emmels
X
FB(-)

Ober-
Emmels

Wallerode
XX
18 VG

Vielsalm
23

Hinderhausen

Rodt

ST. VITH

23

Joubiéval
XXXX
FTH Pz
23 DEC

Salmchâteau
23

Commanster

Crombach

Galhausen

Cierreux
Rogeny
23

Moldingen

Grufflange

XX
62 VG

Bovigny

Salm

23 DEC

Beho

Thommen

Maspelt

Deiffelt
LXVI
XXX
LVIII Pz

Burg Reuland

GERMANY
BELGIUM

erain

Gouvy
Elms/1130
XX
560 VG

Ourthe

Huldange

BELGIUM
LUXEMBOURG

LVIII Pz
XXX
XLVII Pz

BETWEEN THE SALM AND THE OURTHE
21 - 23 December 1944

⊓⊓⊓⊓⊓ U.S. positions, morning, 21 Dec

⫽⫽⫽⫽ Adjusted U.S. positions, evening, 23 Dec

══════ U.S. army or corps or division dividing line

━━━━━ German army or corps or division dividing line

◯ German concentrations, morning, 21 Dec

23 ◄- - - Axis of German armored units

23 ◄━━━ Axis of German infantry units

Bérismenil's village priest suspect that those who had just rung the bells in his church were German soldiers, back again more than three months after their ignominious rout. Advance troops had sounded the bells merely to signal their safe arrival to the main body of the 116th Panzer Division and had then taken off like lightning. The division's artillery claimed possession of Bérismenil in a matter of hours. Vindictive guns abruptly answered the puzzled priest's questions as they began blazing away at La Roche and Samrée. By six o'clock on Wednesday evening, all of Samrée was in German hands, including six smoldering houses.[3]

The road to Hotton was now wide open. Around three o'clock on Thursday morning, in pitch darkness and dense fog, German reconnaissance vehicles gave inhabitants of Beffe, almost six miles northwest of Samrée, a rude awakening. Heavy armor continued to roll through the village all day, and tanks displaying big black crosses made buildings and their inhabitants shudder without reprieve. German troops claimed part of the safest shelters that evening and bedded down with the civilians. There was nothing anybody could do about the brash intrusion. In the farm of the Desramaults, a soldier lay down on a heap of straw, next to Joseph's eighteen-year-old daughter Renée. The German went to sleep with the girl's hand in his. No one dared object.[4]

German troops also reached Trinal long before the cock crowed on Thursday. The village's sixty or so inhabitants first thought the new arrivals were Americans. Several moments passed before Léa Collard realized that she was staring the enemy in the face again. Her husband had been deported to Germany as a political prisoner in July. Ever since that fateful summer day it was she and her two young sons who had taken care of the farm's hard labor. She immediately ordered the eldest, fifteen-year-old Marcel, to hide in the hayloft and to keep from showing himself until she told him it was safe to do so. Léa Collard was determined not to lose another of her men to the hated Boches. Before noon, packs of enemy guns were spewing fire from the trembling village. A cannon in Mrs. Collard's courtyard left the horses wide-eyed and the cows bellowing with fear.[5]

From Trinal it was only a stone's throw to Werpin. Here, as in many surrounding villages, most able-bodied men had played it safe and taken to the road as soon as news had reached them of a large-scale German attack launched from behind the West Wall. One of the first to leave his flock had in fact been Father Laloux himself. Werpin's priest was known to have been involved in the resistance. He, like the others, feared brutal reprisals from the enemy. What made the mood particularly nervous among the men in this area was the memory of the German withdrawal in the autumn. The 2nd SS Panzer Division in Erezée and Fisenne on September 9 had arrested six presumed members of the resistance and had executed them without as much as an interrogation. Still, when military vehicles halted in Werpin in the morning darkness of December 21, Renée Lhermite, too, automatically assumed they were American. The eighteen-year-old girl had learned to appreciate the way the GIs doted on her. She rushed to the soldiers and with a coy smile asked them where the Boches might be by now. The faces staring back at her seemed set in stone, their contemptuous mouths parting slightly to spit abusive words in a guttural language. Renée backed away and fled to her parents' house.[6]

Elements of the 116th Panzer Division pushed on to Mélines that Thursday morning. Two reconnaissance half-tracks rushed past the village and got as far as Ny. Three Panzergrenadiers burst into the Jadin home in search of something to drink and eat. Seventeen-year-old Renée stumbled into the kitchen just in time to tear portraits of Churchill, Roosevelt, and Stalin from the wall. The Germans left with a pail of water and all the bacon they could carry.[7]

Mélines itself was a hamlet of no more than a few handfuls of scattered farms. It was important only because it sat astride a decent road that led straight into Hotton, some three miles to the west. Half-tracks pulled up to the Beaufays farm between four o'clock and five o'clock in the morning. Panzergrenadiers violently kicked the door. An angry Mr. Beaufays threw on some clothes and drowsily descended the stairs ready to tell the Americans off for their impudence. Just as he set foot on the last step, two bullets ripped through the front door and slammed into the hallway's rear wall. A pale and trembling Mr. Beaufays needed little prodding from his nocturnal guests to spill what little he knew about the Americans in the vicinity.[8]

The day before, eighteen-year-old Florent Lambert and two other boys from Mélines had decided they would leave their village before dawn on December 21. They had waited too long. They were about to assemble at the Buron farm around seven o'clock when all hell broke loose. The rattle of small arms and the pounding of artillery engulfed them from all sides. The boys rushed to the farm's cellar with their heads down. Barely ten minutes later, Panzergrenadiers stormed the Buron farm. The boys and two women, one of them holding an infant, climbed the cellar stairs with raised hands to show that there were only civilians in the farm. The Germans yelled at them savagely, but all they apparently wanted to know was if there were any Americans left. Then they calmed down and behaved as if the inhabitants were invisible. Later that day the Germans turned the Buron cellar into a command post. Officers barged in, telephone wire was strung, maps laid out on a table. Boys, women, and baby withdrew to the small adjoining cellar where heaps of potatoes lay stored in gloomy darkness.[9]

German officers at the command post in Mélines had only one concern: to seize Hotton at the earliest time possible. With its eight hundred inhabitants Hotton did not at first glance look like an objective that could have sparked interest in military planners. But the town was cut in two by the Ourthe River, and both sections were connected by a bridge. It was this sturdy two-way bridge, put in by U.S. Army engineers to replace the one that retreating Germans had blown up in September, that made Hotton crucially important to the 116th Panzer Division on its way to the Meuse.[10]

Hotton was defended by no more than a platoon of the 51st Engineer Combat Battalion and a handful of support troops from the 3rd Armored Division. Civilians, and former members of the resistance in particular, had begun abandoning their town as early as Monday, December 18. On Wednesday, the Americans in Hotton, alarmed by stories of German infiltrators, took drastic measures to tighten security. The circulation of civilian vehicles was prohibited, the remaining inhabitants were no longer allowed to leave town, and the identities of civilians crossing the bridge were subjected to careful scrutiny from GIs aided by local gendarmes. By the end of the day, some ten civilians thought to be suspicious were locked up in the town's fishing-rod factory. Yet, despite the nervous atmosphere, more than five hundred of Hotton's inhabitants went to bed that evening confident that the Americans had everything under control. After all, in May 1940 the Germans had been in Hotton barely thirty-six hours after crossing the frontier; now, five days after the start of their counteroffensive, they could still only be heard in the distance.[11]

On the left bank, on Thursday morning, December 21, two elderly ladies, Mrs. Lobet and Mrs. Colle, blissfully ignorant of the danger approaching Hotton from the other side of the Ourthe, got dressed for the seven o'clock Mass. The service had just started when on the right bank German troops burst into the houses on Hotton's outskirts. They wanted information on the Americans and demanded food. A woman in the Verdin farm pleaded with the soldiers to leave them at least something to eat. She was slammed into a corner by an officer. "Our men haven't eaten in eight days," he snarled. "They come first."[12]

At 7:30 A.M. mortars and machine guns suddenly opened up on Hotton's bridge and the buildings around it. The attack came as a surprise to soldiers and civilians alike. In the chapel on the left bank a flabbergasted Father Marquet abruptly halted his service. He knew what the noise meant, and memories surged to the surface of how retreating Germans in September had set fire to part of Hotton, including the town church. He turned around and, drawing a large cross in the air with a trembling hand, offered the churchgoers general absolution. Then he handed one of the faithful a strongbox containing the silver chalices. In a nearby garden Mr. Jacquemart lowered the box into a hole together with his best bottles of wine. He covered the treasure with straw and quickly pulled the earth over it.[13]

The battle for Hotton lasted three days. Tanks and Panzergrenadiers of the Windhund division repeatedly stormed the bridge. Each time the elite troops were stopped by American engineers, clerks, and mechanics who had at their disposal no more than a handful of bazookas. They were reinforced by two platoons of Shermans from the 3rd Armored Division that slipped into Hotton after dark on the first day. The tanks arrived with the help of a civilian from Ny who jumped on the lead tank and piloted the Americans across a back road. At the end of the second day the 116th Panzer Division disengaged and was rerouted to La Roche, which, the Germans had learned, the Americans had abandoned. Foot soldiers of the 560th Volksgrenadier Division continued the attacks and managed to get close to the bridge, but they never seize it.[14]

Damage to the town was significant but not disastrous; it was mainly limited to buildings on two roads on the right bank that led to the bridge. Despite bitter fighting, the number of civilian casualties remained remarkably low. Before noon on the first day, Auguste Collard had been mortally wounded by shell fragments while fetching straw to make his family more comfortable in their underground shelter. On the second day, Raymond Richel was killed in his kitchen, probably by one of the Panther tanks roaming the rue Haute alongside the Ourthe. The next day, a mortar shell exploded close to Alexandre Lobet just as he emerged from his cellar. GIs rushed him to an aid station in

Hotton and then to a hospital in Marche, but there was nothing the surgeons could do to save him. Worse carnage among the civilians was prevented by the fact that much of the enemy's heavy artillery had failed to keep pace with the armor. That gray skies and fog had kept Allied fighter-bombers at bay for much of the battle undoubtedly also played a role in keeping Hotton's civilian casualty rate down.[15]

Before midnight on December 23, Americans from the 517th Parachute Infantry Regiment and the 509th Parachute Infantry Battalion had driven the last Germans from Hotton's right bank. The paratroopers were part of the reinforcements that had been rushed into the gap between the Ourthe River and the 82nd Airborne Division, which was guarding the rear of the troops in St. Vith at the Salm River. They and two regiments of the 75th Infantry Division had been sent to complement the 3rd Armored Division with foot soldiers. These forces, together with the 84th Infantry Division that was getting into position behind the Ourthe, now formed an extension of the defensive northern shoulder that stretched as far northeast as the Elsenborn Ridge.[16]

From this section of the northern shoulder, too, increasing concentrations of artillery began to put tremendous pressure on the enemy. And when the skies at last cleared on December 23, growing packs of Allied aircraft joined them in wreaking havoc. American artillery was already hitting back at the Germans in Trinal during the afternoon of December 21. Phosphorus shells immediately set fire to the Guébel farm. A rain of American shells caused so much damage the following day that the Germans forced at least one civilian to help clear rubble. The uninterrupted shelling prevented the villagers from burying Mrs. Leduc, who had died of natural causes on December 18 and was laid out in her bedroom. On December 23 the lull that the villagers had been praying for finally materialized, and everyone headed for a wooded area on the bank of the Ourthe. Some of the elderly had to be pushed in wheelbarrows; a man too frail to carry his suitcase dragged it along on a rope. The villagers stayed in the woods for more than four days. Fires were built at the risk of attracting fighter-bombers and from time to time had to be shared with German soldiers roaming the area. On December 27 the inhabitants of Trinal at last succeeded in crossing the Ourthe and finding refuge in Rendeux. When they finally returned to their village in January not a single building remained standing and Mrs. Leduc's corpse had been buried under the rubble.[17]

American artillery had begun to reach farther southward and started pounding Beffe at dawn on December 22. People fled to the cellars and stables and were soon joined by inhabitants from the nearby hamlet of Magoster. Many flocked to the four solid shelters beneath the presbytery. With much of the village already pulverized or ablaze, the barrage increased in intensity the following day. In the evening, news spread that Marie Docquier and Emile Latour, a lumberjack and father of three sons, had been killed. The scared civilians hung on to their shelters until Christmas morning. Then shells of such heavy caliber began to plow into Beffe that the situation became untenable. Father Renson prepared the villagers for an escape in the direction of the Bardonwez flour mill, which lay hidden in woods on the Ourthe bank. At nine o'clock, just after a shell had ripped open the presbytery's back wall, the barrage lifted long enough for the inhabitants of Beffe and Magoster to stumble to Bardonwez in temperatures far below freezing. The community had barely organized itself at the mill when a band of German soldiers showed up demanding laborers to dig trenches for them. They rounded up fifteen of the strongest men. Panic-stricken villagers hurriedly provided the men with some food before watching them be marched off. Over the next few days the forced laborers all trickled back to the mill, frozen to the bone but otherwise unharmed.[18]

For two long weeks the refugees from Beffe and Magoster lived on melted ice and bread made with flour stored at the mill. All the while American forces continued to pummel their villages and many others on the Ourthe's right bank. The day after Christmas fighter-bombers struck at German troops holed up in Bérismenil. They set ablaze two houses; slugs from their machine guns badly wounded a young refugee from Liège. On December 27 a bomb hit the center of the village causing still more destruction. Five days later, in the shelters that remained intact, the inhabitants of Bérismenil quietly made room for a stream of refugees, at least one of whom was ill with highly contagious diphtheria. The unfortunates had come down from Dochamps after the Germans had ordered them out of their homes. Twenty people thronged the presbytery's basement; twenty-six shivering civilians pressed against each other in the mayor's cellar.[19]

None of the overwhelming American firepower was any good to Task Force Hogan. Sent out in the direction of La Roche by the 3rd Armored Division on December 20 to reconnoiter the area, the task force of some 400 men had become surrounded at Marcouray, a village of about forty houses three miles upstream from La Roche. Marcouray in normal times counted some 140 souls, but most of the men of arms-bearing age had fled as soon as they had heard the first rumble of shelling at Samrée. They remembered all too well the wrath of the enemy the previous September when, in retaliation for attacks launched by the maquis, German soldiers had torched half the houses in nearby Marcourt and had executed a total of 13 suspected resistance fighters in both villages. As soon as Task Force Hogan had pulled into Marcouray in the afternoon of December 22, relentless German shelling had made people seek cover in three of the village's sturdiest cellars. The trapped Americans prohibited anyone from leaving Marcouray. Around noon on Christmas Day, Lieutenant Colonel Hogan called Father Chariot to his command post. The Texan told the priest that he had just received orders to break out after dark and head for the American lines on foot. To avoid panic, he wanted Father Chariot to keep the news from his flock until his troops had vanished. Once that had happened, the priest was to urge the villagers to strip tanks and trucks of all that was useful rather than have it fall in German hands.[20]

Large numbers of enemy troops arrived in Marcouray the following day. They robbed the villagers of all the food they could find and of all things American. Other than that they behaved. But the villagers' ordeal was far from over. During the night of December 27 the Americans greeted the enemy with ferocious shelling that destroyed at least four houses and mortally wounded one woman. The following day, fear of more shelling and a lack of food drove most villagers to seek refuge in Marcourt. Disaster struck the ill-fated communities again three days later. On New Year's Eve German soldiers got drunk and aggressive. They demanded the company of girls and harassed several of them. Around midnight two soldiers with alcohol on their breath arrested Joseph Piret and Louis Adams, both refugees from Marcouray, possibly because they had tried to protect the girls. Pistols in hand the Germans forced both men to walk in the direction of the church cemetery. Louis Adams tried to escape but was shot in the head. A bullet in the neck ended the life of Joseph Piret. Ten days later, a cadaverous Louis Adams, blood caked on his face, was discovered in the cellar of his own home in Marcouray. Dazed and in shock, he had staggered back to his village and laid himself down on the cellar floor expecting to die. GIs rushed him to a hospital in Huy where doctors gave him a second life.[21]

American troops liberated Marcouray after the start of the large-scale Allied counteroffensive on January 3. Long before then, however, GIs with the support of massive artillery to their rear had started nibbling away at the edges of the German positions near Hotton. Long lines of infantrymen were filing through Hampteau on December 25. They belonged to the 75th Infantry Division, which had never seen action. Villagers were pained to see how young and insecure these GIs were. Some called out to the Belgians to pray for them on Christmas Day. They marched on to Werpin, where they installed artillery to keep the pressure on the Germans while trying to establish contact with the soldiers of the 517th Parachute Infantry who had just captured Mélines.[22]

The people of Werpin did not have long to savor their second liberation. Made nervous by sporadic shell fire and the possibility of a German counterattack, officers of the 290th Infantry on the first day of the new year called a meeting of the heads of the village's households in a barn near the church. There they announced that the following day all villagers were to assemble and leave for Soy and Fisenne. There were to be no exceptions, and those who resisted could expect a heavy fine. All were devastated by the news that they would have to leave behind farms and cattle, and some uttered loud protests. But at eight o'clock the following morning, a column of more than eighty elderly, women, and children began the two-mile trek through snow and the wreckage of battle. At the column's head and tail American guards—bayonets fixed to their rifles—made sure that the dejected bunch, hunched under heavy bags, arrived at their destination.[23]

2 While American forces were staving off German attacks at Hotton, a new threat developed some fourteen miles east of the Ourthe town at Baraque de Fraiture. The place took its name from the nearby village of Fraiture and was nothing more than a crossroads with three farmhouses and their outbuildings. But this crossroads, located in the marshy and wooded Hautes Fagnes, was one of the most vital in the Ardennes. For at Baraque de Fraiture the roughly east-west highway from Salmchâteau to La Roche crossed Highway N-15, the major north-south route connecting Liège with Houffalize and Bastogne.

On Friday, December 22, German troops reached Highway N-15 north of Houffalize and some six miles south of Baraque de Fraiture.

They belonged to the 2nd SS Panzer Division. The veteran division, also known as *Das Reich*, had acquired a reputation for brutality in Russia as well as in Normandy. It had razed the Norman village of Oradour-sur-Glâne, murdering more than six hundred of its inhabitants, including women and children. During its retreat to Germany in September 1944 it had also committed several crimes in the Ardennes. Because of the failure of the SS troops to get across the Elsenborn Ridge, General Dietrich had ordered Das Reich to plunge into the same gap through which the 58th Panzer Corps had passed. From there it was to move up Highway N-15, capture Baraque de Fraiture, and seize Manhay. The division was then to veer northwest to protect the north flank of von Manteuffel's Fifth Panzer Army to which the main effort had now switched.[24]

American commanders were not sure of Das Reich's intentions on Highway N-15. Many in fact thought that the SS division's true objective was Liège, a major supply hub behind which lay the headquarters of the First Army. They knew, however, that German troops on the highway had to be halted at all cost. But the Allies had only a handful of mostly airborne troops to spare for the defense of Baraque de Fraiture. The 2nd SS Panzer Division did not wait for them to get stronger. On Saturday morning, December 23, the hardened outfit hurled itself against the enemy at the crossroads. Most of the farms' inhabitants had fled to Fraiture as soon as the Americans had begun reinforcing the intersection. Retreating Germans in September had set fire to at least one farm and had threatened some of the men with execution; no one had wanted to relive the horror of those days. SS troops were in control of Baraque de Fraiture and its smoking ruins by Saturday evening.[25]

The following afternoon the elite panzer troops also captured the village of Fraiture. They immediately rounded up six men and boys. They marched them to a command post in tents just south of the Baraque de Fraiture crossroads. Officers interrogated the civilians about the strength of the American forces in the vicinity and the nature of their vehicles. The questioning done, they left them standing in the snow for a while. Then they let them go.[26]

When dark came the Americans retaliated by hammering Fraiture with their artillery. Two shells pulverized the cellar that belonged to the Gille family, snuffing the lives of four women and a fifteen-month-old baby. Marie Baccus was still alive, but just barely. The explosion had virtually severed both her feet. Accompanied by her brother, the Germans drove the victim to a hospital in Luxembourg. There her brother was forced to say goodbye. He never saw his sister alive again.[27]

Despite continued shelling, SS troopers requisitioned a cart and a couple of Fraiture's youngest men to collect the corpses of comrades killed in the surrounding woods. They also ordered the farmers to furnish one animal each as a contribution to their food stocks. Increasingly, however, more and more animals simply vanished. Some of the female refugees in the village tried to make their way back to their farms at Baraque de Fraiture to watch over their cattle. German troops promptly arrested them and hurried them to La Roche to have them out of the way.[28]

Beyond Baraque de Fraiture, tanks on Highway N-15 would be hemmed in by dense forests on both sides, thus threatening to become sitting ducks for mounting swarms of fighter-bombers. To avoid this, General Lammerding, commander of the 2nd SS Panzer Division, decided to send his troops in the direction of Manhay by way of small roads fanning out through the woods on either side of the highway. The new plan made Odeigne, a village just west of the highway with a population of some four hundred, a prime target.

Many of Odeigne's young men had fled on December 21, and some would eventually get as far as Brussels on their bicycles. Two days after they had gone, SS troops in pitch darkness attacked the village with vehemence. Within hours part of the presbytery lay in ruins and the Thomas home in ashes. Hidden by the fog, Mr. and Mrs. Thomas with their seven children managed to escape to a nearby wood. Nestor Bastin was cut down on his doorstep by a burst from a machine gun and would die a week later. Battle briefly carried over into the next day. Civilians who dared show themselves to the frenzied German troops paid a high price. A bullet from an SS pistol killed seventy-five-year-old François Dessy. Another one took the life of fifty-five-year-old Alfred Fagnant in front of the entry to his cellar. By noon on Sunday, December 24, the last remnants of American resistance at Odeigne were erased. In home after home anxious civilians from the top of their lungs cried, "Civilians! Civilians!" as soon as they heard the butts of rifles force in their doors.

On Christmas Day swarms of starving SS troopers roamed the village in search of food. They stripped dead GIs of their jackets and shoes. That same day, and the day after, American artillery replied angrily from beyond Manhay, gutting many of Odeigne's buildings. Allied fighter-bombers joined in the punishment of German troops in and around the village on December 27. Many terrorized families fled to the presbytery's cellars, and most of the sick and wounded were taken there too. The vicious air attacks came on top of the discouraging news for the Germans that their comrades were being driven back from inroads made just west of Manhay. Some SS soldiers in Odeigne snapped under the mounting pressure and turned against the civilians. Late in the afternoon, a vengeful trooper hurled a grenade into the cellar of the Wuidar home, killing four members of the family. The following day soldiers claimed the presbytery's solid cellar for themselves and drove the crowd of refugees, including the sick and wounded, into the open. Before the panic-stricken group could locate another shelter, an American shell had claimed the life of eighty-year-old Jean Nandrin.[29]

In the village of Malempré, a knot of secondary roads on the other side of the vital highway and still closer to Manhay, people's ears had pricked up when the radio on Saturday, December 16, had announced that the Germans had launched a counterattack on Belgium's eastern border. On Sunday unease had grown as the radio began to refer to the enemy operation as nothing less than a counteroffensive. Things had remained relatively calm until Wednesday when the muffled bark of guns could be heard through the thick mist. That same day part of a task force from the 3rd Armored Division had taken up position near the village. On Thursday the distinct sound of explosions had drifted in from Odeigne. Then the thunder of battle had begun to roll in from the direction of Baraque de Fraiture.

The rumble swelled by the hour on Saturday. To the inhabitants of Malempré there was no doubt now that the storm was heading their way. Some of the village's young men said goodbye to their families in the afternoon and reluctantly took off. The first German shells hit Malempré around nine o'clock that evening, damaging the school and two houses. The following morning, December 24, tension reached fever pitch. More American troops arrived at the village and dug in. They were mostly battered and exhausted men from the 7th Armored Division, just pulled out from the salient at St. Vith. The GIs were suspicious of everything and everyone, and in the course of the day arrested several villagers for reasons that were unclear. The din of battle continued to creep closer. For the inhabitants of Malempré it was still hard to believe that the Germans, so ragged and dejected in September, were not only back again, but were actually routing what had looked like the best-equipped army in the world. In the early afternoon, however, what lingering doubts remained were brutally dispelled when a jeep pulled up and discharged two captured German soldiers for questioning. Villagers flocked to the prisoners and stared at them as if they were the ghosts of people long dead.[30]

The 2nd SS Panzer Division unleashed its troops against Malempré late on Christmas Eve. For several hours the village was a whirlpool of hellish noises and violent shocks while the inhabitants held on to each other in their cellars. By midnight the racket ebbed away at last. Only the metallic crunch of German hobnailed boots remained. Apprehensive villagers came up from their shelters on Christmas Day to find Malempré teeming with SS troops. The Germans combed house after house in search of food and clothing and anything else they could use. They even broke into the sacristy to reappear again with white Mass vestments over their uniforms as part of their snow camouflage. Many villagers could not keep from crying at the sight of such irreverent scenes and the thought of what was to happen next.[31]

Ironically, the inhabitants of Malempré found the SS troops reasonably well behaved during the first days of the occupation. "They were correct with us," one village woman recalled, "as long as we gave them what they wanted." In fact, with the front line not far away, the first to threaten the villagers were the Americans. Shells began to rain down on Malempré around ten o'clock in the morning of December 26. Fighter-bombers swooped down not much later that day, demolishing several enemy vehicles as well as Joseph Philippe's home. Early in the afternoon, twenty-nine-year-old Elisabeth Leruse was the first to fall victim to an American shell when it pierced a stable wall and exploded inside. Her parents wrapped her body in a shroud, gently placed it on the living-room table and, bent with grief, retreated to their cellar.[32]

Jules and Joseph Collignon, meanwhile, were in a painful quandary. They realized that fleeing Malempré while under fire might cost them their lives. But they knew the outcome could be the same if they decided to stay. The brothers had lived on a farm near Commanster when the Germans invaded Belgium in May 1940. To avoid conscription in the German army after the Reich absorbed the Ostkantone, they had gone into hiding in Malempré where they had family. If the

SS troops found out that they were draft dodgers, their wrath would be terrible. The brothers decided to risk escape some two hours after Elisabeth Leruse was killed. They walked in the direction of Fraiture holding tools they hoped might pass them off as lumberjacks. But the Germans could hardly be fooled by loggers pretending to be at work on a battlefield. In no time triumphant SS troopers arrived in Malempré with Jules and Joseph Collignon in their midst. First they took the cowering brothers to the presbytery. After a brief interrogation, SS soldiers marched the pale young men out of the village and to the edge of a wood. They told the brothers to look away; then killed them both with a bullet in the neck. Jules was twenty-nine years old; his brother Joseph was twenty-one years old.[33]

As the execution of the Collignon brothers showed, the continuous nerve-racking bombardments, as well as the crumbling foothold at Manhay, caused the behavior of the SS troops in Malempré to turn nasty and unpredictable. Some of the hardened soldiers cracked. In the wake of the first devastating bombardment on December 26, for example, civilians in one cellar watched a wild-eyed officer gesticulate furiously to no one in particular, while one of his subordinates kept mumbling to himself, "Alles Kaput. Alles Kaput." (Everything is lost. Everything is lost.) Other soldiers vented their frustrations on the civilians. In one cellar an SS trooper threatened to kill all of the "terrorists" after finding some weapons nearby that had clearly been abandoned by GIs. Soldiers pulled Arthur Collignon from his shelter and took him away with a rifle pressed against his back. He returned a little later relieved that all they had wanted him to do was find them some alcohol.

More and more SS men, meanwhile, were drawn to the relative safety of the robust cellars, and they did not shrink from throwing the civilians out if there was not enough room. It was Maria Collignon's baby son that sealed her fate and that of her family when he kept crying throughout the night despite an officer's furious admonitions. The following morning the annoyed soldiers promptly ostracized the family from their own home. Still, amid such heartless behavior, individual SS men from time to time surprised the villagers with the simplest of human gestures. The surgeon, for example, who took two of Mrs. Noirhomme's jugs and later in the evening unexpectedly returned to drop one off filled with fresh water. Or the soldier in the local syrup factory who, even when phosphorus set the giant shelter and aid post on fire and civilians and wounded comrades struggled to get out in a mad panic, took time to lift a frail octogenarian into his arms and carry her to safety.[34]

Amid SS harassments great and small American artillery fire continued to claim the lives of Malempré's civilians. On December 27, a shell lacerated Joseph Samray. Germans took him to a hospital near Houffalize, where he died two days later. On the last day of 1944, a shell exploded in the courtyard of the farm where earlier artillery had already claimed Elisabeth Leruse. The blast mangled a village woman, Lydie Daco, and instantly killed a refugee who had come from as far away as Liège. Stunned villagers dragged Mrs. Daco, her strangely twisted body smeared with blood and dirt, back to the cellar. There they were to watch her suffer for three days until the Americans managed to take the village back.[35]

On December 24, the 7th Armored Division's battered Combat Command A, just back from the St. Vith salient, was ordered to Manhay to help defend the village against the SS thrusts from Odeigne and Malempré. The Americans were at the end of their tether and confusion reigned. Of the civilians who had yet to leave Manhay, some, on the advice of concerned GIs, now packed their bags and belatedly left for Vaux-Chavanne, a village about a mile and a half to the northeast. They were joined by villagers who had been ordered out of those homes located near vital crossroads. Later in the day, however, a new order suddenly came, this time strictly prohibiting civilians from leaving their shelters.[36]

The reason why troops in Manhay now wanted the unsuspecting inhabitants to stay indoors was that they were planning to leave the village that night. To build a more solid northern flank, the Allied command earlier that day had decided to pull back troops from the Salmchâteau–La Roche highway. They were to fall back to the road connecting Manhay with Trois-Ponts. The shortened line on its right would tie in with the defensive positions of the 3rd Armored Division between Hotton and Manhay. On its left it would mesh with solid positions already established at Stavelot and Malmedy and on the Elsenborn Ridge. The 7th Armored Division was to leave only an outpost at Manhay. The rest of Combat Command A was to withdraw and occupy high ground behind the village.[37]

Unaware of Allied plans, the 2nd SS Panzer Division attacked Manhay just as American armor was putting into action the complicated maneuver of withdrawal under cover of darkness. German shelling was so ferocious that it shook concrete grit from cellar roofs and blew away the wooden railroad ties that villagers had used to barricade their windows. In the morning hours of Christmas Day, a shell exploded against the window of Jules Massin's cellar, killing his eighteen-year-old son and a fifty-six-year-old neighbor. The village descended into chaos with the American withdrawal turning into a rout. Across Manhay, inhabitants were being flushed from their cellars. First by blasts pouring in from two sides; then by SS troopers claiming the shelters for themselves and in their impatience even forcing some of the civilians out through the windows. The Laurents poured from the cellar beneath their combined grocery and hardware store that two direct hits had nearly destroyed. In a reflex, fifteen-year-old Louis asked if he should try and return to retrieve the money. "To do what," his father asked resignedly, "we'll never need it again. We are going to die."[38]

Panic-stricken villagers surged onto the road to Vaux-Chavanne in pitch darkness. Some waved white flags. It did not do them much good. Bullets mowed down thirty-one-year-old Léon Danloy and his slightly older sister, Thérèse. A single explosion sufficed to cut short the lives of Mrs. Brasseur and nine-year-old Marcelle Lesenfants. In Vaux-Chavanne, which remained just inside the new defensive line, nervous Americans systematically checked the identities of the hollow-eyed refugees and made a few arrests. The mayor and inhabitants did all they could to take care of the traumatized neighbors trickling in throughout the night. The following day, afraid that the same fate might befall Vaux-Chavanne, some refugees immediately got going again to destinations farther north. In the evening, one such group, on its way to Bomal, arrived at an isolated farm serving as a command post. An American chaplain assembled soldiers and civilians in the courtyard and gave them absolution. Then he handed each of them a rosary and a religious medallion.[39]

Meanwhile, losses accumulated over a period of five days were beginning to make the 2nd SS Panzer Division lose steam while promised support from other SS panzer divisions failed to materialize. Adding to the division's problems, more than two hundred artillery pieces were now trained on the roads in Manhay from behind the strengthened northern flank, while increasingly active fighter-bombers prevented the Germans from bringing up most of their own artillery. Two days after Christmas, troops of the 517th Parachute Infantry readied themselves for the attack that was to dislodge the Germans holed up in Manhay. "I have never seen a bombardment like the one that preceded our attack," a paratrooper recalled much later. "The explosions merged into a continuous rumble, one could not distinguish separate bursts anymore." By nightfall Manhay was in American hands again. Bulldozers had to be sent in to trace roads through the giant heap of rubble that had once been a village.[40]

That the paratroopers managed to wrestle Manhay from armored SS troops by nightfall of December 27 had much to do with the fact that Das Reich had been told to disengage earlier that day. They were now to leave the sector around Baraque de Fraiture to the 9th SS Panzer Division that had at last begun to move up the Lienne Valley to the east. Instead they were to join what was left of the 560th Volksgrenadier Division in the Aisne Valley to their west.

3 The Lienne River meanders northward roughly parallel with the N-15 to its left and the Salm River to its right. Just south of the Lienne's source stretches the Salmchâteau–La Roche highway. In the evening of Saturday, December 23, just after the fall of St. Vith, the Führer Begleit Brigade launched itself from Salmchâteau. The elite outfit was under orders to support the 2nd SS Panzer Division by attacking along its right flank near Baraque de Fraiture. As the highway from Salmchâteau to Baraque de Fraiture was still defended by outposts of the 82nd Airborne Division, the Führer Begleit Brigade chose to advance along the secondary roads just south of it.

The armored column under cover of darkness rumbled from Provedroux to Langlire and from there, along even smaller roads, to Bihain. At dawn on Sunday the Germans looked down on Regné from the hills south of it. The hamlet was located just north of the highway and sat astride the secondary road leading straight to Fraiture, the village the Führer Begleit Brigade was to attack in order to support the 2nd SS Panzer Division at Baraque de Fraiture. The capture of Regné was vital to the Germans.[41]

The hamlet's inhabitants were unaware that the enemy was spying on them from the hills on Sunday morning. Most of the remaining men were tending their cattle in the barns. Many women were busy baking cakes and cookies for Christmas. In a matter of minutes shells wiped away the peaceful scenes, causing panic-stricken people to stampede to cellars and stables. The sprinkling of paratroopers in Regné stood no chance against the armor, and by noon the hamlet was in

German hands. Early in the afternoon, however, paratroopers and tanks from the 9th Armored Division, the latter just back from the St. Vith salient, launched a counterattack. Fighter-bombers swooped down on Regné to support the push. They went after the tanks that tried to hide as close to the buildings as possible. In the stable of the Mathieu farm a large number of villagers pressed closer together. The adults prayed. Eleven-year-old Jeanne and Roger, a boy her age, continued to play cards—pretending that there was not a battle going on around them. One bomb blew the adjacent tank to pieces; another ripped the stable apart. Roger was killed instantly. Fire raced through the rubble and flames licked at Roger's corpse. People darted in all directions and the wounded wailed. Acrid smoke mushroomed over the hamlet. With all the force still in her, Jeanne grabbed her mother's left arm and dragged her away from the burning stable. The woman was unconscious and blood gushed from her body's horribly mangled right side. Late in the afternoon Regné belonged to the Americans again. They loaded the many wounded civilians into ambulances and sped them to Esneux. There, Jeanne's mother succumbed to her wounds in the hospital.[42]

That same night the Americans suddenly abandoned Regné again. They merely responded to the order that made the 82nd Airborne Division pull back from the entire stretch of highway between Baraque de Fraiture and Salmchâteau to a stronger line farther north running from Manhay to Trois-Ponts. The Germans returned to Regné unopposed on Christmas Day. In village after village along the highway German reoccupation now materialized in similar fashion. Helpless civilians watched as an uninterrupted stream of Wehrmacht and SS troops began to flow by from behind the Salm River.

Enemy troops generally behaved well along this axis of advance. German medics in Ottré immediately obliged when Joseph Maréchal one night asked them to assist his wife who had gone into labor; by late morning the soldiers had helped deliver a healthy baby girl. Joseph Petitjean was less happy with the arrival of two armored cars near his farm in Regné. SS troops spilled from the vehicles, massacred eight chickens, and told his wife to pluck and cook them. After they had eaten, however, one of the SS troopers motioned Mr. Petitjean to follow him. In his vehicle the German had a bag filled with scarves and blouses and other civilian objects. From it he pulled a pair of children's shoes and handed them to the farmer.[43]

War and troops brought the usual inconveniences. Refugees

flooded the villages along the highway as they poured in from Fraiture and from as far away as Vielsalm and St. Vith. More and more soldiers, meanwhile, had to be billeted in the villages. When German troops arrived in Hébronval on Christmas Day, soldiers hurriedly assigned families lodgers by marking their doors with chalk. Germans in Petites-Tailles drove the inhabitants together in a few places and simply claimed the rest of the village. As American firepower increased, the soldiers did not flinch from chasing civilians from the most solid shelters, either. In Ottré they drove women, children, and the elderly from the humid quarries and shamelessly took their places around the makeshift stoves.[44]

Neither did the Germans hesitate to call upon villagers to perform all kinds of onerous tasks. Four women each morning had to assemble at the gendarmerie in Petites-Tailles to peel potatoes for the occupying troops. In Provedroux men were requisitioned to hack dead GIs from the ice with pickaxes and bury them. Farmers from Langlire worked long and hard to replace a bridge over the Ronce with a wooden structure and to fill a huge bomb crater in a nearby road. Civilians who refused to perform such tasks were made to see sense at gunpoint. Armed soldiers could bully civilians in any way they wanted. In a home in Joubiéval, SS troops, annoyed by the display of Mr. Willem's Great War medals, snatched the frame from the wall and hurled it to the floor. Three SS men who stopped their armored car at the isolated Masson farm near Langlire had the most odious of intentions. Reeking of alcohol, they burst into the house, grabbed Mr. Masson's wife, Yvonne, and dragged the screaming and kicking woman to their vehicle. Only when the arrival of another vehicle startled them, did the SS men let go of their victim.[45]

The withdrawal of the 82nd Airborne Division to a new line between Manhay and Trois-Ponts invited the German occupation not only of villages along the Salmchâteau–La Roche highway, but also of much of the Lienne Valley north of it. Droves of refugees from the German-speaking part of Belgium had alerted inhabitants of the valley to the seriousness of the German offensive at an early stage. Rumors were soon circulating up and down the Lienne of German brutality toward civilians. People readily believed them. Everyone in the area vividly remembered what the passage of German troops had brought in September. During the German occupation the vast dense forests between the Salm River and the Liège-Houffalize highway had harbored numerous resistance fighters, and many had struck at the Germans while retreating. In at least two instances in the Lienne Valley, German soldiers had avenged comrades in ruthless fashion. In Bra-sur-Lienne seven people had been executed and several homes set ablaze in response to the resistance, which had wounded one German and captured three others. In La Chapelle troops of the SS panzer division Das Reich, in reprisal for the death of one of their men, had shot seven civilians without so much as a hearing. With such horrors etched on their minds, many of the valley's able-bodied men had disappeared long before the withdrawal of American paratroopers on the night of December 24.[46]

The German troops that poured into the vacuum on Christmas Day belonged to the 9th SS Panzer Division. After their unsuccessful attempt to cross the Salm River at Grand-Halleux, troops from the Hohenstaufen division moved into the Lienne Valley from the direction of Vielsalm. They were to head as far as Werbomont and then to swing west in the direction of Hamoir where they, too, were to cross the Ourthe and protect the offensive's northern flank. In the early morning of December 25, SS troopers ordered all of Sart's men to assemble. They marched them to Petit-Sart. There they added three men to the group and told the twenty-five prisoners to line up in front of the hamlet's monument to the Great War dead. The ashen-faced men were convinced they had only seconds left to live. Then suddenly came the order to get going again. The soldiers took the prisoners with them in the direction of the valley. The armored column pushed on to Lierneux, where large numbers of troops installed themselves in and around the village. SS troops requisitioned even the large psychiatric institution, ousting many of the hapless patients from their rooms and herding them into the building's basement.[47]

The division's spearheads, meanwhile, continued their rapid push. In the hamlet of Baneux they promptly arrested an inhabitant wearing the cap of a forester. Perhaps mistaking him for a member of the maquis, the SS troopers almost beat and kicked the life out of him. Several miles farther north, in Amcomont, they seized another civilian, forcing him to accompany them to the village of Reharmont. There the Germans let him go, obliging the man to grope his way back home across the darkened battlefield. At a stone's throw from Amcomont, in Hierlot and La Chapelle, SS troops rounded up all male inhabitants between the ages of twenty and fifty-five. No one knew why. Shells had just destroyed a couple of vehicles, and perhaps the Germans feared the villagers were directing American artillery fire. Or perhaps the SS troops had been briefed about the region's reputation for resistance and simply wanted the men out of the way. After checking their identities, soldiers marched twenty-three of them down to Verleumont, where they herded them into a building that already bulged with the prisoners from Sart and Petit-Sart. The frightened men joined each other in prayer while awaiting their fate.[48]

As darkness fell on Christmas Day, SS troops stood before Bra-sur-Lienne. Situated on the road that connected Manhay with Trois-Ponts, the village formed part of the new defensive line that the Americans were to hold at all costs. Soldiers of the 82nd Airborne Division had poured in from positions farther south throughout the night of December 24. Father Mossay had held three Masses on Christmas morning. Civilians and GIs had thronged the church, and the Americans had donated large sums of money they thought they might never have a chance to spend again. Later in the day an American officer had broached the news the villagers had feared most: at dawn all civilians were to leave their homes for safe havens in the rear. The village priest had been asked to help organize the evacuation. Bra's young men, mindful of what had happened in their village in September, had taken to the roads several days earlier. They had rubbed up against incoming American reinforcements, however, and many had been arrested and kept for questioning. But the evacuation that had been planned for Tuesday morning, December 26, went smoothly. Trucks showed up to help carry children and elderly to their new destination. Only four farmers received permission to stay behind to take care of the village cattle. In less than two days, these four men, too, would flee from the horrors of the front line.[49]

The 9th SS Panzer Division failed to break through the American defenses at Bra. But the occupation of the Lienne Valley south of Bra brought hardships to the civilians in many forms. The SS troops did not have enough warm clothing and thus ransacked homes in search of blankets, sweaters, and socks. But they were, above all, starving, and they plundered all the food they could find, sometimes forcing civilians to hand goods over at gunpoint. By the end of December, many of the valley's inhabitants and refugees were lucky if they had some potatoes left to eat.

What the Germans also lacked desperately, here as elsewhere in the Ardennes, was the firepower of the Allies. From the sky over Lierneux fighter-bombers on December 27 swooped down on the

multitude of enemy vehicles and the houses they were hugging, causing panic among soldiers and civilians alike. Among the casualties at
Lierneux were at least two inhabitants, one of them the village priest.
So browbeaten did artillery and aircraft leave the Germans at
Verleumont that they no longer kept an eye on their civilian prisoners
and at last allowed them to trickle back to their homes.[50]

By the end of December, nowhere in the Lienne Valley were the
Germans safe from air attacks or from the artillery concentrated in
ever larger numbers on the northern flank. It left the SS troops more
jittery and irritated by the day. In La Chapelle they requisitioned men
to dig trenches. In Jevigné, a mile northwest of Lierneux, they evacuated most of the male inhabitants, with the exception of a few farmers
and the sixty-one-year-old village priest. Soldiers came to pluck Father Fenaux from one of the cellars in the evening of December 30.
Relations with the outspoken priest had been tense since the arrival
of the SS troops in Jevigné. Now they accused him of having sent
signals from the church tower to direct American artillery fire. There
was not the least shred of evidence and despite severe beatings, Father Fenaux denied all charges. SS troopers dragged the bruised priest
away and finished him off with a bullet through the temple.[51]

4 Life in the communities behind the Allied northern shoulder
could not have contrasted more sharply with that in the villages
occupied by the Germans. People were awed by the tremendous
buildup the Americans were accomplishing in record time. In Noiseux,
some four miles downstream from Hotton, GIs in two days and two
nights threw two bridges over the Ourthe, one of which was capable
of carrying tanks of more than forty tons. People on Christmas Day
claimed they counted five hundred pieces of artillery in and around
their village. The guns' roar made houses tremble and windows shatter.

In Fisenne, a hamlet just behind the defensive line at Erezée, youngsters watched the daily ritual of trucks arriving and GIs unloading
lemonade, beer, coffee, chocolate, oranges, potatoes, rice, sugar, cheese,
butter, eggs, bacon, and corned beef. They rarely went home empty-
handed. On Christmas Day the Americans, amid the massive concentration of artillery in Noiseux, felt optimistic enough to throw a party
for the hosts and their children. First they livened up the town hall
with a huge decorated tree. Then followed what a clerk in Noiseux's
official war chronicle described as "abundant distribution of candy,

chocolate, chewing gum, cheese, canned fruit, meat hash, cookies, coffee, cigars and cigarettes, tobacco, soap, and even blankets and shoes." "Great joy," the chronicler concluded, "for the children." But Noiseux's adults, too, must have slept soundly that night, convinced that, despite the temporary setback, the Americans were sure to win the war.[52]

Chapter 10

Between the Ourthe and the Meuse

"We are as astonished as we are desperate."

1 Having hit a brick wall at Hotton in its attempt to seize the town's bridge over the Ourthe, corps commander General Krüger ordered the Windhund division to pull back once again and this time to try its luck at La Roche. The 116th Panzer Division on December 23 slowly wound its way through the small, crooked streets of La Roche and over a single bridge that the Americans had damaged in retreat. As soon as the division reached the other side, the armored columns swung northwest toward the highway connecting Hotton with Marche-en-Famenne. They were under orders to cut this artery without delay. This would isolate American troops in Marche, a vital road center. More importantly, it would allow German armor to pour onto the open ground of the Condroz plateau and head for the Meuse at Namur along Highway N-4. Nowhere was the distance from the Meuse to Brussels and Antwerp shorter than at Namur. There was nothing to separate Namur from the Belgian capital and port but plains and rolling hills. The sheer thought of so much space made the veteran German tankers chomp at the bit.[1]

People in the villages just in front of the Marche-Hotton highway would remain unaware that the enemy had flung a steel fist their way until it hit them on the evening of December 23. They had, nevertheless, been sick with fear ever since they had first heard the muffled sound of guns on December 16 and the accompanying rumors of a big German push. The locals here had good reason to be more afraid than others. Early in September 1944, in step with orders from London, resistance fighters from both the Armée Secrète and the *Front de*

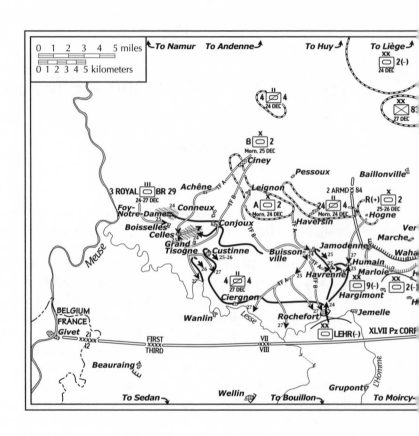

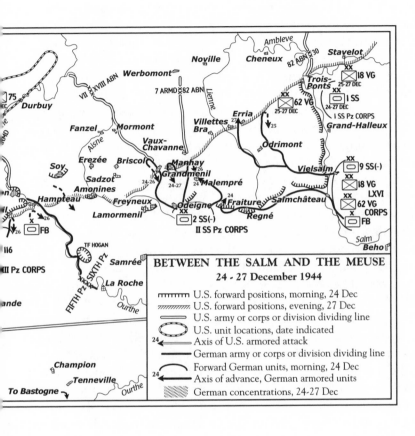

Amblève

Noville   Cheneux   82 ABN 30   Stavelot
                                                                XX
Werbomont⊡   Trois-   ⊠ 18 VG
VII XVIII ABN   Ponts   XX 25-27 DEC
75   7 ARMD 82 ABN   XX 62 VG ⊠ I SS
Durbuy   Villettes Erria 25-27 DEC 24-27 DEC
                                                              I SS Pz CORPS
Fanzel   Mormont   Vaux-   Bra   27   25   Grand-Halleux
                      Chavanne   Odrimont
          Erezée Briscol   Mannay 26   XX
Soy   Grandmenil 26   Vielsalm   ⊠ 9 SS(-)
     Sadzot   24-26   24-27 24   XX
     Amonines   Malempré   ⊠ 18 VG LXVI
Hampteau   Freyneux   24   Fraiture Salmchâteau   XX
         Lamormenil   Odeigne   Regné   ⊠ 62 VG CORPS
    X 26   XX   X FB
    26 ⊡ FB   ⊡ 2 SS(-)
                              II SS Pz CORPS   Salm
116   Beho
              TF HOGAN
III Pz CORPS   Samrée
                La Roche
                Ourthe
ande

BETWEEN THE SALM AND THE MEUSE
24 - 27 December 1944

⊓⊓⊓⊓ U.S. forward positions, morning, 24 Dec
⁄⁄⁄⁄⁄ U.S. forward positions, evening, 27 Dec
▭ U.S. army or corps or division dividing line
◯ U.S. unit locations, date indicated
24◀━ Axis of U.S. armored attack
▬ German army or corps or division dividing line
◠ Forward German units, morning, 24 Dec
24◀▬ Axis of advance, German armored units
▓ German concentrations, 24-27 Dec

Champion
  Tenneville
To Bastogne ↴   Ourthe

FIFTH Pz SIXTH Pz

l'Indépendance had poured from their camps in the region's dense forests to harass the retreating Germans with all available means. Stung by these actions, SS troops on their way back from France on September 6 had abruptly stopped. They had organized themselves and early in the afternoon set out to flush the maquis from some fields and woods near the village of Verdenne. They cornered six men suspected of being "terrorists" and shot them without asking questions. Convinced that some had escaped and were hiding in Verdenne, the frenzied SS sent four armored vehicles into the village. They raked house after house, killing one man and maiming another. The soldiers finished their job by setting fire to twenty-eight homes. Then they moved back to Champlon-Famenne. There they set still more buildings ablaze, meanwhile demanding food and alcohol from the inhabitants. Drunk and furious, the SS soldiers took a hostage with them to Marche, placed the man with his face against the front wall of the fire station, and shot him with a bullet in the neck. A pained Father Hanin had watched the execution from his house across the road. All he had been able to do was give the victim absolution from behind the window.[2]

Villagers had heaved a huge sigh of relief when American troops arrived in the area two days later. They soon felt safe enough in the presence of the tall, well-equipped, and easygoing soldiers to set about rebuilding their lives. Farmers in Verdenne gathered in their crops and cleared the rubble. Those who had escaped the destruction accepted the less fortunate civilians into their homes and opened the barns to their animals. The only note of discord during life under the GIs had been the death of Father Dernivois, Marenne's parish priest, who in October had been run over by an American truck while driving his Gillet motorcycle.[3]

When the alarming sound of German guns erupted on December 16, however, few GIs remained in this farming area. After four days of unbearable tension during which the rumble had inched ever closer, villagers heaved a new sigh of relief when American reinforcements reached Marche in the form of the 84th Infantry Division, an outfit that in November had undergone a costly baptism of fire in the battle for Aachen. For GIs of the 334th Infantry who were sent to the Verdenne area just northeast of Marche, digging in proved exceedingly difficult in the frozen soil of the Ardennes. But civilians there were so happy with the protection the Americans had come to offer that some joined them in scooping foxholes from the stubborn earth. A few miles farther west, at Serinchamps, the mood turned panicky when a company of the 333rd Infantry readied itself to move out again under orders to help defend the divisional headquarters farther back at Baillonville. The Americans had a great deal of trouble calming down the terror-stricken mayor and priest who were determined to prevent them from leaving.[4]

On Saturday, December 23, a thin American line was firmly in place on high ground just forward of the Marche-Hotton highway that it commanded. By afternoon, troops of the 116th Panzer Division were already in possession of Lignières and Grimbiémont. Here the Germans hurriedly set up their bases and aid posts, taking over the village buildings and requisitioning from the civilians whatever they needed. Nothing more than dense wooded areas separated Grimbiémont from the American line. That line was anchored on Verdenne and Marenne, villages situated on the small roads that formed the key to reaching the highway. The Germans wasted no time in probing the defenses. In mid-afternoon an American patrol returned to Verdenne with two Germans it had surprised near the village. While they were being interrogated in the home of Joseph Dony, anxious villagers dropped by hoping to learn more of what the enemy was up to. Some failed to restrain themselves and shouted insults at the prisoners for the grief their countrymen had caused them on September 6. Meanwhile, German artillery had found the range of the villages perched on the ridge. An explosion in Verdenne wounded Lea Galloy, and medics had to come to the anguished woman's rescue. American artillery responded with increasingly intense fire in the direction of the woods and the road from Grimbiémont. In their cellars that evening, Verdenne's inhabitants knew they had to leave soon—if they still could.[5]

The following morning, however, things were much worse. More than one hundred Panzergrenadiers under the cover of darkness had managed to slip through the American line and sneak into the woods behind Verdenne. German shelling intensified at dawn. Ignoring the danger, at noon villagers rushed to an American field kitchen where they were given food, chocolate, and cigarettes. Backed up by half-tracks and a handful of tanks, at dusk large numbers of Panzergrenadiers emerged from the woods north of Grimbiémont and stormed Verdenne. It took the German assailants seven hours of pitched battle to gain control of the village. The spent American defenders fell back to a line scarcely half a mile north of the village. The villagers hunkered down in shelters beneath the surface.[6]

For Verdenne's inhabitants, Christmas Eve of 1944 brought the ultimate perversion of the message of peace for all. By midnight, the Germans in and around the village were preparing for a predawn push against Bourdon, the hamlet that straddled the Marche-Hotton highway and was key to its control. The commander of the 84th Division was determined to stop the attack before it took place. Heavy artillery fire was brought down on Verdenne almost immediately. If German shelling had been bad for the civilians, American firepower was still worse. With many of the village's cellars rendered useless as a result of the SS rampage in September, people pressed together in the few solid shelters that remained. Cellars rapidly grew still more crowded as American shells set houses ablaze, forcing people to flee to their nearest neighbors. Members from three different families dashed from the soaring heat engulfing their communal shelter. They plunged into the icy night hoping to find refuge in the Jacob home across the street, one of the few buildings still standing in their part of the village. But the Germans had already claimed its cellar and turned it into an aid station. The desperate villagers could think of nothing better to do than to hide outside between the house's baking oven and the adjoining cemetery wall and to hold on to each other. At long last they succeeded in finding a more secure place inside the Jacob home. There they had the company of a Panzergrenadier left behind by his comrades on a table to die. For what seemed like an eternity the numbed civilians were forced to listen to the soldier crying for his mother. Then American shelling became so ferocious that the villagers crept away behind doors and furniture and hid beneath the bloodstained table.[7]

American reinforcements from the 333rd Infantry arrived north of Verdenne by midnight. An hour later, they joined men from the 334th Infantry in an effort to take back Verdenne from the Germans. Skirmishes could soon be heard to the north and west of the village. Panzergrenadiers, their nerves in tatters, acted increasingly hostile toward the civilians in the Jacob home, threatening to take hostages with them should they be forced out. Meanwhile, American troops slowly worked their way down the village, clearing house after house. By the time they reached the Jacob home, the Germans were still holed up inside. The infantrymen who burst into the house at dawn could not have been more different from the GIs the villagers had known in the previous months. Their faces dirty and unshaven, their eyes bloodshot, they struck twenty-one-year-old Albert Gaillard as a bunch of "bandits." Rifles and grenades at the ready, the Americans shoved soldiers and walking wounded into one corner of the house. Desperate to avoid being mistaken for the enemy, the villagers at the top of their voices kept screaming, "Civils! Civils!" In a nearby house, an alert woman managed to warn the GIs that civilians were mixed up with some fifty German soldiers in the cellar by pinching her child until it cried.[8]

American troops needed the better part of Christmas Day to mop up Verdenne. The Germans even managed to launch a counterattack in the afternoon, supported by close to a dozen tanks. Aircraft were called in to help stem the attack. Fighter-bombers incinerated not only some of the Panthers but also the houses they were hiding against. Only later in the day, when haggard American soldiers found time to share chocolate and cigarettes, did the trembling civilians begin to calm down. Of the few houses that had remained standing in September, nineteen had been pounded to rubble, while nine others were smoldering heaps of ashes. At least four civilians had been wounded. Two of the elderly had died from stress and emotion.[9]

The following morning, villagers were packing their bags to get away from an uninhabitable Verdenne. The Herman family braved the biting wind on the road to Marenne, only to be stopped at the village's edge by a menacing German tank around which a number of wounded Panzergrenadiers lay gathered. The nervous civilians placated the enemy with pieces of chocolate and were soon allowed to continue their way to American-held Marenne. The Germans who had inched so close to Marenne formed part of a large concentration of troops from the 116th Panzer Division trapped in the woods around the château northeast of Verdenne. Most had received nothing to eat since Christmas Eve, and some were risking capture by the Americans in Marenne by sneaking up to farms just to snatch some eggs.

Still, the strong unit pride of the Windhund soldiers made up for the miserable condition they were in. Time and again they rebuffed attempts by the Americans to clear the woods. In the cellar of the château de Verdenne, Baron Charles de Radzitzky d'Ostrowyck (a Belgian of Polish origin), his daughter Elisabeth, and fifteen other civilians heard the rooms above their heads change hands five times. When the Americans at last succeeded in wresting the château from the enemy, not even the emotional pleas from the baron's daughter could stop the frenzied soldiers from gunning down their German prisoners. Then, early in the afternoon of December 26, no less than five battalions of artillery coordinated their fire. In less than ten minutes they poured massive amounts of explosives and phosphorus into the Verdenne pocket. The merciless barrage finally broke the back of what was left of the veteran fighting force. The Americans sent a truck convoy to Verdenne and took all of the ill-fated village's inhabitants to reception centers in Marche-en-Famenne.[10]

2 While the 2nd Panzer Division was still engaged in fighting just north of Bastogne, its reconnaissance troops at dawn on December 20 had reached the bridge over the west branch of the Ourthe at Ortheuville. The small group of American defenders failed to blow the bridge, and by nightfall the Ourthe crossing was in German hands. Marie du Bus de Warnaffe spied the soldiers from her château in the nearby hamlet of Roumont. "There is a dense fog," she scribbled in her diary, "that seems to be the accomplice of these pigs. The soldiers pass without end. We are as astonished as we are desperate." All through December 21 and 22, however, the 2nd Panzer Division was unable to exploit its success at Ortheuville for lack of fuel. Troops piled up across the bridge and in front of it. Soldiers moved in and out of the château du Bus de Warnaffe to eat, wash, shave, and plunder. They shot a hog and carved up the bloody carcass on an antique desk in the study. When an outraged Marie de Warnaffe complained about the soldiers' behavior to an officer, he laughed in her face and told her this was war.[11]

By nightfall on December 22, enough fuel had arrived for the division to resume its advance along Highway N-4 connecting Bastogne with Marche. The two-day delay, however, had allowed the 84th Division to reinforce Marche and push out a screen south of the town.

Until the arrival of these infantry troops on Wednesday, December 20, the American garrison in the small town of Marche had been made up of Civil Affairs personnel, a handful of combat engineers, large numbers of mechanics, and a sprinkling of soldiers on leave. In the early evening of Sunday, December 17, nervous officers and MPs plucked all of them from Marche's movie theaters and from the living rooms of families with whom they were having dinner. The tram from Bastogne unloaded the first refugees on Monday. When on Tuesday morning the GIs could be seen evacuating Marche's many repair shops, the inhabitants panicked much as they had done in May 1940. Classes were adjourned; parents rushed to pick up their children at school, and many packed their bags and poured out of town. Among those who decided to stay, word spread to assemble for prayer at the chapel of Notre Dame de Grâce. At three o'clock in the afternoon, a large group had gathered at the designated spot and humbly beseeched Our Lady to have mercy on them.[12]

A V1 had exploded near Marche's hospital on Tuesday night. Another one hit the town shortly after dawn. The sound of artillery could be heard in the distance later in the day. Anxiety grew in leaps and bounds. GIs herded refugees into movie theaters to prevent spies from infiltrating; people in prison for collaboration were carted off to the rear; patrols checked and rechecked the identities of inhabitants. A town crier hurried through the streets to announce that no civilians were allowed outside from right after dusk until shortly before dawn. That night yet another V1 had sent a shock wave through town.

Only on Thursday had Marche's inhabitants regained some courage as they watched reinforcements from the 84th Division and 909th Field Artillery Battalion enter their town. Their fervent prayers on Tuesday appeared to have been answered after all. Grateful civilians set about brewing coffee, distributing gallons of the hot drink to frozen soldiers sent to their rescue all the way from Germany. At their convent, Carmelite nuns hailed the olive-drab saviors equally enthusiastically with hot soup. "Are there many Germans out there?" the mother superior wanted to know from a soldier. "Oh yes!" the GI affirmed. "We will pray for you," the nun had assured him. "Thanks," the soldier had replied. "Yes, pray a lot."[13]

In the afternoon of Friday, December 22, troops of the 2nd Panzer Division began probing the defenses just south of Marche. Meeting determined American resistance at the Hologne crossroads and again at Marloie, the Germans abruptly swung west, leaving behind only some blocking forces. The division's spearhead now plunged into the gap between Marche and Rochefort, the latter situated seven miles to the southwest. The armored troops were impatient, irascible, and unpredictable. At Hargimont they snatched eighteen-year-old Albert Durand from his bicycle for wearing GI clothing and insignia. When the boy naively tried to explain that these had been given to him by American friends, the Germans beat him to a pulp, dragged him to a nearby barn, and fired two bullets into his neck. Still in Hargimont, a soldier at night dragged a screaming fifteen-year-old girl from the Simal home. The girl fought her violator tooth and nail until he finally beat her into submission with his helmet. Speed allowed the soldiers to get away with their crimes. Already on Saturday, the head of the column reached Buissonville, five miles beyond the Marche-Rochefort highway. From a distance of no more than fourteen miles cross-country, Dinant on the Meuse enticingly beckoned German armor to make even more haste.[14]

On Saturday, too, dozens of shells were raining down on Marche. The first ones had begun hitting Marche just before dusk on Friday, causing an immediate power outage. Now one of the explosions badly mauled Alfred Gérard, who was to succumb to his wounds more than a month later. Another one on Sunday morning ripped off Antoinette Martin's arm. GIs rushed her far north to a hospital in Nandrin but could not prevent her from dying the same day.

Fearing a breakthrough at any time, American troops that Sunday extended Marche's curfew hours and threatened to shoot on sight anyone out on the street after dark. The following day, Christmas Day, to the consternation of the inhabitants, nervous GIs placed mines across all main entryways into town, rendering even the sidewalks unsafe. During lulls in the shelling, more and more civilians fled the town in total disorder.

The ring of American artillery around Marche, meanwhile, was blasting the assailants from all directions. Artillerymen, naked to the waist despite the biting cold, worked their weaponry until it was red-hot. People in cellars near the batteries were told to keep windows and doors open to prevent them from being ripped apart. They were given gum to chew and advised to sit through the hellish barrages with cotton wool in their ears.[15]

Like the artillery concentrations at Elsenborn and Manhay, massive fire support helped infantrymen save the day at Marche, sparing it from much worse destruction. Still, for some in Marche the misery the Germans had once again caused was too much to bear. Sixteen-year-old Tony Fautré and his father stood at a crossroads gaping as vehicle after vehicle passed with Germans taken prisoner at Verdenne. Something suddenly forced a jeep to slow down. Before anyone could stop him, Mr. Fautré had leaped at the vehicle and with his fist smashed one of the POWs squarely in the face. An American guard immediately pulled his gun. By way of explanation, Mr. Fautré with his right arm demonstratively raised the empty sleeve dangling on his left. The GI understood and lowered his gun. He had no way of knowing that the Germans had cost Mr. Fautré his arm more than a generation ago, during the Great War.[16]

3 In Bande, a village on Highway N-4 between the Ourthe and Marche, the inhabitants on December 17 had listened to the news of a major German offensive with too much incredulity to act. Many of the young men had decided to wait and see. Refugees from the Bastogne area continued to pour in from across the Ourthe until the evening of Wednesday, December 20, when reconnaissance troops of the 2nd Panzer Division seized the bridge at Ortheuville and stopped civilians from crossing. Among the last refugees to arrive in Bande on Thursday were Father Musty and the exhausted boys from the Bastogne seminary who were in his care. By now word had spread that the Americans in Marche were not letting anyone through because of fear of infiltrators. Encouraged by the warm reception and the presence of more young men in Bande, Father Musty and his eight students had decided to stay and take some rest.[17]

They were still in Bande when early on Friday afternoon the first vehicles of the 2nd Panzer Division raced by on the highway to Marche surprising them all. Refugees and villagers now had no choice but to sit out the offensive in Bande. That seemed not such a bad predicament at first. The armored spearheads hurried by, carrying battle to the Americans far to the northwest of Bande. What remained of the 2nd Panzer Division in the village on the highway by Saturday, December 23, were support troops who, by all accounts, behaved correctly toward the civilian population.[18]

That same Saturday, however, a unit of some twenty-five to thirty men under cover of darkness slipped into Bande. They wore uniforms with the insignia and patches of the Sicherheitsdienst (SD), the security service of the SS. Most were Germans, but some spoke French and had been recruited from the Walloons, Brittany, the Alsace, and Switzerland. The shadowy group stayed away from the houses and farms that coalesced around the church on top of a gently sloping hill. Instead, they moved into the charred ruins of homes and shops hugging either side of Highway N-4 at the foot of the hill. The men were on a special mission closely related to the blackened skeletons along the Grand 'Rue.[19]

A feverish atmosphere had gripped Bande early in September 1944. German troops had been retreating along the highway through the village for weeks. The Allies were said to be only days away. Word spread that a group of Belgian resistance fighters from the Armée Secrète had moved into the dense forest south of Bande. The villagers were so excited that some defiantly displayed the Belgian flag even before they were liberated. On September 5 the resistance attacked a nearby ammunition depot and killed three soldiers. The Germans had had enough. The following day troops sealed off the thirty-five houses along the highway, chased the inhabitants into the streets, and then set about torching the buildings. One man was shot and killed when he broke free and tried to escape across the Wamme River. The others were spared their lives. But the villagers never forgot that the last soldiers to pull out had shaken their fists and yelled, "We'll be back!"[20]

The SD unit that had sneaked into Bande on the night of December 23 appears to have been under orders to take care of September's unfinished business. On Sunday morning, the SD men went from house to house, arresting all the men aged seventeen and over. They assured the fearful men and their families that they were merely to come along for routine identity checks and that they would all be back for Christmas dinner. Guards marched the group of some seventy men down the hill to the Marche-Bastogne highway and put them together in the remains of the Rulkin sawmill that had been destroyed in the September reprisal. Early that afternoon, the prisoners were joined by still more men, this time from Grune, a village just west of Bande. They had been arrested by agents from the same SD unit. "You are scared of the SS, Madame," a German soldier remarked to a worried woman in Grune after the men had disappeared from sight. "You are right. We too are afraid of them."[21]

The questioning of the prisoners in the sawmill began around one o'clock and lasted until dusk. The interrogators consulted notes from time to time and seemed well informed about what had happened in the vicinity of Bande in September. But they wanted to know much more. They asked for the names of members of the underground forces. They inquired about who in the area had been affiliated with Communist organizations. Villagers who were not forthcoming with information or denied allegations were thrashed with a bamboo cane. Meanwhile, the SD men, intent on having a good time that Christmas Eve, allowed some of the prisoners to go home to fetch them some drinks. One of the Germans told Mr. Toussaint that he and his son would be set free if he could provide them with twenty bottles of wine and three bottles of cognac. When the farmer returned with the ransom, he was astonished to hear that he and his son were now indeed free to go. But Mrs. Tournay, who brought liquor to try and bribe one of the officers into releasing her nephew, had come in vain. "Don't bargain with me," the officer fumed. "I am not a Jew." One of the 2nd Panzer Division's officers decided to intercede himself and see if he could "arrange things." But he soon returned from the sawmill thoroughly discouraged. "Those men are strangers," the Wehrmacht officer announced. There was nothing he could do. There was nothing Father Musty could do either. When he tried to intervene on behalf of his students, a German officer put a gun to the priest's chest and barked: "You, black crow, get lost!"[22]

As darkness fell, some ten SD men armed with rifles and burp guns marched thirty-three of the youngest prisoners (all between the ages of seventeen and thirty-two) to the café de la Poste across the highway. While the prisoners held their hands behind their heads, the guards robbed them of watches, rings, and money. Some asked to keep their rosaries, but their tormentors refused to listen. They organized the victims into three rows. A guard put his hand on the shoulder of the last man in the front row. He led him to the charred Bertrand home behind the prisoners. An officer shot the condemned man in the neck as soon as he entered the door and with a jerk of his knee hurled him into the gaping cellar. By now the villagers knew what their fate would be. But, dusted by light snow, their rigid forms remained nailed to the ground, as if the victims had decided they were dead already.

Within less than an hour, thirty-two bloody corpses lay tangled in the cellar of the burned-out house. Eleven of the victims were teenagers; three of those were students of Father Musty. Only twenty-one-year-old Léon Praille had succeeded in summoning enough courage to escape. He had punched his guard in the face with all his might before reaching the slaughterhouse. The surprised executioners had opened fire as he darted away. But they had missed. Léon hid in the woods before making his way back to Bande, where he would disappear in his uncle's hayloft until the Allies arrived two weeks later. He alone would live to tell the horrid tale of the executions on Christmas Eve in Bande.[23]

The SD on Christmas Day returned to the sinister cellar in Bande with Georges and Raymond Malempré, two brothers from Roy, a village a couple of miles north of Bande. They executed both young men on the very spot that had seen so much bloodshed the day before, bringing the number of corpses in the cellar to thirty-four. Two days later and some miles east of Roy, German security forces (some say the SD, others the Gestapo) arrested Joseph Philippe and Georges Robinet in Hodister. Their corpses would remain hidden in a wood scarcely half a mile from their village for almost two months.[24]

4 While its support troops witnessed the SS security forces' purges in and around Bande, the 2nd Panzer Division's spearheads were embroiled in a life-and-death struggle in front of Dinant. On the evening of Saturday, December 23, advance elements of the veteran outfit gained control of Conneux and Conjoux. They immediately began probing in the direction of Celles and Foy-Notre-Dame, villages at a distance of no more than four miles from the Meuse that sat on the two main roads into Dinant from the east.

The villagers in the area were taken by surprise. The young men of Celles had not realized the urgency of the danger until early on Saturday afternoon. They had grabbed some clothes and food, jumped on their bicycles, and hurried to the heavily guarded Dinant bridges in the hope of being allowed through before it was too late. The villagers who stayed behind instinctively flocked together to discuss their options. As the rumble of guns grew louder, word spread that they should all seek refuge in the crypt beneath the massive walls of the ancient village church. The elderly, children, and women clasping babies hurriedly made their way to the sacred place.[25]

As night fell, British officers of the veteran 3rd Royal Tank Regiment organized their command post at Sorinnes just north of Foy-Notre-Dame. Their unit formed part of the British XXX Corps that was to block the enemy at the Meuse. The officers were trying hard to determine where and how far the Germans had penetrated their sector. Baron Jacques de Villenfagne, an inhabitant of Sorinnes who had proved his mettle in the Armée Secrète, volunteered his services. He asked his cousin Philippe le Hardy de Beaulieu to join him. Covered in white rags held together with safety pins, they scouted the snowy woods they knew so well with only the moon as a guide. They slipped into villages asking questions, listened to the sharp sounds of guns in the frosty air, and observed the movements of vehicles and men. They were back at their château in Sorinnes by four o'clock on Sunday morning. For over an hour they briefed the British officers on the exact locations of German positions and the fattest targets for their artillery. At seven o'clock sharp, British and American guns opened up with an earsplitting roar. Eighty minutes later, as the sluggish sun rose at last, the British attacked the nose of the Bulge in the direction of Foy-Notre-Dame.[26]

That same day, hardened American troops of the 2nd Armored Division readied themselves to join the British in blunting the German spearhead. Combat Command B assembled at Ciney, some six miles northeast of Celles. Like the British, the Americans were eager to learn more about the precise locations of the enemy. A Belgian army officer liaised between the American commander and Ciney's telephone operators. An electrician was called in to restore some of the lines the resistance had systematically destroyed on the eve of liberation. In a matter of hours operators were talking to civilians who found themselves in the path of the 2nd Panzer Division. Among them were a farmer in Conneux, the owner of a château in Conjoux, and a post official at Ychippe. Some continued to whisper valuable information to Ciney from under the very noses of the armored troops.[27]

While the Allied counterattack against the tip of the Bulge gathered strength, villagers in the area braced themselves against the shock. In Hubaille, a hamlet just north of Celles, people from their cellars watched the enemy who had arrived before dawn. Spotter planes hovered over the area like vultures, forcing the Germans to spend much of Sunday hiding their vehicles against walls, in sheds, and under leafless trees. Artillery pieces and antiaircraft batteries were quickly brought into position. Tanks bulldozed the fences, ripped through hedges, and even crushed the village's splendid cherry trees. In Celles, meanwhile, Jules Schelbach, the local grocer, had taken command in the church's crypt. He had made sure that enough food from his store had found its way into the catacomb before dawn. He had even had the foresight to install a number of pails in the darkest corners for sanitary purposes. Father Caussin, a veteran of the Great War, managed to reassure the people with his sublime calm. The priest asked the villagers to pray for Saint Hadelin. He was an Irish missionary from the seventh century who was believed to have founded Celles and introduced Christianity to the area when Germanic infidels still ruled it. Morning had scarcely broken when the 2nd Panzer Division arrived. German tanks with their unholy black crosses reclaimed Celles as their own.[28]

The 2nd Panzer Division's reign in the area was to be very brief. Early on Monday afternoon, Christmas Day, the British captured Foy-Notre-Dame with little opposition. The 2nd Armored Division that same afternoon closed two pincers around Celles. Ferocious fighting erupted as the Americans moved in. While artillery devastated the woods east of Celles, Allied fighter-bombers lashed out at whatever dared move inside the pocket. Houses and farms caught fire. Some villagers broke free from the crypt in suicidal but vain attempts to extinguish the flames and save the cattle. Tanks and infantry reached the village by late afternoon. Taking no chances, they raked the buildings with gunfire. People in the crypt listened to the church windows being blown to smithereens. Afraid that the soldiers would mistake them for the enemy, a chorus of shrill voices rose from the catacomb indicating they were civilians. Suspicious, rough-looking combat soldiers motioned the refugees to come up and step out of the church single file. As the villagers brushed past their liberators, they whispered tremulous words of thanks. At that, some GIs at last managed to crack a smile. Others were lining up to see Father Coussin, eager to confess their sins with the help of a pocket dictionary.[29]

The following day, the 2nd Armored Division began to sweep the woods east of Celles. As Allied aircraft prevented reinforcements from getting through, the fate of the proud 2nd Panzer Division was all but sealed. On December 27 the battered troops made a final desperate attempt to break out. No more than 600 got away. By mid-afternoon, resistance in the Celles pocket had been eliminated, and the German chances of crossing the Meuse had been dashed. The 2nd Armored Division had killed 900 Germans. The mop-up resulted in more than 1,200 prisoners. Villagers in Hubaille, a hamlet of a mere seven homes, were burdened with so many German soldiers who were wounded or just eager to surrender that they sent some men to Celles to ask the Americans for help. GIs walked away from Hubaille with a column of more than 200 prisoners.[30]

The mood in Celles turned grim when GIs herded prisoners wearing parts of American uniforms (gloves, shoes, coats—anything to keep them warm) into a separate corner of the square and pointed a machine gun at them from a half-track. News of the Malmedy massacre had spread rapidly. The prisoners guessed what the Americans were thinking. As if on command, they hurried to take off to the last scrap clothing that was American. Father Coussin pleaded with the GIs not to stain their victory with cruel reprisals. Was it the authority of the gray-haired priest in his black cassock that made them change their minds? Whatever the reason, the Germans walked away from Celles alive, though some left scarcely dressed, and many were made to trudge through snow and sleet barefoot.[31]

5 Meanwhile, to the south of Celles the 2nd and 116th Panzer Divisions had been receiving support from another formidable armored fist in the fight to reach the Meuse. Pulled out of the battle for Bastogne with the exception of one of its Panzergrenadier regiments, the Panzer Lehr Division had captured Morhet and on Thursday, December 21, was briskly rolling down the road to the Ourthe. In the morning reconnaissance troops overtook knots of refugees from the Bastogne area. Apparently considering them security risks, the Germans halted several of the men, leading them away to a nearby wood. Twenty-year-old Gilbert Guillaume was the first of twenty-two men to undergo a body search. The soldiers frowned as they thumbed through his papers. They handed the young man from Longchamps a pickax and led him away. The body searches continued for a while and then the soldiers lost interest and moved on. But no one ever found a trace of Gilbert Guillaume.[32]

The following day, Panzer Lehr's commander, Gen. Fritz Bayerlein, ordered his troops that were in front of the Ourthe to fan out north and south of the St. Hubert road. To the north, a column headed for Amberloup in search of a river crossing. On its route lay the Redemptorist monastery of Beauplateau, a hamlet of Tillet. Most of the clergy and novices had fled two days earlier. But more than a dozen had stayed to look after the building and help take care of the civilians who had sought refuge in its labyrinthine cellars. By the time the Germans arrived on Friday, no fewer than 171 civilians were hiding in the monastery's belly. Around noon, just as GIs from an artillery unit were blowing up guns and ammunition in preparation for retreat, an ambulance screeched to a halt in front of the monastery. Three heavily sedated patients were hurriedly carried out on stretchers. The GIs had been wounded at Bastogne, the medics explained, and were in too bad a shape to continue the bumpy ride. Could the Redemptorists ask the Germans to look after them?

No more than an hour later, the first Panzergrenadiers arrived in Beauplateau. The Redemptorists immediately informed them of the presence of American battle casualties. But the enemy had other things on their mind, and the medical assistance they promised never materialized. Afraid that the presence of enemy soldiers in the monastery might soon anger German troops and cause them to take reprisals, the Redemptorists finally decided to hide the three soldiers in a closed-off section on the second floor. Though they were hungry and cold themselves, clergy and civilians secretly slipped upstairs to assure a constant vigil at the side of the GIs. With deep sadness they watched the soldier from North Carolina die on Christmas Day. Their grief was assuaged only by Lester Reed's awakening from a coma several days after arriving at Beauplateau. Somehow the Belgians at the monastery would succeed in keeping Reed and his comrade alive until the Americans fought their way back on January 2.[33]

While a column of Panzer Lehr crossed the Ourthe at Amberloup on Friday, December 22, another column to the south of St. Hubert road reached as far as Moircy. Though the Americans had damaged the village's bridge, German troops requisitioned a civilian and his horse to help repair the span, and not much later they were crossing the Ourthe here, too. In Jenneville, located on the Ourthe just northeast of Moircy, astonished inhabitants saw the first German troops arrive late on Friday afternoon. At the sight of the first armored vehicle, ten-year-old Marcel Lassence, on the lookout at the village entrance, thought his heart had stopped beating. Then he recovered and yelled: "There they are!" Marcel's father tried to disappear from sight, but the vehicle was too fast and had him cornered in no time. "Since when," an officer asked in a sugary voice, "have your American friends left?" "Two days ago," Mr. Lassence said, answering the question truthfully. The Germans relaxed. They caught the smell of soup and told Marcel's mother to serve them a cup. But none of the frozen soldiers dared put their lips to the hot broth before they had made the boy's father take a sip to show them it was not poisoned.[34]

At about the same time the German scout cars showed up in Jenneville on Friday, reconnaissance elements reached St. Hubert. They reported the absence of any organized American defense. By midnight, the head of Panzer Lehr's column was nosing its way from Moircy into the vital road center west of the Ourthe. More tanks and troops continued to pour into the town from the direction of Moircy and Amberloup on Saturday. Some 3,500 people called St. Hubert their home in normal times, but the approaching sound of guns on Wednesday had triggered a mass panic that had affected the town much more than the surrounding villages. Frantic people, young and old, had grabbed some belongings and abandoned St. Hubert on bicycles and on foot, pulling and pushing carts and wheelbarrows. Despite orders to stay put, many of the town's officials and gendarmes had joined the fleeing crowds without a backward glance. Though they had been imprisoned by the Germans in July 1944, Mayor Ernest Zoude and

Father Schméler, one of the town's senior clergymen, had made the courageous decision to stay with their people.

St. Hubert fell to the enemy with barely a shot fired. But if the town was spared destruction, it did not escape systematic looting. German troops claimed they had not eaten properly in four days and proceeded to pick the town clean of all the food they could find. During the next few days, according to inventories drawn up by town officials after the battle, occupation forces requisitioned or stole 25 tons of potatoes, close to 19 tons of meat, 4 tons of wheat, 3 tons of fruit, more than 2 tons of flour, and more than a ton each of sugar and preserves. In addition, they seized more than 3,000 bottles of wine and liquor. But the plunder did not stop there. To protect themselves against the snow and worsening cold, the soldiers also took 117 stoves, 155 mattresses, 313 men's suits, 336 pairs of shoes, 1,784 sheets, and close to 4,000 undergarments. On Sunday, December 24, Mayor Zoude was informed that, because it had been established that his people were tuning in to British stations for news, all radios would have to be handed in. By evening the Germans had thrown some 180 radios onto a pile in the town hall.[35]

Lacking sufficient gasoline to continue their march, Bayerlein's troops were stuck in St. Hubert until noon on December 23. Then the spearheads were at last able to get going again, this time in the direction of Rochefort, the last sizable town between them and the Meuse at Dinant. In the villages in front of Rochefort, people who had decided to flee had done so long before Panzer Lehr launched itself from St. Hubert on Saturday. In Bure, a village of some seven hundred inhabitants, a small panic had broken out when exhausted, mud-covered refugees began shuffling through and Luxembourgers in a crowded bus stopped long enough to paint a horrid picture of the fate of their beloved home town, Clervaux. By Thursday, dozens of Bure's young men had taken to the roads.

Bayerlein's armor had Bure in its sights early on Saturday afternoon. The sound of cannon and machine guns drove almost all of those who remained in the village onto the small road leading up the hill to what the locals called "the château." The imposing building looking down on Bure was, in fact, the *Alumnat*, the home of the Assumptionist Fathers and a well-known boarding school. Though most of the clergy and pupils had fled and no more than a dozen of them remained on December 23, within a matter of days the solid cellars of the Alumnat were housing close to six hundred frightened civilians. Most of them would stay there for nearly three weeks and make do with not much more than coffee, herbal tea, and soup (the Germans were to cart off most of the Alumnat's potatoes and coal).

In the village of Resteigne, a few miles west of Bure, there was no religious fortress on a hill to turn to for safety. But, as Bayerlein's troops closed in, people filled the church to overflowing and together prayed for protection. Then they hurried home and dragged mattresses, blankets, and food to their own cellars or those of their neighbors. Some were so scared and so unsure of how to defend themselves in battle that they could be seen digging holes in their gardens—just in case.[36]

To the relief of the villagers, Panzer Lehr's occupation of Bure and Resteigne was achieved without much violence. In fact, there were few, if any, American troops left in front of Rochefort to put up a fight. In Jemelle, for example, a village some two miles from the town, American troops hurriedly had pulled out some days earlier. The retreat had been so chaotic that in the schools and theaters that had housed the GIs, panic-stricken civilians found not only abandoned blankets and helmets, but wallets and glasses too. Late on Saturday, all that Jemelle's inhabitants could do was watch German troops take up positions for the strike against Rochefort. Many were ousted from their homes to make space for exhausted soldiers who had not been warm for days. Within hours of Panzer Lehr's arrival, Mrs. Laurent and some of her neighbors were among those evicted. Mrs. Laurent grabbed her four children (aged one, two, four, and twelve years) and in the dark groped her way to a neighboring farm. The following morning soldiers forced her and her family out on the streets again. They finally managed to find refuge in a drafty quarry from which only Mrs. Laurent dared make an occasional run to nearby farms in search of milk for her children.[37]

Around midnight, meanwhile, Panzer Lehr had launched its attack against Rochefort. Patrols had sent word that this town also appeared undefended. This time, however, they were wrong. As part of the screen that the 84th Infantry Division had organized south of Marche, one of its battalions had taken up position as far away as Rochefort. The mission of this small force was not an all-out defense of the town but, more realistically, to delay the enemy for as long as possible. Rochefort numbered about as many inhabitants as St. Hubert, though in the days preceding the attack it had taken in some 250 refugees. With the exception of former members of the resistance who feared reprisals (they had shown themselves to be extremely effective and lethal in this area between June and September 1944), the vast majority of Rochefort's population had stayed. Most likely it was the presence of a battalion of GIs that made the difference between the panic in St. Hubert and the relative calm in Rochefort. The American commander imposed a curfew from six o'clock in the evening to seven o'clock in the morning. He also made sure to appoint two English-speaking civilians as liaisons between himself and the town's authorities.[38]

The presence of the infantrymen certainly made a difference to Ninette Bouchat. She had been publicly honored as a member of the resistance not long after the liberation in September. A single denunciation might suffice for the Germans to have her executed. She too would have fled, had it not been for her aged mother whom she felt she could not leave behind. Late on Friday afternoon, however, a platoon of soldiers—none of them more than twenty years old—had taken up position in Mrs. Bouchat's street. They understood her fears, pointed to their bazookas and antitank gun, and told her not to worry.[39]

But the cockiness of young riflemen, faked or real, did not suffice to turn the tide at Rochefort. As there were not enough American troops to defend all of the buildings, Bayerlein's men under the cover of darkness managed to penetrate the town fairly easily. The battle that ensued, however, was fierce. Slowly and grudgingly, the Americans fell back house by house and street by street. By mid-morning the order came to withdraw to the western part of town. The GIs tried to hold on to buildings on one side of the town square, with the Grand Hôtel de l'Étoile as their key bulwark. Panic now gripped the inhabitants. People dashed from their homes in last-minute attempts to find safety elsewhere. Some joined the already overcrowded vaulted cellars beneath the Cistercian abbey of St. Remy, just north of the town. Others sought cover in the sturdy buildings belonging to the Trappists and the Sisters of St. Vincent de Paul. Many rushed to the natural caves that dotted the area, which, in peacetime summers, had formed a major tourist attraction. But in the midst of winter, the caves appeared the gloomiest and dampest places on earth, and the slimy cavities could make many hundreds disappear from sight while withstanding the fiercest shelling. So people, some wearing no more than a night robe or pajamas, continued to flock to the Rochefort, Fays, and Falizes caves and to what locals had long known as the "Maulin Hole." Among them in the faint morning light were Mrs. Bouchat and her mother. The antitank platoon in her street had not been able to do more for Ninette Bouchat than help her bury her resistance papers in the garden.[40]

All through the morning of Sunday, December 24, troops and tanks engaged in heavy street fighting. The Grand Hôtel de l'Étoile was ablaze. So was the hôtel Biron. Flames from a burning vehicle in the town square leaped to an adjacent building and before long, fire was raging in a dozen buildings. Away from the center, thick smoke billowed from many other buildings, among them the château Della Faille. Utter confusion reigned. One moment people saw GIs dash past their cellar window; then Germans burst in asking for papers and food and information on the Americans. Debris, tangled cables, and wrecked equipment littered the streets. German and American corpses lay sprawled on the pavement or slumped in doorways. Civilians who dared show themselves were certain to court disaster. In the rue de France, Berthe Salvé dashed upstairs to gather some belongings only to have a bullet pierce her head. As her desperate mother and brother tried to carry her to a civilian doctor, crouching GIs in the street snapped at them to hurry up. At about that same time, a machine gun mowed down an old woman who had ventured out into the same street. It was early in the afternoon when orders came down for what remained of the haggard American battalion in Rochefort to withdraw to Marche.[41]

There was no reason for the inhabitants of Rochefort to rejoice on Christmas morning. Their town was firmly in the hands of the Germans again. Soldiers were breaking into the houses and dragging away radios, bicycles, mattresses, blankets, clothing, and all the food they could carry. They did not bother about the raging fires and allowed the buildings to burn to the ground. With the sound of artillery reverberating on all sides, civilians thought it safer to remain cooped up in spaces that often allowed only children to stand up. To make life in the cellars still more difficult, water from ruptured mains began to seep through the walls. In more and more homes, meanwhile, water from the tap was exuding a disgusting smell, the result of broken sewers spilling their contents.[42]

For the Panzer Lehr Division, Christmas Day brought no rest. Early in the day, troops were sent a few miles northward in an attempt to dislodge units from the 2nd Armored Division from Havrenne, Humain, and Buissonville so as to reopen key roads to the threatened 2nd Panzer Division at Celles. Despite heavy fighting, Bayerlein's troops got nowhere as they hit a steel curtain of Allied fire. The villagers were nevertheless made to pay a heavy price. In the wake of the battle for Humain, civilians were so enraged by the senseless destruction that in one place they were seen pelting the face of a dead German with clods of frozen earth.[43]

The following day, corps commander von Lüttwitz ordered the column to fall back to Rochefort. Panzer Lehr's retreat was tacit acknowledgment that Hitler's gamble had failed in full view of the vaunted Meuse. It was the beginning of the end for the German troops in the Bulge. An end that would be painfully protracted—and merciless to soldiers and civilians alike. On December 26, Bayerlein's tanks and half-tracks in Rochefort maneuvered themselves beneath trees, into barns, and alongside houses. Exhausted troops silently waited for the Allied answer to come. It was to the skies that they looked most nervously.[44]

6 Allied aircraft had swung into action over the nose of the salient as soon as the skies had cleared to a cold blue on December 24. Whereas medium and heavy bombers wiped St. Vith from the map on December 25 and 26 to help stall the offensive on the north flank, still more medium bombers on December 26 and 27 were to attack major towns in the Ourthe Valley. Their blunt mission was to reduce the towns to rubble, thus making their key bridges impassable and transforming the vital road centers into choking points. Houffalize was only one of two main targets. The other was scenic La Roche, a town of some 1,900 people and, in ordinary times, one of Belgium's most popular tourist attractions. With only seventeen miles separating it from Rochefort to the west, La Roche was a major thoroughfare for German supplies and reinforcements intended for the spearheads near the Meuse. To blot out this town was to sever the spearheads' lifeline and make them wither up front.[45]

La Roche had been liberated by Americans of the 4th Infantry Division on September 9, 1944. Within weeks the place had been transformed into a bustling garrison town dotted with depots and repair shops. Relations with the American troops were excellent. Preparations for La Roche's first free Christmas in five years brought GIs and civilians still closer together. Soldiers volunteered as singers and musicians to liven up night Mass. For Christmas Day the military had planned a large banquet as well as a popular ball, and La Roche's inhabitants were invited to both events. Weeks before Christmas, the population was talking about little more than food, balls, songs, trees, and decorations. GIs had asked the town's girls to design and produce several hundred menus for the big day. The girls worked feverishly to please the good-looking foreigners. "What joy," sixteen-year-old Myriam wrote in her diary on December 15. "What exhilaration."[46]

No one in La Roche was prepared for the cruel chain of events to be set in motion the following day. Radio news on Saturday talked of a small German offensive. On Sunday evening, however, the show in the town's movie theater was suddenly interrupted and GIs on leave were ordered to join their units at once. The next morning, disbelieving townspeople looked on as the Americans disassembled depots and repair shops, loaded their trucks, and began pulling out. On Tuesday, December 19, long columns of refugees from Houffalize and St. Vith and from as far away as the Grand Duchy of Luxembourg trudged by. Though cold and exhausted, they were too scared to halt even for a while. The unnerving spectacle caused large numbers of La Roche's inhabitants to pack their bags and join the exodus. They fled not a day too soon. The following morning, artillery of the 116th Panzer Division, then on its way to Hotton, opened up on La Roche from the vicinity of Bérismenil. The surprise bombardment wounded many GIs and at least three civilians. One of the latter, Véronique Saenens, was in such a bad way that American medics had to rush her to a hospital in Bertrix, where she would die from her wounds more than a month later. Meanwhile, Father Liégeois lay dead in front of the church in the rue Châmont; he had been killed by a sudden shell burst shortly after saying morning Mass. The fear that had rapidly built up over the past days now exploded into panic, and civilians poured from the town all day long.[47]

Two days later, on Friday afternoon, tanks of the 116th Panzer Division were rumbling through town. By now no more than an estimated 450 civilians remained in La Roche. Sixteen-year-old Myriam and her cousins hurried home. They tossed an American flag, a dress displaying the British national colors, and the unfinished menus for the Christmas banquet into a box and buried it in the vegetable garden. That night, rather than preparing Christmas in La Roche, the Americans were shelling the town.[48]

On Sunday night, six German officers and NCOs gathered around the dinner table at the Gutt home to celebrate Christmas Eve. They ate and drank and sang as if there were no tomorrow. In the cellar beneath their feet, twenty-two people were quietly saying their prayers.

The next day, people in La Roche dashed to morning Mass despite the dangers. The priest held a service just long enough to offer general absolution to the crowd of pale and drawn faces. Later that day, agents of the dreaded Nazi security forces descended on the town hall and fanned out to make their first arrests of people suspected of having been involved with the resistance. They locked them up for an interrogation that was never to be.[49]

The wave of bombers that appeared over La Roche around mid-morning on Tuesday, December 26 caused the inhabitants no concern. They instantly recognized them as Allied aircraft and knew they were carrying death and destruction to the enemy's homeland. "Still more eggs for Germany," Mrs. Quinet called to her aunt from the kitchen, a satisfied grin on her face. She had barely finished her sentence when a thunderous roar violently shook the town. Mrs. Quinet dropped everything and rushed to the basement stairs. As she reached the bottom step, a terrible explosion lifted her off her feet and smashed her into a crate of bottles. A couple of hours had passed by the time she regained consciousness. The blast had ripped off all her clothes. Her mouth was gritty with dust and plaster. Deep cuts covered her body and especially her head. She stumbled to the cellar window and called out for help. A priest, two civilians, and a German soldier came to her aid and pulled her into the street. She gazed at the destruction around her and fainted.[50]

Mrs. Quinet had no memory of the second wave of bombs that hit La Roche just minutes after the first one. Together they had pulverized the Faubourg bridge and much of the built-up area around it. The Marquet tannery, an imposing construction of solid brick and concrete, had collapsed and crushed at least eighteen people who had earlier fled to its huge basement to escape shell fire. Of the magnificent château des Agelires south of the town, nothing remained but a heap of burning rubble fueled by copious amounts of white phosphorus. Some fourteen people had disappeared in the furnace. La Roche's inhabitants, many of them wounded, roamed the streets, not knowing what to do or where to go. Slowly groups began to form that set off for the Strument farms and the Halleux tannery on the outskirts of town. Some walked more than six miles through driving snow and sleet before collapsing in one village or another. Still others hid in La Roche's lead mine, thronged the cemetery's chapel, or camped in the surrounding fields where they built makeshift huts. Long after sundown, people could be heard begging for help from cellars buried by rubble. Joseph Binet was killed and several other civilians wounded when a bomb with a delayed fuse went off while they were trying to offer help at the Marquet tannery. Later that night, a shaken uncle told Myriam and her cousins that they had just seen worse things than he had during the Great War.[51]

Though the bridge and vicinity had been destroyed, La Roche had not been pounded to a choking point where all circulation was prevented. Around mid-afternoon on Wednesday, the bombers again appeared in two waves. This time they made sure to finish the job. As there were no precise targets, the aircraft simply blanketed the town with their heavy bomb loads. For the people on the ground the effects were disastrous. One bomb pierced the town hall, igniting a large cache of American TNT in its basement. The explosion that followed destroyed an entire block. More blasts pulverized the St. Joseph school, burying all of the wounded civilians in doctor Jacquemain's improvised basement hospital. Bombs also plowed into the nursing home, ignoring the Red Cross flag on its roof. People rushed to the aid of the terrorized survivors, wrapped them in blankets, placed them in carts, and then on slippery roads pushed them to a nearby school. When that school, too, caught fire, the elderly had to be evacuated again, this time to a hotel that was still standing. Several of them died of fear and exhaustion before they got there. In the days that followed, five more succumbed to dysentery. There was no other place for the withered bodies to be laid out than the coal cellar.[52]

Again a stream of survivors fled to neighboring farms and villages. Some of them had arms, legs, or heads bandaged and had to be supported; others, motionless, were carried away on stretchers. Piles of rubble blocked all through traffic for two days. Then the Germans began to clear some areas with the forced labor of civilians. Perhaps in response to this activity, Allied bombers again attacked the town on the first day of the new year. Earlier that day, four men of the Vidick family had judged it safe at last to return to La Roche to check the damage to their home from the first bombardment. The third and final bombardment cynically buried three of them under what was left of their home. They were the last victims of the air raids on La Roche, bringing the total number of civilian dead to eighty-seven.[53]

7   While Allied aircraft pulverized the pivotal Ourthe towns, American ground troops were readying themselves for counterattacks aimed at sealing off the salient's nose. The main thrust from the

north was to be in the direction of Rochefort. At dawn on December 27, aircraft began a merciless bombing and strafing of the town and surrounding villages. Allied artillery joined in with all its might, pummeling even the town center. "[A] terrible explosion," Mrs. Van Pelt scribbled in her journal, "a shell has exploded in the living room, demolishing part of the façade. . . . Everything is destroyed, chandeliers, doors, dishes, crystal. . . ." Only a rear guard now remained of the Panzer Lehr Division in Rochefort. Morale was low. The soldiers were exhausted and talked little. They were running out of supplies and took what they needed from the civilians. Alcohol was more popular than food, and discipline suffered as a consequence. Two drunk soldiers attacked Mrs. Henrotin. Only the firm intervention of an officer saved her.[54]

That night, patrols of the 83rd Infantry Division began groping their way toward Rochefort. A fierce battle raged throughout the following day and night. Buildings were on fire. In streets, homes, and gardens soldiers fought with grenades, bayonets, and knives. Terrorized civilians tried to make themselves invisible in underground shelters. Some three hundred refugees held on to each other in the orphanage of the Sisters of St. Vincent de Paul. In the large farms on Rochefort's outskirts, some cellars were spacious enough to allow cooking and a stove; some even harbored cattle and horses. In town, however, many were too small for adults to stand; they were damp and sometimes without light. Sandbags blocked the cellar windows, making the air grow foul. Hygienic conditions became worse by the hour. People risked their lives to get their hands on some food. Parents burned gas in cans to heat milk for their infants, while those without fuel simply held the feeding bottles between their legs in vain attempts to make the vital drink more palatable.[55]

At dawn on Friday, December 29, there was a lull in the fighting and people from all parts of town used it to rush to the neighboring caves. There they joined more than one thousand civilians, some of whom had already been there for about a week. The thick rocky ceiling was sure to withstand any shelling, and the din of battle could not be heard so deep beneath the earth. But the living conditions were appalling. Apart from some scarce candles and oil lamps, there was no lighting, and people could not tell day from night. Bottles were used to collect the icy water from dripping stalactites. Some slept on mattresses, but most had to make do with straw. People had brought blankets, a few even their fur coats, but the humidity made it impossible to remain warm and dry. Food stocks were running low. Some of the men undertook dangerous runs to nearby farms only to return with some apples and carrots. A family of eleven children saw no choice but to kill the goat they had brought with them and ended up eating much of the meat raw. Chronic darkness and nagging hunger caused people to become depressed, nervous, and short-tempered. Acute claustrophobia drove several insane. One man launched himself at a girl, almost pushing her into a dark crevice. People managed to subdue the crazed assailant, leaving him tied up at the entrance of the cave, where they took turns feeding him. To make matters worse, the Lomme River flooded its banks, causing so much water to seep into the "Maulin Hole," one of the main caves, that it had to be evacuated.[56]

The fighting in Rochefort briefly flared up early on Friday afternoon as the last of the German troops pulled out. Ironically, with the enemy gone, terror for the civilians inside Rochefort increased. While Allied artillery continued to pound the town as if the Germans were still there, enemy guns now joined the barrage to prevent the Americans from getting a firm hold. Rochefort's inhabitants were caught in the cross fire. None of them cared if the shells, many of them incendiaries, were friendly or enemy, for the flames and the rubble they caused looked alike. Fires raged in the town's northern section and devoured much of the center. Acrid smoke and the stink of phosphorus prevented people from abandoning their cellars. A courageous townsman, Auguste Pigeon, twice slipped into the Allied lines to beg the soldiers to hold their fire because all the Germans had gone. At 9:30 in the evening the guns fell silent at last and Rochefort was liberated again. Neither the American infantrymen nor the British soldiers who replaced them during the last days of December compared well with the friendly GIs who had been garrisoned in Rochefort earlier that month. Hardened combat troops, they struck the population as callous and uncaring. They did break some of the ice, however, when they insisted on providing every child that emerged from Rochefort's frigid caves with a sizzling baked potato.[57]

With the firemen gone and the water mains ruptured, Rochefort continued to burn for three days. When the smoke finally cleared away, the town was barely recognizable. Ninety percent of its 940 homes had been destroyed or seriously damaged. Close to forty civilians had lost their lives in less than a week of fighting. Those who had survived the storm inside Rochefort picked through the rubble in a daze.

The mayor had to requisition inhabitants to help remove the many corpses of combatants and noncombatants alike. Long after the battle, people clearing rubble were still using special products to help wipe the nasty phosphorus from their callused hands.[58]

Just as the British began replacing GIs of the 83rd Division at Rochefort around the turn of the year, American infantry of the 87th Division jumped off from Freux for their attack against the southern flank of the salient's extremity. Their objective was to seize Bonnerue so as to block the main road leading into St. Hubert from Morhet in the east. Not only would this sever the last supply line across the Ourthe, but it would also trap the Panzer Lehr Division, most of which by now had fallen back to St. Hubert.[59]

Aircraft had begun softening up Moircy, the first village on the road from Freux to Bonnerue, as soon as the skies had cleared on December 24. On the night of Friday, December 29, a mighty concentration of artillery was let loose on Moircy to pave the way for the infantry attack. The blasts made trees bend and in Freux shook snow from the roofs and shattered the windows. For the next few days, Freux's inhabitants, some seven hundred in peacetime, were prohibited from leaving their homes except between nine and ten o'clock in the morning and two and four o'clock in the afternoon. Arrangements were made for medics to be sent to the sick and to infants needing special care. At least one civilian was shot for violating the curfew and ignoring the guard who hailed him. The man turned out to be deaf.[60]

The Americans attacked at dawn on Saturday. They had to push back the Germans house by house. Exhausted, their nerves frayed, the GIs behaved toward the civilians in Moircy with increasing rudeness and suspicion. During house searches they forced inhabitants, rifles against their backs, to enter the rooms first. At the public fountain they ordered Joseph Lassence to drink some water before daring to quench their own scorching thirst. By noon the Americans were in control of no more than half the village. Sensing that the enemy was not about to let go of Moircy, the GIs in their part of the village proceeded to round up all the civilians they could find. Armed guards herded between seventy and eighty people to the Leriche home, locked them in, and warned them that anyone who dared come out would be shot.[61]

Dusk had barely set in when Panzer Lehr launched a vicious counterattack. In the midst of the destruction and confusion that night, groups of terrified civilians somehow managed to break free from the village, cross enemy lines, and reach American positions at Freux. There, rather than being received with open arms, they were subjected to a series of harsh interrogations. Suspicious officers even called on inhabitants of Freux to see if they indeed recognized their dialect and perhaps even knew the refugees. Still, anything was better than being stuck in Moircy while the battle raged. A shell fired by a tank horribly mangled Marcel Fraselle's ankle, but there was little time to properly treat the wound. Shrapnel ripped into Raymonde Nicolay's leg; she needed a blood transfusion, but the medics could not give her one as the few bags they carried were strictly for soldiers only. Raymonde was lucky enough to make it to an American hospital in the rear. Marcel, however, was fated to succumb to gangrene. On the last day of 1944, the Germans finally gave up on Moircy. On New Year's Day, GIs at last set free the prisoners in the Leriche home, who had gone seventy-two hours without heat or food. In the stacks of frozen dead that the GIs put together soon after, Moircy's inhabitants noticed two civilian-clad corpses. Eugène Godenir and Henry Pinson had both fallen victim to shell fire. Mr. Pinson died not knowing what had happened to his son after German soldiers had arrested him in Moircy on December 26. It would take until February for the body of twenty-three-year-old Victor Pinson to be recovered from a wood near Hardigny, north of Bastogne and some eighteen miles from his father's grave.[62]

From Moircy on New Year's Day the Americans edged to Jenneville. For the inhabitants the chaos of battle that Monday obscured the line between friend and foe. Before she had time to think, Lisa Leitz found herself feeding and comforting a German soldier. He was seventeen years old, unarmed, and crying. Fearing for the safety of close to thirty refugees in her cellar if the GIs found an enemy soldier among them, Mrs. Leitz advised the sobbing boy to walk to the American lines and surrender. When, on the other hand, American infantrymen appeared in Jenneville, it seemed to the villagers that the GIs behaved "as if they were in enemy territory." They forced civilians at gunpoint to lead the way in house searches, smashed the furniture to bits, and threw it out of the windows.[63]

Battle's fury and madness drove civilians to the security of Freux not only from Jenneville, but in increasing numbers also from Bonnerue, the village that sat on the road from Morhet to St. Hubert and formed the end objective of the 87th Infantry Division's push.

Aware of the vital importance of Bonnerue, Panzer Lehr troops answered each American attack with an equally determined counterattack. Germans who held on to the north of the village drove civilians up the road, through drifts of snow and sleet, to Amberloup. Americans on the other side of the village flushed the inhabitants from their cellars and pointed them to safety beyond Jenneville. Inside Freux's tiny grocery store, haggard refugees thronged together eager to buy peace of mind. In front of a makeshift altar, lit by candles, and accompanied by a solemn boy in white altar clothes, they went down on their knees and prayed. The battle for Bonnerue had still not been decided when, on January 3, 1945, the Allies began their big, final push against the Germans in the Bulge.[64]

Meanwhile, in Moircy American troops that followed in the wake of the hardened combat soldiers were reminding the people again of the kind, fun-loving GIs they had known before the Germans launched their counteroffensive on December 16. In front of the Nicolay home, an open-air Mass brought soldiers and civilians together in heartfelt prayer. But not all activities shared by Belgians and Americans were so solemn. GIs also cordially invited Moircy's inhabitants to a Laurel and Hardy movie shown at the Fraselle farm. The wild laughter in the barn soon proved as cathartic as the most earnest prayer.[65]

Part III

The Tide Turns

Chapter 11

Counterattack from the South

"We are all greatly discouraged in our cellar."

They approached from the south like thunder. The inhabitants of Luxembourg City instantly knew whose troops they were. Soiled trucks, menacing cannons, and tanks like primal beasts made streets vibrate and houses tremble. A chilling wind swept the capital beneath gray skies. But the civilians could not be kept inside. "Patton! Patton!" they yelled as they strained their necks to catch a glimpse of the famous general's hardened soldiers.

While American and British troops were bracing themselves for a clash with German spearheads in front of the Meuse, Patton was rushing forward two armored and three infantry divisions from his Third Army in the Saar region to tear into the enemy's southern flank. On December 22 Patton's five divisions launched a combined offensive on a front extending from the Luxembourg border with Germany to just inside Belgium some thirty-five miles farther west. The divisions were to shield the Luxembourg capital, break through to besieged Bastogne, and clear as broad an expanse as possible east of that corridor, thus cutting off some of the enemy's vital supply lines.[1]

On Patton's extreme right flank, troops of the 5th Infantry Division relieved what remained of the battered 4th Infantry and 9th Armored Divisions between Echternach and Eppeldorf. The 5th Division, which had taken heavy casualties in the battle for Metz in the autumn, began gaining momentum on Christmas Eve. Long before sunup on Christmas Day, a massive barrage softened up the infantrymen's targets. Waldbillig was in American hands within hours. The fight for Haller, slightly more than two miles farther north, was

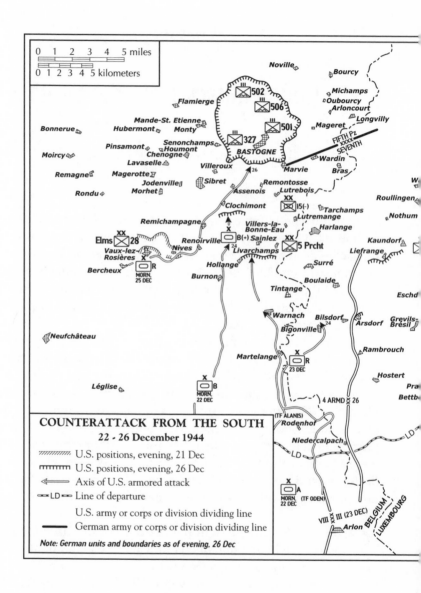

Noville
Bourcy
Michamps
Oubourcy
Arloncourt
Flamierge
502
506
501
Mande-St. Etienne
Hubermont
Monty
Mageret
Longvilly
Bonnerue
Pinsamont
Senonchamps
Houmont
Chenogne
327
Moircy
BASTOGNE
FIFTH Pz
SEVENTH
Lavaselle
Wardin
Remagne
Magerotte
Villeroux
Marvie
Bras
W
Jodenville
Sibret
Remontosse
Lutrebois
Rondu
Morhet
Assenois
Lutremange
Roullingen
Clochimont
I5(-)
Tarchamps
Nothum
Remichampagne
Lutremange
Harlange
Villers-la-
Bonne-Eau
Kaundorf
Elms 28
Renoirville
B(+) Sainlez
5 Prcht
Liefrange
Vaux-lez-
Rosières
Nives
Livarchamps
Surré
Bercheux
R
MORN,
25 DEC
Hollange
Burnon
Boulaide
Eschd
Tintange
Warnach
Bilsdorf
Grevils-
Brésil
Neufchâteau
Bigonville
Arsdorf
Martelange
Rambrouch
R
23 DEC
Hostert
Léglise
B
MORN,
22 DEC
4 ARMD 26
Pra
Bettb
(TF ALANIS)
Rodenhof
Niedercalpach
LD
LD
A
MORN,
22 DEC
(TF ODEN)
VIII III (23 DEC)
Arlon
BELGIUM
LUXEMBOURG

COUNTERATTACK FROM THE SOUTH
22 - 26 December 1944

////// U.S. positions, evening, 21 Dec

⊓⊓⊓ U.S. positions, evening, 26 Dec

⇐ Axis of U.S. armored attack

LD Line of departure

U.S. army or corps or division dividing line

German army or corps or division dividing line

Note: German units and boundaries as of evening, 26 Dec

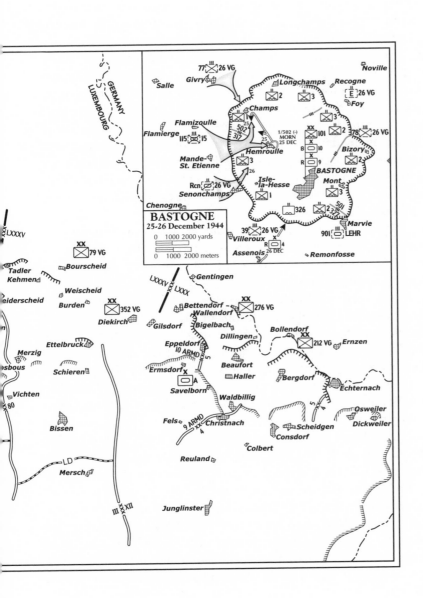

BASTOGNE
25-26 December 1944

0   1000 2000 yards

0   1000 2000 meters

Noville

Salle
Givry
77 26 VG
Longchamps
Recogne
E 26 VG
Foy

Champs
2
3

Flamizoulle
502
3/7
25
25
1/502 (-)
MORN
25 DEC
101
2
378 26 VG

Flamierge
115 15
XX
B 10
X
R 9
Bizory
2

Mande-
St. Etienne
3
BASTOGNE

Rcn 26 VG
Senonchamps
26
Isle-
la-Hesse
1
Mont
3
501

Chenogne
326
2 3
Marvie
901 LEHR

39 26 VG
Villeroux
R 4
901

Assenois 26 DEC
Remonfosse

GERMANY
LUXEMBOURG

LXXXV
79 VG
XX

Tadler
Kehmen
Bourscheid

Weischeid
eiderscheid
Burden
352 VG
XX
Diekirch

Gentingen
LXXXV LXXX

Bettendorf
Wallendorf
276 VG
XX

Merzig
Ettelbruck
Gilsdorf
Bigelbach
Dillingen
Bollendorf
212 VG
XX
Ernzen

osbous
Schieren
Eppeldorf
10 ARMD
Beaufort
Bergdorf

Vichten
Ermsdorf
X
Haller
Echternach

80
A
Savelborn
Waldbillig
Osweiler
Dickweiler

Bissen
Fels
9 ARMD
4
Christnach
Scheidgen
Consdorf

LD
Reuland
Colbert

Mersch

III XII
Junglinster

more dogged. Volksgrenadiers made the GIs fight for each house and every cellar. By the time the battle had been decided, light was beginning to drain from the sky. As German troops continued to threaten Haller from the surrounding woods, the Americans hurried to remove civilians from the front line to avoid mix-ups and confusion. They forced a number of reluctant villagers to join a column of German POWs in the dangerous trek to Waldbillig. The remaining inhabitants were rounded up and herded into the church. There they were kept under armed guard with barely enough blankets to keep them warm. Only the following day, after heated discussions with the village priest, did the Americans agree to let the people return to their homes. They were given just enough time to gather some things and pack. When darkness came, they were marched to some trucks outside the village and whisked off to the rear.[2]

Guided by centralized direction systems, American artillery kept pounding targets with ferocious intensity day and night on December 26. While cannons discharged ample amounts of white phosphorus, fighter-bombers plunged from the clear skies to release into the inferno everything from fragmentation bombs to napalm. In the early morning hours of December 27, troops of the 5th Division captured Beaufort without too much opposition. Almost all of the dazed people in the cellars turned out to be women and children. Despite the pitiless destruction the GIs had rained down on them, the villagers were tremendously happy to see them. Until shortly before the American attack, a Kommando of the Gestapo had sown terror in the small agricultural community. On Saturday, December 23, the security agents had arrested all men aged between eighteen and forty-five—a total of thirty-eight villagers. First they had locked them up in the church, and then they had transferred them to a large basement, where they had grilled the men about the resistance, the militia, and the Americans. During the night, one of the prisoners had managed to escape. The infuriated Gestapo had immediately retaliated by shipping the others off to prisons in Germany. Even during the worst hours of American shelling and bombing, the villagers' minds had been filled with unmitigated dread of the Gestapo and nagging worry about their victims' fate.[3]

By the time they liberated Beaufort, troops of the 5th Infantry Division controlled all of the territory that the 4th Infantry and 9th Armored Divisions had held before the onset of the German counteroffensive, including Echternach. They were now on the Sûre River's southern bank, digging in to await orders for the even bigger push to be coordinated with troops building up north of the Bulge. Though the battle was far from over, evacuated farmers in the rear could hardly wait to get back to the liberated villages, even if located uncomfortably close to the front. Forty-six-year-old Arthur Funck was one of twenty farmers who as early as December 27 received permission from the Americans to return to Waldbillig. Every morning, the farmers left the host villages on their bicycles, accompanied by a gendarme. Danger and thick snow slowed them down so that at times it took the men two hours to reach their homes. At around four o'clock each afternoon they had to abandon cattle and farms again and return to the rear, where they arrived exhausted long after dark.[4]

On the last day of the year, German artillery suddenly opened up on the American lines with renewed vigor. Beaufort was pummeled until deep into the night, so that the Americans the next day decided to have the village evacuated, with the exception of no more than twenty-five inhabitants and their priest. Around noon on December 31, farmers in Waldbillig had been pinned down for about a half an hour. They had all escaped unharmed, however, and the brave men, with permission of the Americans, dutifully returned to tend their cattle the next day. What should have been Waldbillig's dawn of peace, turned into a nightmare at noon, when more German shells suddenly ripped the village apart with barely a warning. When the stinging wind gradually whipped smoke and dust away, it revealed the lifeless bodies of two farmers. Near them, a third villager lay panting, his lungs pierced with shrapnel. Elsewhere, a fourth man, his body mangled by metal shards, was cringing from pain. Mathias Frisch and an American soldier risked their lives to drag him back to the relative safety of a nearby house.

Farmer Arthur Funck remained unscathed that fateful Sunday. But he was less fortunate the next day, when he pushed off for Waldbillig once again, this time determined to take his cattle to safety in Christnach. He did not get much farther than Heffingen. In one of war's many ironies, a giant American truck ran him over on his bicycle, leaving him unable to continue his war journal for weeks, let alone take care of his troubled farm.[5]

2 On the 5th Division's left, one of General Patton's steel fists threw a punch in the direction of the Sûre River in a sector running from Eppeldorf to just east of Ettelbrück. The 10th Armored Di-

vision also received the welcome support of massive preparatory artillery barrages. On the division's right flank, an estimated 2,100 shells plowed the area in and around Eppeldorf on December 24 and 25. As if by a miracle, the remaining villagers were spared serious harm, even the farmers who dodged shells to get just a bit of food or water to the animals bellowing in anguish in their stables. But when the first Americans arrived in Eppeldorf on the day after Christmas, there were no flags or flowers or cries of joy like there had been in September. People just stared at the ruins and carcasses and openly wept.[6]

For the inhabitants of Moestroff, a village northwest of Eppeldorf, cut in two by the Sûre, Christmas brought the cruelest of times. The first Americans arrived around midnight on Christmas Eve. The following day, they cleared all of Moestroff south of the Sûre, but could only watch helplessly as the Germans strengthened their grip on the part of the village north of the river. As darkness came on Christmas Day, Moestroff had the misfortune of being pounded by artillery from both sides of the Sûre. Before the day was out, most of the inhabitants of the northern part of the village had left for Bettendorf on German orders. More than sixty of them would spend the next three weeks holed up in the grain elevator of the Zettinger mill.

On the right bank, American troops delayed evacuation of Moestroff for as long as they could. But each new day made life in the village more unbearable. Power lines had been cut. Moreover, the water main had been blown with the bridge, forcing villagers to draw water for themselves and their animals from local springs with buckets, something that became increasingly dangerous as the enemy sighted his guns ever more carefully.

On January 2 the Americans finally decided that evacuation could no longer be postponed. Strict security measures were announced to avoid drawing fire. The villagers were to leave under cover of darkness and received instructions to be ready by six o'clock in the evening. No wagons were allowed. Neither could any of the cattle come along, though three inhabitants were granted permission to stay behind to look after the farms. Shortly after six o'clock, a sad column of villagers, loaded down with bags and suitcases, shuffled up the steep, slippery road to Keiwelbach, a hamlet about a mile south of Moestroff. They had been briefed beforehand not to make a sound, not to carry torches or lamps, not to light even a cigarette. The sick and elderly made it to Keiwelbach on the backs of GIs. Just as no one expected them anymore, American trucks rolled into Keiwelbach. Heading for

Mersch, a town some ten miles to the southwest, the open trucks disappeared into the icy night with their frozen human cargo huddled together for comfort more than warmth.[7]

In Mersch the Moestroff evacuees were at least safe. For the villagers on the German side who had been forced to exchange Moestroff for Bettendorf on Christmas Day, the ordeal of artillery fire would continue unabated until the Americans liberated the village on January 18. By that time, shells had snuffed the lives of some seven villagers, most of them during desperate attempts to care for their animals. At least two more civilians died of wounds or illnesses that could have been cured had there been a doctor to care for them.[8]

For the people trapped in Diekirch, a town located on the far side of the Sûre and the 10th Armored Division's left, the long road of suffering began in earnest on Christmas Eve, when American artillery started barking in unison and increasing numbers of shells spewed their incendiary bile of white phosphorus onto streets and buildings. Of a total of four thousand inhabitants, only an estimated one thousand had failed to flee. The curl of smoke from a chimney sufficed to invite retribution, making even the preparation of food hazardous. Spotter planes maneuvered between towering columns of smoke to radio more destruction down on anything and anyone foolish enough to appear in the open. Before long, German soldiers in several places were erecting wooden signs bearing macabre skulls and stark warnings against movement during the day.[9]

In some streets, houses soon were awash with white phosphorus dripping down the fronts "like oatmeal." Maddened with fear, civilians abandoned their own and their neighbors' basements to flock instead to the spacious cellars of the town brewery. Carved partly into a rock, its big malt cellars well below ground level with arched roofs buttressed by solid pillars, the brewery offered the reassurance of a medieval bulwark. Still, many of the refugees were elderly, and they did not fare well in an environment of bitter cold and humid drafts, where damp stone floors were covered with nothing more than straw and a few blankets. Chilled to the bone and racked with fear, many of them died in the days that followed. For the remainder of the siege, their bodies, placed in rough-hewn coffins without lids, were stored in an adjoining cellar. Freezing temperatures prevented the corpses from decomposing. The survivors, meanwhile, grew inured to death nearby.[10]

There were more heartrending scenes in the cellars of the town hospital run by the Sisters of St. Elisabeth. By Christmas Eve, sisters and orderlies had carried all of the elderly and sick down the stairs to a variety of small cellar rooms. As wounded from Diekirch and surrounding villages swelled the number of patients and staff to nearly 160, it became impossible to provide all of the needy with beds or even mattresses in the cramped spaces. While wounds interminably oozed blood and pus and incontinent elderly soiled themselves over and over again, nurses were running out of bandages, clean sheets, and fresh clothes. Only one toilet bucket was available to hold the vomit and excreta of the ten to twelve patients in each room. As the pipes had frozen, water could be had only by melting snow. Refugees who flocked to the hospital found the stench so overwhelming that it made them retch.

Freezing cold, lack of hygiene, and the shortage of medicines caused the nurses to lose patients at an alarming rate. Equally troubling was that the staff did not know how to dispose of the bodies. The first two they tried to bury in the garden. An orderly put identification notes inside empty medicine bottles, tied a bottle around each corpse's neck, then wrapped the bodies in a sheet. But the digging of even shallow graves took so much time and was so often interrupted by shelling that the sixteen victims who followed were simply laid out on the cold floor of another cellar room.[11]

The Volksgrenadiers in Diekirch responded to the increasingly aggressive American shelling by strengthening their defensive positions in anticipation of the attack they knew would inevitably follow. They had no qualms about rounding up civilians to help them accomplish that dangerous task more rapidly. With explosions reverberating across town, Germans forced townspeople to clear snow-clogged roads, dig rifle pits and trenches, and prepare firing positions for heavy mortars. Soldiers in the rue de l'Hôpital corralled a number of boys, set them to work on a brick farmyard wall with picks and heavy hammers, and proceeded to install a heavy machine gun in the resulting bunker-like position.[12]

Much greater friction between soldiers and civilians resulted from increased competition for food and other essentials. The Germans robbed houses of all the stoves and cookers they could find for their bunkers and dugouts. They emptied clothing stores, collected bed linens, and desecrated even churches in search of the white garb of priests. Soldiers who sheltered two horses in a stable belonging to Michael

Preisen asked the farmer to keep a close eye on the prized animals so that no other unit would steal them. But it was in the hunt for food that the Volksgrenadiers showed themselves most ingenious, and not a day went by without the squealing of hogs and squawking of poultry. Meanwhile, civilians fanned out across town to comb every nook and cranny of houses, farms, and shops in search of something to eat. Sixteen-year-old Emile Post was one of them. Before long, he was snatching piglets, chickens, and rabbits out from under the hungry Germans' noses. His excitement at the finds in butcher Masseler's shop could not be spoiled even by the meat's sickly green color. After thoroughly cooking it, the people who lived in the cellar with Emile ate it with as much relish as gratitude.

There was also gratitude for the many others in Diekirch who, despite gnawing hunger, did not shrink from sharing. For a couple of refugees from Vianden, for example, who used the remaining flour supplies at the Fischer bakery to prepare loaves of bread for anyone who could get there. For the owners of the Thilmany farm, always willing to part with some of their milk to help the people hiding in the packed brewery. But also for those German soldiers who broke severely rationed stale bread with famished noncombatants.[13]

By the beginning of the new year, for a Volksgrenadier in Diekirch to share anything with anyone was to make a sacrifice. Pulling infantry carts and even baby carriages, ragged and starving soldiers from Diekirch began to roam as far back as Fouhren in search of blankets, stoves, and food. On at least one occasion an unrelenting officer chased them off for the sole reason that they did not belong to his unit.[14]

3 On the morning of December 22, the newly arrived troops of the 80th Infantry Division jumped off from a line of departure just north of Mersch. Positioned on the left of their comrades from the 10th Armored Division, they were to engage the Germans along that part of the front running from Ettelbrück to Mertzig.

On the division's right, American artillery had been blasting Ettelbrück, a town of some one thousand hearths, as soon as the 352nd Volksgrenadier Division had captured it on December 20. When Patton's counterattack began two days later, the shelling became furious and merciless.

Inside Ettelbrück, an estimated three hundred inhabitants had been unable or unwilling to join the exodus on December 19. Most of them were elderly, some too bedridden to make it to the shelters, the minds and bodies of others too fragile to cope with long days of cold and fear in cellars that were as dark and dank as graves. For the six hundred patients in the town's sanatorium, their minds in disarray long before the war, the chaos and stress of battle caused even worse suffering. Outsiders were not able to fathom the depth of their anguish in those terrible days. But the Sisters of St. Elisabeth knew that what their patients needed above all was as much order and routine as the exceptional circumstances would permit. That meant they had to provide them with food at regular times, but the mental institution's bakery and kitchen had been built on one side of the road to Schieren, and several of the patients' pavilions were located on the other side. To attempt to cross that road several times a day with shells bursting all around was to invite disaster. Orderlies and technical staff, all of whom had volunteered to stay behind, agreed with the sisters that the only way to reach the patients with food, was to crawl to them in their underground shelters through the narrow passageway of cables and pipes beneath the Schieren road. For days on end, caretakers moved back and forth with the tirelessness of worker ants. But the patients got their meals without the staff suffering many casualties. Only twenty-four-year-old Sister Hildegunde was unfortunate enough to fall victim to shrapnel. She was killed on December 23 while baking more bread that was to be carried across.[15]

The Volksgrenadiers began to withdraw from Ettelbrück the day after Sister Hildegunde's death. The following morning, the population's Christmas present arrived in the form of American infantrymen. People came out of hiding, however, to find that freedom was the only thing of importance that the soldiers could give them back. Of the town itself, artillery and fighter-bombers had left little standing. Half of the buildings were either razed or irreparably damaged. The church, hospital, and agricultural school all lay in ruins. Bridges, water mains, and power plants had been destroyed. Bloated cattle lay among the debris in streets that had become unrecognizable. Men and women could be seen picking through the rubble crying. Ettelbrück's civil authorities, in the month following the arrival of the Germans on December 20, would register the deaths of seventy people, whereas in normal times for that same period fifteen deceased would have been the average. Some thirty of those who perished that winter died as a direct result of battle. Many of the others were elderly who wasted away from the illnesses and anguish that only war knows how to inflict.[16]

While soldiers of the 80th Division prepared to wrestle Ettelbrück from the Germans, to the west their comrades were making rapid progress in the direction of Heiderscheid. By nightfall on December 23, the infantrymen had overrun the village, thereby cutting off the vital Ettelbrück-Bastogne highway. The Americans tried to restore some normalcy in the newly liberated communities. In Heiderscheid, Civil Affairs officers quickly promoted the village priest to acting mayor. But normalcy was hard to come by with more batteries massing in fields and gardens to fire into the Bourscheid bridgehead, where the Germans were flexing their muscle just south of the Sûre.[17]

Worse than the shells pounding Bourscheid were the Allied fighter-bombers that were let loose on Christmas Eve. An attack at mid-morning that Sunday convulsed the village with panic. Volksgrenadiers scattered and dived into whatever shelters were available; in some cellars they unashamedly threw the civilians out. Villagers soon were abandoning Bourscheid in disorganized droves for places they hoped would be safer. More than a dozen made it to the mill outside the village. Around thirty hid in the railroad depot. Close to one hundred disheveled people flocked to the cellars of the imposing Fischeid farm. Those who chose to cling to their village were proved wrong in a most brutal fashion when the fighter-bombers returned on Christmas Day. One of their bombs whistled its way to the Lemmer house, plunged through roof, floors, and vaulted cellar ceiling, then exploded with terrible force. Weeks would pass before the frozen remains of the Lemmer parents, their two teenage children, a neighbor, a refugee from Aachen, and a nineteen-year-old Luxembourg deserter were reclaimed from the rubble. In the days following the air attack, desperate Volksgrenadiers took over the Fischeid farm as well as the railroad depot. They forced refugees young and old to disperse as far north as Clervaux.[18]

Christmas Day was to be an equally disastrous day for the inhabitants of Kehmen. Insignificant in size, the village had the misfortune of being situated on the main road linking Heiderscheid with Bourscheid. If the Americans wanted to crack the Bourscheid bridgehead, they had to capture Kehmen. On the other hand, if the Germans were set on holding out south of the Sûre, they had to deny the Americans access to the village. At first, fate had seemed to smile on Kehmen's farmers. Some American shells had shaken the village around noon on December 23. Then, following a short but dreadful spell of house-to-house combat, Kehmen shortly after nightfall had been liberated with little damage and no casualties.

But fate turned sour on Kehmen overnight. On Christmas Eve the Germans from Bourscheid launched a counterattack and drove the Americans back. The following day the Americans struck back with a vengeance, pounding the village with their most frightful weapon. White phosphorus in no time was eating its way through roofs, fodder, and haystacks, reducing at least eighteen farms to ash. As plumes of dark smoke climbed into the sky, horrified Volksgrenadiers buried themselves in cellars packed with civilians. Too full of fear to feel shame, they ordered the villagers out of their shelters. By sundown, almost the entire population of Kehmen was desperately groping to find safety in the snow-swept fields and woods. Some villagers set out to reach the American lines. Others were chased in the direction of the German positions and headed for Welscheid. All of them were fair game for machine guns and artillery on both sides spitting death at anything that moved in the darkness and confusion. Five villagers did not make it out of Kehmen's bitter woods and fields alive. Not long after Christmas, Kehmen became no-man's-land. It would stay that way until the Americans came back on January 21.

Death's harvest in Kehmen on Christmas Day had been wantonly random as the thaw revealed in 1945 when it pulled back the shrouds of snow from woods and fields. Up to the fresh skies stared the uncomprehending faces of Maria Hecker, a spinster aged forty-four; Peter Bonert and his wife, both in their seventies; and Thérèse and Bertha Rippinger, teenage sisters.[19]

4 Early on Friday morning, December 22, fresh American troops from the 26th Infantry Division jumped off from the line of departure at Bettborn in tandem with comrades of the 80th Division on their right. They were faced by elements of the 352nd Volksgrenadier Division, and German resistance became steadily worse as reinforcements arrived from the *Führer Grenadier Brigade,* a force of some six thousand troops, many of whom had fought with the Grossdeutschland Division on the eastern front.[20]

None of this, however, could prevent the men of the 26th Division from making steady progress toward the Sûre. While on the division's right troops inexorably gained ground in the direction of Esch-sur-Sûre, on its left the Americans were making even better progress as long columns of troops and tanks swiftly pushed ahead along the road to Rambrouch. Thousands of GIs on Friday night bedded down in a chain of villages stretching northwest from Ospern to Eschette. In

Hostert, they arrived a day too late to save Nicolas Urth. The Germans had apprehended the man, a member of the resistance and Miliz, on Thursday and carried him to an unknown destination. His mutilated corpse would be discovered in a shallow grave in Bigonville long after the battle.[21]

Before dawn on Saturday, guns pointing at Rambrouch and beyond began a deafening roar that lasted until the following morning. When American troops captured Rambrouch late on Sunday, five homes were still burning, the girl's school had been obliterated, and two civilians lay dead among the ruins. In Arsdorf, a village two miles farther north, people who had not fled with the others, most of them on sledges pulled by cows, spent Christmas Eve praying and crying in their cellars. Germans and Americans began battling for their village early on Sunday evening. Five buildings were ablaze in no time. The Barnich family only realized what was happening when thick smoke started filling their cellar. Father, mother, and daughter crawled into the street choking. They stumbled into the cross fire and were cut down almost instantly. Badly wounded, surrounded by American and German casualties, the three of them were left to lay in the snow for hours. By the time an American ambulance whisked the family away it was clear that Mr. Barnich did not have much longer to live.[22]

In the wake of a devastating barrage causing the village mill to receive twenty-seven hits in one night and leaving one civilian dead, the Americans on Christmas Day reclaimed Insenborn and its thirty homes just south of the Sûre. The soldiers lost no time in installing the local priest as Insenborn's new mayor; then they turned their attention to more urgent matters: the crossing of the river. By evening the Americans had built several bridges while pouring bombs and shells on the enemy on the other side as fast and as hard as they could. Much of the center of Bavigne went up in flames and people fled to the woods where at night a hard frost made their blankets stiff like cardboard. In Liefrange, a village on the Sûre's northern bank, one of countless explosions made a barn wall collapse, crushing two teenage boys. Liefrange was the first village the Americans succeeded in entering on the far side. The battle for what was a collection of no more than twenty-four houses began in the afternoon of December 26 and lasted throughout the night. The enemy made the GIs fight for every building. The Americans cleared one of them with hand grenades only to find a woman and a boy dead inside. The warm blood of Mrs. Hoffmann and her son Mätti slowly blended into a single puddle.[23]

From Liefrange on Wednesday, December 27, the Americans pushed on to Mecher. There they regrouped to move against Kaundorf. Kaundorf had been under relentless artillery fire for more than thirty-six hours, but the barrage that preceded the attack on Wednesday afternoon was like nothing the inhabitants had experienced before. People cowered in their cellars, covered with dust and plaster shaken from the ceilings. At least six buildings were burning. Some civilians could not stand it any longer and broke free from the shelters to head for the woods. Twice the Germans counterattacked and threw the enemy out; twice the Americans clawed their way back. By the end of the day, the Germans had given up on Kaundorf. As if by a miracle, no civilians were hurt. In the cellar of the Schiltz home, the door swung open to reveal two GIs at the top of the stairs. "Nix Nazis?" they called down. "Nein!" the packed bunch assured in one voice. The soldiers descended with their fingers on the trigger. Though they tried to resist, they could not stop one of the women from squeezing them tight and rewarding them both with a loud kiss. A sigh of relief rippled through the crowd.[24]

On Thursday the men from the 26th Division extended their bridgehead north of the Sûre as far as Nothum, barely two miles southwest of the strategic town of Wiltz. There the advance halted and the troops dug in to await General Patton's orders for a renewed push early in the new year. In preparation for the fresh advance, however, artillery batteries massed along the division's front line to soften up the ground still to be taken. From Mecher alone guns fired an estimated 2,500 shells each day in the direction of Berlé, a key village in front of Wiltz. So violent and continuous was the roar of outgoing fire in and around Dellen that ninety-four-year-old Barbara Bomm, whom the entire village had hoped would live to be one hundred, succumbed in a matter of days to stress and fear.[25]

For the civilians on the receiving end, things were still worse. As soon as the first barrages erupted, Berlé's village priest threw his violet stole around his neck and dashed from cellar to cellar to offer his people at least the consolation of general absolution. By the time the Americans captured the village in January, Berlé was one of the most devastated places in the Grand Duchy of Luxembourg.[26]

Though low on ammunition, the Germans north of the Sûre continued to harass the newly liberated communities with shell fire that was as murderous as it was unpredictable. In Mecher, one shell cut a boy to pieces as it caught him by surprise in bed. Another one mortally riddled a small girl with shrapnel. Yet another sudden blast ripped off a young woman's legs. She bled to death beside her son who was missing a foot. "We are all greatly discouraged in our cellar," an inhabitant of Kaundorf, liberated more than a week earlier, scribbled in his journal on January 4, 1945. "Nothing seems to improve." For things to get markedly better, the inhabitants would have to wait until the fall of Wiltz. But that was more than two weeks away.[27]

5 Also to be pitied were the Luxembourgers who remained at the mercy of the Nazi security forces even while the Americans were pushing the front line toward them. On Friday, December 22, the day that Patton's troops began their first assault on the salient, agents from the Gestapo Kommando in Clervaux descended on Crendal, where they arrested Ernest Lamborelle and his two sons, Georges and Michel. All three were accused of having molested a family suspected of collaborating with the German occupier during the liberation in September 1944. The sons, moreover, were charged with membership in the resistance and Miliz. Father and sons were badly mistreated and locked up in Clervaux, where they were joined almost immediately by Jean Heck. A farmer, Mr. Heck had been taken away by the Gestapo during a raid in Weiswampach aimed at seizing his brother, Jean-Pierre. As they had failed to capture their intended victim, the frustrated agents had grabbed Jean as a hostage instead. All four prisoners were taken away on Christmas Day. Their corpses were discovered not far from Clervaux around the middle of February 1945. Each of them had a bullet hole in the neck.[28]

On Christmas Eve, a severed telephone cable belonging to the Wehrmacht invited terror to the tiny village of Binsfeld. Unable to find out who was responsible for the presumed act of sabotage, the Gestapo snatched ten male hostages from their homes and loaded them onto a truck. They took the hostages, too, to their sinister headquarters in Clervaux, and kept them in frigid cells with barely any blankets, food, or water. On the first day of the new year, a truck whisked the unfortunates away to Germany. It was the beginning of months of unmitigated suffering in which the starving hostages were marched from prison to prison and in between were forced to perform heavy labor. Of the ten hostages, Michel Meyers never returned to Binsfeld.

His brother, Bernard, did. But exhausted from protracted hardships, he died at the age of thirty-three, even before the summer of 1945 had come to an end.[29]

On the second day of 1945, hours before the Allies were to commence their coordinated, all-out offensive against the German bulge, the Gestapo, seemingly undaunted by the turning tide of the battle in the Ardennes, launched their own offensive in the villages of Munshausen and Marnach, just southeast and east of Clervaux. In no time they rounded up five men suspected of involvement in the resistance and Miliz. The prisoners were trucked to an unknown destination. Four of their bodies were discovered early in February, not far from Troisvierges. These men, too, were shown to have been executed in cold blood, their necks smudged with entry wounds from bullets fired at close range. The fifth victim, twenty-year-old Aloyse Stelmes, was carried off to Germany, where he died in Giessen not long after his liberation by American troops.[30]

During the first days of January 1945, even as the final Allied counteroffensive had begun gaining momentum, Nazi security forces operating from Troisvierges, in the northern tip of Luxembourg, continued to round up victims as if in a frenzy. Nine men and women, among them farmers, a teacher, and a cook, were taken from their homes in Hoffelt and Hachiville, villages close to the border with Belgium. The men were charged with having ties to the resistance. The women were accused of having harbored American stragglers. All of them were hastily driven away in passenger cars. On a dirt road in the vicinity of Stockem, they were told to get out and start walking in the direction of Clervaux. No one ever saw them again. The dark forests between Stockem and Clervaux have refused to unearth the mystery of what happened to the nine missing to this day.[31]

Chapter 12

Lifting the Siege of Bastogne

"In the cellars, we pray, we beg, we forget to eat."

1 Like moths to a flame, GIs in the icy night of December 22 were drawn to a house near a demolished bridge in the town of Martelange. The house, pockmarked by bullets and shells, had only two good rooms left. In the upstairs room, half a dozen men with rifles and packs slumped on the double bed and floor. Close to seventy Americans packed the downstairs room. The elderly Belgians who owned the house had a good fire going. They were feverishly brewing coffee in a vain attempt to keep canteen cups full and the soldiers' bodies thawed. The homey atmosphere was abruptly spoiled when a furious lieutenant burst in and "threatened to court martial anyone not on the road in five minutes."[1]

The frozen soldiers belonged to Combat Command A, one of three 4th Armored Division battle groups. The house the GIs had sought shelter in lay near the Sûre River. Their column had started rolling on the highway from Arlon at dawn. It was part of the much bigger assault against the German southern flank that Patton had unleashed that morning. But the 4th Armored Division had received the specific order of breaking through to Bastogne and to do it fast. On the first day, however, that had been easier said than done. Martelange was not quite half the distance from Arlon to Bastogne. But the town's two bridges had been blown up by American engineers to delay the enemy advance during the first days of the German offensive. And now German soldiers of the 5th Parachute Division at the Sûre showed themselves possessed with a grim determination to block the main southern highway into Bastogne for as long as possible. By nightfall on December 22 casualties among the armored infantry at Martelange were so high that some of the 704th Tank Destroyer Battalion's men were told to stand by as replacements. Only in mid-afternoon of the next day was a Bailey bridge built over the Sûre. At that point, twelve long miles still separated Combat Command A from a Bastogne desperate for relief.[2]

Combat Command B was making much better progress on the secondary roads west of the Arlon-Bastogne highway. It had launched itself from Habay-la-Neuve early on December 22 and by dawn the next day stood poised to take Chaumont, a village only six miles from Bastogne. A regiment of the 5th Parachute Division had descended on Chaumont in the night of December 21 when the village was already swollen by refugees from Bastogne and Marvie. The Germans had barged into bedrooms, plundered straw, and begun stoking fires in rooms everywhere. "They are real bandits," Maria Lozet noted, "all boys of between 17 and 20." "We are," they smugly informed the villagers, "going to push the Americans back to America." They would not do quite that, but supported by some fifteen heavy tank destroyers and assault guns, the uniformed boys stood fast and were to battle the Americans for three long days.[3]

The battle sucked Chaumont into a vortex of destruction. On Saturday, December 23, Americans plowed the village with shells and bombs before sending in infantry and tanks. Still, by nightfall the GIs had been hurled back again. Flames soared from the homes of the Dessoys, the Davids, the Hormans, the Lozets, the Paquays, and the Charneux. The school, too, was ablaze. Félicien Rosières and his wife were dead. So was Marie Horman. Jacques Vermer had come from as far away as Verviers to search for food in the countryside; the German counteroffensive had caught him by surprise and kept him trapped at Chaumont. A shell found him behind the wall of a stable and took his life. Battle raged so violently on Sunday that the thirty or more refugees in the Materne cellar pledged in unison to erect a chapel for the Holy Virgin and live more piously if only their lives were spared. Around noon on Christmas Day, another American barrage shook Chaumont, announcing yet another assault. Explosions rocked the Materne cellar, cracking the walls and dislodging window frames; a German chaplain and medic joined the refugees in their prayers. By dusk the Americans were in control of Chaumont. The GIs were exhausted, disheveled, and bearded. They smashed all the German guns they could find. Then they brought bacon and coffee and implored the villagers to fix them a hot meal. The next day, an American ambulance came to pick up a number of wounded civilians. Five of them would die in the weeks to come. One of them was Alfred Materne, the mayor of Bastogne who had thought it safer to seek refuge with relatives in a village hard to spot on any map.[4]

With Chaumont in the hands of Combat Command B, enemy troops in the anticipated path of the armored column were getting nervous and irritated. In the night of December 25, a crying baby at the Bouzendorff farm in Salvacourt, some three miles north of Chaumont, refused to let German soldiers catch some much-needed sleep. The high-strung men threatened to harm the inhabitants if they did not make the infant shut up at once. Someone hurried to the cow stable and squirted milk straight into the nursing bottle. Tension temporarily ebbed as the child drank it all and went to sleep.[5]

That same night no one could find sleep in what was left of Sainlez. Three miles east of Chaumont, and just east of the Arlon-Bastogne highway, the battered village stood in the way of Combat Command A, whose tanks had pushed as far as Warnach by Christmas Day. From Warnach it was no more than four miles to Sainlez. A good number of rounds had begun to tear up Sainlez on December 23, the day Combat Command A had crossed the Sûre and crisp wintry skies had finally allowed spotter planes to help direct the artillery. The following day, the first aircraft had lashed out at Sainlez to help pave the way for the armored spearhead. By Christmas Eve not a single house had remained untouched. One explosion had dealt a farmer a serious head wound while he was feeding his pigs; another had killed a villager on his way back from tending cattle that belonged to refugees from the grand duchy.[6]

On the eve of the Nativity most civilians had found refuge in three of the village's most robust shelters. Around forty villagers had flocked to the Goosse farm. The Bihain farm had become home to some seventy people. Close to the church, the Grégoire forge formed the rallying point for yet another community. Beneath the vaulted ceiling of the forge's nearby stable hid twenty-two people, fifteen of them refugees from Marvie. Their number had jumped to thirty in the afternoon, when room had to be made for widower Joseph Didier and his seven daughters aged six to sixteen years old. American aircraft had set their house on fire and acrid smoke had chased them from the cellar they had been forced to share with German soldiers. Father and children had barged into the Grégoire shelter, their mouths and noses covered with wet rags.[7]

A German tank late on Christmas Eve had hidden under a tree between the Grégoire forge and stable. At dawn on Christmas Day, the black cross on the tank's side glared at the refugees in the stable as if pointing to their tomb. Within minutes American fighter-bombers swooped down on their steel prey. Three bombs pulverized the tank as well as the immediate vicinity. So powerful were the blasts that the turret was catapulted onto the roof of a neighboring house. The Grégoire complex was swept away entirely. Virtually nothing remained of twenty-nine of its thirty inhabitants. Only Marie Gossiaux survived. German soldiers found her badly burned and in a state of shock on the bottom of a gaping crater. They carried her to a nearby house and left her in the kitchen to be treated by the inhabitants. The villagers did not know how to relieve her pain except to daub some cream on the wounds. They knew even less how to soothe her mind as she deliriously called out for Maximilien and Francis—her children, aged seven and two, who had vanished with the Grégoire shelter. They were only two of twelve children incinerated together with the German tank that day.[8]

The lightning thrust to Bastogne that Patton had had in mind for the 4th Armored Division (he had promised to be in the town by Christmas) was degenerating into a slogging match because of the tenacity of the German paratroopers. To strengthen the attack, Combat Command R was hastily dispatched to the division's left flank and ordered to make an additional stab at Bastogne along the highway leading into the town from Neufchâteau. This third armored column launched its attack against Bastogne from Vaux-lez-Rosières on the morning of December 25. Hoping to skirt the strongest German defenses, its commander ordered tanks and troops off the highway and onto the secondary roads.[9]

Four artillery battalions mercilessly hammered the first village to show up in the path of Combat Command R. It turned out not to have been an exaggerated precaution: tanks and armored infantry stormed Remoiville at the end of the barrage to find an entire battalion of paratroopers dazed and in so much disarray that they allowed three hundred men to be taken prisoner. Remoiville lay in ruins and its inhabitants were found to be as shell-shocked as the German paratroopers. Amazingly, however, the hundreds of shells fired that Christmas Day had not claimed a single civilian life in the solid cellars. Compared with the carnage that a handful of bombs had caused earlier that day in Sainlez, it was another stark reminder of why civilians feared air attacks above all else.[10]

Combat Command R was forced to invest much of the morning of December 26 in the grim battle for the next village on the map. Artillery pummeled Remichampagne's farms and nearby woods. Sixteen P-47 fighter-bombers of the 362nd Fighter Group joined the fray, lashing out at anything that moved. By noon, half the village was on fire. At a crossroads south of the village, the Zabus farm was also burning. Together with refugees from Bastogne, the Zabus family poured out of the cellar and into the courtyard where, much to their surprise, they bumped into American soldiers. The GIs tried to get the cattle out of the burning stables. When that failed, they mowed the animals down with their machine guns. The soldiers were tense and impatient. They asked civilians to point out the enemy's hiding places. Ten-year-old Guy Zabus watched how GIs with carbines and grenades flushed two Germans from the Léonard farm. The first one came out with his hands above his head. The second one defiantly kept his arms next to his body. The Americans hurled themselves at the German and beat him with the butts of their rifles until he, too, obeyed. Guy continued to look on as the Americans next tried to dislodge the enemy from the Delhaisse farm. One German surrendered right away. But another refused to come out for quite a while. When he finally did, the young paratrooper turned out to be wearing parts of an American uniform. Four or five GIs dragged him across the courtyard, tied him to a pole with a cable, and shot him on the spot. Guy Zabus witnessed the execution without any particular feeling of horror or injustice, "as if all that," he later remembered, "belonged to the logical order of things."[11]

Though two of Remichampagne's inhabitants had lost their lives two days earlier, the others somehow remained spared on the ferocious day of the liberation itself. Around three o'clock in the afternoon of December 26, Combat Command R from Remichampagne rolled into Clochimont. The column took the village fairly rapidly, leaving only one civilian, seventy-six-year-old Joseph Meunier, dead in its wake. Frightened by the sound of battle, almost all of Clochimont's inhabitants a few days earlier had sought protection in the reassuringly strong stables of the Verlaine farm. There Mrs. Gillet, the wife of Assenois's teacher, had given birth on Christmas night.

The child had not come into the world under a lucky star, however, and due to the lack of proper medical care, died soon after.[12]

The only village now remaining between Combat Command R and Bastogne was Assenois. The leading armor surged ahead on a secondary road. Artillery at 4:35 P.M. threw its weight behind the attack by lobbing more than four hundred rounds on the village and nearby woods. While armored infantry engaged in fierce combat for Assenois with a mixture of paratroopers and Volksgrenadiers, Sherman tanks cut through the village and headed straight for Bastogne. Tankers of the 4th Armored Division at 4:50 P.M. were shaking hands with engineers from the 101st Airborne Division.[13]

Arthur Leclere, one of Bastogne's youthful "vagabonds," happened to be in the town's marketplace when the long-awaited Shermans arrived. He watched how a sentry in the middle of the main square raised his arm to stop the tanks, took his time to salute solemnly to the crews, then directed them to the Grand'Rue. Tuesday at dusk, news that the siege had been lifted spread like wildfire among the civilians in Bastogne's sepulchral underground. The following morning, airborne officers in the château at Isle-la-Hesse, inside Bastogne's perimeter, got together and kindly invited their hostess to join them. Baroness Greindl and the relieved paratroopers smoked a tasteful American cigarette to celebrate the news.[14]

2 Many of the men who enjoyed a cigarette with Baroness Greindl that day would be dead before the new year. For if the siege of Bastogne was lifted on December 26, the battle for the town not only continued, but increased in ferocity. The fighting that followed the siege would cost the lives of many more civilians, too, and would again reap innocent victims mostly in Bastogne's perimeter of countryside and villages.

The 4th Armored Division first set to work securing the exceedingly fragile American corridor leading into Bastogne from the south. How precarious that corridor was during the very first days, Mr. Mutschen learned soon after he set out for Bastogne from Remichampagne. His father had refused to leave Bastogne with the rest of the family when the Germans began their encirclement, and Mr. Mutschen was anxious to check on the eighty-five-year-old man. He had just reached Assenois when a shell exploded near the Laval farm and several tiny shards pierced his stomach. Mr. Mutschen stumbled around for help until two GIs noticed him and with a jeep drove him to a hospital in Martelange. Surgeons retrieved two fragments from his arm, and an operation revealed five perforations in his intestines. Without adequate medical treatment, Mr. Mutschen's wounds, innocent though they had looked on the surface, could have proved lethal.[15]

More and more of Combat Command R's troops hastily followed in the track beaten by its spearhead. Mrs. de Coune's château in Assenois was soon filled with American soldiers from cellar to attic. The veteran tankers struck her as rough-hewn and surly. To make room for more soldiers, they removed the furniture by throwing it out the windows. They simply told Mrs. de Coune that their army would settle matters after the war. The Civil Affairs personnel that arrived a little later proved more caring. Where needed they quickly appointed interim mayors from among trusted civilians to help restore order in the newly liberated villages. When several children in Assenois, including Mrs. de Coune's, began running high fevers, Civil Affairs, fearing an epidemic, rushed in trucks and evacuated the stricken families to the rear.[16]

While troops of the 4th Armored Division were feeding into Bastogne along the Neufchâteau axis from the southwest, Combat Command A was still struggling to reach the town via the southern highway from Arlon. Just east of that highway, and five miles south of Bastogne, American artillery and aircraft incessantly continued to blast the ill-fated Sainlez until December 27. Incendiaries in the afternoon of December 26 set the Goosse and Bihain farms, the village's most crowded shelters, ablaze. Soon Sainlez's smoking cellars and stables were spewing dozens of villagers, Luxembourg refugees, and German paratroopers. Close to forty civilians trekked more than a mile across snow-covered fields to hide in the Wagières wood; few carried food or blankets.[17]

Most of the people who fled the Bihain farm were drawn to the Fonteny wood, a patch of spruces facing the Arlon highway about half a mile from Sainlez. Here the villagers got caught up in the cross fire between German and American artillery. In a blind panic the group tried to reach the less-exposed eastern fringes of the wood. They were about to cross a small stream when a series of explosions shook the earth and splintered the spruces around them. A dazed Mrs. Rollus clawed her way through a tangle of branches to check on her family. Shrapnel had mangled her husband's knee and her daughter Gisèle's foot. The marble stillness and strangely contorted bodies of daughter Josée and son Marcel, eleven and six years old, immediately told her that they were dead. Villagers, many of them wounded, dragged themselves across the icy stream. Mr. and Mrs. Rollus had no choice but to follow and leave their dead children behind in the blackened snow. One woman carried Gisèle. Another carried Mrs. Rollus's badly wounded fourth child, two-year-old Ghislaine. It took them five hours to reach Honville, a village just a mile and a half southeast of Sainlez. By that time Ghislaine Rollus had bled to death.[18]

The second liberation of Sainlez and its vicinity in no way resembled the first liberation three months earlier. Many of the liberated had nothing left to cheer about. And the weary liberators who arrived on December 27 were a far cry from the boyish victors of September. In the nearby village of Livarchamps a farmer noticed that the roughened combat troops were "in a foul mood." From the handful of villagers who remained in Sainlez, gruff and irascible Americans wanted to know only one thing: Where were the damned "Boches"?[19]

On the day the first Shermans arrived in Bastogne, more American divisions were rushed into the corridor to help widen it in westerly and easterly directions. But the tenacity with which German troops held on to both shoulders promised that here, too, much suffering was in store for civilians. Already on December 26, Allied air raids set much of Lutremange, a village east of the Arlon-Bastogne highway, on fire. Most of the two hundred villagers disappeared into the area's dense forests. However, farmer Léon Lafontaine never made it. He had been forced to watch the hungry flames engulf his life's work and suffered a lethal stroke.[20]

In Villers-la-Bonne-Eau, a short distance from Lutremange, most of the sixty-five inhabitants, with the exception of the young men who had fled on December 18, had gathered in the cellars of two farms. On December 27, artillery and aircraft so punished the village that three families decided they would be better off in the nearby woods. What happened to the Garcias on their way to the Bernaï forest was almost a carbon copy of the horror that had befallen the Rollus family in Sainlez the day before. Though it wounded three other people in the group, a shell appeared to have singled out the Garcia family in particular. One of its jagged tentacles instantly struck down sixteen-year-old Flore. Another let her youngest brother live, but not without taking part of his arm. Sizzling hot metal punctured Marie's lung, shattered her father's jaw, and came close to ripping off Mrs. Garcia's arm. Flore's body had to be left behind while the wounded dragged themselves back to Villers. They were put up in the corner of a shelter harboring forty other refugees, all of them painfully impotent in the face of the victims' dreadful moans.[21]

Slightly farther north, artillery and fighter-bombers were gutting Lutrebois and Losange in preparation for an attack by the 35th Infantry Division. Farmers drove cows, horses, and pigs from burning stables only to see the crazed animals massacred in the surrounding fields. German troops joined the civilians in their cellars; in one such shelter in Losange, the determined rattle of enemy typewriters hammering out battle reports mixed weirdly with the disruptive roar of explosions. On December 29 American ground troops launched their attack after an intense fifteen-minute barrage. The small-arms fire of the assailants could be heard shortly after noon. Fearing for their lives, civilians in a cellar in Losange succeeded in persuading German soldiers to step outside and join the battle by playing on their sense of honor. However, it did not prevent an American from aiming a grenade at their cellar window. Though the device exploded prematurely and took no casualties, the villagers burst out of the shelter wailing. For a horrifying couple of minutes they had no choice but to witness the battle firsthand until they decided to reenter their shelter.[22]

Still in Losange, at the height of battle, a German soldier strode into the cellar of the Roland home. He announced that for him the war was over, handed his pistol to Mr. Dewere, and vanished again. Mr. Dewere quickly hid the weapon under a pile of potatoes. A little later American infantrymen burst into the cellar. They scared the villagers, chasing them from the cellar and putting Mr. Roland and Mr. Dewere against a wall. Only after careful scrutiny of their identities were they free to go. By dusk of December 29 Lutrebois and Losange were back in American hands. So was Remoifosse, about a mile northwest of Lutrebois. But Victorien Lefèbvre did not launch himself at the GIs to thank them. Beside himself with rage, he demanded to know why earlier that morning their air force had thought it necessary to scorch much of the village, including his father's farm.[23]

On the other side of the corridor, enemy troops were jittery as far away as Mande-St.-Etienne, nearly four miles northwest of Assenois. The inhabitants received an unequivocal order from the Germans at dawn on December 28 to have their village evacuated before nine o'clock that morning. They were to seek refuge in Flamierge, a village a couple of miles farther to the rear. The villagers did as they were told, bent against the biting wind, and arrived in their new home with nothing but the clothes on their backs. Many settled in Flamierge's abandoned homes. Neighbors were kind enough to provide them with flour, bread, and milk.[24]

The arrival of so many newcomers left the Germans in Flamierge edgy. The following day, the occupiers came upon some American grenades in the Féron farm. The find was not necessarily suspicious as GIs had been in Flamierge before the German counteroffensive. But the agitated German soldiers immediately spoke of "franc-tireurs" and "partisans" and decided to investigate. They arrested four refugees from Mande-St.-Etienne who were staying in the Féron farm. Next, four men from Flamierge were rounded up, too. All eight of them were herded into the local forge. A heavy machine gun stood trained on them in the entrance. Later that day women were allowed to bring the prisoners some hot drinks and sandwiches. In the evening the soldiers took the suspects to the Dubuisson farm for interrogation. The village heaved a deep sigh of relief not long after, when it learned that the men had all been released unharmed. Some claimed Mr. Dubuisson had secured their release by talking to one of the Germans in his own dialect. Supposedly, farmer Amand Dubuisson had picked it up near the soldier's hometown while he was a prisoner during the Great War. The story was never confirmed, however, because three days after the prisoners' release a bomb obliterated farm and farmer. Perhaps the truth is less poetic and questioning simply showed the German soldiers that mounting pressure was making them see ghosts.[25]

Still west of the corridor, but closer to it, the pressures became as unbearable for the civilians as they were for the German troops. On December 27 a task force of the 9th Armored Division slammed into the enemy flank alongside the Neufchâteau highway. To keep this vital artery open it was particularly crucial that Sibret be taken, as the village virtually touched the highway and the Germans had been sending reinforcements there. On the day of the American attack, Sibret, already badly damaged by an air raid on Christmas Day, was subjected to furious shelling until about noon. The incessant blasts, shrieks, and blows were almost impossible to bear. "In the cellars," one of the numbed villagers wrote, "we pray, we beg, we forget to eat." By the time tanks and troops descended on the village, some fourteen houses had been ripped apart. Forty cows and three horses had perished at the Lonchay farm alone. At least eight buildings had collapsed, the rubble forming a chaotic grave for three of the village's civilians. The battle for Sibret raged throughout the afternoon and into the night. Then the Germans vanished into the woods and, dressed in bulging bedsheets, stole back in the direction of Chenogne.[26]

Chenogne's prolonged agony began with a tragic death on the day the Americans took Sibret. One of the Panzergrenadiers who were cleaning their rifles in the kitchen of the Burnotte farm accidentally pulled the trigger of a loaded weapon. The bullet wounded forty-four-year-old Irma Burnotte so gravely, it was soon decided that if she wanted to survive an ambulance would have to take her to the rear. Among those filing past Mrs. Burnotte to say a tearful goodbye were her six children. The ambulance did not leave until noon the next day. German medics told the family that Mrs. Burnotte would be cared for in St. Hubert. But war's maelstrom somehow took the ambulance in the opposite direction, causing the vehicle to become stuck in Brachtenbach, Luxembourg. It was there that Mrs. Burnotte died later that day with not a soul to comfort her.[27]

Many more of Chenogne's people were to die lonely deaths within the next forty-eight hours. The German ambulance taking so long to evacuate Mrs. Burnotte had everything to do with the attack the Americans had launched from Sibret on the morning of December 28. Heavy shelling kept villagers hunkered down in cellars and vaulted stables for much of the day. Yet despite the preceding barrage, the Germans managed to thwart an attempt by the 9th Armored Division to seize the village and by nightfall that Thursday were still in control of Chenogne.[28]

On Friday morning American armor readied itself for another assault against the unfortunate village. The air force was called in to pave the way because intelligence had identified a large number of tanks belonging to the Führer Begleit Brigade that had just arrived. Fighter-bombers angrily swooped down early in the afternoon. For what seemed an eternity, the aircraft worked the village over with guns roaring, then splattered their targets with incendiaries. The Germans scattered. Civilians huddled inside their shelters. By the time the marauders flashed out of sight, five tanks were ablaze, as were at least eleven of Chenogne's homes.[29]

One of those homes belonged to the Zabus family. Mr. and Mrs. Zabus and their three children—Marie-Josée, Gisèle, and René, aged twelve, ten, and eight, respectively—rushed to join some ten other people determined to make it to Lavaselle, just over a mile west of Chenogne. About halfway into their journey, near the hamlet of Mande-Ste.-Marie, the group emerged from the woods. They had barely begun to traverse the windswept fields when a machine gun opened up on the suspicious line of dark shapes, mowing them all down in long greedy bursts. Mr. Zabus lay still and felt the cold penetrate his skin. Blood oozed from his shoulder and melted a hole in the snow. For a long time he was afraid to move for fear of drawing more fire. Then he finally gathered his courage and groped around to find his family. He located his wife only to find she stared through him. Marie-Josée and Gisèle were dead, too. His youngest child, face as white as the icy crystals touching it, was missing a foot. The mauled stump ended in a giant pool of blood. Mr. Zabus could not immediately tell if his son was alive or not. Five other shapes had disentangled themselves from the carnage. They urged Mr. Zabus to return to Mande-Ste.-Marie for help.

The survivors made it as far as the Mars farm. It was filled with refugees. Tormented by the thought that his son might still be alive, Mr. Zabus rocked back and forth, begging for help. A couple of volunteers attempted to reach the scene but were driven back by a hail of fire and German soldiers ordering them out of sight. The following day, American troops near Mande-Ste.-Marie stumbled across the snow-shrouded bodies of eleven civilians. Only one of them was still alive. It was not eight-year-old René Zabus, but fifty-year-old Charles Pinsch. He was rushed to a hospital in Arlon but could not be saved.[30]

Close scrutiny of the military situation near Mande-Ste.-Marie that Friday, December 29, makes it almost certain that the refugees from Chenogne fell victim to bullets from an American machine gun. Still, some of the survivors would forever insist that they were shot at from the German side. But, then again, how could they ever have believed that eleven innocents were mistaken for the enemy by those who had come to set them free? To have accepted that would merely have heaped trauma upon trauma.[31]

As the corridor was being widened, some of the troops and inhabitants inside Bastogne could at last be evacuated. Some 260 of the worst American wounded were rushed out of Bastogne the same night the siege was lifted. The first civilian casualties were whisked away by American ambulances early the following day. That day groups of

Bastognards risked squeezing through the narrow corridor along the highway to Neufchâteau. Toward the evening many of them were brushing past the battle for Sibret. On Thursday, December 28, a tall American officer halted his jeep at the Institute of Notre Dame. He asked to see Madeleine and Gisèle Logelin and showed the girls a note. In it their father told them that their family in Florenville, a town on the Belgian-French border astride the Bastogne-Neufchâteau highway, was safe and well. The officer told the girls that he had come to take them home. They were the first of the boarding school's pupils to be reunited with their parents since the beginning of the siege.[32]

3 On Friday word had spread in Bastogne that the entire population was going to be evacuated. The girls at the Institute of Notre Dame rejoiced when they learned that American trucks were coming to take them out first. Several of them were ill and running a fever; all of them desperately wanted to be back with their families. By dusk, however, no vehicles had shown up. Immensely disappointed, the girls once again settled down for an uncomfortable night in their school's underground corridors.[33]

The previous two nights had been relatively quiet inside the town and, with the siege lifted since Tuesday, the Bastognards did not expect darkness to be much different that Friday, December 29. But early in the evening a strange hum approached Bastogne from the sky as it had done on Christmas Eve. Flares again bathed the streets in a stunningly bright light. Muscles tensed as the whistle of the first bombs pierced the air. Seconds later deafening roars shook the town. Fires ignited in several places. They formed enticing beacons for the three German raids that were to follow before dawn. The air attack was far heavier than that of Christmas Eve. When morning came, entire blocks were ablaze across town. Some one hundred houses had collapsed or were about to crumble. In the rue du Sablon a bomb had hit the command post of the 10th Armored Division, killing five officers. That few, if any, civilians were seriously harmed in what was Bastogne's worst punishment from the air was nothing short of a miracle.[34]

But many of the townspeople reasoned that their luck might run out if they stayed longer. On the morning of December 30, between 1,500 and 2,000 terrorized civilians pushed through Bastogne's southern gate and onto the highway to Neufchâteau. Most were on foot. Only a few had loaded a bicycle or horse-drawn cart or had bothered to pack at all. At a frighteningly short distance to their right, the front line meandered along the route of escape for five excruciating miles. People walked as fast as they could. Some went too fast, collapsed, and had to be picked up by American ambulances. In the midst of battle there were few American vehicles available to speed up the evacuation. Nevertheless, on Sunday evening, December 31, two trucks managed to whisk to safety a group of thirty boarding-school girls, escorted by several lay teachers and Sister Raphaël. By that time most of Bastogne's refugees had arrived safely at Neufchâteau and other peaceful havens nearby.[35]

That the refugees made it to these safe havens was yet another miracle. For at dawn on December 30, German troops launched a coordinated attack against the American corridor into Bastogne. The air raids against Bastogne the previous night had been ordered to support the hammer blows that were to follow on the ground from both easterly and westerly directions. On the same morning that von Manteuffel wanted his troops to sever the corridor, however, Patton had his divisions catapult themselves from the area for a major attack. They were to swing around Bastogne on both sides and claw deeper into the southern flank of the German bulge. In Saturday's early-morning fog, the attacking armies thus clashed head-on west and east of the corridor. The effects were horrendous for soldiers and civilians alike.[36]

In the corridor's western shoulder it was again Chenogne that became the focal point of the battle. Despite the support from fighter-bombers, soldiers of the 9th Armored Division had failed to capture Chenogne the previous day. Now a large number of the Führer Begleit Brigade's surviving tanks, supported by Panzergrenadiers and Volksgrenadiers, tried to break out of the village in an effort to reach Sibret and cut the Neufchâteau highway. Inexperienced troops of the 11th Armored Division were rushed in to help stop them.

The battle for Chenogne would rage for four long days. The village changed hands so many times that the inhabitants lost count. Close to fifty people hid in a stable of reinforced concrete that was part of the Mars farm at Mande-Ste.-Marie, about half a mile from Chenogne. Among them were Mr. Zabus and other survivors of the machine-gun massacre of December 29. Several of them were badly wounded, and they were soon joined by half a dozen other unfortunates, among them Ernest Mayon, with fragments of a shell in his back, and Mrs. Marthus, her eye sliced by shrapnel. Medics from neither army were able to stay long enough to offer much help. But Germans did manage to transport Raymond Meunier to a hospital after an explosion hurt his spine, and GIs during another assault took his brother, André, to treat his frozen feet.

Eighty other civilians had found refuge in the cellar of the Burnotte farm inside Chenogne. They had to make room for a rapidly increasing number of wounded soldiers. On Sunday, December 31, word reached the villagers that Maria Caprasse and Catherine Hubermont, two of Chenogne's young women, had perished in the battle. People considered the sad news listlessly. Those whose stomachs still accepted food downed a gruel of boiled milk and potatoes. To quell their thirst, they scooped snow and let it melt in their parched mouths.[37]

At the first dawn of the new year, thirteen artillery battalions laid down a massive barrage on Chenogne; then troops of the 11th Armored Division launched what would be the decisive assault on the village. For the civilians inside the Burnotte cellar the situation became untenable. Dozens of German soldiers had barged into their cellar to escape the fiery barrage. The Americans were fighting their way into Chenogne house by house. Infantrymen aimed grenades at the Burnotte farm. They soon stepped aside to let a tank do the job. Within minutes the Sherman had set fire to the building. Acrid smoke billowed into the cellar in ever thicker waves. People stumbled, coughed, pushed each other. Some villagers snapped and yelled at the Germans, accusing them of preferring the sacrifice of civilians over surrender.

At last the trapped Germans decided to give up. A jumble of soldiers and civilians pushed toward the front door. A German waved a white flag and stepped into the cold. Soldiers of the 11th Armored Division immediately mowed him down. What happened next is not entirely clear. GIs apparently continued to pick off enemy soldiers as they emerged from the Burnotte farm trying to surrender. The civilians were allowed to escape from the farm unharmed. Those who came through the front door were herded away in the direction of Sibret. Some fled from the back of the farm and hurried to the village of Poisson-Moulin. Mr. Moncousin did not know that his daughter was among the latter. He kept waiting for her until American soldiers forced him to join ten German prisoners and lined them up not far from the Burnotte farm. Sensing trouble, Mr. Moncousin quickly showed the Americans his identity card. The reflex saved him his life. The GIs told him to leave for Sibret right away. He had not gone far when he heard shots fired near the Burnotte farm. He turned around just in time to see the prisoners fold and hit the snow.[38]

Mopping up Chenogne continued for most of the next day. The mayor was the first to return on January 3. He found thirty-one of the village's thirty-two houses in ruins and the carcasses of three hundred cattle. In a meadow in front of the Burnotte farm he came across a neat row of what he claimed to be the corpses of twenty-one German soldiers. The total number of prisoners killed at Chenogne on New Year's Day is impossible to establish. Some American soldiers have claimed that there were as many as sixty. What is clear is that word had been passed down during the final assault on Chenogne not to take prisoners and that the Americans in this tiny Ardennes village had committed a serious crime of war.[39]

While men of the 11th Armored Division engaged the Germans at Chenogne on December 30, comrades on their left pushed on to Lavaselle and in the afternoon clashed with more troops of the Führer Begleit Brigade in the village of Houmont. The battle for the tiny farming community lasted until evening. The Americans responded to the stubborn German defense with an increasingly blind fury that failed to distinguish between the enemy and the civilians in their path. Artillery and tank fire set some fifteen farms ablaze. Two villagers climbed to roof of the Poncin farm in a desperate effort to put out the flames. A Sherman tank immediately opened fire on them. The civilians slid to the ground and ran for cover. A burst from the tank's machine gun shredded Emile Closquet's knee. Villagers dragged the man to the nearest cellar. By the time the Americans were able to look at his leg, all they could do was amputate it above the knee.[40]

One of the farms on fire in Houmont was that of the Zabus family. From it poured several people who failed to find a safer haven than the nearby barn. Among the unfortunates in the flimsy shed were seventy-year-old Joseph Châlon, seven members of his family, and their domestic help, Pierre Engelmann. They had barely escaped from battle and their own burning farm the previous day in Chenogne. For the traumatized family to have to go through it all once again proved to be too much. In a fit of terror they darted from the barn, not knowing where to go. For a few moments they remained invisible in the billowing smoke. Then they tore loose from the cloaking cloud. American machine gunners probably mistook them for soldiers trying to escape battle. A hail of bullets was sent their way. Of the nine escapees only one managed to drag himself back to the people who had remained in the shed. "They are all dead," he murmured in disbelief. "They" were Joseph Châlon, his three daughters, three grandchildren, and Pierre Engelmann.[41]

The GIs in Houmont were in a vicious mood. They fired at cellars showing as much as the flicker of a candle. They weaved in and out of shelters, shining torches on the refugees' faces, brusquely checking and rechecking identities. The Americans finally evacuated the entire village during the first days of the new year; in part because it was a shambles, but also because they distrusted the presence of noncombatants. Father Lallemant, the village priest, stayed behind for a few days to watch over the civilian wounded who remained to be picked up. All the while suspicious American guards escorted him wherever he went.[42]

On the other side of the corridor, two German divisions that had newly arrived at Bastogne were thrown against the Arlon highway. One was the 167th Volksgrenadier Division, which had been rebuilt with Luftwaffe replacements after its near destruction on the eastern front. This hybrid outfit operated in tandem with the 1st SS Panzer Division, or rather what remained of it after its furious struggle in the Bulge's northern shoulder. The villages and dense forests that formed the scene for the German attack against the corridor's east flank were punished with atrocious shelling from both sides. Of the four hundred villagers in the Lutrebois-Lutremange-Villers triangle, an estimated thirty perished.[43]

The Germans had been ordered to sever Bastogne's vital artery at all costs, and civilians who stood in their way could count on being dealt with swiftly. On the day of the attack, December 30, Auguste Forman, one of Lutremange's inhabitants who had taken to the woods the day after Christmas, slipped back to his village, probably in search of food. He stumbled into some German soldiers who took him for a spy. The young man had no papers to show; he had left them with his mother in the forest. The Germans shot him on the spot. Revenge for yet another failed effort to break through is all that can be found to have motivated an SS lieutenant at a house in Lutrebois when on January 1 with his weapon he motioned two men in their thirties to step outside. Ernest Zévenne bolted at the first opportunity. His ears rang with the shot that killed his friend Marcel Colson.[44]

Ground troops hated to be troubled by civilians in the midst of combat and did what they could to have them out of the way as soon as possible. In some places east of the corridor, German soldiers personally escorted groups of civilians on forced marches away from the combat zone. They rounded up villagers in the woods near Lutremange, for example, and took them across the border with Luxembourg. The march was so grueling that people searched the pockets of dead soldiers for food and even drank greedily from streams exuding the smell of phosphorus, which had seeped from incendiary shells.[45]

One of the most dramatic evacuations in the area took place at Villers-la-Bonne-Eau. By January 1 it was clear that the attempt to cut the corridor had failed. It left the Germans frustrated and dejected. It also made them dangerous and unpredictable. On New Year's Day the occupiers barked at the able-bodied men of Villers to abandon the cellars and seek shelter elsewhere. Two days later, three Germans at gunpoint plucked some thirty of the remaining civilians from their shelters. The soldiers were frantic and prickly. First they wanted the civilians to dig them some kind of air-raid shelter at the edge of a wood. Then they suddenly abandoned the project. They herded the villagers together and pushed off in the direction of Luxembourg.

The ragtag column was a sorry sight. At its head the Germans put an older woman, Marie Francis, who was made to display a white flag. Behind her, elderly, women, and children trudged through the deep snow. The end of the plodding line was formed by those members of the Garcia family who had survived the vicious shell blast on December 27. Mr. and Mrs. Garcia, badly injured themselves, tried to look after their baby daughter, who suffered from meningitis, as well as their youngest son, who had part of his arm ripped off. Ten-year-old Jean was unharmed and did his best to support his nine-year-older sister, Marie. A punctured lung prevented the girl from walking fast, and each time she heaved her chest, blood seeped through the bandage. She had lost her shoes and, half-shuffling, half-dragged, struggled to keep up with the rest, her frozen feet without feeling.

The villagers from Villers were hostages more than evacuees. Their German guards showed no compassion. They pushed the unfortunates with their machine guns and dealt blows whenever the pace slackened. On their way out of Tarchamps, the hostages found some potatoes and ate them raw, their first food in two days. The group was abandoned at the Luxembourg village of Derenbach, some nine miles northeast of Villers. There one of them was killed in an Allied air raid. German troops ordered them to move on to nearby Oberwampach, where the villagers begged some meat from soldiers who were cutting up a cow, but the stonehearted Germans chased them away. Mrs. Garcia did not survive the time at Oberwampach. Her daughter, Marie, died in an American hospital not long after the liberation. A similar fate befell the group's five-year-old Denise Lafontaine.[46]

As the German attack against the corridor petered out, American troops hurried to evacuate more civilians. The inhabitants of Lutrebois under the cover of darkness on January 5 slid toward the Losange wood in groups of five. There, as promised by an American officer earlier that day, three trucks were waiting to take them away from the front line. By that time the Americans had rushed more people out of Bastogne, too. Convoys had arrived on January 2 and 3 to pick up the town's elderly and sick. A jeep had whisked away at least one pregnant woman. Trucks also took to safety all of the Institute of Notre Dame's remaining pupils and most of its sisters. On January 3, Bernadette Dumont, one of the boarding-school girls, watched the desolation to her left as their icy truck rolled down the highway to Arlon. "A poor man in the snow, not far from a half-demolished house," she observed, "watches over some 50 cows tearing bark from shredded trees." Her blank eyes remained fixed on the scene of misery until it receded into a gray blur.[47]

4 On the day that the Americans drove Bernadette Dumont and her fellow pupils southward, more misery descended on Bastogne from the north. On orders from Hitler, von Manteuffel gathered several divisions for what was to be a final and desperate attempt to dislodge the Americans from the crucial town. The 12th SS Panzer Division had been channeled southward to launch the key attack from Bourcy in the direction of Mageret and Bizory.

These villages, northeast of Bastogne, had already witnessed much fighting in the past couple of days as the 6th Armored Division had just come to wrest them from the Germans. American aircraft and artillery had plowed the area with explosives. Napalm bombs and phosphorus shells had set fire to building after building. People in Horritine had fled to the solid cellars of the village tannery. Adults and children in Michamps had formed chains to try and save their farms with the trickle of water from buckets. A shell had killed a one-year-old child in the arms of his father just hours before the Ameri-

cans captured Neffe. Also in this area, GIs struck the civilians as completely different soldiers from those before the German offensive.
Combat soldiers who entered Neffe on the last day of 1944 looked
menacing and testy. They brusquely frisked the civilians and forced
some to lead the way in house searches. Only when no more Germans
could be found did the GIs lighten up.[48]

German morale had begun to crack under the relentless American pressure. Villagers in a cellar in Oubourcy on January 2 saw how
an officer had to threaten seven soldiers with his pistol to make them
join the fight outside. But the German mood changed overnight with
the arrival of what was left of the 12th SS Panzer Division. Despite
having been mauled in the northern shoulder, Hitler's callous elite
troops continued to believe they could make the battle go their way.
For a while at least, it seemed they were succeeding. On January 3,
the first day of the German attack and the day after the Americans
had liberated the village, SS troops recaptured Michamps. They introduced themselves to the civilians as "those who never withdraw."[49]

What the new arrivals lacked in food and equipment, they made
up for in arrogance and brutality. In Oubourcy's Dutroux farm, SS
soldiers pillaged, burned family papers on the wooden floors, and
destroyed religious images. They intercepted a villager on her way
back from the stables with fresh milk and took their share without
listening to the woman's story about eight needy children down in
the vaulted cellar. People in the charred ruins of Arloncourt were
dirty, lice-ridden, and suffering from diarrhea. They were also hungry, as most potatoes had either frozen or burned. The SS did not
care. One day they requisitioned the men to dig trenches. The next
they made them replace their horses and had them pull cords attached to ammunition wagons. In their staging area at Bourcy, SS
troopers with their pistols killed the last chickens, hogs, and cattle
that remained on the farms. Villagers asked the Wehrmacht to intervene, but the soldiers in gray readily admitted they were afraid to
do so. Each evening in the cellar of the Maquet farm, adults and
children tried to still their hunger, thaw their insides, and calm their
nerves all at once by downing a small ration of warm wine spiked
with a pinch of sugar.[50]

Control over the villages northeast of Bastogne remained shaky
for the 12th SS Panzer Division. Oubourcy had been captured from
the Wehrmacht by GIs of the 6th Armored Division in the afternoon

of January 2, only to be retaken by spearheads of the SS that evening. But the SS troopers realized that while their outfit had been terribly weakened, American armor was bound to hit back with its full weight. The prospect left the SS tense and edgy. It also made them exceedingly suspicious of the civilians in Oubourcy. For reasons that are not clear, SS soldiers on January 3 rounded up a number of civilians for interrogation. One of them was Ernest Charneux, a refugee from Arloncourt, who was holding his granddaughter when arrested. No one knows what the SS accused him of, but Mr. Charneux suddenly broke free from his interrogators, fled into a nearby house where he put down his grandchild, and then dashed into the fields leading to Arloncourt. He had not gotten far when the SS shot him.[51]

Already on January 4, the second day of the attack, it was clear that the Germans were getting nowhere from the north either. Bracing for the American counterattack that was bound to come, the SS troops hastily tried to get as many civilians as possible out of their way before the clash. They ordered the inhabitants of Oubourcy and Horritine to leave immediately for Michamps. Two days later, on January 6, the Germans wanted the civilians to move even farther back: they now flushed everyone from the shelters in Michamps and barked at them to head for Bourcy. In twos the people in a long line snaked out of Michamps and into the glacial cold. The thunder of artillery and tanks echoed from all sides. Mr. Widart in a reflex had thrown the family's silverware in some of their bags. Now, out on the battlefield, it seemed a ridiculous thing to have brought and he abandoned the superfluous weight behind a tomb at the village cemetery. By the time the refugees began to trickle into Bourcy, the village lay hidden in stygian darkness. The oldest people, slowed by exhaustion, did not arrive until the next morning.[52]

Meanwhile, at the SS division's rear, the Gestapo, seemingly unfazed by the fact that the tide was turning against them at Bastogne, calmly bided their time, like spiders waiting for prey to hit their web. Their vicious trap snagged thirty-year-old Fernand Maquet as soon as he entered Bourcy on the evening of January 6. He had fled with the other young men of the village early during the offensive. But he had heard of the havoc Allied bombs had wrought on Bourcy and wanted to check on his parents. Two Gestapo agents snatched him away early the following morning. They dragged him to their lair, where they questioned him between beatings. Before the day was over, Fernand Maquet lay dead in a meadow between presbytery and cemetery. His back and neck were specked with scarlet, fang-like holes.[53]

On the 12th SS Panzer Division's right, the 340th Volksgrenadier Division had gotten as far as Foy along the highway from Liège before grinding to a halt. Northwest of Bastogne, the 3rd and 15th Panzergrenadier Divisions, battered in the Vosges and around Aachen and never fully refitted, were having no more luck than their Volksgrenadier and SS brethren. It was not for want of trying. Battle was most ferocious in the villages near the highway to Marche. Many soldiers on both sides paid with their lives for possession of the road. But civilians were charged a heavy toll as well. That was particularly true in Flamierge, just north of the highway. Between January 4 and 8 the village changed hands at least six times. During a lull in the fighting on January 5, nine civilians, most of them refugees from Mande-St.-Etienne, hurried up from the cellar of the Bever farm. Frozen to the bone, they got the stove going and put their numb feet against its hot metal sides. It was then that another barrage took the village by surprise. A shell dropped through the roof of the farm, landing virtually on top of the kitchen stove. Seven people were killed instantly. The other two were horribly wounded. One of them was thirty-eight-year-old Marie Collard. The blast had ripped off one of her stockinged feet. There was nothing the other civilians could do but watch her bleed to death.[54]

Though the final assault against Bastogne received no support from the Luftwaffe, the number of German shells reaching the town increased again for a short while. Most of them were fired by field guns to the north, but each afternoon a giant railroad gun emerged from a tunnel at Schimpach in Luxembourg and joined the deadly chorus by hurling a couple of heavy-caliber projectiles onto Bastogne across a distance of some seven miles. Relatively few civilians inside Bastogne had fallen victim to bombs and shells during the battle because they had remained hidden in the vaulted cellars. But with the siege lifted for over a week and discipline relaxed, enemy artillery managed to sneak up on its prey a few more times. Christiane Viroux on January 5 volunteered to fetch some medicines from a nearby pharmacy for an elderly lady in one of the collective shelters. In the small rue St.-Pierre, the thirteen-year-old ran into Jeanny Duteille. Much had happened since they had last seen each other, and the teenaged girls lingered for a chat. A terrible explosion wiped away the conversation, flinging both girls into a store's windowpane. Jeanny was left dazed with bruises and scratches. But her friend had incurred a severe head wound. American medics rushed Christiane to a field hospital in Remoifosse. By the time her alarmed parents arrived in the village, they were told their daughter had been hurried to a hospital in Virton. The girl would die there before the day was over. She might have been Bastogne's last civilian casualty had not Emile Maron three days later decided to snatch some air outside the Institute of Notre Dame. A shell greedily swallowed the unsuspecting fifty-six-year-old together with three American soldiers.[55]

5 By January 8, barely five days after it had started, the final German push against Bastogne had fizzled out. That same day Hitler at last agreed to a limited withdrawal from the tip of the Bulge to a line anchored on a point some five miles west of Houffalize. It was the first reluctant admission by Hitler that the counteroffensive in the Ardennes had failed.[56]

Patton relaunched the offensive from around Bastogne with his III and VIII Corps on January 9. One of the units that began battering its way northward that day was the 705th Tank Destroyer Battalion. One of its soldiers was Gaëtan Delecaut. He was a rather awkward GI. Gaëtan spoke little if any English for he was not from Boston or Seattle or Columbus, Ohio, but from Brussels. His helmet and uniform were ridiculously ill-fitting, but that could not be helped for an eleven-year-old.

Gaëtan's parents had decided to send him to the peace and calm of the Ardennes after a V1 had killed his cousin early in December. The German counteroffensive had caught the boy by surprise at Monaville, some three miles north of Bastogne. During the final assault from the north early in January, the 9th SS Panzer Division had joined the four other divisions and launched itself at Monaville and Longchamps. In the melee that followed, Gaëtan had become separated from the other civilians; an explosion had erased the memory of who he was; and American soldiers had decided to adopt him. They had even come up with a new name for the lost son: Marcus January.

When the combat soldiers were told to move out in a hurry on January 9, they could not find it in their hearts to leave the boy behind. They took their adoptive comrade with them, back through the Ardennes, and all the way into Germany. They made sure he received a weapon, warm clothing, and plenty of food. For Gaëtan's real parents the nightmare that had started in Bastogne on December 16, 1944, would last until the summer of 1945. Only then did they learn that their son was still alive and that he was patiently awaiting demobilization in his unit's camp in France.[57]

Chapter 13

Eliminating the Bulge

"It was like the end of the world."

The attack that Patton's troops set in motion from the south on January 9, dragging child-soldier Gaëtan Delecaut along, was part of a much broader, carefully coordinated action against the enemy bulge in American lines. If until early January the battle in the Ardennes was the German offensive phase, the Allied offensive phase started in earnest on Wednesday, January 3, with simultaneous attacks from the north and the west launched first. The reduction of the German salient would take the better part of that frigid month, official Allied histories not declaring the Battle of the Bulge over until January 28, 1945.[1]

The flattening of the Bulge was at least as grim as the events that had hammered the salient into being. In terrible winter weather that at times reached blizzard conditions, German troops, though increasingly demoralized, slowly and expertly fell back to the West Wall, resisting every step of the way with a tenacity that on occasion "defied explanation." Trapped near vital crossroads and inside villages and towns that the opposing troops coveted for their warmth as much as anything else, the hapless civilians of Belgium and Luxembourg in January 1945 suffered at least as much as the soldiers.[2]

1 The First Army was to attack from the north to link up at Houffalize with Patton's Third Army from the south. The burden of that attack fell on the shoulders of the VII Corps. It was to push in a southeasterly direction between the Ourthe and Lienne rivers with five divisions, a cavalry group, and multiple artillery units— a total of close to one hundred thousand troops. Their main axis of advance was the highway from Liège, which, at Baraque de Fraiture,

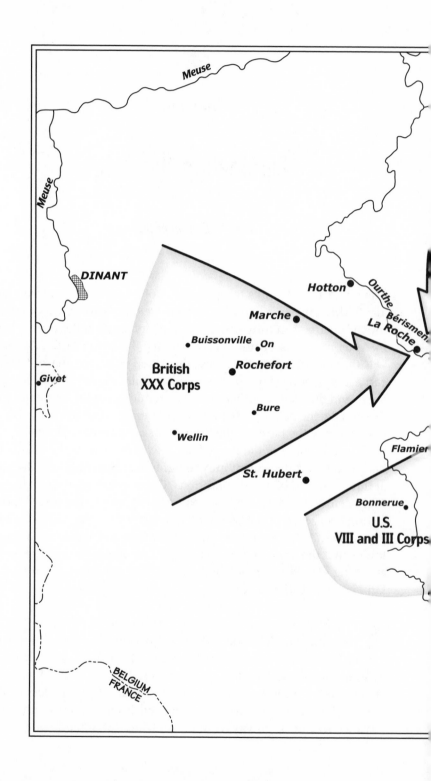

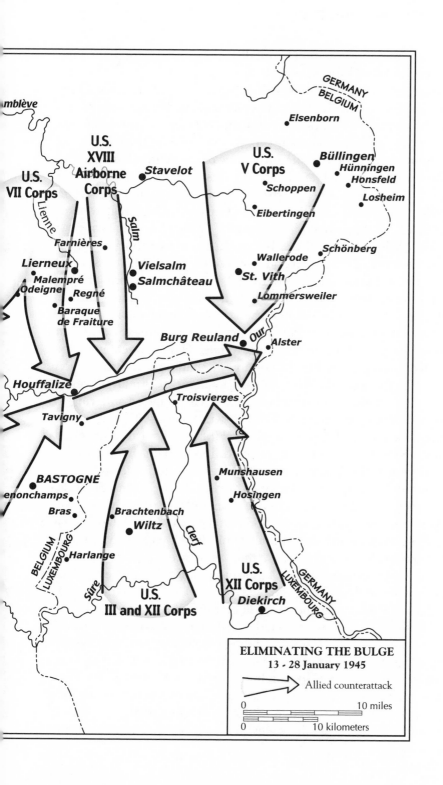

mblève

GERMANY
BELGIUM

Elsenborn

U.S.
XVIII
Airborne
Corps

Stavelot

U.S.
V Corps

Büllingen
Hünningen
Honsfeld

U.S.
VII Corps

Schoppen

Losheim

Lienne

Salm

Eibertingen

Farnières

Schönberg

Lierneux
Malempré
Odeigne

Regné

Vielsalm
Salmchâteau

Wallerode
St. Vith

Baraque
de Fraiture

Lommersweiler

Burg Reuland

Our

Alster

Houffalize

Troisvierges

Tavigny

Munshausen

BASTOGNE
enonchamps
Bras

Hosingen

Brachtenbach
Wiltz

Clerf

BELGIUM
LUXEMBOURG

Harlange

U.S.
XII Corps

GERMANY
LUXEMBOURG

Sûre

U.S.
III and XII Corps

Diekirch

ELIMINATING THE BULGE
13 - 28 January 1945

Allied counterattack

0   10 miles

0   10 kilometers

some nine miles northwest of Houffalize, intersected the equally vital east-west highway from Salmchâteau to La Roche.

Several days before the jump-off on January 3, artillery began blasting the 2nd SS Panzer Division and two Volksgrenadier divisions standing in the way of the VII Corps. In the hamlet of Florêt, a hellish barrage on Saturday, December 30, finally made the nerves of the inhabitants snap. Some forty people poured from one of the main cellars and ran for the woods. It was a fateful decision. First, American shells rained down on them. Next, when, in the dark, they tried to make it back to their village with the casualties, nervous German soldiers began shooting at anything that moved in the spooky light of burning farms. At least five civilians were killed: a boy and a girl of five and eight years old, two brothers of nineteen and twenty-one years old, and a forty-eight-year-old mother of nine children. Later that night, the Germans ordered the villagers to head for safety in Lansevin, a village farther south. Some of the badly wounded had to be left behind. One of them, an elderly man, would succumb to his injuries the next day. From Lansevin people set out for Lierneux to fetch civilian doctors for the wounded among them. But the community had none to spare. Even then one of the wounded men refused to allow a German officer to take him to a military hospital farther east. He preferred suffering to the uncertain fate of being whisked away to enemy soil.

Soldiers of the 3rd Armored and 83rd Infantry Divisions liberated the ravaged Florêt without too much additional damage on January 3, the first day of the Allied counteroffensive. They immediately rushed the wounded to hospitals as far away as Huy, Antwerp, and Brussels, where doctors could not prevent one more villager from dying.[3]

The task force that captured Florêt on the extreme left flank of the VII Corps crawled south along the left bank of the Lienne with Lierneux as its objective. Following fierce German resistance, it captured Baneux late in the afternoon of January 4, finding a handful of the less than a dozen homes on fire. The next day Jevigné fell to the Americans, but the villagers were made uneasy by liberators who appeared to be "in a state of shock" and were "not kind." As the GIs approached Lierneux, the Germans in some of the surrounding hamlets resisted with devastating effect. In the battle for La Vaux, for example, a dozen or so of the sixteen homes went up in flames. Then, on January 6, the Germans abandoned Lierneux, allowing the task forces in the Lienne Valley to seize their main objective without much of a fight.[4]

Confusion reigned in the valley in the days following the second liberation. American ambulances took care to rush civilian casualties to hospitals but often did so without informing their families of their destination. In some cases it took anxious relatives weeks of frantic inquiries before they learned where the patients were being treated and how they were doing. As well as entire villages, the Americans decided to evacuate Lierneux's mental institution, whose fragile patients had suffered more than anyone from the nerve-racking shelling and bombing. Packed with 190 male patients, one convoy of army trucks headed for the peace and security of an institution in Tournai, while another set off with 160 women to Munsterbilzen. Even now the madness of war managed to catch up with the patients. During a stop in a suburb of Charleroi, civilians mistook the men huddling together for warmth in the backs of the trucks for German POWs. Seething with anger, people thronged the vehicles, hurling insults and trash at the cringing shapes.[5]

Those civilians in the valley who were authorized to remain in their homes soon discovered that having combat soldiers for guests was no pleasure, even if they were allies. Though the GIs were generous with food, they behaved "not always very correct" and thought nothing, for example, of throwing chairs, tables, and cupboards out of the windows for firewood or even of answering the calls of nature in the relative warmth of the rooms.[6]

During the first day of the offensive, on the right of the Americans in the Lienne Valley, another task force composed of men from the 3rd Armored and 83rd Infantry Divisions engaged in a bitter fight for Malempré with troops of the 12th Volksgrenadier Division just east of the Liège-Houffalize highway. The fiery morning barrage that preceded the American attack shook the village like an earthquake. In one of the cellars some thirty ashen civilians were holding on to each other. As the shelling intensified at least as many Volksgrenadiers joined them. Packed together, the air growing foul, the strain became unbearable. Then, suddenly, a German soldier burst into the cellar crying. Two of his comrades had just been killed outside. He pulled a pistol, put it against his head and, in the middle of the crowd, shot himself. People hid their faces, praying they might be allowed to forget the horrifying scene.

When the GIs finally stormed the village, the Germans made them fight for every building. In at least one case the Americans bluntly responded to the enemy's stubborn refusal to abandon a house by setting it on fire. As soon as the battle died down late in the afternoon, nervous and exhausted GIs barked at the civilians to hurry and come out of their shelters. Most of them were crying when they emerged. They would have been hard put to tell if it was from fear or relief. Nothing much remained of Malempré at the end of the day. The fury unleashed by SS troops on Christmas Eve, the unforgiving shelling by the Allies, and the battle for recapture earlier that day had caused terrible damage. Sixty-nine of the village's 74 houses were destroyed, the village church had been ripped apart by at least seven shells, and the carcasses of 13 horses and 116 cows lay spread about.[7]

Two days later, the Germans in Regné, a village on the La Roche–Salmchâteau highway under increasing American artillery fire, forced several farmers to evacuate to Hébronval. Later that day, however, sixty-six-year-old Léocadie Laurent and her sister slipped away to try to reach their farm and care for the animals. They had not gone more than two hundred yards when an exploding shell slammed them to the frozen ground. By the time her sister had recovered and returned with help, German soldiers were already caring for Léocadie. But there was nothing they could do to help her live another day.[8]

GIs recaptured Fraiture on January 6, encountering only one civilian, an elderly person who had been allowed to stay behind when the Germans had ordered the villagers to evacuate to Baclain four days earlier. The battle for Regné the following day was brutal, leaving most of the village charred and ruined. The villagers here paid a heavy price for not having been evacuated: six corpses had to be lowered into makeshift coffins that were stored in the icy church until the end of the battle.

That same day, from Regné the Americans immediately pushed on to Hébronval along the highway to Salmchâteau. On their farm between both villages, sixty-three-year-old Mr. Thérer and his daughter made the mistake of leaving their underground shelter to have a quick peek from their living room to see what was going on. At the exact moment that they opened the front door an American shell blast violently threw them back. Joseph Thérer was bleeding profusely from multiple wounds. His twenty-three-year-old daughter, only slightly injured herself, frantically attempted to stem the flow of blood with improvised tourniquets. A German soldier needed all his powers of persuasion to convince her that her father was dead. The next day, with Hébronval firmly in the hands of the GIs, Mr. Thérer's coffin was placed in the church next to that of Léocadie Laurent.[9]

American combat troops in and around Malempré parted with whatever they could spare to aid the civilians. They handed out chocolate and rations while mobile canteens arrived to distribute hot soup. In some places the GIs even provided the inhabitants with overshoes and socks. Troops who had captured some thirty horses from the Germans at Fraiture made sure they went to the local farmers. But the Americans themselves lacked sufficient heat and systematically smashed any furniture made of wood to feed their fires and keep warm. It bothered the villagers that the soldiers seemed to derive pleasure from the destruction.[10]

The pain and destruction wrought by the Germans, however, was infinitely worse, even as they withdrew. On January 10, vengeful German guns fired shells at the newly liberated village of Regné, setting fire to the Lambert farm. Marie-Louise Lambert and her parents darted to the stables to untie the bellowing cattle. On their way back, a violent explosion blew the earth out from under their feet. Marie-Louise's father, hit in the head, was dead in an instant. Her mother, bleeding from a nasty abdominal wound, lived just long enough to lift her head and see what had happened to her husband. Two GIs managed to drag the corpses to a nearby farm. But they failed to console twenty-five-year-old Marie-Louise.

On January 13 a wagon slowly rumbled along the road from Hébronval. On it rested the coffins with the remains of Mr. Thérer and Mrs. Laurent. The wagon halted at Regné, where people gathered and respectfully unloaded the coffins. They put them next to those in the church that held Marie-Louise's parents and the six other civilian victims awaiting a final resting place.[11]

At the start of the new year, troops from the 2nd Armored and 84th Infantry Divisions on the other side of the Liège-Houffalize highway were also readying themselves for the attack in the direction of the vital road from La Roche to Salmchâteau. Closest to the Liège-Houffalize highway, Task Force Disney was to capture Odeigne, a small village having the misfortune of being located on a crucial knot of secondary roads. The shelling of Odeigne that began on the night of January 2 was in proportion to the village's military importance. On Wednesday the barrage continued so ferociously that people were unable to leave their cellars to get food and water. In some shelters desperate villagers agreed to draw straws to decide who would venture outside to fill buckets with snow. The following night the Germans chased several families from their cellars and ordered them to head south to the village of Les Tailles. Hampered by the cold and snow, terrorized by explosions and shooting in the pitch dark, the group of twenty people, among them many elderly and a three-month-old baby, struggled for five hours to cover the six miles of forest roads to the rear.

They were the lucky ones. Just before dawn on Thursday a shell pierced the cellar of Prosper Thomas and tore it apart. Four villagers were killed instantly, three others were injured so badly they would not live to see the second liberation. The dawn slaughter was immediately followed by an American attack. The Germans responded by getting the civilians out of their way and herding close to one hundred people into a single village stable. By nightfall the GIs were in control of the lower part of Odeigne. Savage house-to-house combat continued until the Americans took the rest of the village around noon the following day. The last Germans to hold out hid in the church tower. Five of them were killed while resisting. A sixth soldier surrendered. His captors dragged him to the nearby cemetery and shot him, too.

Once they had calmed down, the Americans agreed to drive a villager with a leg injury to the nearest hospital. There was nothing, however, that they could do for Marie-Thérèse Fagnant, an eighteen-month-old child who was suffering from bronchopneumonia. She would die before the first day of liberation had come to a close. The Americans were determined to get the villagers to safer and healthier environments as soon as possible. In the next few days they brought in trucks and evacuated many of Odeigne's inhabitants to places like Melreux, Barvaux, and Comblain.[12]

A week after the jump-off, GIs of the 84th Infantry Division finally linked up with soldiers from the British 51st Division at La Roche, some eight miles south of the line of departure. That same day American infantry and armor captured Samrée, a key village located on the highway from La Roche to Salmchâteau. Even before the Germans lost Samrée, the Americans had begun to spill across the La Roche–Salmchâteau highway farther east. The preparatory shelling there had caused devastation in the tiny communities. American artillery erased a large part of Bihain, including seven houses swallowed by the eerily bright flames of phosphorus. Capricious fate decided that the barrages would take the life of only one civilian in Bihain, while just one shell claimed the lives of many in Baclain. That particular shell on January 9 happened to pierce a stable of the Urbain farm where some twenty civilians were huddling together. The carnage was horrific. Death came almost instantaneously to nine people; two others were pulled from the rubble alive only to die in the following days. At least four of the victims were teenagers. Ironically, all of the eleven casualties were refugees who had hoped to outrun danger. Eight of them were evacuees from Fraiture; the three others had come from as far away as Vielsalm and Luxembourg.[13]

The particularly ferocious shelling in this area was part of the attempt to dislodge remnants of the 2nd SS Panzer Division. That outfit had withdrawn from the Baraque de Fraiture crossroads and was now engaged in a tenacious rearguard defense. The arrival of these callous troops brought the civilians still more hardship. The Volksgrenadiers who had been there before the *Waffen* SS had shown themselves so weary and inoffensive that some of Sterpigny's inhabitants had voluntarily shared some of their soup with the men. Now, however, frustrated young SS troopers were stealing animals and demanding food at gunpoint. But American artillery dealt harshly even with Hitler's most fanatic troops. In a matter of days, many of them were dead or badly mutilated. People in the cellar of Sterpigny's Caprasse farm were horrified by the sounds escaping from the improvised aid station upstairs. "The kitchen," one inhabitant remembered, "was full of dying who cried, screamed, and called for their mothers."[14]

Nevertheless, when on January 15 American troops reached as far as Sterpigny, the SS still managed to put up stiff resistance. By the time the village was firmly in American hands again, the cries from the aid station in the Caprasse farm's kitchen had changed to English and to calls for mothers far away in another country. It was a heavy blow to the civilians to find that battle's unforgiving nature had left some American combat soldiers as callous as the Germans they had just driven out. Inhabitants of Bihain reported the first liberators to be "in a state of extreme agitation." Dirty, disheveled soldiers coldly proceeded to requisition the village's homes, sometimes leaving only one room to an entire family. At the end of the battle for Langlire, too, villagers found the GIs "inflamed." That these soldiers thrashed their furniture to build fires and warm themselves without asking questions, some were willing to accept, heartrending though the destruction was. That some of the liberators also tried to violate their women, however, no one in Langlire could understand or condone. Civilians stealing their first glances at the newly arrived GIs in Taverneux on January 18 later vividly remembered that the soldiers looked "enraged." Hardened and angered by two weeks of ceaseless German resistance, troops from the VII Corps now hovered on the outskirts of Houffalize.[15]

Combat forces in the newly liberated villages to the immediate rear, meanwhile, failed to cope with the urgent demands for medical assistance with which the civilians besieged them. Many wounded needed to be transported to hospitals. And many more, especially the very young and the elderly, suffered from illnesses like croup, diphtheria, and infections of the airways and lungs. Immediately following the liberation of his village on Sunday, January 14, for example, the mayor of Bérismenil made the rounds to see which of his inhabitants needed medical assistance. He counted no fewer than 120 people with serious illnesses in a small village where in the wake of battle there were neither civilian doctors nor supplies of medicine. Overburdened American officers gruffly ignored the mayor's desperate pleas for a military doctor until he began warning them of epidemics that would also hurt their soldiers. Even with help from American medical personnel, however, many of the weakest died from illnesses that had been left to fester for too long. In Odeigne, for example, neither evacuation nor medical assistance could prevent at least one infant and three people older than seventy from dying in the three weeks following eighteen-month-old Marie-Thérèse Fagnant's death on the day of liberation.[16]

Around the turn of the year, troops from the British XXX Corps relieved Americans in the sector between the Meuse and a line running from Hotton to an area near Bure. On January 3 these troops joined the Allied counterattack and, on the right flank of the American VII Corps, began pushing in the German salient's nose.

The line of departure for the 53rd Welsh Division ran from Hotton to Marche. The troops' main objective was La Roche on the Ourthe. In the area of assembly, civilians eyed the newcomers with keen curiosity. At first sight the British struck them as more martial and disciplined than the laid-back and somewhat slouchy Americans. They were also more distant, and officers appeared to be in a different class from the enlisted men. Most remarkable, however, was the parsimony with which they treated their personal equipment, which was strikingly sparse and rudimentary in comparison with that of the Americans. The GIs who had moved out of Bourdon by truck had left sleeping bags and many other items on the sidewalks. The British gladly seized it all before American quartermaster units even had time to arrive. The nuns in Marche's Carmelite convent were flabbergasted to find that all the British soldiers had to keep themselves warm were tin biscuit boxes filled with fuel. They so pitied the new soldiers' "poverty" that they hurried to drag two old stoves from the attic to help make them more comfortable.[17]

The British immediately began to evacuate civilians from key villages in the area like Verdenne, Champlon, and Hollogne. In places like Marche where civilians were allowed to stay, the most urgent need was the removal of mines. The Americans had made liberal use of the devices to defend the town in December, and now they were claiming casualties among civilians and British troops alike. Frozen soil, however, made clearing mines extremely difficult and the job proceeded at an excruciatingly slow pace. The British in some places even had to thaw the soil with hot water to get at the fiendish explosives. In the vicinity of Marche's railway station, exasperated soldiers decided simply to blow up the mines, damaging many houses and angering the inhabitants. But the exigencies of war allowed little room for receptiveness to civilian grievances. The impending offensive, for example, demanded rapid road repairs, and British troops at Verdenne thought nothing of utilizing for that purpose bricks salvaged from wrecked houses that were stacked in neat piles awaiting reconstruction. Moreover, the roads became the almost exclusive property of the military. In places behind the lines as far away as Ciney, British authorities had mayors post warnings that no vehicles could be parked in the roads and that cyclists, pushcarts, and horse-drawn wagons were to keep to the extreme right side. Pedestrians were to stick to the sidewalks at all times.[18]

Shivering troops were also quick to take possession of all homes from which the civilians had fled or been evacuated. In the midst of war's ceaseless destruction they cared little about keeping civilian premises clean and tidy. In living rooms and bedrooms they burned fuel in open canisters blackening the walls with soot. They cut carpets and tacked them to shattered windows. Cans spilling food and juice piled up in corners. By the time British troops left the primary schools of Noiseux, the buildings were thoroughly trashed. Stoves were broken, doors damaged, curtains ripped off, coat hooks torn from the walls. Soldiers had strewn library books and teaching materials about in the snow, "while," according to one municipal report, "smashing them malevolently." Owners of a knife factory in Marche needed days to clean up after the British, risking their lives to do so with grenades, mines, and other explosives that had been left behind in the straw bedding. But not all of the soldiers were inconsiderate about the damage. A group of twelve soldiers left a note in a home in Marche thanking the owner for the use of his place and apologizing for the mess they had made and been unable to clean up. "You know," the note ended, "we are here one moment and somewhere else the next."[19]

On January 3 British troops began their tortuous advance to La Roche through thick snow and savage wind. In Marche the roar of heavy British artillery backing up the infantry sounded even more thunderous than that of the Americans. Awed civilians in Hotton felt the foundations of their homes tremble when the big guns opened up. The merciless blasts of outgoing fire in Noiseux shattered nearly all of the village's windows including those of the church.[20]

By Friday, January 5, the sound of exploding shells inside La Roche had become virtually incessant and fires were raging violently in what remained of the town after the air raids. An estimated seven thousand shells would fall in and around the town before the Allies managed to liberate it again a week later. The barrage did nothing, however, to deter an SS Sonderkommando from going about its gruesome business. During house-to-house identity checks on January 4, they arrested three refugees from St. Vith whom they charged with having been members of the resistance: Lucien Hennes, chief of police; Edgard, his son; and André Fagnoul, his son's friend. The two younger men had also been members of the St. Vith police force. All three had fled on the advice of the Americans, only to get trapped in La Roche. They were taken away never to be seen alive again.

The Germans in La Roche on January 5 set fire to the hôtel Royal, in reprisal for the owner's alleged aid to Communists. More arrests followed two days later. Most were released after tense interrogations, but La Roche's mayor, Jean Orban de Xivry, and two of his nieces were hurried into a car and whisked away in the direction of the Grand Duchy of Luxembourg. The nieces were released after a few days; the mayor did not return from Germany until April. He was much more fortunate than the policemen from St. Vith. Their bodies had been discovered in the woods of Wibrin several weeks after their arrest. The police chief had been severely beaten and then shot in the neck at close range. The other two had been executed in similar fashion.[21]

For the inhabitants of La Roche, Nazi security forces and Allied artillery alike were a source of constant terror. Most of the remaining civilians had withdrawn to the cellars or fled to outlying farms. No fewer than one hundred people, for example, thronged together in two rooms and a stable of the farm of Petit Strument. In the town's dank and dark basements, meanwhile, civilians bunched together covered in blankets and coats. While the women tried to keep the shelters clean and prepare food, men ventured outside in search of firewood, potatoes, flour, and preserving jars. Because the water mains had been ruptured almost everywhere, people turned to the Ourthe for drinking water, but this was heavily polluted by filth and debris. Hunger made people slaughter even cows wounded by shelling and contaminated with phosphorus. Dysentery became so rampant that people were soon tearing paper from the walls in desperate efforts to keep clean. A town doctor as well as a local member of the Red Cross went from shelter to shelter to provide what little aid they could to the ill and wounded. The Germans occasionally managed to transport the more badly injured civilians to military hospitals outside La Roche.[22]

German troops began withdrawing from La Roche on January 8, mining the roads behind them and halting at farms to requisition what little food remained. Three days later, Scottish troops of the 51st Highland Division, which had taken over from the 53rd Welsh Division, at last entered La Roche from the west. There was little cheering this time. Most civilians were not only at the end of their tether but also still hiding from what now were incoming German shells. The Scottish troops were overcome with tremendous pity for the ghostly people who during the following days slowly emerged from their shelters, wan and wobbly on their feet. They gave them all their rations of chocolate and even parted with their blankets. One soldier retrieved a rosary from the rubble and silently handed it to a teenage girl.[23]

The Scottish troops soon linked up with Americans from the VII Corps at La Roche. By the time the German guns fell silent, only four of La Roche's 639 homes remained intact, and at least 114 civilians were dead. La Roche was such a heap of rubble that American bulldozers were called in to blaze narrow trails where once had been the town's main roads. Locals would never forget that even the swallows appeared disoriented when they returned the following spring and found not a barn standing in which to build their nests.[24]

To the southwest, on the right flank of the Welsh and Scottish troops, the 6th Airborne Division moved up front between Marche and Wellin on January 2. The British paratroopers were to attack along the axis from Givet to St. Hubert. The soldiers in the red berets struck the civilians as hardened and callous. They thought nothing of taking from the population what they were lacking. If that, to a degree, had also been the case with the Americans who had been there before them, the GIs at least had compensated for it by sharing the many items they possessed in ample quantities. By comparison, British troops appeared to have nothing in abundance. Within days of their arrival in Buissonville, a village located some five miles behind the front line, complaints poured in about damages caused by paratroopers. In a claim filed with the British army after the battle, one farmer described how in a matter of two days the chilled paratroopers had burned not only his coal, but also anything made of wood, including hay rakes, bean poles, cart axles, plough handles, fences, floors, and four antique oak cupboards. Gone also were implements like spades, hoes, pickaxes, and hammers. Another inhabitant attested that on his property British soldiers in red berets had "destroyed by burning 24 beehives with cells and in perfect condition." "I understand the matter," the plaintiff emphasized in his statement, "but it is to me a great loss."[25]

When paratroopers jumped off from their line of departure on January 3, their efforts to break through to St. Hubert soon centered on the village of Bure, where a sizeable rearguard force of Panzer Lehr made a stand to cover the division's withdrawal. The battle for Bure began in earnest on Thursday, January 4. By then, however, Bure had already been suffering heavy shelling for several days. If the imposing Alumnat, where most of the village's civilians were hiding, had managed to withstand some thirty direct hits by Thursday, some of the refugees' minds were cracking under the strain. Children were crying hysterically. One woman seized a boy and tore at his hair, shrieking wildly that she wanted to pluck her rooster. Another woman with a vacant stare was lost entirely in polishing her shoes with jelly.[26]

Still more maddening was the sound of furious hand-to-hand combat in Bure that continued during five days of ferocious attacks and counterattacks. Those who could still think clearly knew that the priority was to replenish the Alumnat's rapidly diminishing stocks of food. Amid the confusion, never knowing who was in control of what part, young men began slipping into the smoke-filled village in search of food. Some hid in stables to milk cows; others hurried into houses to empty pantries. Finding the jittery paratroopers as dangerous as the Germans, the men nevertheless found the courage on at least two occasions to transport badly wounded paratroopers up the hill to the Alumnat in pushcarts and wheelbarrows. British soldiers first seized the Alumnat on Thursday night, but were thrown out the following day. The Germans withdrew on Saturday, leaving the Alumnat in no-man's-land for another three days. Living conditions in the huge shelter steadily worsened. There was no heat, no light, and no water except that drawn from an old pump in the courtyard at great risk. A terrible outbreak of diarrhea soiled the cellars, causing a gagging stench. People were caked with dirt and swarming with lice. They were hungry, exhausted, and delirious. Then on Tuesday, January 9, a British officer appeared. He came not a day too early to announce deliverance.[27]

The refugees emerged from the Alumnat to find 119 of their 166 homes destroyed or badly damaged. They were fortunate, however, to count no more than four casualties in their midst. The villagers rightly attributed their luck to the Assumptionist Fathers' bulwark on the hill.[28]

For the refugees in Bure, the arrival of the British could not have been more timely. For hundreds of young men in the area, however, the paratroopers came too late. Increasingly unnerved by the Allied push, the Germans became distrustful of the able-bodied men whom they feared would aid and abet the enemy at the first opportunity. Wehrmacht patrols on January 6 and 7 began rounding up all men aged seventeen to forty-five. Twenty were marched out of Jemelle, 50 were taken away in Hargimont, 90 were rounded up in Forrières, and another 125 in On. Few of them were given a chance to dress for the cold; only the men from Forrières were told to grab some food. In columns closely guarded by German soldiers the men wound their way eastward to Champlon, where all of the prisoners assembled. Despite continuous Allied shelling, the men were immediately put to work. They cleared wrecked vehicles from the roads and shoveled snow. Between 70 and 80 men were sent to Bande to help with bridge construction. Chilled to the bone, the prisoners worked for two long days before being given their first meager meal.[29]

While the prisoners were laboring away, Odon Marlère and three other men from On were being interrogated at Wibrin by SS officers of Einsatzgruppe L that was operating from Houffalize. Mistrustful of what the German soldiers had in store for them, they had made the mistake of ignoring the call for men their age to step forward. They had been found out in the late afternoon of January 7 and, suspected of clandestine activities, handed over to the security services in Wibrin. The interrogation terminated, the four men from On and another one they did not know were loaded onto a truck and driven to a nearby wood. The unknown man was taken away first. Odon Marlère heard a shot followed by the heavy thump of a body. Then Mr. Chauvier disappeared and the sequence of nauseating sounds repeated itself. Now it was Mr. Marlère's turn. He felt the cold steal press against his neck. Though he never heard the fatal shot, he thought he could feel blood spurt from his mouth. Then everything went dark.

The sound of a truck engine made him come to. Odon Marlère left a trail of blood in the snow as he crawled on all fours until he reached a barn with hay. There he hid for four days, quenching his thirst with snow. Mustering his last strength, he finally dragged himself from the barn to a farm where people were kind enough to take him in. He was happy to learn much later that Mr. Bolle and Mr. Martin had been able to escape as well.[30]

At around the time that Odon Marlère was rescued, the group of unfortunates at Champlon was split in two. One column was fed into the German lines north of Bastogne, where they were forced to dig trenches in view of the Americans. Shell fire killed at least two of the prisoners and wounded several others. One of the Belgians protested to a German officer that it was illegal to employ civilians for military tasks. The officer shot back that "for the Germans the laws did not exist." On January 19 the prisoners reached the Luxembourg border and were told they could go home.

For the other group, meanwhile, the agony continued. They were marched to the East Cantons where shell fire killed one of them and injured another who was sped off to Germany. When the others reached the German border they were ordered to dig trenches in the West Wall. On the last day of January the prisoners were suddenly released. By that time only a few dozen of them remained as most had managed to flee. When this haggard group tried to enter the American lines at Habscheid on February 2, however, violent shelling took the lives of five men. They had to be left behind only yards away from where they would have been free again.[31]

While the battle for Bure raged, American troops of the 87th Infantry Division, part of Patton's VIII Corps, continued the bitter fight for Bonnerue, a hamlet located thirteen miles southeast of Bure and on the other side of St. Hubert. The fight there had erupted as a result of the limited counterattack launched near the end of December to cut off the nose of the German salient. At Bonnerue, too, elements of Panzer Lehr were covering the division's retreat, and they were doing so with like determination.

Having been thrown out the day before, the GIs managed to gain complete control of Bonnerue in the early morning of January 3. Expecting new counterattacks, they ordered some two dozen civilians hiding in the Dermience farm to evacuate immediately. They were not allowed to take anything with them. Some did not even have time to get dressed for the cold. An American soldier with a mine detector set off through the fields to Jenneville, the civilians snaking behind him single file. Lucie Dupont's baby carriage got stuck in the snow, and she had to continue with the child bundled in her arms. From Jenneville they were directed to Moircy and from there to Freux. American trucks in Freux sped them off to Paliseul where villagers finally took the exhausted refugees in.[32]

Just hours after the villagers had left the farm, Panzer Lehr launched the first of a series of furious counterattacks. Four days later, columns of smoke trailed up into the sky over Bonnerue and the hamlet was back in German hands. One of the homes on fire was that of Félicie Philippart. In its cellar two dozen civilians had sat bunched together for twelve days, plagued by lice, skin infections, croup, and dysentery. Now they were frantically trying to wriggle themselves free through a narrow window. German soldiers helped drag them out, yelling all the while to hurry up. Outside they threw blood-stained blankets over their shoulders and ordered them to head for Tonny. One woman had to be carried on the way; an exhausted man passed out and died shortly after. Heavy artillery pounded the Germans in what remained of Bonnerue for two days. When the Americans recaptured the hamlet on January 10 at least ten homes and barns were reduced to ashes and another nine to dust.[33]

With Bonnerue firmly in their hands, troops of the 87th Infantry Division rapidly swept northwest in a wide arc. In the morning of January 11 they linked up with British soldiers of the 6th Airborne Division just north of St. Hubert. That very day paratroopers in Bande learned of the terrible crime that had taken place there. Medical personnel of the 9th Battalion helped with the gruesome task of recovering the thirty-four corpses from the cellar, laying them out, and placing them in coffins. All a British officer could utter in the presence of Father Musty as they watched the sinister row of victims was: "Why?"

The paratroopers provided transport and a guard of honor for the funeral. None of the hardened and callous soldiers present would ever forget the incontrollable sobbing and wailing rising up from Bande that day.[34]

Battle, meanwhile, stoically rolled on, crushing in its path village after village. Vesqueville, for example, which the Americans of the 87th Division entered in the afternoon of January 11 as they tightened the noose around St. Hubert, was in ruins. That only a few inhabitants had fallen victim to the heavy American shelling was due largely to the protection the village's solidly built cellars had offered. The farmers' valuable animals had not enjoyed such safety, however. The explosions had been so powerful that they had hurled sheep and pigs onto the roofs. More than a hundred dead animals lay strewn about. Many had been cut to pieces by shrapnel. Others had died in their stables from thirst and hunger. It took ten villagers two days to clean up the carcasses of what had been their livelihood.[35]

The Americans finally liberated St. Hubert in the evening of January 12. The shelling that had preceded the town's capture had caused few casualties. The abbatial town boasted a great number of exceptionally solid cellars that had served as shelters holding up to five hundred people at a time. But hunger had been gnawing at the inhabitants since the Germans had picked the town clean in December. Most had not seen a crust of bread for almost three weeks. When the GIs brought them liberation at last, St. Hubert's inhabitants were too weary even to cheer.[36]

3 As the net closed around St. Hubert, the rest of Patton's VIII Corps, together with part of his III Corps, relaunched the American push against the enemy's southern flank that had begun on December 22 and ground to a halt by the start of the new year. At least eight divisions in and around Bastogne, including Gaëtan Delecaut's unit, jumped off on January 9 determined to link up with the First Army's VII Corps at Houffalize.

In the area west of Bastogne, where the 17th Airborne Division clashed with the 3rd Panzergrenadier Division, inhabitants of Flamierge on the first day of the renewed offensive were ordered to evacuate immediately. Resenting their eagerness to make it to the American lines, the Panzergrenadiers instead pointed the civilians north to Tronle, the next hamlet in the German rear. That this left them less safe was cruelly illustrated that same day when in neighboring Salle in just a few hours three different shells killed three members of the same family: sixty-five-year-old Catherine Lepage, her slightly younger husband, Henri, and their thirty-one-year-old daughter, Alice.[37]

Two days later, Salle's twin village, Trois Monts, was hit even more severely. Twenty-five civilians sat pressed against the warm animals in the stable of the Flock farm when a shell pierced the roof and went off in their midst. Cries and moans floated up with the smoke and dust. The stable was a slaughterhouse. Seven people, among them refugees from Flamierge and Bastogne, lay dead in the rubble. Nine others, including an inhabitant from Salle, had sustained terrible injuries. Six animals had been torn apart by the explosion, rendering the scene still more ghastly. The Germans immediately set to work on the wounded in their aid station in the Leriche home. But there was not much they could do for fourteen-year-old Fernand Lambert, a refugee from Flamierge with two bleeding stumps for legs, who was brought in from the stable by his father. Soldiers rushed the boy to a hospital in Luxembourg together with Mr. François, a villager whose eye had been pierced. Fernand Lambert died shortly after his arrival, the eighth fatality of a single shell.[38]

The Americans captured Trois Monts on January 12, the day after the massacre. The weary paratroopers spent most of their time there transporting victims of their own artillery to the hospital in Arlon. The day after, they captured Givroulle, where inhabitants thought the dirty, bearded paratroopers looked like the *poilus* of the Great War. On January 14 the Americans linked up at the Ourthe with Scottish troops of the 51st Division who did not look much different.[39]

On the other side of Bastogne, some of the most ferocious fighting centered on Harlange, a village to the southeast, just across the Belgian border in Luxembourg. Here, the 5th Parachute and 167th Volksgrenadier Divisions were fighting for their lives against two American infantry divisions, an armored division, and a cavalry group that were corralling the Germans into a pocket. As the ground troops tightened the noose, artillery and air forces pounded the area mercilessly, obliterating not only enemy troops, but also much of the civilian communities in which the soldiers had hunkered down.

According to some estimates, in the densely wooded triangle of Lutremange-Lutrebois-Bras alone, American batteries poured close to one hundred thousand shells. So many of the explosives fired against

Harlange were loaded with white phosphorus that soon even the snow appeared to be ablaze. Allied fighter-bombers roamed the skies over the pocket like hawks in search of quarry. In the early afternoon of January 10, for example, they pounced on German vehicles and troops in Bras. By the time they had finished strafing and bombing, not only military targets had been blown apart, but homes and farms, too. Sixty-three-year-old Victorien Bastin never made it to the cellar in time and was killed when the kitchen collapsed on him. His wife was stumbling down the stairs when an avalanche of rubble rolled in, crushing her. The attack left several more villagers badly injured. The air raids on Tarchamps, meanwhile, had been so frightening that German soldiers hid among the civilians in the cellars, forcing furious officers to come down and chase them out.[40]

The combined effects of air and artillery on the villages in the pocket were devastating. By the time American troops reached Harlange on January 10, some sixteen civilians lay dead, many of them in coffins that had yet to be buried. The GIs took Tarchamps the following day to find around sixty of its seventy houses either destroyed or severely damaged and at least eight civilians dead. When a little later Americans in Tarchamps marched a POW to the rear, an enraged villager threw a brick at the German's head. In Wardin, recaptured on January 12, 80 percent of the buildings were in ruins. With the fall of Bras that same day, the pocket was finally closed.[41]

The exhausted GIs showed themselves jittery and suspicious toward the inhabitants while mopping up enemy remnants. Civilians in Bras who reported that four Germans were still hiding in their cellar found the GIs distrustful. First the Americans ordered all of the refugees out of their shelter, then they forced one of them to descend again and return with the soldiers himself. A villager in Lutremange got into serious trouble when GIs happened across a pair of valuable German binoculars that he had hidden in a heap of potatoes. Suspected of espionage for the enemy, he was arrested and manhandled before being released again.[42]

American military authorities ordered the worst hit villages in the pocket to be evacuated as soon as possible. This not only bought the soldiers peace of mind, but it also enabled the civilians to escape to healthier environments. The inhabitants of Bras assembled in the snow on January 14. In subzero temperatures they waited several hours for the American trucks to arrive. When they finally did, several vehicles turned out to lack protective tarps. It took several more hours to drive the civilians to Luxembourg. There they received their first hot meal in twenty-eight days. Harlange, too, was completely evacuated. In Wardin, however, in spite of the massive destruction, not everyone was eager to leave. When Mrs. Anna Felten resisted, two GIs grabbed her and forced her into the waiting truck. Still, even while evacuated, many weakened people, especially the elderly, continued to die. In the next four months, for example, that was true of at least five of Tarchamps's inhabitants, all of them in their seventies.[43]

At about the same time that an air raid killed husband and wife in Bras inside the Harlange pocket on January 10, fighter-bombers caused a still greater tragedy in Benonchamps. A village just north of the pocket, Benonchamps had somehow managed to escape fatalities until January 9. That day, however, the war began to catch up with a vengeance. First, a shell chose seventeen-year-old Jean Beauve as its victim. Then, on that fateful Wednesday, January 10, the menacing drone of Allied aircraft made frightened villagers hold on to each other in their shelters. The attack that followed was horrendous. Fighter-bombers streaked past the roofs, the noise unbearable. Bombs tore at earth and foundations. The aircraft pulled away, then returned again, releasing more explosives by the dozen. "It was," recalled one witness, "like the end of the world!" Of the church only the tower remained standing. One bomb ripped apart the Michat home, obliterating both Mr. and Mrs. Michat. Another one so thoroughly pulverized a stable of the Guillame farm that of the twelve civilians buried under the rubble nothing could be found afterward but small pieces of bone, skin, and clothing. Of the twelve people who perished in the stable, ten belonged to only two families. Mr. Emile Schmitz died with his two sons, Hilaire and Jean. Mr. Guillaume's home became a grave for himself, his wife, Marie, and their five teenage children, Marie-Louise, Adolphe, Etienne, Camille, and Joseph.[44]

American troops fought their way into Benonchamps from Wardin on January 14. The following day they busied themselves with the dispatch of the village's wounded to hospitals in the rear. One of the wounded was a twenty-year-old girl called Marie. She was barely alive. She had not been injured in the bombing raid, but by a shell burst ten days earlier. Shrapnel had ripped the flesh from her shoulder and fragments sat lodged against her spine. For two long weeks she had been enduring unspeakable pain without sedatives. In all that time, German soldiers had not been able to change her bandages on more than four occasions. The stink of rotting flesh had nauseated the people around her. She had moaned and screamed so heartrendingly that her grandmother had begged God to take her life instead. The eighty-five-year-old woman was granted her wish on January 19. Many months later Marie returned from the hospital alive.[45]

On the day that medics rushed Marie to the rear, the infantry pushed forward to the villages northeast of Bastogne. Phosphorus and explosives had so devastated them that the GIs were incredulous to find civilians still present in the charred remains. At Oubourcy, for example, starving and dazed civilians barely seemed to notice the liberators. From this sector, too, the American military evacuated people as soon as possible. When the harrowed inhabitants of Arloncourt finally arrived in Offagne in army trucks, their appearance scared their hosts.[46]

While their comrades were pushing back the Germans west and east of Bastogne, two more American divisions engaged the enemy north of the town and closed in on Houffalize. The 11th Armored and 101st Airborne Divisions crept forward supported by heavy artillery fire. A particularly furious barrage pounded the unfortunate villages in the troops' path on January 13, killing one civilian in Engreux, and one in Bonnerue, and crushing a villager beneath the rubble of his home in Mabompré. Another shell that same day mauled a man in Vellereux who died of his injuries several weeks later.[47]

The hardened combat troops who followed behind the barrages at first appeared not much kinder to the inhabitants than their artillery. Soldiers of the 11th Armored Division in Bonnerue treated the villagers with so much suspicion that one woman was convinced the Americans "believed they were in Germany." The paratroopers who captured Neufmoulin on January 16 looked like savages. Hung with grenades, and with their rifles pointed at the inhabitants, they searched every nook and cranny before relaxing just enough to offer the civilians some of their food. Of that they appeared to possess limitless quantities compared with the miserly Germans. Rations for the soldiers of the 340th Volksgrenadier Division who had just been chased from Neufmoulin had been down to some 300 grams of bread and 30 grams of fat a day. Only days after the arrival of the American paratroopers in nearby Foy, however, incredulous villagers were gaping at boxes piled up high against the chapel wall. Every single one of them was stuffed with mouthwatering chocolate, one of the rarest of commodities in wartime Europe.[48]

With American troops now on Houffalize's southern edge, the sound of battle slowly died down in Bastogne. In the late afternoon of January 15, several German rounds once again thrashed Bastogne's Franciscan church. They were among the last enemy shells to mutilate the ill-fated town. Artillery duels continued to be heard in the distance throughout the night, but began to fade to a soft rumble the following day.[49]

After weeks of hiding in shelters as dark as they were damp, people in and around Bastogne stepped into the faint winter light to survey the toll of war. Amazingly, inside the town itself incessant shelling had claimed the lives of relatively few civilians as these had managed to find protection in plenty of solid cellars. Of the estimated 3,000 civilians surrounded in Bastogne, 17 were killed, 40 badly wounded, and 70 slightly injured. The real price in terms of civilian lives, however, had been paid in Bastogne's perimeter. In the eighty villages and hamlets located within a six-mile radius of the town, close to 350 civilians had perished as a direct result of battle. The number of wounded in the perimeter is impossible to establish. Many more in and around Bastogne died of illnesses related to deprivation, fear, and stress. The most cautious estimate puts the number of those who died of such causes in December 1944 and January 1945 at one hundred.

The material damage was tremendous both inside Bastogne and in the villages and hamlets surrounding it. Of the town's 1,250 homes, 250 were totally destroyed and another 450 made uninhabitable. Most others were at least partly damaged. In Bastogne's perimeter 656 homes and farms were completely devastated and another 1,300 seriously damaged. An additional 1,500 stables and 1,400 barns had been razed to the ground.[50]

While the noise of battle receded at Bastogne, American troops stood poised to enter Houffalize from the south as well as the north. By this time, however, it was not so much a town that was awaiting them, but rather a giant mass of blackened rubble. The bombardments of December 26, 27, 30, and 31 had done their part to make Houffalize unrecognizable. But it was the massive bombardment of January 6, three days after the start of the coordinated Allied effort to erase the Bulge, that had virtually wiped the town from the banks of the Ourthe.

During the first days of the new year, dozens of people had returned to Houffalize from the woods to rejoin those who had refused to leave and had managed to survive four harrowing bombardments. By the evening of Friday, January 5, between 300 and 350 people hunkered down in the cellars of those parts of the battered town that had remained largely intact. They thronged together in about a dozen communal shelters, the largest of which were the Poncin tannery (holding 115 refugees) and the presbytery (harboring 98 people). Around 3:20 that night, all suddenly awakened as one. Hearts faltered when the all-too-familiar hum of heavy bombers could be heard approaching once again. Within minutes bright flares lit the sky over Houffalize, turning night into day. Almost immediately the sharp glare was followed by chains of fierce flashes as 93 British Lancaster bombers began unloading 1,307 bombs weighing a total of 507 tons.[51]

The objective of the bombers was to choke the one remaining escape route for the Germans west of the Ourthe. The civilians in their underground shelters were not aware of the Allied reasoning behind the bombing. But even if they had been, the cold military logic would have provided no comfort whatsoever. The bombardment lasted exactly twelve minutes, but to those caught in the middle of the cauldron it seemed like a century. The explosions felt like "an immense earthquake." The noise was that of "a formidable rolling thunder" squeezing hearts and throats tight. People in the presbytery's cellar were shaken about like leaves. The door at the top of the stairs was ripped from its hinges, cellar windows were blown to bits, and the roofs were lifted off presbytery and church and smashed to the ground.

A bomb plowed through the thick ceiling of the crowded tannery, burying people beneath dust and stones. Fourteen-year-old Andrée Thiry was suffocating. She realized she was dying. Though she could sense life ebb away, she did not suffer and somehow felt at peace. Then suddenly another explosion hurled her to the surface and made her breathe again. In the dirt next to her were her father and one of her sisters. They too were still alive. Through woods and fields their father rushed them to safety in Fontenaille. Andrée later learned that her mother, brother, and two other sisters had died in the tannery's rubble, together with most of the other refugees there. Her last memory of her mother was of the American chocolate bar that she had taken with her to the shelter and each night had allowed her children to eat small crumbs from.[52]

Explosions continued in Houffalize long after the British bombers had disappeared. Phosphorus kept igniting fires throughout town. From as far away as Engreux, the sky over Houffalize could be seen glowing red-hot. It was, observed a woman in Mont, "a vision of hell." Those who stumbled from their cellars early on Saturday morning, January 6, were scarcely able to fathom the havoc war had wrought from the air in less than half an hour. "It is unimaginable," one survivor later tried to explain. "There were flames everywhere, explosions, piles of wreckage, trees, overturned trucks; it is unthinkable, when one has not really experienced it." There simply was no town left. Street after street had been wiped away. The huge tanneries were razed to the ground, their damaged vats leaking acid. The Ourthe had burst its banks. Age-old trees were shorn to jagged stumps. Not a single distinguishing mark remained, except perhaps the roofless shell of the thirteenth-century church. With 90 percent of the town now utterly destroyed, Houffalize in the most literal sense had become the "choking point" that the Allies had wanted it to be.[53]

In less than half an hour on January 6, 1945, 118 civilians perished in the explosions, the crumbling buildings, the fires. Forty-eight of them were men, 70 were women. Many of the town's families were decimated. In some six cases they ceased to exist altogether. Of the Hoffmann family, for example, forty-six-year-old Guillaume and his forty-year-old wife, Irma, died with their four children: Marie Madeleine, René, Lucien, and Suzanne, aged sixteen, fifteen, fourteen, and thirteen, respectively. Harrowed survivors fled to the fields and woods where they hid in caves and barns or built primitive shelters. They swelled the numbers of those living in the open since the first bombardments, and in certain places enough huts arose to form communities of up to 300 refugees. Others, like Andrée Thiry and her father and sister, poured into the surrounding villages throughout Saturday. Many were badly injured. Some had terrible burns on their hands from frenzied digging through phosphorus-coated debris in search of family, friends, and neighbors. Crazed by pain and despair, not a few refugees collapsed upon arrival. Several would die in the following days.[54]

For the next ten days, the survivors in their cellars, caves, barns, and huts waited to be liberated in the most appalling of conditions. For most there remained nothing to eat but frozen potatoes. As phosphorus had contaminated even the snow, many began drawing water from a river polluted with debris and corpses. Ignoring the danger from mines and haggard German soldiers, men stumbled through thick snow in search of food. Some of the farmers in the surrounding villages were not ashamed to cash in on their suffering, demanding extortionate prices for a loaf of bread. Others gave away what little they could: a few potatoes, a crust of bread, some vegetables. The Dislaire family was part of a group of twenty-nine living in huts near the Ourthe. They subsisted on what they had carried with them in sacks: potatoes and bread baked before Christmas. When one of them returned from a farm with a slab of cow meat, the survivors ate most of it raw as they were too afraid to make a fire that might attract bombs or shells. People were soon suffering from dysentery and paratyphoid. They were ailing with diphtheria and made increasingly itchy with scabies and lice. Women from the local Red Cross tried to help where they could, but they were overwhelmed and without medicines there was little they could do.[55]

The fate of the survivors was made worse, meanwhile, by American gunners. They seemed unaware that there was nothing left to destroy in Houffalize and continued to pummel town and woods with artillery shells as they drew nearer from the north and south. In the night of January 10 alone, one civilian in a Houffalize cellar counted at least two hundred exploding shells. More frightening still was the German troops scattered in and around Houffalize. Bombardments and shelling had cracked their morale, causing discipline to collapse. Deserters, many of them Austrians, Czechs, and other non-German nationals, roamed the forests and begged civilians to hide them. Those who decided to continue the fight cared less and less about the local population. They forced women in Houffalize to perform kitchen duty amidst shell fire. In Engreux they ordered men to clear roads and humiliated women by having them wash their clothes. In Tavigny they requisitioned all men between sixteen and fifty as well as a number of girls and set them to work digging trenches in the cold for two days, with American artillery barking nearby and Allied aircraft overhead. On more than one occasion they sexually harassed local women and girls. But the starving Germans were most dangerous when searching for food. A soldier in Vellereux fired a shot at Stéphanie Voz for protesting when she caught him stealing eggs. In Tavigny eighteen-year-old Ghislaine Collette watched as her mother argued with a bunch of Germans to let her keep at least some of the chickens they were about to cart off. Before the eyes of her daughter, one of the soldiers silenced Mrs. Collette with a bullet that tore into the flesh close to her heart. Both the woman from Vellereux and Mrs. Collette later died from their injuries in American hospitals.[56]

The GIs who were gathered north and south of Houffalize on January 16 had not the faintest idea of what had befallen the civilians they were about to liberate. Patrols from the 2nd and 11th Armored Divisions linked up near the town just before noon that day. By the early morning of January 18 American troops were in control of all that remained of Houffalize. The stink of the charred heap of rubble hiding countless corpses in its twisted bowels sickened the soldiers. Still more upsetting was the sight of survivors drifting through the ruins like specters, their faces gaunt and ashen, and their eyes frighteningly hollow and empty. Some appeared to wander about aimlessly. Others were looking for their dead. Without tools, without disinfectants, without coffins, they went about the gruesome task of recovering corpses from the dirt and burying them again in resting places worthy of their memory. There was nothing more the combat troops could do for the survivors than feed them soup and hand out canned goods. Army bulldozers, meanwhile, were called in to trace roads through the moonscape that would allow the war to march on.[57]

American ambulances immediately rushed the injured and seriously ill to hospitals. Next the remaining civilians received orders to evacuate, and on January 21 and 22 American trucks drove them away to places like Marche, Bomal, and Bertrix. No more than a few dozen inhabitants were allowed to stay. They joined hands with a team of seventeen rescue workers from the Belgian Red Cross who arrived from Brussels five days after the evacuation. Together they worked day and night to recover as many bodies as quickly as possible. Lack of equipment, however, and the stubborn refusal of wreckage and frozen earth to release their victims made the work agonizingly slow. The workers on January 29 reported no more than 22 corpses recovered and identified. Not before the evening of February 1 did the first truck arrive from Bastogne with the much-needed coffins. The nauseating job continued for several weeks. The total number of victims from the five bombardments of Houffalize eventually added up to 189. On March 23, 1945, a glum city council gathered and in a few terse phrases declared virtually the entire town a demolition site.[58]

5 Away from the Bulge's nose, nearer its waist, American troops between the Lienne and Salm Rivers on January 2, 1945, prepared to join the coordinated Allied attack scheduled for the following day. They belonged to the 82nd Division of the XVIII Airborne Corps, and the seasoned paratroopers made quite an impression on Mr. Jamar in Chevron as they lined up in freezing temperatures and deep snow fully equipped and ready to board trucks for the front. "All these soldiers," the elderly notary observed, "have a very warrior-like and martial appearance and they remind me of Roman soldiers."

At least one officer in Chevron was acutely conscious of his army's superiority. Confronted by a villager about the disappearance of food and several objects from his home on the eve of the Americans' departure, the paratrooper lectured the man "that the Americans in Belgium are carrying almost all the weight of the war, without help from the Belgian or French soldiers, and the liberated Belgians should not complain if the war causes them some inevitable detriments." "He is," Mr. Jamar emphasized in his journal that night, "absolutely right!"[59]

Unlike Mr. Jamar, however, the civilians in the path of the Americans as they cleared the Lienne's right bank from tenacious German troops found the behavior of the callous paratroopers much harder to accept. Villagers complained of a lack of discipline, of liberators wantonly destroying property, of soldiers burning coal and wood (as well as furniture) oblivious to the needs of the civilians. Rather than noble Romans, the liberators reminded a disappointed inhabitant of Brux of "vandals." They "acted like savages," a civilian from Provedroux corroborated, "and we regard their behavior towards friends with some bitterness."[60]

The paratroopers in turn proved extremely suspicious of the civilians. Armed to the teeth, they burst into homes in La Chapelle and forced the inhabitants, rifles pressed against their backs, to go before them into cellars and other possible German hideouts. As soon as the area was firmly back in American hands, Joseph Martin in Hierlot decided to try and make his way to a civilian doctor in Lierneux to have his feet treated for frostbite. He never got there. GIs arrested him on the way, affronted the former Belgian soldier by locking him up with five German POWs, of whom two were SS, and subjected him to rigid interrogation. They finally ordered him to hobble back to Hierlot.[61]

If the toughened paratroopers were suspicious of Belgian inhabitants, they more than once proved unforgiving of enemy soldiers. Ci-

vilians in Odrimont witnessed how one German threw down his rifle
and raised his hands. A frenzied paratrooper drew a knife from his
boot, lurched at the prisoner, and fatally stabbed him in the chest.
Another German prisoner was killed in the hamlet of Amcomont despite valiant efforts by the villagers to deliver him into the hands of
the Americans safely. The German, a father of four, had deserted earlier and been allowed to hide in a stable. Two courageous civilians
walked the unarmed soldier to a group of paratroopers to explain the
situation. Before they even had a chance to open their mouths, one of
the Americans slowly turned around, aimed his rifle at the German,
and coldly took him out.[62]

In such a climate of suspicion and brutality, it was paramount to
have the civilians removed from the front lines as swiftly as possible.
Many villages in the Lienne Valley received orders to evacuate as soon
as trucks became available. Arbrefontaine, for example, was captured
on January 4. Four wounded civilians were immediately rushed away
in ambulances. In the night of Saturday, January 6, the Americans
trucked the remaining inhabitants to Chevron, where they were to
await further transportation. Chevron's churchgoers woke up to a
distressing scene the following morning. "These poor people," Mr.
Jamar scribbled in his journal, "wrapped in shawls and surrounded
by bags of all kinds, were sitting in the pews; around the stove children were crying and lamenting. What a sad sight, images of all the
sad things resulting from war."[63]

Slightly further to the east, still more people had been moving back
and forth with the tide of war. One could, in fact, write the history of
battle in the Salm Valley merely by examining the ebb and flow of
refugees at the château de Farnières.

Located on the left bank of the Salm, just two miles southwest of
Grand-Halleux, the château and adjacent buildings had been donated
by a family of noble blood to the Salesian Fathers for educational purposes. The first refugees, inhabitants of Grand-Halleux, had begun to
arrive at the imposing château as early as December 18. Three days
later it had been decided to have most of the Salesian Fathers as well
as the students and gardeners evacuate from the institute in small
groups. Combatants from both sides were soon to designate the
château as the main refuge for civilians in the area. Withdrawing
American paratroopers, for example, on December 24 had already
ordered several villages on the Salm's left bank to evacuate to Farnières.

By Tuesday, December 26, the number of refugees at the institute had swelled to nearly six hundred.[64]

Still more arrived as the Germans began to ready themselves for the Allied counterattack. They were eager to have the civilians out of the way so that they could at the same time take their homes and food. On the last day of the old and the first day of the new year, German troops expulsed almost all who lived in the Salm Valley between Trois-Ponts and Grand-Halleux, forcing people out of their homes in villages east of the river as far away as three miles. On January 2 the occupier ordered mass evacuation of both banks of the valley as far south as Salmchâteau. In villages and towns everywhere, German posters threatened inhabitants disobeying the order with summary execution. A number of civilians nevertheless succeeded in staying in or at least near their homes. Some feigned illnesses leaving them bedridden; others obtained permission to stay put because they had infants or elderly in their care. Close to 250 people from Vielsalm, a town with a population of some 4,000 in normal times, fled to the nearby slate quarries, where they would live in deep dank galleries until the liberation. Hundreds more trekked southward through the valley in the hope of finding safety in villages south of the highway from Salmchâteau to La Roche. Another 200 people, however, decided that the religious institute at Farnières would offer them the best protection.[65]

Those who made it to Farnières, their limbs frozen, their meager belongings in wheelbarrows and on carts, could indeed count themselves among the more fortunate refugees in the area. By January 4 no less than 798 people thronged together in the institute's cellars and ground-floor rooms. But the Salesian Fathers had experience running a large organization and tight ship. The few priests who remained received invaluable assistance from a "council of elders" that was formed among others by the mayor and the local doctor. Food was a first concern. Though it had to be rationed, shortages never became particularly acute. This was partly because the Salesians also ran an agricultural school and partly because the Germans respected the château as an essentially civilian refuge and thus did not plunder potatoes and vegetables. Occasionally, too, stocks were replenished with a heifer or hog brought in by farmers or with food scrounged from nearby villages. The latter was a dangerous undertaking: Mrs. Pirotte, for example, stepped on a mine during a search for food and was brought back horribly mutilated; she died a couple of hours later. A team of some ten women took control of the kitchen and worked tirelessly to feed all under the Salesians' roof. Though the electricity had been cut off, heating was never too serious a problem as the Germans also refrained from touching the institute's large stocks of coal and wood. Hygiene was a headache, though, especially when mass usage clogged the toilets. Health was by far the most serious concern. Doctor Fransolet had his hands full caring for the ill, the wounded, the dying, and mothers in labor. He did what he could to prevent epidemics, isolating a girl that arrived with diphtheria, and doing the same with a child brought in with scarlet fever. He even risked his life slipping back into Grand-Halleux to look for medicines left behind by the Americans.[66]

The daily struggles and inconveniences were not, however, exacerbated by direct military threats to the shelter. The most dangerous days were those when the Americans returned to battle it out with the Germans for control of the valley. Infantry attacks were invariably preceded by fearsome artillery barrages. One such barrage on January 5, for example, made a store in Salmchâteau collapse, crushing nine civilians, all of them refugees from a hamlet near Grand-Halleux and four of them children. Farnières, too, around that time was being rocked by shell fire, but the institute managed to escape serious damage. On Sunday, January 7, American paratroopers emerged from the forests and approached the château single-file. The Fathers Salesians hurried to inform them that the buildings housed only civilians, assuring them there was not a single German inside.[67]

As the paratroopers swept the Germans from the Salm's left bank and began penetrating east of the river, civilians poured from the château to try and reach their homes and farms. They were shocked to find that their liberators were far from happy to see them there. A group of refugees who tried to return to Arbrefontaine on January 9 found their village filled to the rafters with American troops and were obliged to retrace their steps to Farnières that same day. Even homes that were not off limits to the inhabitants often turned out to have become uninhabitable. People returned to Farnières from villages throughout the Salm Valley with complaints of American troops dragging away beds and mattresses, burning furniture, smashing china, scattering household goods into the snow, and generally displaying a lack of discipline that upset many.[68]

Anticipating still more refugees as fresh troops from the 75th Infantry Division arrived to relieve the paratroopers and continue the offensive east of the Salm, the American military announced on January 10 that the refugees in Farnières were to be evacuated to Liège and the Herve plateau. The only ones allowed to stay were the Fathers Salesians, kitchen and hospital personnel, the sick and elderly, and 25 men to take care of cattle in the area. All others had to go without exception. On the very day of the order, 160 people in long lines shuffled through snow and woods to vehicles awaiting them in Arbrefontaine. Two days later, a convoy of thirty trucks, all but two without protective tarps, pulled up to the institute and carried off another 570 refugees.[69]

They had barely gone when the first batch of fresh refugees, some 50 people from Mont, arrived at the château on orders of the Americans. The following day, January 13, they were joined by 60 people from Ennal and Petit-Halleux. More people arrived a day later from Goronne, La Comté, and Sart. Among them was an upset priest from Goronne who railed "against the barbarians of the new world" for uprooting them. By Wednesday, January 17, the institute was again harboring more than 470 people. As late as January 25 the Americans sent 40 refugees to Farnières from Francheville, to which they had earlier been evacuated by the Germans from their homes in Commanster, a village not far from St. Vith.[70]

Still, no matter how forlorn and uprooted, the villagers passing through the refuge at Farnières were infinitely more fortunate than those forced to flee the valley to the area south of the highway from Salmchâteau to La Roche. Tossed about from village to village without protection, many of the refugees here fell victim to increasingly furious Allied firepower. So unbearable was the shelling in Petite Langlire on January 10, for example, that Germans flushed the Offergeld family into the open to take their cellar. Panicked by explosions, desperate with fear, the refugees from Vielsalm clawed their way into a small stone building that looked like a chapel. A middle-aged Volksgrenadier, his rifle pointed northward through a slit, stared at the horrified parents, their three trembling children, and wailing baby. Then the German soldier embraced the father and started crying.[71]

6   On the southern flank of the Bulge, opposite the XVIII Airborne Corps, those troops of the American III Corps that were not part of the push to Houffalize from Bastogne, aided by one division from the XII Corps, were embroiled in the bitter battle for Wiltz, a

town with a population of about four thousand. Patton's offensive against the strategic town, located ten miles east of Bastogne inside the Grand Duchy of Luxemburg, had come to a halt in sight of the objective by the end of December. The attack resumed on January 6. It was the beginning of two weeks of ferocious fighting in which the Germans defended Wiltz with a tenacity reminiscent of that of the Americans in Bastogne. The effects on the villages and hamlets in Wiltz's perimeter were as disastrous as they were for those surrounding the Belgian town.[72]

Artillery and aircraft had been pummeling the enemy positions south of Wiltz relentlessly since the holdup and continued to do so right up to the attack on January 6. The civilians paid a heavy toll along with the Germans. In Roullingen, for example, the Germans evacuated the entire village except the Wolter family. On the first day of 1945, Mrs. Wolter, her fourteen-year-old son, and one of her uncles lay dead under the rubble in their cellar. By the time of the American attack, artillery fire against Nocher had already left one villager blind and four others dead. Most had become casualties while trying to tend their cattle.[73]

At dawn on January 6, soldiers of the 80th Infantry Division renewed the attack with a push southeast of Wiltz. Exhausted, disheveled, chilled to the bone, the GIs took Goesdorf before noon. Afterward, they guzzled liters of brandy served by the villagers and hurriedly peeled potatoes, wolfing them down raw with some salt. In the afternoon they stormed Dahl yelling and growling, their bayonets fixed. House-to-house fighting left eight-year-old Hilda Grethen dying; blood emptying from an artery in her neck. One of the hardened GIs responsible for Hilda's death was inconsolable, begging the girl's mother for forgiveness.[74]

That same day, the Americans stalled in front of Nocher. They laid siege to the village for nearly two weeks. Trapped, seventy civilians were forced to undergo the traumatic experience; all of them packed together in a single farm, fifteen in one cellar and fifty-five in another. There was barely enough air to breathe, only watery soup to survive on, no chance to care for cattle. Some 150 shells struck the village each day. German batteries from the snow-covered heights noisily fired back, their gunners wearing gold-trimmed white vestments taken from the church. Aircraft dived on Nocher, repeatedly bombing and strafing it. Worse than anything else was the burning phosphorus, dripping from roofs, seeping into cellars, releasing sickening fumes.

In the evening of Sunday, January 14, Germans chased the civilians in Nocher from their cellars and ordered them to Kautenbach. Deep drifts of snow slowed the villagers down. Phosphorus fallout forced them to dive for cover more than once. Children wailed hysterically; elderly collapsed and refused to go on. It took the group of seventy six long hours to cover four miles. In Kautenbach they had trouble finding a shelter, finally settling in a drafty cellar on the Wiltz River, its walls shiny with ice. There they stayed for ten days, begging bread from German soldiers, eating cow meat riddled with shrapnel, robbing shoes from corpses. The Germans showed little sympathy for the refugees, at one point even forcing the weakened men out into the street to have them shovel snow to facilitate their retreat. GIs of the 80th Division liberated Kautenbach on January 24, allowing the haggard refugees from Nocher to return home three days later. There they found only thirteen of forty-four hearths still inhabitable.[75]

While the Germans desperately tried to stave off the GIs southeast of Wiltz, aircraft and artillery increasingly pounded the area northwest of the town in preparation for an attack with American troops bearing down from Bastogne. Here, too, the effects of so much firepower were devastating for soldiers and civilians alike. Germans in Noertrange commandeered the sturdy cellars, chasing the villagers into the more vulnerable stables and barns. Three civilians were dead when the occupier on January 11 ordered most of the people of Noertrange to disappear altogether. They stumbled to Niederwiltz, crazed by fear and wrapped in bedsheets in the hope that these would leave them invisible in the thick snow. Of the few people they left behind, four more would perish from Allied fire before the liberation.[76]

Early in the afternoon on Saturday, January 13, fifteen fighter-bombers peeled off in the direction of Brachtenbach. Panicked by the thunderous roar, the Philippart family rushed from their cellar, sprinting to the shelter of a nearby home they thought more solid. The aircraft lashed out at the village with blind rage, leveling eleven buildings, badly damaging three others including the school. They killed so many German soldiers that their comrades did not have time to bury them all. They also killed eleven civilians. Among them were Mr. Philippart and his three young children. In one of war's cruel ironies, the raid had left the home that the Philipparts had abandoned untouched.

Fate dealt harshly with yet another family in Brachtenbach. Mrs. Mersch's oldest son was one of the unfortunates who had perished in the air raid on Saturday. On Tuesday, as they crossed the street to a nearby farm, it was shell fire that took the mother and her three eldest daughters by surprise. Smoke and dust cleared to reveal four corpses. Three were those of Mrs. Mersch's daughters. The fourth belonged to a woman who had stepped into the street to hand the mourners a freshly baked loaf of bread. Mrs. Mersch survived unharmed, sentenced to a life of unfathomable grief.[77]

Despite fierce preparatory fire, the going remained tough for the American infantry. The battle for the small but key village of Oberwampach, for example, erupted on January 16 and was to last three days. House-to-house fighting and repeated German counterattacks with tanks destroyed much of the village, adding five more civilian dead to the three who had fallen victim to American artillery earlier. Among the battle casualties was five-year-old Marcel Shilling. The boy was killed by shrapnel together with the selfless American sergeant who had tried to carry him to safety across the road and away from his burning home.[78]

The scenes the GIs witnessed as they pushed from village to village were heartrending. In the twin villages of Niederwampach-Schimpach, two Allied air strikes on Christmas Day and New Year's Day had set close to half the buildings ablaze with fire bombs. American artillery had completed the job. When ground troops arrived on January 15, no more than five of about sixty homes remained intact. Though many people were ill and diphtheria was rampant, it took a week before ambulances could get them to hospitals. Four people died in the days after they were liberated.[79]

Infantry captured Noertrange on Sunday, January 21, to find the corpses of seven civilians in the church. Only four were in coffins; the others lay covered in sheets. Jeeps brought four more coffins with civilian dead to the church from nearby Grümelscheid. Out of a population of 320, the twin villages of Brachtenbach-Derenbach by the time of the second liberation that same Sunday had buried 39 killed by shells, bombs, disease, and deprivation. Wrapped in blankets and sheets, 17 of them had been lowered into a mass grave on January 18. A shell had plowed into the grave the following morning, refusing to leave the victims in peace even in their final resting place.[80]

Still on Sunday, January 21, the Americans finally managed to capture the town they had been fighting for. After weeks of ferocious battle they entered Wiltz without opposition as the Germans had decided to withdraw the previous day. Artillery and fighter-bombers had caused significant material damage to the town. Out of 922 houses, 44 were totally demolished and another 253 badly damaged. Yet, as at Bastogne, the number of civilian casualties at Wiltz was light compared with those killed in the perimeter. Of an estimated two thousand civilians hidden in solid cellars during some five weeks of fighting, thirty-two perished as a result of battle or the deprivation and disease it engendered. Two days after Wiltz's liberation they were all lined up in coffins for the official burial ceremony. Comparisons with the grief of those in the perimeter did nothing to assuage that of the victims' relatives and friends in Wiltz's icy cemetery.[81]

Around the time the Americans captured Wiltz, the last of the dreaded SS security Kommandos slipped back across the German border from the northern tip of Luxembourg as stealthily as they had gone about their sinister business in the rear of the armed forces. Even while falling back, however, they had marked their trail with blood and suffering, arresting, deporting, and executing people suspected of membership in the resistance or Miliz, deserting the armed forces, or any other kind of disloyal behavior.

The list is brutal in its monotony. Four men arrested in the vicinity of Beiler and Leithum on January 6 were put on transport to Germany. Three of them returned after the war. The fourth, Alphonse Dhur, a farmer, perished in a prison convoy to Dachau. On January 8 or 9 the Gestapo in Vianden arrested seventy-eight-year-old Jean Bous and eighty-one-year-old Margaretha Thielen. Husband and wife were driven off to a wood near Clervaux and told to enter it arm in arm. Both were shot in the neck at close range. Another married couple, Michel Elsen and Elise Arendt, were arrested in Enscheringen on January 10 and deported to Germany. Allied troops liberated Mr. Elsen in March but came too late to save his wife. They also failed to arrive in time for one of three people from Troisvierges sent to Germany as prisoners on January 12: an SS Kommando on March 26 executed Emilie Schmitz near Hirzenhain together with eighty other women and six men from all over Europe. Much later, in the summer of 1945, people in a pine wood near Vianden discovered the corpses of three men. German troops in Merscheid had delivered two of them, Felix Martzen and Frantz Weiler, into the hands of the Gestapo on January 9. A similar fate had befallen the other, Michel Menster from Bettendorf, on January 13, five days before the return of the Americans. All three had been punished with a bullet in the back of their heads.[82]

From Wiltz American troops pushed farther north into the Clerf Valley. There they ran into the enemy's last defensive line in Luxembourg. Running north-south, parallel with the West Wall, it ran along the heights on the Clerf's east bank. The Germans had been preparing it for weeks with help from civilians requisitioned in the surrounding villages and forced to shovel snow, dig trenches, and build machine-gun emplacements. In the Clerf Valley, too, the gruesome fate that civilians suffered at the hands of both occupiers and liberators caused the GIs heartache in village upon village. In Siebenaler, for example, they learned that two teenagers of the Maintz family had died of diphtheria for lack of medical assistance. Troops of the 26th Division took the key town of Munshausen after three days of merciless fighting. Three-quarters of its forty-five homes by that time were largely destroyed, most of them burned. Artillery had killed seven of the villagers it was supposed to liberate. Of the Rodesch family, five-year-old Leo was the only one to see the Americans enter Munshausen on January 27. His father and mother, his uncle, his ten-year-old sister, Trinchen, and his eleven-year-old brother, Nicolas, were no longer there. All in a flash had been wiped away by a single shell that had struck their home two weeks earlier. The boy was too numb with shock to register the liberation.[83]

7 Close to the base of the Bulge, the V Corps from the north joined the Allied offensive almost two weeks after the concerted attack had gotten underway. Spearheaded and flanked by infantry of the veteran 1st, 2nd, and 30th Divisions, the 7th Armored Division began fighting its way back to St. Vith on January 15.

Massive concentrations of artillery had ceaselessly hammered the area north of St. Vith in the two weeks preceding the attack. The shelling grew steadily worse as the ground troops inched closer. The forty-five remaining civilians in Hünningen trooped together in the cellars of a handful of the most solid farms. And it was only there that they could continue to take care of the animals. The precious livestock elsewhere had to be abandoned. By the time the Americans captured the village, 90 percent of its cattle had disappeared, died of hunger and cold, or fallen prey to shells. Artillery fire killed so many German soldiers in Honsfeld that corpses began to contaminate water sources and wells, giving rise to cholera-like diseases. "Every single day it was the same," remembered Mrs. Düchers of Schoppen, "shelling . . . shelling. . . ." People in their cellars in Schoppen became so isolated that they lost all notion of what was happening with their neighbors or whether indeed they were still alive. Only the occasional visit of the local priest, dashing from shelter to shelter to offer Communion and take confession, brought some of the much-awaited news of what was happening to the village above their heads.[84]

Shells, unlike bombs, only rarely managed to penetrate the rock solid cellars so typical of the Ardennes homes and farms. Still, artillery regularly sneaked up on civilians as they abandoned their underground sanctuaries to grab something in the upstairs rooms, get water from a well, or care for their animals. And so, by ones and twos and little handfuls, the list of casualties from shelling steadily added up. A direct hit on the Jenniges home in Wallerode on January 19, for example, killed one man and one woman, claiming the eye of yet another woman. In one of the worst instances in the area, a shell the following day struck a house in Crombach, taking the lives of four members of the Zeyen family. Even in a village as tiny as Rodt, possibly as many as eight civilians fell victim to artillery fire in a series of incidents throughout January.[85]

The merciless shelling frayed the German soldiers' nerves and, together with the air attacks, seriously disrupted their supply lines. As a result, troops in the area, a mixture of paratroopers, Waffen SS, and Volksgrenadiers, became increasingly unpredictable in their behavior even toward the German-speaking Belgians whom the Nazis had claimed belonged to the Reich. German soldiers systematically plundered food, taking from houses and farms whatever else they could use. They forced farmers to get their horses and wagons and haul equipment, made civilians shovel snow from the roads, ordered inhabitants of Heppenbach to dig trenches, and requisitioned men in Eibertingen to erect machine-gun emplacements. Peter Fleming, the ten-year-old in Rodt who on December 22, against the advice of his father, had donned a Hitlerjugend cap, proudly returning a confident soldier's "Heil Hitler" salute, suddenly felt sorely disappointed by the Führer's troops. He angrily threw his German cap into the fire, exchanging it right away for much smarter-looking headgear that the GIs had left behind in December.[86]

Those GIs were drawing inexorably closer. And with them the battles that would claim still more civilian casualties. Stubborn fighting on both sides pinned the villagers between a rock and a hard place. American tanks, for example, rolled into Deidenberg on January 20. Mrs. Michels scraped all of her courage together and, holding one of her children by the hand, walked toward the lead vehicle. "Nix Soldat?" a tanker demanded to know. "No," Mrs. Michels answered truthfully. For a few seconds the tank did not move. Then, suddenly, one of the crew motioned Mrs. Michels to step aside. They fired a shot and, almost instantly, a second one. Both shells slammed into the Müller home. Mr. Müller survived the explosion. But his wife and two of his three children were dead. No one in the village ever learned why. That very day the same question remained unanswered for the parents and sister of Elisabeth Johanns in Eibertingen. Captured by the GIs a day earlier than Deidenberg, German guns opened up on the village just when the American batteries had fallen silent. One of them caught twenty-three-year-old Elisabeth off guard at the horse stable. She died with her family kneeling over her.[87]

In an act of bittersweet revenge, troops of the 7th Armored Division on January 23 at last recaptured St. Vith. They barely recognized the town the Germans had forced them to abandon about a month earlier. There were no more houses or stores, only a pockmarked moonscape of stone and dust. Instead of the hustle and bustle of people, there was only the hush of giant graves of rubble hiding countless frozen corpses. Where once trucks and horse-drawn wagons had lumbered by, American bulldozers had to scrape paths through tons of wreckage and debris.[88]

With St. Vith back in American hands, armor and infantry now lunged eastward from the corridor they had carved. As always, artillery spewed fire from behind their backs in support. They did so most literally as copious amounts of phosphorus rained down, setting ablaze villages and towns. "Even the snow seemed to be burning," Mrs. Mertens said of the war's last days in Büllingen. So panicked were some in Amel that they took the dirty smoke and strange smell to be signs of a gas attack. In Möderscheid, the tiniest of hamlets, phosphorus set several homes and barns on fire, killing one woman with its toxic fumes.[89]

The veteran American ground troops, well aware of the fighting qualities of their opponent, refused to take risks, preferring to be safe rather than sorry. In doing so, they more than once made civilians pay the price. The battle for Wallerode lasted three days. On the first day the Gilles home caught fire. From it poured Mrs. Gilles as well as Mr. and Mrs. Wiesemes and their two sons. They stuck to a roadside ditch trying to reach a nearby home. They were about halfway there when the metallic sound of rapid rifle fire rang out. Mrs. Wiesemes collapsed with a shot through her lung. Looking up from the bottom of the ditch, she could see that her sons were safe. But her husband was dead and Mrs. Gilles mortally wounded. The group of five remained pinned to the ground for three long hours. Helped by her sons, Mrs. Wiesemes finally made it to the nearby house, where she received treatment. As the battle finally neared its end on the third day, tense GIs moved through the streets emptying their guns at anything that moved. One of the bullets seriously injured Hermann Dupont. The Americans rushed him away in an ambulance as soon as they could. They did the same with Mrs. Wiesemes. As the ambulance pulled out of Wallerode, she caught a glimpse of her husband's corpse next to the road where it had been for three days. Mrs. Dupont waited three years to find out what had happened to her husband. Completely in the dark about where the Americans had taken him, she finally learned in 1948 that he had died and was buried in a cemetery in Spa.[90]

"You sure should be glad you live in the States," a private from the 86th Chemical Mortar Battalion wrote to his father on January 24, "and not over here." The GIs could not but feel sorry for the civilians in and around St. Vith. At the same time, however, they were also very suspicious of the German-speaking Belgians. In the wake of liberation, there followed a series of wrongful arrests. In one case, farmers wearing GI clothes because they had no others were arrested. In another case, a monk was mistaken for a spy because he had changed his robe for civilian clothing to work in the monastery's stables. American troops in Eibertingen took drastic measures to make themselves feel more at ease: they ordered all men aged fourteen to sixty to relocate to a village in the French-speaking part of Belgium far to the rear.[91]

8 Patton ordered the XII Corps to join the attack from the south and capture northern Luxembourg three days after the start of the drive on St. Vith from the north. Involved in static warfare from positions south of the Sûre since late December, the 4th and 5th Infantry Divisions in the week before the attack on January 18 massed their troops and had corps and divisional artillery blast the area north of the river.

Alerted by all this activity that the final push was near, the Germans decided to remove the civilians from the northern bank of the Sûre as rapidly as possible. They designated Brandenbourg as the assembly point for the evacuees. Located about three miles north of Diekirch, the village lay hidden in a deep valley and in the long shadow of an imposing medieval castle. For the people of Erpeldange, Ingeldorf, and Bettendorf, the order to pack up and leave came on Sunday, January 14. If German planning for the evacuation was systematic, however, its execution amidst the chaos of an impending attack faltered. In Ingeldorf and Bettendorf, civilians ignored the order, soldiers were too preoccupied with preparations for the looming battle to enforce it, and the evacuation never took place. For the inhabitants of Erpeldange the order to move out was issued on Sunday evening. They, too, hoped to avoid evacuation, knowing full well that liberation was a question of days and that a trek to the rear with constant shelling was more dangerous than hunkering down in underground shelters. But in Erpeldange the Germans refused to take no for an answer. Shortly after midnight, eighteen elderly and ill were carried to one of the village's cellars. All others assembled at the church and, guarded by German soldiers, left for Brandenbourg with three horse-drawn wagons. Deep snow and shell fire slowed them down, allowing them to cover only four miles in four hours. The following night some men returned to Erpeldange with the wagons to fetch the eighteen remaining villagers for a trek to Brandenbourg at least as arduous.[92]

Diekirch, meanwhile, was suffering the full wrath of American artillery more than any other place on the Sûre's northern bank. "Shell after shell comes our way," a tormented Michael Preisen wrote in his diary in the last week of the siege, "it is almost beyond endurance; the walls are full of holes and no longer strong." More and more of these shells were incendiaries, splattering white phosphorus onto roofs and walls and setting entire blocks on fire. From his vantage point alone, Mr. Preisen on one particular day observed "15 to 20 different places burning simultaneously." To seal the German escape routes, American batteries and fighter-bombers poured most of their deadly loads into the northern part of Diekirch. This was where the brewery and hospital happened to be located, their cellars packed with civilians. A nightmare descended on Félicie Lanners in the town brewery. On Saturday, January 13, her mother died from a lung infection. A week earlier her aged father had died from a heart attack when shells exploded right in the brewery's courtyard. Her parents' bodies and several others were laid out in the open in one of the malt works' icy storerooms. But Félicie insisted they be laid to rest in coffins. She risked her life darting to a nearby carpenter. They returned with the coffins to find a German soldier in the storeroom. He had placed a candle before the bodies and was praying. When he saw the civilians, he slunk away without speaking a word. Félicie Lanners took a knife and carved the names of her parents in the coffin lids. Word came down on Tuesday for the inhabitants of Diekirch, too, to evacuate to Brandenbourg. Few heeded the German order, but some forty harrowed refugees in the brewery did. Félicie was not one of them. She decided to stay with her parents and watch over them.[93]

At dawn on Thursday, January 18, American troops crossed the Sûre along a stretch running from Ettelbrück to Reisdorf. On the northern bank civilians whom the Germans had failed to get rid of just days earlier now stood in the way of the liberators. GIs who captured Gilsdorf that Thursday quickly rounded up all remaining inhabitants, herded them into two large cellars, and made sure to put guards at the doors. In Bettendorf conditions in which the civilians lived proved so appalling that American officers got involved as soon as the fighting ceased on Thursday. They ordered ambulances to speed the injured and sick to hospitals in Luxembourg City. Notes were made of what the people said they needed most urgently. The following day Bettendorf received quantities of foodstuffs, yeast, salt, and burning fuel.[94]

For the civilians inside Diekirch the street fighting that erupted on Thursday was as frightening as the endless shelling and bombing. "Nebelwerfers howled, machine guns hammered, rifle shots cracked," remembered Forester Zeyen, "all hell had broken loose." Mortar battalions fired smoke shells to shield the infantry, but people in the town brewery mistook the wisps of fog that reeked of chemicals for gas and cried alarm. When shooting suddenly erupted around the Haentges home and shattered the windows, everyone inside dropped to the floor. The door was kicked from its hinges with a crash. Two men holding weapons peeked inside. Emil Grosbusch recognized two American soldiers. "I jumped right up," he explained, "and wanted to hug them." They stopped him with their rifles in his stomach, pinned him against the wall, and made him hold his hands up. Only when one of the women assured them in English that he was not German did the GIs back off, but only reluctantly.[95]

Infantrymen of the 5th Division who entered Diekirch's brewery on Friday morning looked straight through Félicie Lanners and the other wretched civilians in the cellars. They searched every nook and cranny and took off again without ever saying a word. Then medics and a chaplain came to take care of the civilians. They gave them hot meals and warm clothing. "The chaplain blessed the dead and held a Mass, with a generator serving as altar," Félicie Lanners vividly remembered. "Even the toughest men cried when they realized that they were finally free."[96]

The chaplain warned, however, that the danger was not yet over. From the north now, German shells pummeled the Sûre's north bank, striking parts of Diekirch until as late as January 23. By that time many of the villages and towns near the river lay in ruins. Of the approximately 1,100 homes in Diekirch, 174 had been demolished, most by fire. Another 650 homes were damaged but declared inhabitable. When things had quieted down, forty-six civilian casualties were lowered into the ground in an official burial ceremony in Diekirch's cemetery. Nine had perished in shrapnel and phosphorus. Thirty-seven were elderly who had failed to withstand the stress and cruel deprivations of war.[97]

With Diekirch completely in American hands on January 19, battle quickly shifted from the Sûre's northern bank to the main road leading north from the town to Hosingen. Artillery and aircraft smashed up anything that looked even remotely like an enemy target, creating havoc among the long columns of retreating troops. The German soldiers looked exhausted and disheveled. They roamed farms famished. There remained so little fuel that each of their vehicles could be seen towing another. Demoralized and testy, they requisitioned civilians to help clear roads leading east to the West Wall. In Merscheid all men aged fifteen to sixty-five and all women between seventeen and forty-five were ordered out of their cellars. They were told to shovel snow and dig graves for dead comrades.[98]

In village after village along the road to Hosingen, American troops uncovered untold civilian suffering. In Bastendorf, for example, twenty-six of the seventy-six homes were destroyed or badly damaged. Much more of a disaster for this farming community, however, was the fact that almost all of its animals had either been killed or taken away by German soldiers: 409 head of cattle, 45 horses, 310 hogs, 5 sheep, and close to 1,500 poultry. In Brandenbourg, the German collecting point for evacuees, the GIs ran into civilians who were half-frozen and half-starved, the eyes of many emptied by worry and fear. Medics all over the area had their hands full treating injuries, many caused by shrapnel, others by phosphorus that had dripped from the sky and burned holes in the skin. The sick formed an equally worrisome problem. As soon as American troops liberated Merscheid, Joseph Turpel begged them to have a look at his children, all nine of whom lay in a dank cellar terribly ill. Medics of the 5th Infantry Division instantly diagnosed them with diphtheria. One of the children, Margrit, died before an ambulance had a chance to arrive. The soldiers helped the anguished father bury his daughter in the garden. They sped the other children to a hospital in Luxembourg City. There the medical staff was able to save all except Bernadette.[99]

Total evacuation was the only answer to the chaos and disruption in many a town and village. The spread of disease in Merscheid and lack of food made the Americans decide to have trucks remove the inhabitants to the rear right away. No more than a dozen men received permission to stay behind to watch over what remained of the village and its animals. Before long, three of them were ill, too, and had to be carried off to the Luxembourg capital. Hoscheid, a dozen of its inhabitants killed in the fighting in January and forty of its sixty-one homes uninhabitable, was evacuated on January 26. In a few of the convoy's army trucks the inhabitants of Schlindermanderscheid sat packed together. They had been through this uprooting experience before, earlier in January, in horse-drawn wagons ordered to Hoscheid by the Germans. The Americans unloaded them in Luxembourg City exhausted and filthy, too apathetic to respond to the sight of their country's proud capital.[100]

9 As infantry from the XII Corps pushed into the northern tip of Luxembourg through knee-high snow at the end of January, troops from the III and VIII Corps swung sharply northeast to help drive the enemy troops back into the Reich behind the West Wall. Some five American divisions now converged on Burg Reuland in Belgium's German-speaking East Cantons.

Remnants of the German armies that had smashed into the Allied lines in December desperately tried to extricate themselves from the rapidly shrinking Bulge. They were being torn to pieces, however, by Allied aircraft and artillery that rained destruction on anything that dared move or looked slightly suspicious. Once again the demands of war denied the luxury of differentiating between enemy soldiers and the civilians they were inevitably mixed up with. Fighter-bombers roamed the skies so aggressively that the Germans hurried to have entire areas bathed in artificial fog.[101]

Civilians in the area had their own ways of making themselves invisible. They had learned earlier in the month how destructive air-craft could be during the air force's attempts to sever German supply lines. American fighter-bombers on January 8, for example, had swooped down on Weweler. In a matter of minutes they had released some eighty bombs that had wiped away the village center in a fun-nel of smoke and dust, had damaged all other buildings, and had left three young women dead. In an air raid on the bridge and railroad in Steinebrück five days later, a single bomb had sufficed to efface the Schmitz home and with it a mother and four children. Those civilians in Steinebrück, however, who at the time of the air strike had been hiding in a nearby slate quarry, remained unscathed. They wisely stayed there until the Americans arrived at the end of January.

Many others in the area decided to withdraw to similar dank but solid shelters to survive the endless pounding. Between forty and fifty civilians in Schönberg, for example, fled to a quarry and trooped to-gether in one of the horizontal shafts. By the time of the liberation the air had grown so foul and was so lacking in oxygen that candles could barely be kept lit. Living conditions in Lommersweiler's railroad tun-nel were hardly more comfortable. Countless civilians, many of them refugees from St. Vith, had flocked to the disused tunnel fearing new air raids. At first the villagers were kind enough to bring them some food while the refugees were able to go out to cut wood for fuel in the drafty shelter. But in the last days of January ferocious shelling put a halt to all that as it prevented the tunnel dwellers even from scooping snow for drinking water.[102]

For a while German soldiers had shared the Lommersweiler tun-nel with the civilians. But then enraged officers had discovered them and kicked them out. German troops were now a mere shadow of what they had been when they jumped off for the surprise offensive on December 16. Deserters roamed the woods, imploring civilians to hide them. On the roads to the West Wall vehicles stood bumper to bumper for miles. Troops passed them on foot, on bicycles, on horses. The Germans were starving, chilled to the bone, infested with lice. They made food, wood, hay, clothing, watches, and tools disappear. They suffered from dysentery that forced them dishonorably to empty their bowels next to the roads, in the preserving jars of farms, even in churches.[103]

German aid stations could no longer cope with the influx of maimed soldiers. Cella Förster in a farm in Bracht became nauseated by the bloody bandages, amputated limbs, and excreta piling up in the vegetable garden. Inside she had to tread carefully to avoid stepping on casualties crammed together in puddles of blood and urine. She was astonished when suddenly she noticed a civilian among the Germans. The medics were too busy with their own to look after him. With the help of a farmhand she carried the badly injured man to a separate room and cared for him as well she could. He whispered his name and that he had come all the way from the vicinity of Rochefort, where his house had been hit and his son killed. He died a few days later. Mrs. Förster saw to it that he received a proper burial. In his jacket she found a child's shoe, a rosary wrapped around it.[104]

With mind-numbing repetition and voracious irony the senseless killing of civilians continued until the very end. In Alster, a tiny village in sight of the German border, the Becker family rejoiced too early when American infantrymen reached their farm in the afternoon of January 27, searched rooms and cellars, and declared their home safe. The excited daughters hurried away and returned to the kitchen with apples. They were happily watching the GIs munch away when suddenly a handful of Germans launched a counterattack with armor. A shell exploded in the middle of the kitchen. Two daughters were slightly injured and rushed to a hospital in Arlon. The younger of the sisters, Elisabeth, was in too much pain to be moved. She died shortly after midnight, on the day that official Allied histories would later declare to be the last of the Battle of the Bulge.[105]

Epilogue

Rebuilding Elisabeth Becker was just one of an estimated 2,500 civilians killed in Belgium as a direct or indirect result of the Battle of the Bulge. To that number another 500 noncombatants have to be added who perished in the Grand Duchy of Luxembourg. An early survey in 1945 spoke of at least 600 seriously injured civilians in Belgium alone. The total number of wounded for both countries certainly ran much higher, though it is impossible to establish with precision sixty years after the facts. Ironically, roughly one-third of the civilian dead in Belgium were caused by Allied air raids, especially those involving medium and heavy bombers as carried out against towns like St. Vith, Houffalize, Malmedy, and La Roche.[1]

The material damage was disastrous. Not even religious sanctuaries had been spared: in the Belgian provinces of Luxembourg and Namur, for example, 18 churches lay in ruins while 69 others were badly damaged. In the province of Luxembourg more than 5,600 houses were destroyed and 6,900 badly damaged. The province of Liège counted 2,800 homes reduced to rubble and 4,000 damaged. In the province of Namur 270 houses were devastated and 1,900 more or less damaged. In the Grand Duchy of Luxembourg 2,118 homes were wiped away and another 1,411 seriously damaged. All in all, some 11,000 homes inside the salient were left totally uninhabitable, a particularly serious concern in a region where winters tended to be harsh.[2]

Equally disastrous was the fact that the livelihoods of many in this predominantly agricultural region had been wiped out. Together, for example, the provinces of Luxembourg and Liège lost 3,290 horses, 31,864 cattle, and 14,623 hogs, or respectively 30, 23, and 57 percent of the number of animals before the battle. In the twenty-one worst-hit communities these percentages climbed to 65, 44, and 82 percent. Many of the surviving animals were starving because there was nothing to feed them with. Much of what had been harvested in 1944 was lost with the destruction of barns and granges. In Bertogne, for example, 174 of 210 farmers lost their crops, in Flamierge 183 of 258, in Longchamps 175 of 326, and in Longvilly 200 of 300. In places like Houffalize, Grand-Halleux, and several others nothing at all remained of what had been reaped that year.[3]

Myriad other problems plagued the region in the wake of battle. Merciless shelling, for example, had riddled trees with shrapnel, significantly reducing the value of timber and causing sawmills problems until many years after the war. Where white phosphorus, the much used and feared incendiary, had contaminated the soil, grass and crops refused to grow for a long time. In fact, when spring arrived in 1945 and the sun began to warm the earth, the nasty substance was reported to ignite again all over the Ardennes. People in Osweiler had to wait until 1946 for the village's natural spring to be rid entirely of phosphorus residue.[4]

Though the least of people's worries immediately after the war, the loss of administrative and archival materials eventually caused considerable headaches. In St. Vith, for example, the municipal register of births, marriages, and deaths went up in flames with the rest of the town. Copies of the records from 1800 to 1939 had been brought to safety in a citadel in Koblenz, Germany, and survived the war. From 1940 on, however, the German occupier had not bothered to make copies. With the help of inhabitants, newspapers, and radio, it took local authorities two years of painstaking detective work to put together 96 percent of the register for St. Vith and surrounding villages.[5]

Battle in its greed swallowed not only lives but also their histories. In the 1990s, for instance, the Belgian Maubeuge family through patient genealogical research finally managed to trace its ancestors as far back as the early 1700s. That trace unfortunately led them to Marenne, a village close to what had been the Verdenne pocket in 1944. There their hopeful search for family roots abruptly ended when they learned that the local parish records had gone up in flames.[6]

In communities recaptured from the Germans, the American military was the first authority responsible for bringing order to a situation of utter chaos. Civil Affairs units immediately established contact with local authorities to coordinate aid or, in the absence of such authorities, temporarily appointed mayors and other officials deemed reliable. One of the first concerns was to have army ambulances available to take injured and sick civilians to military and civilian hospitals. Another one was to have army trucks supply the civilians with enough food, blankets, clothing, and coal to tide them over the first days. Illnesses formed another headache as they easily flared up in ravaged towns and villages. The Fifth Army, for example, rushed in medical personnel to fight diphtheria while its engineers established water points to help control outbreaks of dysentery.[7]

At the same time, with Civil Affairs units overburdened by more than 43,000 Belgians needing material assistance of some kind and 45,000 Luxembourgers scattered as refugees, the American military worked hard to prevent those inhabitants who had fled west of the Meuse from returning too early. Radio, public address trucks, and newspapers urged people to remain where they were while GIs and gendarmes were posted at the Meuse bridges to enforce restrictions. As early as January 26, 1945, however, a Fifth Army report noted that refugees and evacuees were "understandably anxious to return, and somewhat restive under restrictions on travel." Still, it was early spring before most of the civilians had been allowed to return to their homes.[8]

There was only so much that Civil Affairs personnel could do to help civilians. In fact, there was only so much that they were allowed to do. "Relief," an official policy directive on Civil Affairs operations in northwest Europe starkly reminded, "except as otherwise directed, is limited to that required by military necessity." For much of the vital aid, therefore, civilians had to look to people other than soldiers. The first aid workers to arrive in the recaptured areas on the heels of the American military most often belonged to the Red Cross. In fact, in mid-January the Belgian Red Cross was complaining that mayors were turning to them for help even in matters outside their competence. The Red Cross more than any other organization was to be credited for containing the dangerous and contagious diseases that authorities initially feared would engulf the Ardennes. From Brussels, for example, the Belgian Red Cross by mid-February 1945 had dispatched some two hundred doctors, nurses, ambulance drivers, and administrators to the stricken area to assist volunteers from the organization's local sections. In the Marche-Lierneux-Bastogne triangle they successfully combated the occurrence of dysentery. In Arlon and Givry they set up centers with the specific purpose of preventing croup epidemics. Special measures were taken to deal with the high incidence of pneumonia. At the end of February the Belgian Red Cross was proud to report that the health situation had been stabilized and that "not a single serious epidemic has broken out." Vigilance remained crucial, however, as events demonstrated in the Grand Duchy of Luxembourg when in the summer of 1945 an outbreak of typhus in the village of Consdorf killed fourteen people including a nurse.[9]

Apart from disease control, the Red Cross fulfilled many other tasks. The Belgian organization's all-female Motor Corps, for example, was responsible for the difficult job of carrying civilian patients to hospitals over disintegrated and mined roads. In consultation with the Belgian Ministry for Public Health, the Red Cross coordinated the workings of some seven hospitals in the stricken region. A Red Cross train was made available to take civilian casualties to Brussels where room was made even in the Royal Palace to receive victims. Meanwhile, special teams arrived to recover corpses from the rubble in the most heavily bombed towns and to help identify them. The Red Cross also set up centers of information designed to deal with hundreds of desperate people inquiring about relatives or friends that had gone missing during the battle. The final battle the Belgian Red Cross fought in the Ardennes in the autumn of 1945 was that against scabies, the result of the sickening filth that war inevitably brought in its wake.[10]

The local civil authorities recovered only slowly from the blow of the German surprise offensive. Many officials had fled and returned only gradually. One of the first orders issued by mayors everywhere, often urged on by Red Cross representatives who feared outbreaks of cholera with the arrival of spring thaw, was to have the countless livestock carcasses littering the villages buried or burned as soon as possible. Other than some superficial cleaning up, however, there was not much that mayors and their subjects could do without assistance from the central government. In Belgium, for example, such assistance was provided in the first place by the High Commission for the Defense of the Civilian Population. Responsible for facilitating and coordinating the activities of public services and NGOs, it was organized per province. There it closely cooperated with the governor, paying particular attention to the problem of food supply. Its representatives in many communities virtually served as substitutes for local authorities until by early March the situation had become sufficiently normalized for a directive to change the High Commission's role from an executive into an advisory one. Working shoulder to shoulder with the High Commission was the National Fund for Aid to the Victims. The National Fund, too, was organized per province, but its primary role was to provide more than twelve thousand afflicted families with what they most desperately needed apart from food. To this purpose the National Fund distributed clothing, linen, kitchen equipment, mattresses, and household utensils. Finally, there was the National Work for Children, which sent nurses into the most isolated areas to ensure that children, hit hardest together with the elderly, were adequately taken care of.[11]

Aid poured in from abroad, too. The American Red Cross sent ten trucks and in the hospitals and homes for the elderly in the province of Luxembourg alone distributed clothes and blankets worth 40 million Belgian francs. The British Red Cross presented Belgium with five trucks and fifteen ambulances. The Canadian organization donated large amounts of clothing and blankets. From Switzerland arrived Red Cross representatives to set up programs in schools providing children with milk products, while Swiss families in the Jura opened their homes to the children of devastated Houffalize.[12]

Still more heartwarming was the wave of solidarity that swept across the Ardennes from all over Belgium. In a matter of months a system of "adoption" had been set up in which communities spared by the war pledged to take care of places ravaged in the salient. Belgium's linguistic barriers temporarily evaporated as aid poured in from towns and villages in the Walloons as well as Flanders. Huy took La Roche under its wing, for example. Schaerbeek adopted Houffalize. Aalst did the same with Rochefort; Hasselt with Vielsalm; Bruges with Bastogne; and so on. In a badly devastated village like Grand-Halleux, trucks arrived with food, mattresses, clothes, shoes, utensils, candles, and coal from Clavier en Condroz, St.-Agatha-Berchem, and Eisden. Streets are still named after the benefactors and special ties, official and other, remain to this day. In the pocket of a coat that arrived in Grand-Halleux from St.-Agatha-Berchem in 1945 Marthe Mahaux found a note with an address and a message saying, "Things will be better tomorrow." The note was signed "Léa." The young women got in touch, started meeting, and before long Marthe's brother, André, had married Léa.[13]

Still, despite rapidly multiplying gestures of solidarity and visits from ministers and members of the royal family expressing sympathy, the crucial work of reconstruction took much longer than the inhabitants of the region had hoped. The task was, of course, gigantic, as can best be illustrated by the problems facing reconstruction in Luxembourg, the worst-hit Belgian province. To begin with, the province was totally isolated. Telephone, telegraph, and postal services were a total shambles while the main roads and railroads connecting Luxembourg with the rest of the country had been ripped to pieces. Most secondary roads had been destroyed or chewed up by heavy military traffic. Cars and trucks had all but disappeared. These circumstances made it extremely difficult to supply the province in sufficient quantities with the countless things it needed. Farmers desperately waited for feed, livestock, seed, tools, and wagons. The rural province's few industries remained paralyzed because sawmills and slate quarries lacked sufficient coal and most of the electricity plants had been ravaged. Finally, materials were needed for the rebuilding and restoration of close to 4,000 barns and stables, more than 28,000 homes, 157 acres of road surface, and 158 bridges. To make matters worse, there was such a shortage of laborers all over the Ardennes that German POWs and Belgian collaborators were put to work while thousands of builders were being attracted from as far away as Flanders. Pacifist Mennonites even came over from America to lend a hand in rebuilding, as they did in stricken areas across Europe and Asia after the war. They arrived in Büllingen in the spring of 1947, for example, and stayed there to help in construction as volunteers for two years.[14]

One gets an even better idea of the challenges facing the inhabitants by examining the road to construction in a single community. Of the 153 homes and public buildings in Faymonville, a village in the East Cantons, 81 were completely destroyed, 51 badly damaged, and 21 lightly, leaving not a single construction intact. The condition that the farmers' animals were in was equally discouraging. Of the 1,250 heads of cattle, about 300 had survived, while no more than 100 poultry remained of the 2,500 before the battle. Fields were pockmarked with nearly 26,000 shell holes from which some 30,000 cubic yards of earth had been thrown up. To help the farmers remove carcasses, fill craters, and plow fields, no more than 19 emaciated horses were left of the original 50. No wonder the people of Faymonville were grateful to have farmers in four Flemish villages send aid and accept thirty-six children into their homes for about half a year.

The rebuilding of the first of Faymonville's eighty-one ruins began in 1946. The reconstruction's peak did not occur until 1948, however, with five homes still not restored in 1950. Even then, only the ground floor of most of the new homes was inhabitable, with the rest still to be completed. As late as 1950 only the number of horses and hogs had returned to the levels on the eve of the battle. Five years after the battle poultry had reached just half that level and cattle still only three-quarters.[15]

Most of the reconstruction across the Belgian battlefield was completed by 1953–54, ten years after the battle. By that time, too, much of St. Vith had been rebuilt on its original site, even though some in 1945 had suggested leaving the ruins as a memorial to the madness of war and to start the town anew close to Neundorf. Still, the construction of roads and underground sewers in St. Vith was not entirely completed until 1965.[16]

If the material aspects of reconstruction posed serious headaches, the financial side of the story proved even more frustrating. Initially there was, of course, not nearly enough money available to please everyone in a country that had been ravaged and plundered during four years of war. Even so, administrative foot-dragging and legal hairsplitting needlessly prolonged the financial agony of many, often stretching their patience to the breaking point. Members in parliament representing Bastogne, Houffalize, Manhay, and Vielsalm, for example, for many years tried to get a bill accepted that would at last make the Belgian government cough up almost 100 million francs in war damage arrears dating back to the Battle of the Bulge. They were still trying at least as late as 1999.[17]

The story of reconstruction would be far from complete if mention were not made of the devastating problem of abandoned mines and other explosives. In fact, in the first months after the battle, people were more concerned about these devilish devices than they were about rebuilding or financial assistance. When the mayor of Vesqueville, a village near St. Hubert, decided in late January to have the snow cleared from the roads, most farmers refused to cooperate. They had good reason: so many mines had been sown in the vicinity that they feared the job would cost them their few remaining horses. A quick inventory of the weaponry lying about in Consdorf immediately after the battle, for example, gives an idea of the mind-boggling dangers everywhere in the salient. Inhabitants of the tiny village reported no less than 248 shells, 27 mines (2 of which were heavy Teller antitank mines), 60 *Panzerfausts*, 17 mortar shells, 63 hand grenades, and 4 boxes of rifle ammunition.[18]

Still more dangerous, however, were the killing devices remaining hidden beneath snow and earth. No wonder then that from all over the former salient reports poured in of inhabitants virtually paralyzed by the fear of abandoned explosives. To the civilians the war in a way appeared to continue immediately after the liberation as news circulated of casualty upon casualty. On January 14 the village priest was killed in Champs when he opened a door in one of the homes and set off a booby trap. About a week later a mine killed two refugees on their way home to Ennal from the safe haven of Farnières. On February 4 mines killed two teenage boys in Tillet and another one in Bra. Inhabitants of Grand-Halleux that same day searched the woods for foxholes, digging through the GI trash in hopes of finding canned food, clothing, and blankets. Jean Jacquemart reached for an object when suddenly a terrible explosion made him disappear. Villagers carried back what remained of the twenty-two-year-old in a blood-stained sheet.[19]

While the list of tragic deaths went on and on, people had no idea of whom to turn to for help. American and British troops had other battles to fight, making time for the systematic clearing of mines only when necessary for their own safety. Civilians here and there took it upon themselves to render the devices harmless, often paying with their lives for their courage and lack of expertise. It was the Belgian military that finally began sending experts to the region by mid-February 1945. At first they were small groups belonging to the SEDEEO, a specialized service in existence since before the war. On February 17, for example, a team of no more than fifty arrived to clear explosives the length and breadth of the province of Luxembourg. Belatedly realizing the scope and urgency of the problem, the Belgian government early in April 1945 created the 1st "Ardennes" Battalion, a separate unit of some one thousand men intended solely for clearing mines.[20]

The battalion was made up of professionals as well as conscripts and more often than not formed a sorry sight. Dressed in a mixture of Belgian and Allied uniforms and even civilian clothing, they went about their dangerous jobs poorly fed, underpaid, and without even enough tobacco for comfort. But the Belgian soldiers performed their vital jobs knowledgeably and stubbornly and inhabitants everywhere loved them for it, often putting them up in what was left of their own homes.[21]

Even the soldiers' expertise, however, could not prevent things from going terribly wrong on occasion. Two of the worst incidents took place in the space of a single month in the summer of 1945. On July 27 an American hand grenade exploded, igniting some 900 pounds of shells already loaded onto a truck in Lierneux. The blast made the village tremble, obliterating the truck's chauffeur and two other soldiers. Three soldiers in Moinet on August 30 calmly worked to defuse a device near a haystack close to the road. The explosive blew up in their faces, instantly killing two while maiming another who later died of his injuries in a hospital in Bastogne. Villagers joined the comrades of the fallen in mourning. Lierneux, for example, insisted on organizing a church service in memory of the three silent heroes killed on July 27. The service was celebrated by no less than five priests and attended by almost everyone in the village.[22]

The explosives experts, meanwhile, refused to have the incidents slow them down. The High Commissioner for Luxembourg on April 30, 1945, could report that in his province alone they had eliminated 440 tons of explosive devices, 20,000 of them mines. At the end of September 1945 the Belgian Minister of Defense commended the SEDEEO and 1st Mining Clearance Battalion in the Ardennes for having removed or destroyed no less than 114,000 mines and 5,800 tons of various other dangerous devices. These remarkable results, however, had come at a cost. Counting those who had died at Lierneux and Moinet, fourteen Belgian soldiers had been killed and another forty-eight wounded, many of them suffering loss of limbs and eyes or terrible burns from white phosphorus. The toll of mining clearance in the Grand Duchy of Luxembourg was at least as high. In and around Vianden, for example, so-called *Sprengkommandos* in the spring and early summer of 1945 removed 20,000 mines and 1,000 tons of other explosives. Here alone the work claimed seventeen dead and thirty-four injured.[23]

No matter how hard the experts worked, however, the removal of mines and explosives never went fast enough to prevent more civilians from becoming innocent victims. Before the Sprengkommandos had finished in Vianden, for example, three teenage boys were dead. A local historian has calculated that in Bastogne and its immediate surroundings abandoned explosives in the first five months after the battle claimed the lives of some 40 civilians. Even the incomplete listings of civilian casualties in the Oesling after the battle indicate that mines and other devices in 1945 alone took the lives of at least 34 people while maiming some 13 others. According to yet another source, a total of 165 civilians had died in hospitals across the salient by April 1945 as a result of injuries caused by explosives since the end of the offensive.[24]

The overwhelming majority of these victims were male as they tended to stray furthest from the home to rebuild and farm. Most tragic was that a disproportionate number of the victims were boys aged sixteen or less as they appeared to be more intrigued than girls by military equipment and loved tinkering with it. The consequences could be horrendous. What happened in Steffeshausen on May 30, 1945, is just one example of an endless series of incidents. In one of the tiny village's meadows a group of boys were playing a game with hand grenades when suddenly one of the devices exploded. Two brothers, Peter and Hermann Thiesen, were dead when the alarmed villagers arrived. Emil Heinen and Leo Arimont were badly wounded and rushed to a hospital in Malmedy. Both died that same night. All four boys were aged between ten and thirteen.[25]

The boys from Steffeshausen belonged to a group of at least forty-four civilians mown down by explosives in the East Cantons after the offensive. Several of these incidents occurred as late as 1950, 1951, and 1954. In fact, the latest casualty in the East Cantons to have been found documented was a ten-year-old boy who fell victim to a hand grenade in Nidrum during the summer vacation of 1972. The poisoned legacy has continued to pose problems ever since. In a span of merely five months in 1985, for example, the mining clearance unit of the Luxembourg army had to be called out more than one hundred times. Until this very day, mayors in the former salient at regular intervals are reminding inhabitants to stay clear from any kind of military equipment and to report it to the authorities. It is all they can do to prevent people with just the faintest memory of the Battle of the Bulge from falling victim to it.[26]

Remembering In the Ardennes the most tenacious memories of the winter offensive concern the crimes committed against innocent civilians by individual German soldiers and security agents. The Allies relatively quickly succeeded in putting on trial a number of them. In 1946, for example, the Americans at Dachau sentenced several high-ranking Waffen-SS officers, one of them Jochen Peiper, to long prison terms of which they would eventually serve only a small part. In 1948 twelve soldiers of the 1st SS Panzer Division appeared before Belgian judges in Liège on charges of having committed the Stavelot crimes. Eleven of them received punishments from between ten to fifteen years of forced labor. None of this ever sufficed to take away the pain of those who had remained behind. Even today the dead silence in the

Bande cellar, now a monument, begs an answer to the question of how thirty-four unarmed villagers (the eldest of them thirty-one, the youngest barely seventeen) could have deserved to be executed in cold blood.[27]

Today literally hundreds of Battle of the Bulge plaques, monuments, and museums dot the Ardennes landscape in Belgium and Luxembourg. Some, like the Bande cellar, keep alive the memory of the civilian dead; others that of men who perished clearing mines. Most, however, commemorate the Allied soldiers who returned to liberate the area from Nazi oppression a second time. Too numb with hunger, pain, and fear to applaud their return in January 1945, the inhabitants sometimes were remembering their liberators even before they began rebuilding. On a sunny July day in 1945, for example, villagers in a devastated Grand-Halleux organized a procession celebrating the end of the war. Several of the horse-drawn wagons honored the overseas soldiers in elaborate style. Then the local schoolgirls solemnly passed by, their hats festooned with ribbons in red, white, and blue, their teachers proudly carrying American flags.[28]

On the initiative of the Association Belgo-Américaine, in July 1950 was inaugurated what has remained, apart from the cemetery in Henri-Chapelle, the most impressive monument commemorating the sacrifices American troops made to halt the Germans in the Ardennes. Known as the Mardasson Memorial, the huge star-shaped construction towers over the landscape just northeast of Bastogne at a point thought to be the closest the Germans got to the town during the siege. Chiseled into the monument are the names of all American states and of every American unit that participated in the Battle of the Bulge. The visitor is reminded that the memorial is "dedicated to the lasting friendship between the peoples of Belgium and the United States, who have forged close ties in their common battle against the enemies of free nations."[29]

Gratitude toward the liberators has largely continued to permeate this particular region despite the often serious disagreements in Europe with postwar American decisions in foreign policy. That is not to say that such disagreements have failed to seep even into Battle of the Bulge commemorations. The thirtieth anniversary of the battle, for example, coincided with the end of the divisive Vietnam War. On that occasion one Belgian newspaper pointed out that there might be "diverging viewpoints" regarding diplomacy, but that it should be remembered that soldiers from "the United States in Bastogne were beings of flesh and blood," and that compared to the shared suffering in World War II such disagreements appeared "petty." During the fortieth anniversary, when tensions over President Reagan's policy of nuclear deterrence were at their height, a newspaper in the grand duchy wrote that it should be clear that the Americans had made their sacrifices "not out of enthusiasm for Luxembourg, but out of urgent strategic necessity." That, the paper nevertheless added, "Should not in the least take away from the fact that we owe them thanks." On unveiling a monument in 2001 for GIs killed at Houffalize, a local spokesperson referred to the thorny issues in the Middle East when he reminded the audience: "Even if American policy often raises questions, we should never forget the sacrifice made by all these ordinary boys who were not even 20 years old."[30]

The GIs commemorated at Houffalize in 2001 belonged to the ground troops. A similar ceremony honoring Allied air men who gave their lives in the Battle of the Bulge would be unimaginable not only in Houffalize, as it has remained too sensitive an issue in much of the former salient. In his book on American bombing during the war, Ronald Schaffer shows that the leaders responsible for the air war over occupied Western Europe reached a point where they "subordinated the likelihood of civilian casualties to the promise of military gains." As much as they regretted such casualties, they also regarded them as "inescapable consequences of modern warfare." But many inhabitants of the Ardennes have questioned the necessity and morality of the indiscriminate Allied bombings of several of the region's most important towns. Even in that regard, however, people have found it difficult openly to criticize those to whom they owe their regained freedom. Nelly Simon, for example, a survivor of the horrific bombardment of Houffalize on January 6, 1945, in an interview many years later was very careful to weigh her words when asked about lingering resentments. "There was a feeling, I should perhaps not say this," she hesitated, "there was nevertheless a certain feeling of rancor, . . . we have had the impression for a long time that that was a needless carnage."[31]

Memories of carnage among civilians continued to haunt soldiers, too, long after the Battle of the Bulge. In 1969, during ceremonies marking the twenty-fifth anniversary of the invasion of Normandy, General of the Army Omar N. Bradley took time out from his crowded schedule to pay a private visit to Belgium. The purpose of his visit was

Houffalize. Afterward he explained to the American press that he was one of those responsible for ordering the bombardment of Houffalize. That he had done so without being able to warn the inhabitants had gnawed at his conscience ever since. "There were no visible scars," the Associated Press reported a relieved Bradley as saying after his visit. "In fact, they were prospering." "And," the general added, a burden clearly lifted from his shoulders, "they were genuinely glad to see me. Gave me a grand welcome."[32]

Still another twenty-five years later Herb Copeman did not need a grand welcome in the Belgian village of Schönberg to have the stain removed from his soul. The tortured Australian pilot in 1994 finally decided to go back to the fateful place where he thought he had unwittingly killed several dozen civilians in an attack with his fighter-bomber on a German convoy on Christmas Eve. A tiny war memorial and the testimony of some of Schönberg's elderly inhabitants assured him that no more than four civilians had perished during the offensive and that none of those had died in an air attack on Christmas Eve. "Since then," the veteran pilot confessed, "I have been different in so many ways that are too hard to explain."[33]

Allied veterans of the Battle of the Bulge by no means have remembered the civilians exclusively as victims. Many of the former soldiers have admired the inhabitants for their tenacity and endurance under fire. Veterans of the 75th Infantry Division expressed that feeling most clearly in the plaque they installed near the church in Grand-Halleux. They refused to have it mention only the men in uniform, dedicating it instead "To the memory of courageous American soldiers and Belgian civilians who gave their lives in the Battle of the Bulge." Many veterans have also held inhabitants of the salient as dear friends. Lasting gratitude often sprang from the slightest sign of solidarity assuring the soldiers they were welcome despite the carnage and destruction they brought with them. As with the lieutenant of the 84th Division who in 2003 finally succeeded in identifying the farm near Baillonville where a woman had insisted on baking waffles for some one hundred GIs on New Year's Eve in 1944; or the American veteran who in 1992 in a local Bastogne publication called for help in locating the people of a farm in Michamps. His ears and feet frozen, the inhabitants had invited the soldier to share the warmth of their kitchen shortly after the battle in January 1945. For that smallest of human gestures he had wanted to thank them all those years. Requests from Allied veterans for help from local authorities and media in similar searches have decreased in number only with the waning of their generation.[34]

Perhaps no Allied soldier expressed his gratitude and respect for the civilians he encountered during the Battle of the Bulge in a more fitting way than John Hanlon of Winchester, Massachusetts. In December 1944, John Hanlon, commander of the 1st Battalion, 502nd Parachute Infantry Regiment, desperately needed lots and lots of white cloth for his men at Hemroulle to become invisible in the snow. He turned to the mayor of the tiny village just northwest of Bastogne for help. Victor Gaspar, a man in his seventies with a red face and large moustache, motioned the major to follow him to the church. He rang the bells and soon the alarmed villagers were flocking to the church square. Mr. Gaspar explained the problem and urged them to return as soon as possible with all the sheets they could possibly find. In no time more than two hundred bedsheets were piled up in the square in neat little piles. "We will return them as soon as possible," a delighted Major Hanlon promised. Then he and his men disappeared into battle.

In the autumn of 1947 John Hanlon read an article on Bastogne in a Boston newspaper. In it a correspondent described how the civilians in the area were slowly rebuilding their lives. He also mentioned that an inhabitant of Hemroulle had told him, tongue-in-cheek, that all they were waiting for was for the American who had borrowed their sheets to return them. John Hanlon immediately wrote to the newspaper that he was to blame for the unreturned sheets and that he wanted to make up for the neglect. To Hanlon's utter surprise, in response to his letter packages with sheets began arriving from all over Massachusetts. Other newspapers got wind of the story and eventually it was decided to give people the chance to hand in sheets in person on a Sunday in December. They did so while the churches of Winchester rang their bells.

John Hanlon returned to Hemroulle with the sheets in February 1948. Dressed in their Sunday best, the villagers were waiting for him in the church square. A retired Mr. Gaspar invited the former major to ring the bells. The inhabitants responded with applause. Then they lined up to get back the number of sheets they had parted with almost four years earlier. Each of them warmly shook hands with the veteran. More than one hundred sheets remained and were given to a local home for the elderly.

Hemroulle in a gesture of like respect named John Hanlon an honorary citizen. Moreover, the new mayor refused to let the veteran go home with empty hands. On behalf of the entire village he presented the American with fourteen paintings from Hemroulle's chapel. Each of the churches of Winchester, Massachusetts, as well as the town hall was to get one. Depicting the Stations of the Cross, the paintings carried traces of the battle forever marking the village's own calvary in 1944.[35]

Notes

Works and archival collections that are frequently cited have been identified by the following abbreviations:

ACSL — Archives Communales Somme-Leuze
ARA-AGR — Algemeen Rijksarchief—Archives Générales du Royaume
BRK-CRB — Belgische Rode Kruis—Croix-Rouge de Belgique
CEGESOMA — Centre d'Études et de Documentation Guerre et Sociétés Contemporaines—Studie en Documentatiecentrum Oorlog en Hedendaagse Maatschappij
DOS-SVG — Dienst voor de Oorlogsslachtoffers—Service des Victimes de la Guerre
DVI — *Der verhängnisvolle Irrtum: Hitlers Fehlkalkulation in den Ardennen beschleunigte vor 40 Jahren das Ende.* Eupen: Grenz-Echo-Verlag, 1984.
EuW — Kurt Fagnoul and Hubert Jenniges, eds. *Ende und Wende im Lande zwischen Venn und Schneifel: Augenzeugen berichten von ihren Kriegserlebnissen 1944/45.* St. Vith: Geschichts und Museumsverein "Zwischen Venn und Schneifel," 1995.
FNSS — Fonds National de Secours aux Sinistrés
GAB — Gemeindearchive Büllingen
JdS — Christian Kraft de la Saulx, ed. *Jours de Sursaut.* Vol. 21 of *Jours de Guerre.* Brussels: Dexia, 2001.
KS — *Kriegsschicksale 1944–45: Beiträge zur Chronik der Ardennenoffensive zwischen Venn und Schneifel.* St. Vith: Geschichtsverein "Zwischen Venn und Schneifel," 1969.
RTBF — Radio Télévision Belge Francophone

Preface

1. Marquet, "Bataille," 205–8.

2. Colignon, "Bataille," 273–76; Delvaux, *Celles*, 81–83.

3. De Coune, "Souvenirs," 125.

4. Murray and Millett, *A War To Be Won*, 463–71; Hubert, "Après la bataille," 259.

5. The Ambrose quote is from page 235 of the 1998 Touchstone edition. Colignon, "Bataille," 265–66; FNSS, "Rapport," 17, DOS-SVG.

Chapter 1. The Northern Shoulder

1. MacDonald, *Trumpets*, 160–61; Ian Kershaw, *Hitler, 1889–1936: Hubris* (London: Penguin, 1999), 343 and 514.

2. MacDonald, *Trumpets*, 160–61; Toland, *Battle*, 20; and Eisenhower, *Bitter Woods*, 119.

3. MacDonald, *Trumpets*, 161 and 648–52.

4. Colignon, "Ostkantone," 105.

5. Fagnoul, "Aspects," 186; Colignon, "Ostkantone," 105–6.

6. Colignon, "Ostkantone," 108–10; Fagnoul, "Aspects," 186–87, 190, and 193–94.

7. Toussaint, *Verlorene Jahre*, 14; Fagnoul, "Aspects," 197–202; Colignon, "Ostkantone," 110–13; Toussaint, *Bittere Erfahrungen*, 9–12; and Lucien Cailloux, *Du 15 au 21 décembre 1944*, 9.

8. Blumenson, *Breakout and Pursuit*, 692–96.

9. Fagnoul, "Aspects," 203–4.

10. Jenniges, "Eine Frau," 44–49; Weynand, "Ein Mädchen," 131.

11. Dries, "Streiflichter," 172–74.

12. Blumenson, *Breakout and Pursuit*, 693 and 695–96.

13. MacDonald, *Trumpets*, 28 and 85.

14. Jenniges and Fagnoul, "Manderfeld," 76–77 and 79–80.

15. Toland, *Battle*, 6–7 and 37.

16. Ibid., 30–32.

17. Transcript of Heinzius interview by Peter Thomas, Folder "Interviews," Box W16bis, AA 1207-1208, CEGESOMA; Toussaint, *Bittere Erfahrungen*, 525–26; and e-mail from K. D. Klauser to author, 24 January 2004.

18. Fagnoul, "Angesicht," 157–58 and 162–67. On the attempts by inhabitants of the region to have locals and moderates installed as *Ortsbauernführer*, see Fagnoul, "Aspects," 201.

19. MacDonald, *Trumpets*, 166.

20. Fagnoul, "Rocherath," 168; "Salaires pour les personnes chargées du soin du bétail," Commune de Rocherath, 5 April 1947, R240, GAB.

21. Cavanagh, *Krinkelt-Rocherath*, 90.

22. Ibid., 38, 90, and 142.

23. Fagnoul, "Rocherath," 171.

24. Cavanagh, *Krinkelt-Rocherath*, 118–19.

25. Fagnoul, "Rocherath," 171–72.

26. Fagnoul, "Mürringen," 176–77.

27. Cavanagh, *Krinkelt-Rocherath*, 126–27; Fagnoul, "Rocherath," 171.

28. Gehlen, "Elsenborn," 179–80.

29. Ibid., 180 and 183.

30. MacDonald, *Trumpets*, 409; "Nidrum," 184; and André Cailloux, "Elsenborn," 41–42.

31. "Nidrum," 186; Gehlen, "Elsenborn," 183.

32. Elstob, *Last Offensive*, 262–63.

33. Lejeune, "Hünningen/Büllingen," 99–100; "Übersicht über die Situation in der Gemeinde Büllingen," 28 February 1945, B600, GAB; and "Récit

d'un habitant de Hünningen," 1, de Lilienfeld report 55, 9 March 1945, AA 757, CEGESOMA.

34. Lejeune, "Hünningen/Büllingen," 100–101.

35. Ibid., 101–3.

36. Fagnoul, "Büllingen," 103–4 and 106; MacDonald, *Trumpets*, 404.

37. Fagnoul, "Büllingen," 104 and 107.

38. Ibid., 107.

39. MacDonald, *Trumpets*, 127; Kirch, "Ardennenoffensive," 123–25.

40. Kirch, "Ardennenoffensive," 126–27. Civilians who had cooperated with American Civil Affairs and military government detachments were often the first to be evacuated from places in danger of being overrun. "First U.S. Army G-5 Report," 29 December 1944, 7, AA 17, CEGESOMA.

41. Kirch, "Hilfspolizist," 108–9.

42. MacDonald, *Trumpets*, 389; Kirch, "Ardennenoffensive," 128.

43. Fagnoul, "Büllingen," 106.

44. Kirch, "Ardennenoffensive," 129 and "Hilfspolizist," 109–10; MacDonald, *Trumpets*, 408; and e-mail from K. D. Klauser to author, 12 January 2004.

45. Elstob, *Last Offensive*, 189 and 264; MacDonald, *Trumpets*, 649.

46. Lejoly, *Faymonville*, 50–51, 147, and 179.

47. Rivet and Sevenans, *Civils*, 30–31; Breuer, "Erinnerungen," 115–17; Reuter and Fagnoul, "Schoppen," 113; Lejoly, *Faymonville*, 145; and Toussaint, *Bittere Erfahrungen*, 485–86.

48. Reuter, "Weywertz," 119–20; Reuter, "Tagebuchaufzeichnungen," 133; and "Nidrum," 184.

49. Reuter, "Weywertz," 120–21.

50. Reuter, "Tagebuchaufzeichnungen," 135.

51. Elstob, *Last Offensive*, 265–66 and 321–22.

52. Margraff, "Eibertingen," 292 and "Heppenbach," 286; Toussaint, *Bittere Erfahrungen*, 509.

53. Fagnoul, "Engelsdorf," 151 and "Chronik," 142–43; Ramscheid, "Ondenval," 138–39.

54. André Cailloux, "Elsenborn," 42; Fagnoul, "Engelsdorf," 151 and "Iveldingen-Montenau," 302.

55. Peters, "Massaker," 177; Reuter, "Weywertz," 120; Maniura, "Erinnerungen," 145; and Margraff, "Deidenberg," 295 and "Heppenbach," 284–85.

56. Reuter and Fagnoul, "Schoppen," 113; Fagnoul, "Iveldingen-Montenau," 301; and Margraff, "Heppenbach," 283.

57. Reuter, "Tagebuchaufzeichnungen," 135. See also Reuter, "Weywertz," 123.

Chapter 2. The Peiper Breakthrough

1. MacDonald, *Trumpets*, 197–98; Bartov, *The Eastern Front*, 119–20.

2. MacDonald, *Trumpets*, 182–83 and 197–98; Elstob, *Last Offensive*, 151–52.

3. Signon, "Honsfeld," 92–93.

4. Ibid., 94–95.

5. MacDonald, *Trumpets*, 203–4 and 620–21.

6. Ibid., 207–9.

7. Reuter and Fagnoul, "Schoppen," 112.

8. Signon, "Honsfeld," 95; MacDonald, *Trumpets*, 204.

9. MacDonald, *Trumpets*, 199 and 213–14.

10. Laurent Wilen, "Comment les GI's ont été massacrés," *La Lanterne*, 6 May 1985; Toland, *Battle*, 55.

11. Rogister, "Baugnez," 61.

12. MacDonald, *Trumpets*, 218–20. For the best in-depth treatment of the Malmedy massacre and the postwar trial of the Waffen-SS perpetrators, see James J. Weingartner's *Crossroads of Death* and *A Peculiar Crusade*.

13. MacDonald, *Trumpets*, 220–21; Wilen, "Comment les GI's ont été massacrés."

14. MacDonald, *Trumpets*, 221; Rivet and Sevenans, *Civils*, 39–42; and L.C., "45 ans après le massacre de Baugnez," *La Meuse*, 22 January 1990. One of the GIs who managed to escape from the crime scene later died of his wounds in a Malmedy hospital. That is why the names of eighty-four American victims are engraved on the Baugnez monument. Rogister, "Baugnez," 76.

15. Rogister, "Baugnez," 74; MacDonald, *Trumpets*, 222.

16. Jamar, "My Day," 1–3; Rogister, "Baugnez," 68–71.

17. Laby, *Stavelot*, 32–33; Rivet and Sevenans, *Civils*, 53–54.

18. "Werbomont," Folder 2/Group IX and "Stavelot," Folder 2/Group II, AA 120, CEGESOMA.

19. Rivet and Sevenans, *Civils*, 54.

20. Elstob, *Last Offensive*, 181–82.

21. Henry de Backer, "Extraits de mon journal écrit en février 1945," 2, Folder W16bis, Box W16bis, AA 1207–1208, CEGESOMA; Rivet and Sevenans, *Civils*, 46–47.

22. MacDonald, *Trumpets*, 435 and 436–37.

23. Laby, *Stavelot*, 294; Commission des Crimes de Guerre, *Stavelot*, 11 and 45–46.

24. Commission des Crimes de Guerre, *Stavelot*, 11–13 and 15.

25. Ibid., 14–15 and www.ardentem.free.fr/page14.html.

26. Commission des Crimes de Guerre, *Stavelot*, 15–17.

27. Ibid., 17 and 18–25; Laby, *Stavelot*, 257–58 and 294–95.

28. MacDonald, *Trumpets*, 435–36.

29. Ibid., 436; Warnock, "Story," 2.

30. Commission des Crimes de Guerre, *Stavelot*, 35–39; Bovy and de Lame, *Bataille*, 163. On the very young age of those who committed war crimes at Stavelot, see also Kartheuser, *Documentation*, 63–65.

31. Commission des Crimes de Guerre, *Stavelot*, 27–28 and 29–30.

32. Ibid., 28–29; www.ardentem.free.fr/page16.html; and www.users.skynet.be/bulgecriba/parfondruy.html, 1.

33. Commission des Crimes de Guerre, *Stavelot*, 30–31; Jean-Marc Veszely, "Nous en avons réchappé par miracle," *Le Soir Illustré*, 20 December 1984, 57–58; and Rivet and Sevenans, *Civils*, 48.

34. Commission des Crimes de Guerre, *Stavelot*, 31–32.

35. Ibid., 32–34; www.ardentem.free.fr/page36.html.

36. Commission des Crimes de Guerre, *Stavelot*, 35.

37. Rivet and Sevenans, *Civils*, 55–56.

38. Schrijvers, *Crash of Ruin*, 79–80; "Martyrologe de Stavelot," in Commission des Crimes de Guerre, *Stavelot*, illustration opposite page 31; Laby, *Stavelot*, 257–58; and Eisenhower, *Bitter Woods*, 271. The most detailed list of the civilians who fell victim to German war crimes in Stavelot is in Annex XXIII of Laby, *Stavelot*, 294–95.

39. Laby, *Stavelot*, 268; Hoyois, *L'Ardenne*, 50.

40. Laby, *Stavelot*, 266; 268; Hoyois, *L'Ardenne*, 46–47 and 50.

41. "Stavelot: Mon premier bal," *La Libre Belqique*, 22 December 1969.

42. Henry de Backer, "Evacuation de civils le 28 décembre 1944," 7 May 1983, Folder W16bis, Box W16bis, AA 1207–1208, CEGESOMA and, in the same folder, Belgian Red Cross letter from Jean Masure to Lieutenant Bertrand, 27 February 1945.

43. MacDonald, *Trumpets*, 239–40.

44. Rivet and Sevenans, *Civils*, 77–80; van Caster, "Petit Spay," 225–28.

45. Appendix to de Lilienfeld report of 24 December 1944, AA 757, CEGESOMA; Lucien Cailloux, *Du 15 au 21 décembre 1944*, 39; and MacDonald, *Trumpets*, 243.

46. Grégoire, *Décembre 44*, 146; 161–62; Rivet and Sevenans, *Civils*, 60.

47. Rivet and Sevenans, *Civils*, 60–61.

48. Ibid., 61; Grégoire, *Décembre 44*, 146 and 162–64.

49. Grégoire, *Décembre 1944*, 147 and 151–52.

50. Eisenhower, *Bitter Woods*, 271–72.

51. Grégoire, *Décembre 44*, 152–53.

52. Hanlet, *St-Edouard*, 12.

53. Ibid., 6. For another reference to franc-tireurs at Stavelot made by German soldiers see, for example, Commission des Crimes de Guerre, *Stavelot*, 23–24. The Belgian War Crimes Commission never found evidence substantiating the German claim of franc-tireurs. Likewise, local historian Hubert Laby maintains that, in the many years that he has researched the subject and conducted interviews with eyewitnesses, he has never found any indication that the town's civilians were engaged in armed action against the Germans during the Battle of the Bulge. Laby, *Stavelot*, 270.

54. Hanlet, *St-Edouard*, 7–8; MacDonald, *Trumpets*, 446.

55. Hanlet, *St-Edouard*, 8–9.

56. Ibid., 10–15.

57. Ibid., 15–16.

58. Grégoire, *Décembre 44*, 147, 154–55, and 156–57.

59. Eisenhower, *Bitter Woods*, 277.

60. Commission des Crimes de Guerre, *Stavelot*, 46–47.

61. Ibid., 42–45; www.ardentem.free.fr/page12.html.

62. Rivet and Sevenans, *Civils*, 57; Grégoire, *Décembre 44*, 148.

63. Rivet and Sevenans, *Civils*, 59; Grégoire, *Décembre 44*, 149.

64. Grégoire, *Décembre 44*, 169–71.

65. Rivet and Sevenans, *Civils*, 59; Grégoire, *Décembre 44*, 149.

66. Grégoire, *Décembre 44*, 165–66.

67. MacDonald, *Trumpets*, 459; Rivet and Sevenans, *Civils*, 57; and Grégoire, *Décembre 44*, 166–67.

68. Rivet and Sevenans, *Civils*, 57–58; Grégoire, *Décembre 44*, 167.

69. MacDonald, *Trumpets*, 461; Rivet and Sevenans, *Civils*, 58; Grégoire, *Décembre 44*, 145–46 and 168; and Serge Fontaine, "Décembre 1944: Exercices des sapeurs U.S. à La Gleize," *Echos*, 10 December 1982.

70. MacDonald, *Trumpets*, 461–62 and 463.

71. *Chevron*, 5 and 8.

72. Appendix to a de Lilienfeld report of 24 December 1944, AA 757, CEGESOMA; *Chevron*, 14, 18, and 23.

73. *Chevron*, 6, 11, 12, and 13.

74. Ibid., 24.

75. Ibid., 6, 12, and 16; Appendix to a de Lilienfeld report of 24 December 1944, AA 757, CEGESOMA.

76. *Chevron*, 24.

77. Author interview with Charles Hilgers, 5 August 2002; Crouquet, *Bataille*, 54–55 and 58; Binot, "Malmedy," 157 and 159; Mayérus, "Gendarmerie," 140; and *1944: Un Noël en enfer*, 59.

78. Cole, *Ardennes*, 278; MacDonald, *Trumpets*, 233; Hoyois, *L'Ardenne*, 44; G-5 Report, 29 December 1944, 7 and G-5 Report, 26 January 1945, 3, AA 17, CEGESOMA; Binot, "Malmedy," 164; Mayérus, "Gendarmerie," 140 and 143; and Crouquet, *Bataille*, 58.

79. Crouquet, *Bataille*, 55–56; *1944: Un Noël en enfer*, 61.

80. "Amerikanische Bomben auf Malmedy," 63.

81. Ibid., 67–71.

82. Ibid., 76.

83. Ibid., 76–77; *1944: Un Noël en enfer*, 21–22.

84. *Un Noël en enfer*, 24–26 and 62.

85. "Amerikanische Bomben auf Malmedy," 76 and 79–80; *1944: Un Noël en enfer*, 51.

86. Carter, "Air Power," 10 and 17 note 82; Craven and Cate, *Europe*, 690 and 692; "Amerikanische Bomben auf Malmedy," 73; MacDonald, *Trumpets*, 465; "Liste des victimes civiles des bombardements," in *1944: Un Noël en enfer*, 74–76; Laurent, "Un Noël en enfer!," 24; and Crouquet, *Bataille*, 56–57 and 60–61.

87. *1944: Un Noël en enfer*, 66–69.

Chapter 3. Closing in on St. Vith

1. MacDonald, *Trumpets*, 24, 29, and 101–2.

2. Ibid., 104, 112, 114, and 646–47.

3. Kubiak-Hoffmann, "Harte Zeiten," 225–26; Toussaint, *Bittere Erfahrungen*, 527.

4. Peterges, "Andler," 88–89.

5. Fagnoul, "Schönberg," 84–86.

6. Nilles, "Winteroffensive," 257; MacDonald, *Trumpets*, 345 and 347.

7. Theissen, "Wallerode," 103–7.

8. "Meyerode, Medell," 206.

9. Cole, *Ardennes*, 280.

10. Toussaint, *Bittere Erfahrungen*, 498–500; Margraff, "Born," 306.

11. MacDonald, *Trumpets*, 326; Ellenbecker, "Recht," 310–11.

12. Ellenbecker, "Recht," 310–12 and 322.

13. www.users.skynet.be/bulgecriba/duby.html; Ellenbecker, "Recht," 311.

14. Gosset, "Poche," 101 and 111–12; Ellenbecker, "Recht," 315–16; and Rivet and Sevenans, *Civils*, 31–32.

15. Ellenbecker, "Recht," 315–16.

16. Ibid., 322–23; Fagnoul, *St. Vith*, 13.

17. Cole, *Ardennes*, 284–85; Parker, "Order of Battle," 646–47.

18. Nilles, "Lommersweiler," 222–23.

19. Mayérus, "Gendarmerie," 139 and 144–45.

20. Nilles, "Lommersweiler," 223; "Neidingen," 255.

21. Nilles, "Breitfeld," 226.

22. Toussaint, *Bittere Erfahrungen*, 537–45; Gennen, *Burg Reuland*, 12 and 124.

23. Gennen, *Burg Reuland*, 62, 63 note 1, and 12–14.

24. Ibid., 12 and 13 note 9.

25. Ibid., 100–101; Toussaint, *Bittere Erfahrungen*, 539.

26. Gennen, *Burg Reuland*, 101 and 78. On Nazi propaganda and the subject of African-American soldiers see, for example, Fagnoul, *St. Vith*, 14. See also Schrijvers, *Crash of Ruin*, 138.

27. Gennen, *Burg Reuland*, 103.

28. Ibid., 62, 63 note 3, and 71; "Augenzeugen," 266–67 and 268.

29. Gennen, *Burg Reuland*, 13 note 7, and 78.

30. Ibid., 101, 104, and 106.

31. Ibid., 68.

32. Ibid., 18, 55 note 2, 62, and 124–26.

33. Ibid., 68 and 78–79.

34. Gennen, "Augenzeugen," 267; *Burg Reuland*, 124–25.

35. Schetter, *Saint-Vith*, 15; Fagnoul, "Märtyrerstadt," 312; "Aspects," 205; and *St. Vith*, 47–48.

36. Fagnoul, "Aspects," 186, 193 note 30, 203–4, and 205; letter from the town of St. Vith to CEGESOMA, 8 September 1983, Folder "St. Vith," AA 1211, CEGESOMA; and Fagnoul, *St. Vith*, 50–51 and 60.

37. Graf, "Märtyrerstadt," 247 and 248; Fagnoul, "Aspects," 205; *St. Vith*, 61–62, 123, 64 note 68, 47, and 62. Quote is from Toland, *Battle*, 9. On how American troops experienced their arrival in the East Cantons, see Schrijvers, *Crash of Ruin*, 132–33.

38. Graf, "Märtyrerstadt," 240; Fagnoul, "Aspects," 205 and 206; "Märtyrerstadt," 315; Toussaint, *Bittere Erfahrungen*, 571–77; and Fagnoul, *St. Vith*, 13, 79, 62–64, 65, and 125. Early in January 1945, military authorities made the more than five hundred *Reichsdeutsche* who remained in Malmedy wear yellow armbands. See Binot, "Malmedy," 165.

39. Graf, "Märtyrerstadt," 240; Nilles, "Winteroffensive," 256; and Fagnoul, *St. Vith*, 87.

40. Fagnoul, *St. Vith*, 87–88 and 93; Toland, *Battle*, 34; and Graf, "Märtyrerstadt," 236.

41. Fagnoul, *St. Vith*, 87–89; MacDonald, *Trumpets*, 311; Schetter, *Saint-Vith*, 15–16; Schütz, "Unsere Flucht," 227; and Gosset, "Poche," 101. Quote is from MacDonald, *Trumpets*, 232.

42. Heinen-Drees, "Flucht," 113–20.

43. Rivet and Sevenans, *Civils*, 27.

Chapter 4. The Race for Bastogne

1. MacDonald, *Trumpets*, 137–38.

2. Parker, "Order of Battle," 644–45; MacDonald, *Trumpets*, 130.

3. Rasqué, *Oesling*, 438–39; Melchers, *Bombenangriffe*, 431.

4. Rasqué, *Oesling*, 388–89 and 152–53; Maertz, *Luxemburg*, 149–54.

5. Toland, *Battle*, 10 and 25.

6. Gaul, "Brief Historical Survey," 1–2; Melchers, *Luxemburg*, 433–34.

7. Rasqué, *Oesling*, 142–44.

8. Maertz, *Luxemburg*, 158–59 and 164–71; MacDonald, *Trumpets*, 278–79; Toland, *Battle*, 91–92; and Hohengarten, "Gestapo," 7.

9. Maertz, *Luxemburg*, 163; Rasqué, *Oesling*, 214 and 216.

10. Rasqué, *Oesling*, 428–29; Heinrich, "Zwangsrekrutierte," 101.

11. Rasqué, *Oesling*, 73–74; Melchers, *Luxemburg*, 434.

12. Maertz, *Luxemburg*, 188; Rasqué, *Oesling*, 75–81.

13. Rasqué, *Oesling*, 531–32.

14. *Bastogne: Des civils témoignent*, 192–93.

15. Ibid., 193, 166, and 165.

16. Commission des Crimes de Guerre, *Ardennes*, 31–36; Heintz, *Périmètre*, 107–8.

17. Commission des Crimes de Guerre, *Ardennes*, 26–30; Heintz, *Périmètre*, 108–10; and Rivet and Sevenans, *Civils*, 196–98.

18. Parker, "Order of Battle," 645–46.

19. Rasqué, *Oesling*, 659–60; Gaul, *Americans*, 309.

20. Rasqué, *Oesling*, 547, 549, 550, 545, 246–47, 252, 125, and 502.

21. Heintz, *Périmètre*, 143 and 194; *Bastogne: Des civils témoignent*, 100, 95, and 96.

22. *Bastogne: Des civils témoignent*, 42–43, 46, and 45–46.

23. Ibid., 53–54; Heintz, *Périmètre*, 143.

24. Heintz, *Périmètre*, 47–48; Toland, *Battle*, 140.

25. *Bastogne: Des civils témoignent*, 64.

26. Ibid., 65–66; Rasqué, *Oesling*, 81–82 and 394.

27. *Bastogne: Des civils témoignent*, 220–21; Marshall, *Bastogne*, 106; and Heintz, *Périmètre*, 40, 43, and 196.

28. Heintz, *Périmètre*, 43–44; *Bastogne: Des civils témoignent*, 221–22.

29. Rivet and Sevenans, *Civils*, 192–93; *Bastogne: Des civils témoignent*, 30 and 32–35.

30. *Bastogne: Des civils témoignent*, 69–70.

31. Ibid., 205 and 71.

32. Ibid., 214; de Coune, "Souvenirs," 120–22; and Heintz, *Périmètre*, 189.

33. Bastin, "Sibret," 141–43; *Bastogne: Des civils témoignent*, 321; and Heintz, *Périmètre*, 157–58 and 200.

34. Burnotte, "Noël 1944," 156–57.

35. Brill, "Beauplateau," 99–101; Fourny, *Hiver*, 5, 38, 41–42, and 64–65.

36. MacDonald, *Trumpets*, 488.

37. Franz Legrand, "10 septembre 1944: La 1ère libération de Bastogne," interview by Adrien Lessire, *Le Pays de Bastogne*, no. 3 (September 1991): 2; Lucien Cailloux, "Libération," 4–5; and Fecherolle, "Souvenirs," 126–27.

38. Maria Gillet, "Siège de Bastogne: Souvenirs des jours d'angoisse et des nuits interminables, 18 décembre 44–2 janvier 45," 16–17 December 1944, Folder "Bastogne," Box VI-VIIIA, AA 1207–1208, CEGESOMA; MacDonald, *Trumpets*, 505–6; and *Bastogne: Des civils témoignent*, 436, 445, 463–64, and 465.

39. Gillet, "Siège de Bastogne," 17 December 1944, CEGESOMA; Drossart, "Bastogne," 157; Heintz, *Périmètre*, 66; and *Bastogne: Des civils témoignent*, 436–37, 444, 445, 462, and 498.

40. Gillet, "Siège de Bastogne," 18 December 1944, CEGESOMA; *Bastogne: Des civils témoignent*, 437 and 447.

41. Letter from the mayor of Bastogne to the mayor of Longchamps, 21 October 1948, AA 145, CEGESOMA; MacDonald, *Trumpets*, 506; Lefèbvre, *Bastogne*, 53; and *Bastogne: Des civils témoignent*, 448, 479, and 486–87.

42. *Bastogne: Des civils témoignent*, 115–18.

43. Ibid., 512, 437, and 439; Mayérus, "Gendarmerie," 151–52; Greindl, *Isle la Hesse*, 40; André Dejardin, "Mgr Musty raconte Noël 1944 à Bande," *Vers l'Avenir*, 23 December 1984; and Joss Heintz, "Le 'moribond' Américain a retrouvé ses sauveteurs," Folder "Militairs Américains," Box VI-VIIIA, AA 1207–1208, CEGESOMA.

44. Heintz, *Périmètre*, 66–67.

45. *Bastogne: Des civils témoignent*, 433; Colignon, "Bataille," 276; and Coles and Weinberg, *Civil Affairs*, 816.

46. Heintz, *Périmètre*, 67–68; *Bastogne: Des civils témoignent*, 439 and 487.

47. Raymonde Havelange, "Bastogne," *La Cité*, 23 December 1984; *Bastogne: Des civils témoignent*, 445, 473–74, and 501.

48. Dumont, *Bastogne*, 7–9; Rivet and Sevenans, *Civils*, 182–83; and *Bastogne: Des civils témoignent*, 447, 448–50, and 471–72. See also www.users.win.be/W0005086/traces/soeurs.htm.

49. Heintz, *Périmètre*, 156–57 and 189.

50. *Bastogne: Des civils témoignent*, 451–52.

Chapter 5. The Houffalize Corridor

1. Collette, "Ma guerre," 30–32. Because of power outages, some communities did not even have official news of the offensive four days after it started. Coles and Weinberg, *Civil Affairs*, 813.

2. MacDonald, *Trumpets*, 131 and 133.

3. Toland, *Battle,* 172–73; MacDonald, *Trumpets,* 131; and Cole, *Ardennes,* 203.

4. Maertz, *Luxemburg,* 171–72; Toland, *Battle,* 172; and Elstob, *Last Offensive,* 248.

5. Elstob, *Last Offensive,* 248–50.

6. Rivet and Sevenans, *Civils,* 162–65.

7. Kauffmann, "Mont-Houffalize," 180.

8. Georges et al., "Fors l'oubli," 27–28; Grailet, "Hemingway," 49–50.

9. Kauffmann, "Mont-Houffalize," 181; Dubru, *L'Offensive,* 24 and 295.

10. Dubru, *L'Offensive,* 24–25.

11. Kauffmann, "Mont-Houffalize," 181–82.

12. Lesage, *Houffalize,* 9; Dubru, *L'Offensive,* 27; and Kettels-Crémer, "Tavigny," 191.

13. Dubru, *L'Offensive,* 28.

14. Lesage, *Houffalize,* 10; Dubru, *L'Offensive,* 28–31.

15. Dubru, *L'Offensive,* 28 and 33.

16. MacDonald, *Trumpets,* 535–36; Elstob, *Last Offensive,* 228.

17. Kauffmann, "Mont-Houffalize," 181–82.

18. Dubru, *L'Offensive,* 27–28 and 154; Grandjean, "Ardennes," 198.

19. Dubru, *L'Offensive,* 34 and 39–40.

20. Ibid., 38–40; Collin, "Mabompré," 216.

21. Kettels-Crémer, "Tavigny," 191–92; Collette, "Souvenirs," 184.

22. Collin, "Mabompré," 216.

23. Collette, "Ma guerre," 32–34.

24. Dubru, *L'Offensive,* 30–31 and 33.

25. Ibid., 40, 120, and 122.

26. Kettels-Crémer, "Tavigny," 192.

27. Dubru, *L'Offensive,* 45–47 and 259; Kauffmann, "Mont-Houffalize," 182–83.

28. Dubru, *L'Offensive,* 120 and 122; Kauffmann, "Mont-Houffalize," 182.

29. Collette, "Souvenirs," 184; Dubru, *L'Offensive,* 120–21.

30. Dubru, *L'Offensive,* 31–32, 39–40, and 294; Georges et al., "Fors l'oubli," 27–28.

31. Dubru, *L'Offensive,* 157–58.

32. Ibid., 61–62.

33. Commission des Crimes de Guerre, *Ardennes,* 37–41; Lesage, *Houffalize,* 45, 47, and 49–51; and Dubru, *L'Offensive,* 51–56.

34. Commission des Crimes de Guerre, *Ardennes,* 42–45; Dubru, *L'Offensive,* 66–67.

35. Dubru, *L'Offensive,* 67; www.gouvy.be/fr/Publications/DetailsVillages/text/halonru.html.

36. Dubru, *L'Offensive,* 68.

37. Craven and Cate, *Europe,* 694 and 697–98.

38. Dubru, "Pertes," 195; Collette, "Souvenirs," 184–85.

39. Collette, "Ma guerre," 34–35.

40. Dubru, *L'Offensive,* 259.

41. Lesage, *Houffalize,* 10–11, 55, and 57; Dubru, *L'Offensive,* 108–9, 114, 124, and 255.

42. Craven and Cate, *Europe*, 696; Crouquet, *Bataille*, 71; Rossignon, "Houffalize;" and Dubru, *L'Offensive*, 129–30 and 168.

43. Dubru, *L'Offensive*, 110, 127–28, and 259.

44. Lesage, *Houffalize*, 57 and 60; Dubru, *L'Offensive*, 128–29.

45. Rossignon, "Houffalize"; Dubru, *L'Offensive*, 130–34; and Rivet and Sevenans, *Civils*, 161.

46. Dubru, *L'Offensive*, 99–107, 135, 155–56, and 176.

47. Rivet and Sevenans, *Civils*, 161; Dubru, *L'Offensive*, 170–73 and 260.

48. Dubru, *L'Offensive*, 173.

Chapter 6. The Southern Shoulder

1. MacDonald, *Trumpets*, 146–47.

2. Ibid., 147–49.

3. Rasqué, *Oesling*, 644, 631–32, 640, and 642–43; Gaul, *Americans*, 309–10 and 314–15.

4. Rasqué, *Oesling*, 95–97. On the 5th Parachute Division, see Heilmann, "Ardennen-Offensive," 2–3, AA 484, CEGESOMA; Gaul, *Germans*, 39–40; and Parker, "Order of Battle," 654–55.

5. Rasqué, *Oesling*, 234–36.

6. MacDonald, *Trumpets*, 298 and 301; Heilmann, "Ardennen-Offensive," 3, CEGESOMA; and Cole, *Ardennes*, 209.

7. Maertz, *Luxemburg*, 183; Rasqué, *Oesling*, 677–78; and Toland, *Battle*, 113.

8. Melchers, *Luxemburg*, 314; Maertz, *Luxemburg*, 183; and Rasqué, *Oesling*, 677–78.

9. Maertz, *Luxemburg*, 184.

10. Rasqué, *Oesling*, 164–65 and 582–84.

11. Toland, *Battle*, 207–8, 281–84, 304–5, and 314–15; MacDonald, *Trumpets*, 308–9.

12. Parker, "Order of Battle," 655; Gaul, *Germans*, 22 and 35–36.

13. Gaul, *Americans*, 242.

14. Ibid., 253–54; Rasqué, *Oesling*, 290.

15. Rasqué, *Oesling*, 196–99; Gaul, *Americans*, 246–51 and 36.

16. MacDonald, *Trumpets*, 150; Rasqué, *Oesling*, 286–88; and Maertz, *Luxemburg*, 118.

17. Rasqué, *Oesling*, 181–88; Gaul, *Americans*, 11 and 28.

18. Melchers, *Luxemburg*, 216–17; Gaul, *Americans*, 34–38 and 58; and Maertz, *Luxemburg*, 122.

19. Gaul, *Americans*, 339.

20. Maertz, *Luxemburg*, 122–23 and 124; Gaul, *Americans*, 304, 68, and 275; MacDonald, *Trumpets*, 149 and 356; and Melchers, *Luxemburg*, 223.

21. Gaul, *Americans*, 40; Rasqué, *Oesling*, 191.

22. Rasqué, *Oesling*, 297–98; Melchers, *Luxemburg*, 293; and Maertz, *Luxemburg*, 125.

23. Gaul, *Americans*, 250–51.

24. Melchers, *Luxemburg*, 330–31; Gaul, *Americans*, 98–100; and Maertz, *Luxemburg*, 126–27.

25. Melchers, *Luxemburg*, 331–32; Gaul, *Americans*, 101, 301–2, and 307–8; Maertz, *Luxemburg*, 127; and Rasqué, *Oesling*, 273–74.

26. Gaul, *Americans*, 101 and 146–47.

27. Rasqué, *Oesling*, 191; Gaul, *Americans*, 285, 288–89, 331, and 341.

28. Gaul, *Americans*, 331–32, 329, 342, and 260; Rivet and Sevenans, *Civils*, 148.

29. Parker, "Order of Battle," 654; MacDonald, *Trumpets*, 153.

30. Rasqué, *Oesling*, 218–20; Maertz, *Luxemburg*, 99.

31. Parker, "Order of Battle," 653–54; MacDonald, *Trumpets*, 154 and 365.

32. Melchers, *Luxemburg*, 148–49; Maertz, *Luxemburg*, 67; and Karen, *Kriegsereignisse*, 137, 141, 143, 151–52, 160–61, and 298.

33. Karen, *Kriegsereignisse*, 238.

34. Maertz, *Luxemburg*, 82–85; Karen, *Kriegsereignisse*, 238 and 346.

35. Karen, *Kriegsereignisse*, 346.

36. Hohengarten, "Gestapo," 6–7.

37. Ibid., 6 and 7; Milmeister, "Einsatz," 5.

38. Hohengarten, "Gestapo," 7–8; Rasqué, *Oesling*, 199–200; Gaul, *Americans*, 242, 244–45, and 255; and Milmeister, "Einsatz," 4.

Chapter 7. The Fall of St. Vith

1. Theissen, "Wallerode," 107.

2. Fagnoul, *St. Vith*, 91; "Aspects," 208 note 95.

3. MacDonald, *Trumpets*, 487.

4. Fagnoul, *St. Vith*, 91–92; Graf, "Märtyrerstadt," 236, 240–41, and 248.

5. Fagnoul, *St. Vith*, 125.

6. Ibid., 93.

7. Ibid., 99 and 101.

8. Ibid., 91 and 101; Peters, "Tod," 140–41; and Graf, "Märtyrerstadt," 236 and 240.

9. Graf, "Märtyrerstadt," 236; Fagnoul, *St. Vith*, 93–94.

10. MacDonald, *Trumpets*, 472.

11. MacDonald, "Erinnerungen," 216; Toland, *Battle*, 187.

12. Graf, "Märtyrerstadt," 236.

13. Cole, *Ardennes*, 410–11.

14. Ibid., 411; Fagnoul, *St. Vith*, 95–98.

15. Fagnoul, *St. Vith*, 91–92.

16. Rivet and Sevenans, *Civils*, 27–28; Graf, "Märtyrerstadt," 240 and 243.

17. Parker, "Order of Battle," 646; Elstob, *Last Offensive*, 167; and MacDonald, *Trumpets*, 470 and 475.

18. Flemings, "Erinnerungen," 277–78.

19. Gennen, *Burg Reuland*, 63, 79, 127, 129, and 72; "Augenzeugen," 267 and 269.

20. Dries, "Streiflichter," 172; Gennen, *Burg Reuland*, 81.

21. Gennen, *Burg Reuland*, 81. See also Fagnoul, *St. Vith*, 14.

22. Schütz, "Crombach," 273–74.

23. Nilles, "Neidingen," 255.

24. Dropsy, *Mon village,* 9–10 and 16.

25. Dropsy, "Quelques documents," 15; *Mon village,* 22 and 56.

26. Dropsy, "Quelques documents," 15; *Mon village,* 16, 22, and 28.

27. Dropsy, *Mon village,* 28 and 32–33.

28. Elstob, *Last Offensive,* 245–46; Parker, "Order of Battle," 650–51; and MacDonald, *Trumpets,* 476.

29. Dropsy, *Mon village,* 36–37.

30. Ibid., 31–32.

31. Ibid., 39–40.

32. Jeanpierre, "Grand-Halleux," 1–2.

33. Dropsy, *Mon village,* 42–43.

34. Jeanpierre, "Grand-Halleux," 2.

35. Dropsy, *Mon village,* 42, 51, 52, and 55–56.

36. Ibid., 39 and 51–52.

37. Engels, *Circuit historique,* 1–2; Thill, *Patriote,* 219 and 223–25; and Dropsy, *Mon village,* 11 and 58. At the end of December 1944, Allied command and Belgian government rejected suggestions to rearm the resistance so as to help stem the German offensive. The authorities feared that "in the circumstances confusion might result." SHAEF, 26 December 1944, 11, AA 1230, CEGESOMA.

38. Dropsy, *Mon village,* 56, 62, 63–64, 65, 68–69, and 67.

39. Gennen, *Burg Reuland,* 68, 72, and 127.

40. Von Frühbuss, "Wallerode," 204; Theissen, "Wallerode," 109–10; Ellenbecker, "Recht," 318 and 321–22; Graf, "Hitlers letzte Offensive," 2 January 1975; Toussaint, *Bittere Erfahrungen,* 603–4; and Margraff, "Born," 306 and 309.

41. Schorkops, "Herresbach," 194; Toussaint, *Bittere Erfahrungen,* 505.

42. Craven and Cate, *Europe,* 692–93; Graf, "Märtyrerstadt," 232; Toussaint, *Bittere Erfahrungen,* 580 and 584; and "Amerikanische Bomben auf Malmedy," 80–81.

43. Rivet and Sevenans, *Civils,* 28; Graf, "Märtyrerstadt," 243–44.

44. Graf, "Märtyrerstadt," 235 and 244.

45. Craven and Cate, *Europe,* 700; Fagnoul, "Aspects," 208. Craven and Cate talk of 274 bombers; Fagnoul mentions 294 aircraft.

46. "Interview de Peter Thomas avec Madame Margaret Doepgen à St. Vith," 2–4, Folder "Interviews," Box W16bis, AA 1207–1208, CEGESOMA; Fagnoul, *St. Vith,* 110–11; and Graf, "Märtyrerstadt," 239.

47. Fagnoul, *St. Vith,* 101; "Aspects," 209.

48. Peters, "Tod," 142–43.

49. "Interview Margaret Doepgen," 4–6, CEGESOMA; Fagnoul, *St. Vith,* 111; and Graf, "Märtyrerstadt," 239.

50. Fagnoul, *St. Vith,* 132; Toussaint, *Bittere Erfahrungen,* 577 and 582.

51. One hundred twenty-eight victims were identified as having been inhabitants of St. Vith. Graf, "Märtyrerstadt," 229; Dubru, *Houffalize,* 98, note 42; Hasquin et al, *Gemeenten van België,* Vol. 4, 2760; and Hubert, "Après la bataille," 249. The bombardment of December 25 claimed at least thirty-four civilian dead. See Toussaint, *Bittere Erfahrungen,* 577–84. Special thanks to K. D. Klauser from the historical society *Zwischen Venn und Schneifel* for his help

in estimating the number of civilian dead in St. Vith (e-mails to the author, 8 and 9 January 2004).

52. Theissen, "Wallerode," 108; Flemings, "Erinnerungen," 278; and Gennen, *Burg Reuland,* 129.

53. Nilles, "Galhausen," 253; "Lommersweiler," 223; Fagnoul, *St. Vith,* 110 and 111–12.

54. Gennen, *Burg Reuland,* 109.

55. Fagnoul, *St. Vith,* 112 and 114; Nilles, "Galhausen," 253–54.

56. Graf, "Hitlers letzte Offensive," 2 January 1975; Toussaint, *Bittere Erfahrungen,* 547; Craven and Cate, *Europe,* 696; and Nilles, "Breitfeld," 227.

57. Ellis, *Defeat,* 188; Gennen, *Burg Reuland,* 109, 56, and 72.

58. Nilles, "Winteroffensive," 257–58.

59. Copeman, "Schönberg," 1, AB 1912, CEGESOMA.

Chapter 8. The Siege of Bastogne

1. MacDonald, *Trumpets,* 502–3; Heintz, *Périmètre,* 67.

2. Lucien Cailloux, "Libération," 5; www.users.win.be/W0005086/traces/ monu.htm, 2–4.

3. *Bastogne: Des civils témoignent,* 435–36.

4. Ibid., 429–30; Drossart, "Bastogne," 157.

5. Heintz, *Périmètre,* 68; *Bastogne: Des civils témoignent,* 492–93 and 542–44; and Lefèbvre, *Bastogne,* 93.

6. MacDonald, *Trumpets,* 505; Marshall, *Bastogne,* 138–39; Heintz, *Périmètre,* 69; and requisition form, 26 December 1944, HQ 101st Airborne Division, Office of the Assistant Chief of Staff, G-4, in Folder "Bastogne," AA 145, CEGESOMA.

7. Meurisse, *Croix Noires,* 36–41.

8. Ibid., 41–44.

9. Ibid., 44–46 and 56–57.

10. Lefèbvre, *Bastogne,* 94; Heintz, *Périmètre,* 68; MacDonald, *Trumpets,* 488 and 506–7; *Bastogne: Des civils témoignent,* 37 and 414; and Greindl, *Isle la Hesse,* 47–48.

11. *Bastogne: Des civils témoignent,* 96 and 419–20.

12. Ibid., 72; de Coune, "Souvenirs," 124–26; Rivet and Sevenans, *Civils,* 194; and Marquet, "Bataille," 195–96.

13. See, for example, Rivet and Sevenans, *Civils,* 198; *Bastogne: Des civils témoignent,* 198, 527, and 529.

14. *Bastogne: Des civils témoignent,* 255, 527, and 422; Greindl, *Isle la Hesse,* 57 and 53; and de Coune, "Souvenirs," 124.

15. De Coune, "Souvenirs," 124.

16. *Bastogne: Des civils témoignent,* 207, 167, and 66; Heintz, *Périmètre,* 50.

17. *Bastogne: Des civils témoignent,* 86, 254, 255, 419, and 541; Hinckels, "Mageret," 6.

18. *Bastogne: Des civils témoignent,* 38, 40, 66, 84, 240, and 331; Burnotte, "Noël 1944," 158; Heintz, *Périmètre,* 50; and *Senonchamps,* 18.

19. *Bastogne: Des civils témoignent,* 44–45, 38, 40, 253, and 414.

20. De Coune, "Souvenirs," 122–23; Burnotte, "Noël 1944," 157; and *Bastogne: Des civils témoignent*, 427, 422, 551, and 240.

21. *Bastogne: Des civils témoignent*, 398.

22. Greindl, *Isle la Hesse*, 38; *Bastogne: Des civils témoignent*, 44, 47, and 331; Burnotte, "Noël 1944," 158; Heintz, *Périmètre*, 155; and Marquet, "Bataille," 189.

23. *Bastogne: Des civils témoignent*, 343 and 84.

24. Ibid., 392–93 and 528.

25. Ibid., 551 and 553; Heintz, *Périmètre*, 111.

26. *Bastogne: Des civils témoignent*, 398, 150, 167, and 426–27.

27. Heintz, *Périmètre*, 112–13.

28. Meurisse, *Croix Noires*, 42–43; *Bastogne: Des civils témoignent*, 44 and 410–11.

29. Bertin, *Ruée*, 59–61 and *Bastogne: Des civils témoignent*, 214.

30. *Bastogne: Des civils témoignent*, 85; MacDonald, *Trumpets*, 523; and Heintz, *Périmètre*, 158–59.

31. *Bastogne: Des civils témoignent*, 401–2.

32. Heintz, *Périmètre*, 87–88; *Bastogne: Des civils témoignent*, 530–31.

33. *Bastogne: Des civils témoignent*, 98, 100, and 102.

34. Ibid., 207, 233, 120–21, and 227; Heintz, *Périmètre*, 108.

35. MacDonald, *Trumpets*, 523.

36. *Bastogne: Des civils témoignent*, 125, 206, 71, and 197.

37. Rivet and Sevenans, *Civils*, 177–79; *Bastogne: Des civils témoignent*, 252–56; and R.R., "Il y a trente ans–L'Offensive des Ardennes: Cet Américain qui m'a sauvée," *La Libre Belgique*, 18 December 1974.

38. Bastin, "Sibret," 143.

39. Ibid., 144.

40. R.R., "Il y a trente ans–L'Offensive des Ardennes: Quand la guerre fait rage," *La Libre Belgique*, December 1974; *Bastogne: Des civils témoignent*, 328, 552, 532, 133, and 531.

41. *Bastogne: Des civils témoignent*, 96, 200, and 365.

42. Ibid., 71 and 512.

43. Ibid., 274.

44. Marshall, *Bastogne*, 157; *Bastogne: Des civils témoignent*, 40, 38, and 414.

45. MacDonald, *Trumpets*, 506; Drossart, "Bastogne," 155; and *Bastogne: Des civils témoignent*, 440, 472, 488, 459, and 567.

46. *Bastogne: Des civils témoignent*, 493–94 and 542.

47. Raymonde Havelange, "Bastogne," *La Cité*, 23 December 1984; Toland, *Battle*, 257; Drossart, "Bastogne," 155 and 157; Heintz, *Périmètre*, 68; Dumont, *Bastogne*, 16; and Rivet and Sevenans, *Civils*, 182.

48. MacDonald, *Trumpets*, 506; *Bastogne: Des civils témoignent*, 452; and Havelange, "Bastogne," *La Cité*, 23 December 1984.

49. *Bastogne: Des civils témoignent*, 466 and 439.

50. MacDonald, *Trumpets*, 526–27.

51. Heintz, *Périmètre*, 189 and 74; Meurisse, *Croix Noires*, 47; and *Bastogne: Des civils témoignent*, 533, 456–59, and 466.

52. *Bastogne: Des civils témoignent*, 458–59.

53. Greindl, *Isle la Hesse*, 54–57; Rivet and Sevenans, *Civils*, 185–86.

54. Heintz, *Périmètre*, 111; *Bastogne: Des civils témoignent*, 489 and 501–3; and Drossart, "Bastogne," 157.

55. *Bastogne: Des civils témoignent*, 489.

56. Ibid., 497, 480, and 495; Rivet and Sevenans, *Civils*, 180.

57. *Bastogne: Des civils témoignent*, 550 and 547.

58. Ibid., 490; Heintz, *Périmètre*, 68; and letter from Louise Lamotte, 10 January 1984, Folder "Bastogne," Box VI-VIIIA, AA 1207–1208, CEGESOMA.

59. Drossart, "Bastogne," 156; *Bastogne: Des civils témoignent*, 490, 484, and 488; and MacDonald, *Trumpets*, 522.

60. *Bastogne: Des civils témoignent*, 490 and 525; Meurisse, *Croix Noires*, 243–44; and Rivet and Sevenans, *Civils*, 185.

61. *Bastogne: Des civils témoignent*, 534 and 492; Meurisse, *Croix Noires*, 244 and 248.

62. Marshall, *Bastogne*, 67–68 and 138–39; *Bastogne: Des civils témoignent*, 456, 565, 567, and 573; and Rivet and Sevenans, *Civils*, 181–82.

63. Heintz, *Périmètre*, 73–74 and 75; *Bastogne: Des civils témoignent*, 454–56; and Rivet and Sevenans, *Civils*, 184–85.

64. *Bastogne: Des civils témoignent*, 566–72; MacDonald, *Trumpets*, 507, 511, and 526–27. See also www.users.win.be/W0005086/traces/lemaire.htm; Moërynck, "Marques commémoratives," 25–26.

Chapter 9. Between the Salm and the Ourthe

1. Lambert, *Vallées d'Ourthe et Aisne*, 15.

2. MacDonald, *Trumpets*, 534–36 and 537.

3. Lambert, *Vallées d'Ourthe et Aisne*, 15–16.

4. Ibid., 21 and 22–23.

5. Ibid., 30.

6. Folder 2/Group II, AA 120, CEGESOMA; Lambert, *Vallées d'Ourthe et Aisne*, 46–47.

7. Lambert, *Vallées d'Ourthe et Aisne*, 122–23.

8. Hemmer, *Vallée de l'Ourthe*, 54.

9. Lambert, *Vallées d'Ourthe et Aisne*, 105–7.

10. Hemmer, *Vallée de l'Ourthe*, 102; MacDonald, *Trumpets*, 538.

11. Hemmer, *Vallée de l'Ourthe*, 16–17, 19–20, and 22.

12. Ibid., 59–61; Jacques Rossignon, "Ardennes '44–Leur bataille: Lisette Jamaigne," *La Meuse-La Lanterne*, 4 January 1985.

13. Hemmer, *Vallée de l'Ourthe*, 62–63 and 66; Doucet and Gillet, *Hotton*, 46–50.

14. Hemmer, *Vallée de l'Ourthe*, 94–95.

15. Ibid., 78, 137, 189, 119, and 220–21. A shell blast killed a fourth civilian, Eugénie Pierard, when German troops on December 25 briefly laid fire on Hotton from the other side of the Ourthe.

16. MacDonald, *Trumpets*, 557.

17. Lambert, *Vallées d'Ourthe et Aisne*, 31–33 and 35.

18. Ibid., 23 and 25–29.

19. Francis Collin, "Nadrin, Bérismenil et Samrée: Le journal de l'Abbé

Dasnois," *La Cité*, 30 December 1984; Frankort and Wilkin, "Souvenirs personnels," 22.

20. Lambert, *Vallées d'Ourthe et Aisne*, 88–89 and 94–95; de Lilienfeld report, 17 March 1945, AA 757, CEGESOMA; and Hoyois, *L'Ardenne*, 117 and 119–20.

21. Lambert, *Vallées d'Ourthe et Aisne*, 99–102; de Lilienfeld report, 17 March 1945, CEGESOMA.

22. Lambert, *Vallées d'Ourthe et Aisne*, 41 and 48–50.

23. Ibid., 52–56.

24. MacDonald, *Trumpets*, 541–43 and 557; Parker, "Order of Battle," 650.

25. Rossignon, "Fraiture," 10; Gavroye, *Haute Ardenne*, 195–98.

26. Rossignon, "Fraiture," 10–11; Gavroye, *Haute Ardenne*, 191–92.

27. Monfort, *Carrefours*, 184; Gavroye, *Haute Ardenne*, 192; and Rossignon, "Fraiture," 11.

28. Gavroye, *Haute Ardenne*, 191, 193–94, and 196.

29. "Odeigne," Section: Luxembourg 757, ARA-AGR; Gavroye, *Haute Ardenne*, 166–68, 172–73, and 175–76; Monfort, *Carrefours*, 183; and Rivet and Sevenans, *Civils*, 83–84.

30. Gavroye, *Haute Ardenne*, 182; Monfort, *Carrefours*, 8 and 152.

31. Monfort, *Carrefours*, 8–9; Frankort and Wilkin, "Souvenirs personnels," 23.

32. Monfort, *Carrefours*, 9, 152, and 154.

33. Ibid., 179–80.

34. Ibid., 157–61.

35. Ibid., 9, 152, 179, and 169.

36. Gavroye, *Haute Ardenne*, 148, 154–55, and 143.

37. MacDonald, *Trumpets*, 549–50.

38. Frankort and Wilkin, "Souvenirs personnels," 23; Rivet and Sevenans, *Civils*, 86–87; Gavroye, *Haute Ardenne*, 152–53, 145–46, and 143; and Monfort, *Carrefours*, 181.

39. Gavroye, *Haute Ardenne*, 143, 156, 146, 155, and 161; Monfort, *Carrefours*, 181; and Rivet and Sevenans, *Civils*, 88–90.

40. Rivet and Sevenans, *Civils*, 86 and 88.

41. Gavroye, *Haute Ardenne*, 16–17.

42. Ibid., 255, 258, 262–63, and 280–81.

43. Gavroye, *Haute Ardenne*, 52 and 277.

44. Ibid., 46, 251, 235, and 61.

45. Ibid., 236, 25, 41, 72, and 43–44.

46. Rivet and Sevenans, *Civils*, 73; Folder 2/Group II, AA 120, CEGESOMA; and "Lierneux pendant la guerre," Folder "Lierneux et vallée de la Lienne," Box VI-VIIIA, AA 1207–1208, CEGESOMA.

47. Hemmer, *Vallée de l'Ourthe*, 217; Gavroye, *Haute Ardenne*, 63–64 and 86; and *Lierneux*, 26.

48. Gavroye, *Haute Ardenne*, 119, 84, 93–95, 97, and 63–64.

49. Ibid., 127–29 and 136–38.

50. "Lierneux pendant la guerre," CEGESOMA; Frankort and Wilkin, "Souvenirs personnels," 22; Rivet and Sevenans, *Civils*, 73–74; Schütz, "Unsere Flucht," 227–28; and Gavroye, *Haute Ardenne*, 87, 105, 103–4, and 95.

51. Gavroye, *Haute Ardenne*, 82–83, 109–11, and 115; Commission des Crimes de Guerre, *Ardennes*, 21–25.

52. "Memorandum," 21 and 25 December 1944, ACSL; Francis Collin, "Le Noël des écoliers de Fisenne," *La Cité*, 18 December 1984.

Chapter 10. Between the Ourthe and the Meuse

1. MacDonald, *Trumpets*, 570.

2. "Marenne," Folder 2/Group IX, AA 120, CEGESOMA; Gaillard, "Mon Noël 1944," 132 and 133; Giot, *Verdenne*, 19–23; "Verdenne: Une victime parmi d'autres," *Vers l'Avenir*, 26 December 1984; and "Marche-en-Famenne: Les dernières heures d'angoisse," *Vers l'Avenir*, 26 September 1974.

3. Giot, *Verdenne*, 25; Gaillard, "Mon Noël 1944," 131.

4. Parker, "Order of Battle," 633–34; Giot, *Verdenne*, 31 and 34; Gaillard, "Mon Noël 1944," 132; and Harold P. Leinbaugh and John D. Campbell, *The Men of Company K: The Autobiography of a World War II Rifle Company* (New York: William Morrow, 1985), 130–31.

5. Giot, *Verdenne*, 49 and 51; Gaillard, "Mon Noël 1944," 132–33.

6. MacDonald, *Trumpets*, 570–71; Giot, *Verdenne*, 54, 56, 58, and 60–61; and Gaillard, "Mon Noël 1944," 133.

7. Gaillard, "Mon Noël 1944," 133–34; Giot, *Verdenne*, 70.

8. Giot, *Verdenne*, 70 and 77; Gaillard, "Mon Noël 1944," 134–35; and "Verdenne: Une victime parmi d'autres."

9. Giot, *Verdenne*, 78 and 113; "Verdenne: Une victime parmi d'autres"; and Gaillard, "Mon Noël 1944," 135 and 137.

10. Giot, *Verdenne*, 73 and 88–89; Toland, *Battle*, 274–75; Gaillard, "Mon Noël 1944," 137.

11. De Warnaffe, *Journal*, 22 and 25.

12. *Marche, souviens-toi*, 63; Giot, *Verdenne*, 33; and Guillaume, *Marche-en-Famenne*, 54–55.

13. Guillaume, *Marche-en-Famenne*, 55, 57, and 59; *Marche, souviens-toi*, 63.

14. Lambert, *Vallées d'Ourthe et Aisne*, 247–48.

15. Guillaume, *Marche-en-Famenne*, 59–62 and 64; Lambert, *Vallées d'Ourthe et Aisne*, 230; Giot, *Verdenne*, 78; and *Marche, souviens-toi*, 64.

16. *Marche, souviens-toi*, 57.

17. André Dejardin, "Mgr Musty raconte Noël 1944 à Bande," *Vers l'Avenir*, 23 December 1984; Rivet and Sevenans, *Civils*, 128.

18. War Crimes Commission, *Bande*, 11–12.

19. Ibid., 12–13 and 27–31. See also O. Goffinet, "Noël 44: L'Ardenne martyre," *Avenir du Luxembourg*, 22 December 1984.

20. War Crimes Commission, *Bande*, 9–11; MacDonald, *Trumpets*, 9–10.

21. War Crimes Commission, *Bande*, 13–15; Chardome, "Aventures," 26, AB 758, CEGESOMA.

22. War Crimes Commission, *Bande*, 15–18; Rivet and Sevenans, *Civils*, 128–29.

23. War Crimes Commission, *Bande*, 18–22; Dejardin, "Mgr Musty raconte"; and Rivet and Sevenans, *Civils*, 128 and 130–31.

24. War Crimes Commission, *Bande*, 22–23; Commission des Crimes de Guerre, *Ardennes*, 17–20.

25. "Les gens de Celles se refugient dans la crypte de l'église," 1, Folder "Rochefort et Province de Namur," Box VIIIB-IX, AA 1207–1208, CEGESOMA.

26. De Villenfagne, "Belges," 27–32; Rivet and Sevenans, *Civils*, 136–38; and Isy Laloux, "Celles–Foy-Notre-Dame 1944," *Vers l'Avenir*, 26 December 1984.

27. Ruchenne, "Témoignage," AB 30, CEGESOMA; Thill, *Patriote*, 219–20.

28. *Celles: Noël 1944*, 43; "Les gens de Celles se refugient dans la crypte de l'église," 1–3, CEGESOMA.

29. Alice Alexandre in "Enquête sur les événements de Celles des 22, 23, 24, 25, 26 et 27 décembre 1944," Cercle Historique de Celles, Folder "Rochefort et Province de Namur," Box VIIIB-IX, AA 1207–1208, CEGESOMA; "Les gens de Celles se refugient dans la crypte de l'église," 3–5, CEGESOMA; and Delvaux, *Celles*, 111–12.

30. MacDonald, *Trumpets*, 583; Delvaux, *Celles*, 101–3 and 105; and *Celles: Noël 1944*, 45–46.

31. "Les gens de Celles se refugient dans la crypte de l'église," 5, CEGESOMA; Delvaux, *Celles*, 113.

32. Heintz, *Périmètre*, 167.

33. Brill, "Beauplateau," 100–105; Joss Heintz, "Le 'moribond' Américain a retrouvé ses sauveteurs," Folder "Militairs Américains," Box VI-VIIIA, AA 1207–1208, CEGESOMA.

34. Fourny, *Hiver*, 42–43.

35. Hoyois, *L'Ardenne*, 59–60 and 62; Crouquet, *Bataille*, 49 and 52; and Chalon, "Saint-Hubert," 19–20.

36. "Ruines et résurrection," 1–2; Hoyois, *L'Ardenne*, 58–59; and Rivet and Sevenans, *Civils*, 131–33.

37. Letter from Lucette-Amanda Losseau to RTBF, Folder "Rochefort et Province de Namur," Box VIIIB-IX, AA 1207–1208, CEGESOMA; Laurent, "Jemelloise," 19–20.

38. MacDonald, *Trumpets*, 568–69; Crouquet, *Bataille*, 18–19; and Limbrée, *45 ans après*, 28–29 and 41 and "Résistance à Rochefort," 35–37.

39. Rivet and Sevenans, *Civils*, 109–12; Limbrée, *45 ans après*, 34.

40. Limbrée, *45 ans après*, 37–44; Paul Bouchat, "Rochefort 1944: Le Noël le plus long," *Vers l'Avenir*, 27 December 1984; and Rivet and Sevenans, *Civils*, 111.

41. Limbrée, *45 ans après*, 51–56.

42. Crouquet, *Bataille*, 18; Limbrée, *45 ans après*, 61 and 63.

43. Lambert, *Vallées d'Ourthe et Aisne*, 265–74 and 258; Limbrée, *45 ans après*, 70.

44. Limbrée, *45 ans après*, 65.

45. Craven and Cate, *Europe*, 695–98; Hemmer, *Vallée de l'Ourthe*, 226–27; and Hoyois, *L'Ardenne*, 92.

46. Jean Lefebvre, "L'Offensive des Ardennes: La Roche-en-Ardenne," 5 and 13–14, Folder "La Roche-Samrée," Box VIIIB-IX, AA 1207–1208, CEGESOMA; "La bataille des Ardennes: Myriam y était," 1 January 1985.

47. "La bataille des Ardennes: Myriam y était," 1 January 1985; Lefebvre,

"L'Offensive des Ardennes," 6, 7, and 9–10, CEGESOMA; and Crouquet, *Bataille,* 40–41.

48. Hoyois, *L'Ardenne,* 92; "La bataille des Ardennes: Myriam y était," 1 January 1985.

49. Lefebvre, "L'Offensive des Ardennes," 14–15, CEGESOMA.

50. Rivet and Sevenans, *Civils,* 157.

51. Nollomont, *Région de La Roche-en-Ardenne,* 47; Lefebvre, "L'Offensive des Ardennes," 16–21, CEGESOMA; Crouquet, *Bataille,* 42–43; and "La bataille des Ardennes: Myriam y était," 1 January 1985.

52. Lefebvre, "L'Offensive des Ardennes," 22–25 and 34, CEGESOMA; Nollomont, *Région de La Roche-en-Ardenne,* 47; and Crouquet, *Bataille,* 43.

53. "La bataille des Ardennes: Myriam y était," 1 January 1985; Lefebvre, "L'Offensive des Ardennes," 25–26, CEGESOMA.

54. Crouquet, *Bataille,* 25; Limbrée, *45 ans après,* 65–66 and 89. On drunk German troops in Rochefort, see also Rivet and Sevenans, *Civils,* 114.

55. Limbrée, *45 ans après,* 70–71, 73, and 88; Crouquet, *Bataille,* 22 and 26; and Rivet and Sevenans, *Civils,* 114.

56. Limbrée, *45 ans après,* 73, 75, and 87–88; letter from Marguerite Champenois to cousins in Brussels, 31 January 1945, Folder "Rochefort et Province de Namur," Box VIIIB-IX, AA 1207–1208, CEGESOMA; and Rivet and Sevenans, *Civils,* 112.

57. Limbrée, *45 ans après,* 73–74, 75, and 77; Crouquet, *Bataille,* 19 and 26–28; and Nollomont, *Région de La Roche-en-Ardenne,* 51.

58. Crouquet, *Bataille,* 27–28; Limbrée, *45 ans après,* 74, 75, 77, and 80; Bouchat, "Rochefort 1944"; Hoyois, *L'Ardenne,* 56 and 58.

59. Chalon, "Saint-Hubert," 18.

60. Fourny, *Hiver,* 6 and 16; Jacob, "Sur le front des Ardennes," sections II, IX, and XIII.

61. Fourny, *Hiver,* 6–7, 16–17, 18, 20, and 30.

62. Ibid., 7–8, 28, 40, 20, 21–22, and 24; Jacob, "Sur le front des Ardennes," section VI; and Heintz, *Périmètre,* 172–73.

63. Fourny, *Hiver,* 52 and 53.

64. Ibid., 58, 59, 61, 63, and 49.

65. Ibid., 28 and 34.

Chapter 11. Counterattack from the South

1. Toland, *Battle,* 168; Maertz, *Luxemburg,* 200; and MacDonald, *Trumpets,* 146–47.

2. Maertz, *Luxemburg,* 105–6.

3. Cole, *Ardennes,* 495; Hohengarten, "Gestapo," 8–9; and Maertz, *Luxemburg,* 108.

4. Karen, *Kriegsereignisse,* 459 and 429–30.

5. Maertz, *Luxemburg,* 108–9; Karen, *Kriegsereignisse,* 430 and 434.

6. Maertz, *Luxemburg,* 109; Rasqué, *Oesling,* 221–23.

7. Rasqué, *Oesling,* 472–76.

8. Ibid., 71.

9. Gaul, *Americans,* 281, 320, 286, and 289–90.

10. Ibid., 290–91, 337, 170, and 286.

11. Ibid., 292–94 and 319.

12. Ibid., 348, 299, and 290.

13. Ibid., 343, 334–35, 289–90, 298–99, and 320.

14. Ibid., 265.

15. Maertz, *Luxemburg,* 211 and 213; Rasqué, *Oesling,* 274 and 276.

16. Camille P. Kohn, "Geschichte eines Regimentes und seines Kommandeurs," *The Bulge* (April 2002): 8–9.

17. Rasqué, *Oesling,* 332 and 520.

18. Ibid., 98–102.

19. Maertz, *Luxemburg,* 229–32 and 507–8; Rasqué, *Oesling,* 103–8 and 112.

20. MacDonald, *Trumpets,* 518.

21. Rasqué, *Oesling,* 284–86, 90, and 553.

22. Ibid., 553 and 3–5; Maertz, *Luxemburg,* 246.

23. Rasqué, *Oesling,* 401–3, 256, 218, and 403; Maertz, *Luxemburg,* 247–49.

24. Schiltz, "Kellerleben," 24–27; Maertz, *Luxemburg,* 250–51; and Rasqué, *Oesling,* 404.

25. Rasqué, *Oesling,* 217 and 324.

26. Ibid., 44; Joss Heintz, "Bastogne et Wiltz," *Avenir du Luxembourg,* 21 April 1989.

27. Rasqué, *Oesling,* 217–18; Schiltz, "Kellerleben," 23.

28. Milmeister, "Einsatz ," 3–4; Hohengarten, "Gestapo," 9; and Rasqué, *Oesling,* 614 and 667–68.

29. Milmeister, "Einsatz," 4; Hohengarten, "Gestapo," 9; and Rasqué, *Oesling,* 335–38 and 352.

30. Milmeister, "Einsatz," 3; Hohengarten, "Gestapo," 9–10.

31. Milmeister, "Einsatz," 3; Hohengarten, "Gestapo," 10–11.

Chapter 12. Lifting the Siege of Bastogne

1. www.purpleheart.org/m0597a3.htm, 3.

2. MacDonald, *Trumpets,* 519; www.purpleheart.org/m0597a3.htm, 3.

3. Lozet-Gustin, "Journées tragiques," 136.

4. Ibid., 136–38; *Bastogne: Des civils témoignent,* 268 and 270; and Heintz, *Périmètre,* 94–96.

5. *Bastogne: Des civils témoignent,* 214.

6. Didier-Robert, *Mémoire,* 36–38.

7. Heintz, *Périmètre,* 91–92; Didier-Robert, *Mémoire,* 44.

8. Didier-Robert, *Mémoire,* 44–49; Heintz, *Périmètre,* 92–93, 196, and 198–99.

9. MacDonald, *Trumpets,* 526 and 529–30.

10. Cole, *Ardennes,* 552; Heintz, *Périmètre,* 198.

11. MacDonald, *Trumpets,* 530; Marquet, "Bataille," 193–95.

12. Heintz, *Périmètre,* 198 and 98.

13. MacDonald, *Trumpets,* 531–32.

14. *Bastogne: Des civils témoignent,* 459 and 496; Greindl, *Isle la Hesse,* 57.

15. *Bastogne: Des civils témoignent,* 279–80.

16. Rivet and Sevenans, *Civils,* 194; de Coune, "Souvenirs," 127–29.

17. Didier-Robert, *Mémoire,* 61–62, 64, and 66–67.

18. Ibid., 67–68; Heintz, *Périmètre,* 93.

19. *Bastogne: Des civils témoignent,* 236; Didier-Robert, *Mémoire,* 71–73.

20. Bertin, *Ruée,* 53; Heintz, *Périmètre,* 54.

21. Bertin, *Ruée,* 53; Heintz, *Périmètre,* 53–54.

22. *Bastogne: Des civils témoignent,* 203–4, 206, and 209.

23. Ibid., 210 and 212.

24. Ibid., 379–80.

25. "25 jaar later," *Ons Land;* Heintz, *Périmètre,* 134–35; and *Bastogne: Des civils témoignent,* 379.

26. Bastin, "Sibret," 144–45; *Bastogne: Des civils témoignent,* 307; and Heintz, *Périmètre,* 200.

27. Burnotte, "Noël 1944," 160–61.

28. Ibid., 160–61; *Bastogne: Des civils témoignent,* 325.

29. Burnotte, "Noël 1944," 161; *Bastogne: Des civils témoignent,* 329.

30. Marquet, "Bataille," 200–201; Rivet and Sevenans, *Civils,* 189; and Heintz, *Périmètre,* 115–16.

31. Marquet, "Bataille," 202.

32. MacDonald, *Trumpets,* 532; Meurisse, *Croix Noires,* 51–52; Drossart, "Bastogne," 155; Maria Gillet, "Siège de Bastogne: Souvenirs des jours d'angoisse et des nuits interminables, 18 décembre 44–2 janvier 45," 16–17 December 1944, Folder "Bastogne," Box VI-VIII A, AA 1207–1208, CEGESOMA; *Bastogne: Des civils témoignent,* 460.

33. *Bastogne: Des civils témoignent,* 460–61.

34. *Bastogne: Des civils témoignent,* 459; Heintz, *Périmètre,* 76; and Cole, *Ardennes,* 632.

35. Heintz, *Périmètre,* 121 and 76–77; Gérard Gerardy, "Six journées d'enfer pour Bastogne assiégée," *La Cité,* 21 December 1984; *Bastogne: Des civils témoignent,* 461; and Crouquet, *Bataille,* 34.

36. Cole, *Ardennes,* 632; MacDonald, *Trumpets,* 606–7.

37. Rivet and Sevenans, *Civils,* 189–90; Heintz, *Périmètre,* 116; R.R., "Il y a trente ans–L'Offensive des Ardennes: Quand la guerre fait rage," *La Libre Belgique,* December 1974; and Burnotte, "Noël 1944," 162–63.

38. *Bastogne: Des civils témoignent,* 325; Burnotte, "Noël 1944," 163–65; Heintz, *Périmètre,* 117–18; and Toland, *Battle,* 328–29.

39. Heintz, *Périmètre,* 140, 118, and 123–24; Rivet and Sevenans, *Civils,* 190; Toland, *Battle,* 329; and John W. Fague, *Un endroit parmi d'autres: Un GI parle des combats de Chenogne qu'il a vécus.* Bastogne: Cercle d'Histoire de Bastogne, 1997.

40. Heintz, *Périmètre,* 128 and 186.

41. Ibid., 116 and 126–27.

42. *Bastogne: Des civils témoignent,* 352; Heintz, *Périmètre,* 127–28.

43. Heintz, *Périmètre,* 52, 55–56, 159, and 162; *Bastogne: Des civils témoignent,* 206 and 213; and Bertin, *Ruée,* 58 and 61–62.

44. Heintz, *Périmètre,* 54–55; *Bastogne: Des civils témoignent,* 207–8.

45. *Bastogne: Des civils témoignent,* 228 and 244.

46. Rivet and Sevenans, *Civils,* 200–202; Heintz, *Périmètre,* 52–54 and 201.

47. *Bastogne: Des civils témoignent,* 206, 462, and 489; Heintz, *Périmètre,* 77; and Dumont, *Bastogne,* 27.

48. *Bastogne: Des civils témoignent,* 89, 82–83, and 36; Heintz, *Périmètre,* 195 and 38.

49. *Bastogne: Des civils témoignent,* 91 and 87.

50. Ibid., 92, 99, and 134–35.

51. Heintz, *Périmètre,* 146–47; *Bastogne: Des civils témoignent,* 92 and 100.

52. *Bastogne: Des civils témoignent,* 89, 93, and 82–83.

53. Ibid., 135.

54. Parker, "Order of Battle," 651 and 653; "25 jaar later," *Ons Land;* and Heintz, *Périmètre,* 133–34 and 195.

55. Heintz, *Périmètre,* 77–78; *Bastogne: Des civils témoignent,* 477 and 479.

56. MacDonald, *Trumpets,* 610.

57. Rivet and Sevenans, *Civils,* 186–88; *Bastogne: Des civils témoignent,* 413.

Chapter 13. Eliminating the Bulge

1. Cole, *Ardennes,* 650.

2. MacDonald, *Trumpets,* 616–17 and *Last Offensive,* 53.

3. E-mails from Eddy Monfort to author, 2 June and 9 October 2003; Gavroye, *Haute Ardenne,* 133–34 and 126.

4. Gavroye, *Haute Ardenne,* 111, 120, 116, 87, and 91; "Lierneux pendant la guerre," Folder "Lierneux et vallée de la Lienne," Box VI-VIIIA, AA 1207–1208, CEGESOMA.

5. Gavroye, *Haute Ardenne,* 134–35, 102–3, and 87–88; First U.S. Army G-5 Report, 26 January 1945, AA 17, CEGESOMA; and *Lierneux,* 26–27.

6. Gavroye, *Haute Ardenne,* 120 and 118.

7. Monfort, *Carrefours,* 137, 159, 169, 167, 171, and 153; Gavroye, *Haute Ardenne,* 183–84.

8. Gavroye, *Haute Ardenne,* 260–61.

9. Monfort, *Carrefours,* 147 and 185; Gavroye, *Haute Ardenne,* 266 and 274–75.

10. Gavroye, *Haute Ardenne,* 187–88 and 203; Monfort, *Carrefours,* 147 and 156.

11. Gavroye, *Haute Ardenne,* 256–57, 261, and 275; Monfort, *Carrefours,* 185.

12. Gavroye, *Haute Ardenne,* 169–70, 173, 177, and 167; Monfort, *Carrefours,* 131, 145, and 183.

13. Gavroye, *Haute Ardenne,* 241; Monfort, *Carrefours,* 184–85; and e-mail from Eddy Monfort to author, 13 May 2003.

14. Lambert, *Vallées d'Ourthe et Aisne,* 69; Rivet and Sevenans, *Civils,* 167–68.

15. Rivet and Sevenans, *Civils,* 169; Gavroye, *Haute Ardenne,* 246, 248, and 49; and Dubru, *Houffalize,* 161 and 183.

16. Gavroye, *Haute Ardenne,* 26, 43, 46, and 47; Rivet and Sevenans, *Civils,* 209–10; and Monfort, *Carrefours,* 183.

17. Hemmer, *Vallée de l'Ourthe,* 235; *Marche, souviens-toi,* 62, 61, and 41–42.

18. Hemmer, *Vallée de l'Ourthe,* 237; Guillaume, *Marche-en-Famenne,* 72–73;

Marche, souviens-toi, 62; Giot, *Verdenne*, 137; and "Stationnement et parcage des vehicules," Commune de Ciney, AA 145, CEGESOMA.

19. Hemmer, *Vallée de l'Ourthe*, 238; "Réclamation," 15 February 1945, ACSL; and "État des lieux Hanin-Brasseur" and handwritten soldier note, Commune de Marche, AA 145, CEGESOMA.

20. *Marche, souviens-toi*, 41; Hemmer, *Vallée de l'Ourthe*, 258; and "Séances," 22 July 1945, ACSL.

21. "La bataille des Ardennes: Myriam y était," 8 January 1985; Crouquet, *Bataille*, 44 and 45; Lefebvre, "L'Offensive des Ardennes: La Roche-en-Ardenne," 27 and 28, Folder "La Roche-Samrée," Box VIIIB-IX, AA 1207–1208, CEGESOMA; Commission des Crimes de Guerre, *Ardennes*, 46–51; and Nollomont, *Région de La Roche-en-Ardenne*, 59.

22. Crouquet, *Bataille*, 37–38; Lefebvre, "L'Offensive des Ardennes," 28–31, CEGESOMA; and "La bataille des Ardennes: Myriam y était," 8 January 1985.

23. "La bataille des Ardennes: Myriam y était," 8 January 1985.

24. Lefebvre, "L'Offensive des Ardennes," 35–36, CEGESOMA; Hoyois, *L'Ardenne*, 92.

25. Limbrée, *45 ans après*, 89–90; "Claims for Alleged Looting," submitted by Henri Solot and Louis Pierard, Commune de Buissonville, AA 145, CEGESOMA.

26. "Ruines et résurrection," 2–3; Rivet and Sevenans, *Civils*, 121.

27. "Ruines et résurrection," 3; Rivet and Sevenans, *Civils*, 120–24; and Limbrée, *45 ans après*, 85.

28. Hoyois, *L'Ardenne*, 59.

29. Commission des Crimes de Guerre, *Ardennes*, 53–56 and 58–59; Rivet and Sevenans, *Civils*, 117–19.

30. Commission des Crimes de Guerre, *Ardennes*, 61–62; "Le fusillé vivant," *Le Gaulois*, Folder "Rochefort et Province de Namur," Box VIIIB-IX, AA 1207–1208, CEGESOMA.

31. Commission des Crimes de Guerre, *Ardennes*, 56–59; Rivet and Sevenans, *Civils*, 119–20.

32. Fourny, *Hiver*, 10; Dermience, *Bonnerue*, 25.

33. Fourny, *Hiver*, 10–12, 64, 72–73, 55, and 58; Dermience, *Bonnerue*, 31.

34. Guy Blockmans, "Un para Britannique revient à Bande (Nassogne)," *L'Estafette!*, no. 220 (May 2003): 1–2; Rivet and Sevenans, *Civils*, 129; and Commission des Crimes de Guerre, *Ardennes*, 23–24.

35. Gillard, "Vesqueville," 11 and 12 January 1945, microfilm 46, CEGESOMA.

36. Crouquet, *Bataille*, 50–51; Chalon, "Saint-Hubert," 19.

37. *Bastogne: Des civils témoignent*, 381–82; Heintz, *Périmètre*, 137 and 199.

38. Heintz, *Périmètre*, 136–37.

39. *Bastogne: Des civils témoignent*, 407.

40. Ibid., 219, 74, and 76; Maertz, *Luxemburg*, 309; Heintz, *Périmètre*, 119; and Rasqué, *Oesling*, 611.

41. Rasqué, *Oesling*, 329, 717, and 612; Heintz, *Périmètre*, 193–94, 51, 196, and 200; and Maertz, *Luxemburg*, 326.

42. *Bastogne: Des civils témoignent*, 76 and 227.

43. Ibid., 77 and 67; Rasqué, *Oesling*, 329 and 612.

44. Heintz, *Périmètre*, 162 and 190; *Bastogne: Des civils témoignent*, 60.

45. *Bastogne: Des civils témoignent*, 57, 58–59, and 62.

46. Ibid., 87, 93, and 100.

47. Georges et al., "Fors l'oubli," 65.

48. Dubru, *Houffalize*, 164–65; *Bastogne: Des civils témoignent*, 202 and 186; and Voigt, "340. Volks-Grenadier-Division," 48, AA 484, CEGESOMA.

49. "Chronique des Pères Franciscains," *Le Pays de Bastogne*, no. 1 (March 1993): 7.

50. Colignon, "Bataille," 266 note 7; Heintz, *Périmètre*, 185–86 and 189–201; Hoyois, *L'Ardenne*, 86; and Lefèbvre, *Bastogne*, 129.

51. Dubru, *Houffalize*, 130–31, 137–38, and 148 and "L'anéantissement," 25–26 and 33–36; Hoyois, *L'Ardenne*, 95; Lesage, *Houffalize*, 65; and transcript interview Nelly Simon, 1, A 363–64, AA 1593, CEGESOMA.

52. André R. Meurisse, "Recherches et texte," 4, Folder "Houffalize," Box VIIIB-IX, AA 1207–1208, CEGESOMA; Dubru, *Houffalize*, 137–38 and "L'anéantissement," 21; Rivet and Sevenans, *Civils*, 161–62; and Lesage, *Houffalize*, 85 and 88.

53. Dubru, *Houffalize*, 145, 166, and 139–40; Kauffmann, "Mont-Houffalize," 183; transcript interview Simon, 2 and 4, CEGESOMA; Verbrugghen, "Aide et solidarité," 208–10; Lesage, *Houffalize*, 65–66; and Hasquin et al., *Gemeenten van België*, Vol. 3, 2112.

54. Dubru, *Houffalize*, 108, 110, 102, 104, 173–76, 139, and 143; Lesage, *Houffalize*, 82–88; and Verbrugghen, "Aide et solidarité," 210.

55. Dubru, *Houffalize*, 211–12, 182, 288, and 270; transcript interview Simon, 3, CEGESOMA; Rossignon, "Houffalize," 25; Verbrugghen, "Aide et solidarité," 213; and Lesage, *Houffalize*, 67.

56. Meurisse, "Recherches et texte," 4, CEGESOMA; Dubru, *Houffalize*, 261–62, 184–85, 142–44, 238, 167, and 169; Kettels-Crémer, "Tavigny," 194; Commission des Crimes de Guerre, *Ardennes*, 13–16; Georges et al., "Fors l'oubli," 65; and Collette, "Souvenirs," 185–86. On German aggression while foraging, see also Rivet and Sevenans, *Civils*, 159.

57. Crouquet, *Bataille*, 73–74; Dubru, *Houffalize*, 141, 287, 199, 282, 256–57, and 213; and transcript interview Simon, 2 and 3, CEGESOMA.

58. Dubru, *Houffalize*, 216–18, 211, 276, 270, 250–54, and 98; Verbrugghen, "Aide et solidarité," 208 and 210; and Lesage, *Houffalize*, 66.

59. *Chevron*, 25, 27, and 29.

60. Gavroye, *Haute Ardenne*, 79 and 26.

61. Ibid., 83 and 100.

62. Ibid., 83–86.

63. *Chevron*, 32.

64. Lechat, "Chronique," 27–28; Dropsy, *Mon village*, 113.

65. Dropsy, *Mon village*, 66–70, 72, 115, and 78; Rivet and Sevenans, *Civils*, 170; Marcel Jeanpierre, "The Battle of Grand-Halleux," 2, www.users.skynet. be/bulgecriba/beaty.html; and Remacle, *Vielsalm*, 113.

66. Lechat, "Chronique," 32, 21, 27, 28, 30–32, 35, and 37; Dropsy, *Mon village*, 113–16.

67. Lechat, "Chronique," 32–33; Dropsy, *Mon village,* 74 and 117.

68. Dropsy, *Mon village,* 80–83, 97, and 99; Lechat, "Chronique," 35–37. For complaints from Trois-Ponts and Vielsalm, see also de Lilienfeld reports, 17 January and 7 March 1945, AA 757, CEGESOMA. When the paratroopers were withdrawn to Chevron in mid-January, even a hitherto sympathetic Mr. Jamar in his journal spoke of misbehavior and "straightforward looting." *Chevron,* 35–39. American military authorities themselves corroborated the complaints, reporting "as yet unpublished accounts of wanton pillaging by our own troops." SHAEF Mission to Belgium and Luxembourg, 6 February 1945, AA 1230, CEGESOMA.

69. Lechat, "Chronique," 34.

70. Ibid., 34–37; Dropsy, *Mon village,* 113.

71. Offergeld, "Comme je l'ai vécue," 19 and 32–34. On the fate of the civilians in this area see also, for example, Dropsy, *Mon village,* 81, 83, and 84.

72. Maertz, *Luxemburg,* 413.

73. Rasqué, *Oesling,* 699 and 171–72; Maertz, *Luxemburg,* 388.

74. Maertz, *Luxemburg,* 376; Rasqué, *Oesling,* 310 and 165–66.

75. Maertz, *Luxemburg,* 388–91 and 498–503; Rasqué, *Oesling,* 172–75 and 477.

76. Rasqué, *Oesling,* 511–12; Maertz, *Luxemburg,* 410–11.

77. Rasqué, *Oesling,* 125–30; Maertz, *Luxemburg,* 406–9.

78. Rasqué, *Oesling,* 532–36; Maertz, *Luxemburg,* 401 and 403.

79. Rasqué, *Oesling,* 503–7.

80. Ibid., 512–13, 516, 125, and 130.

81. Maertz, *Luxemburg,* 413–17 and 421; Joss Heintz, "Bastogne et Wiltz," *Avenir du Luxembourg,* 21 April 1989; and Rasqué, *Oesling,* 680–88.

82. Hohengarten, "Gestapo," 11–14; Milmeister, "Einsatz," 5; www.kloster-arnsburg.de/kloster/friedhof.htm; and Rasqué, *Oesling,* 72.

83. Maertz, *Luxemburg,* 429–30 and 440–41; Rasqué, *Oesling,* 551, 483, and 486–87.

84. Lejeune, *Hünningen,* 6; Fickers et al., *Honsfeld,* 10–11; and Reuter and Fagnoul, "Schoppen," 113–14.

85. Von Frühbuss, "Wallerode," 205; Schütz, "Crombach," 274; Flemings, "Erinnerungen," 278; and Toussaint, *Bittere Erfahrungen,* 593.

86. De Lilienfeld report, 9 March 1945, 2, AA 757, CEGESOMA; Graf, "Hitlers letzte Offensive," 28 December 1974; von Frühbuss, "Wallerode," 205; Veiders, *Möderscheid,* 22–23; Margraff, "Eibertingen," 293; and Flemings, "Erinnerungen," 278.

87. Margraff, "Deidenberg," 296 and 299 and "Eibertingen," 294.

88. Fagnoul, *St. Vith,* 131 and 133.

89. Fagnoul, "Büllingen," 107; Küches, "Amel," 291; and Veiders, *Möderscheid,* 23 and 27.

90. Von Frühbuss, "Wallerode," 205–6.

91. Fagnoul, "Büllingen," 107–8 and "Iveldingen-Montenau," 305; Margraff, "Eibertingen," 294. Quote is from www.private-art.com/archive/1945/jan/012445.html.

92. Maertz, *Luxemburg*, 463–64, 480, and 465 and Rasqué, *Oesling*, 72 and 230–31.

93. Rasqué, *Oesling*, 193–94; Maertz, *Luxemburg*, 464 and 469–70; and Gaul, *Americans*, 281 and 320–21. Quotes are from Gaul, 335.

94. Maertz, *Luxemburg*, 463; Rasqué, *Oesling*, 304 and 72.

95. Gaul, *Americans*, 344, 321, and 329–30.

96. Ibid., 321.

97. Ibid., 321; Rasqué, *Oesling*, 194–95.

98. Rasqué, *Oesling*, 159, 141, 411, and 454.

99. Ibid., 22, 24, 136, 277–78, and 457; Gaul, *Americans*, 209.

100. Rasqué, *Oesling*, 457–58, 364–67, and 586.

101. Gennen, *Burg Reuland*, 132.

102. Ibid., 56; Nilles, "Steinebrück," 220–21; Fagnoul, "Schönberg," 87; Graf, "Märtyrerstadt," 243–44 and 247; and Rivet and Sevenans, *Civils*, 28–29.

103. Fagnoul, "Schönberg," 87 and *St. Vith*, 112; Gennen, "Augenzeugen," 269, 265, and 268 and *Burg Reuland*, 65, 72, 82, 130, and 38; Dries, "Streiflichter," 189–90; Rasqué, *Oesling*, 122, 421, and 670–71; and Weynand, "Ein Mädchen," 136.

104. Gennen, *Burg Reuland*, 112–22.

105. Ibid., 49.

Epilogue

1. Colignon, "Bataille," 265–66; Hoyois, *L'Ardenne*, 147.

2. Hubert, "Après la bataille," 250; Hoyois, *L'Ardenne*, 147–50.

3. Hoyois, *L'Ardenne*, 151–54; "First U.S. Army G-5 Report," 10, 26 January 1945, AA 17, CEGESOMA.

4. Jean Lefebvre, "L'Offensive des Ardennes–La Roche-en-Ardenne," Folder "La Roche-Samrée," Box VIIIB-IX, AA 1207–1208, CEGESOMA; Lambert, *Vallées d'Ourthe et Aisne*, 206; Lejeune, "Wirtzfeld," 179; and Karen, *Kriegsereignisse*, 574.

5. Fagnoul, "Märtyrerstadt," 333–34.

6. www.users.skynet.be/wallonia/maubeuge.htm.

7. Bastin, "Sibret," 148–51; Lozet-Gustin, "Journées tragiques," 139; "First U.S. Army. Report of Operations. Annex No. 3," 162 and 165, AA 20, CEGESOMA; and "First U.S. Army G-5 Report," 26 January 1945, 4 and 5, AA 17, CEGESOMA.

8. FNSS, "Rapport," 17, DOS-SVG; "First U.S. Army. Report of Operations. Annex No. 3," 168; and "First U.S. Army G-5 Report," 26 January 1945, 1 and 11.

9. "SHAEF Standard Policy and Procedure for Combined Civil Affairs Operations in Northwest Europe, rev. i May 1944," in Coles and Weinberg, *Civil Affairs*, 679; "Extraits," in Rivet and Sevenans, *Civils*, 246; General Board reports, 13 January and 21 February 1945 and Executive Committee reports, 18 January and 2, 8, and 15 February 1945, BRK-CRB; "Hulpverleen aan oorlogsslachtoffers," *Het Laatste Nieuws*, 22 February 1945; and Karen, *Kriegsereignisse*, 584.

10. "Het Roode Kruis van België in de geteisterde gewesten," *De Gazet van Antwerpen*, 22 February 1945; *Bastogne: Des civils témoignent*, 572–73; Executive Committee reports, 18 and 25 January and 5 April 1945 and General Board reports, 18 October and 22 November 1945, BRK-CRB.

11. *Bastogne: Des civils témoignent*, 42; Graf, "Hitlers letzte Offensive," 30 December 1974; Rasqué, *Oesling*, 587–88; "Gevaar voor cholera in de Ardennen," *De Roode Vaan*, 11 February 1945; "Extraits," in Rivet and Sevenans, *Civils*, 215, 217–19, 220, 225, and 227–28; FNSS, "Rapport," 6–10, DOS-SVG; and Velge, *Oeuvre Nationale de l'Enfance*, 157.

12. General Board report, 18 October 1945, 3, BRK-CRB; "Du charbon pour les sinistrés Ardennais," *Le Soir*, 14 January 1947; Executive Committee report, 18 January 1945, BRK-CRB; Picalausa, "Het Roode Kruis," 3–7; "Une belle fête à la Croix-Rouge," *Journal de Malmedy*, 4 August 1945; and Verbrugghen, "Aide et solidarité," 214–15.

13. Colignon, "Bataille," 271; Dropsy, *Mon village*, 136.

14. "Extraits," in Rivet and Sevenans, *Civils*, 215–49; Karen, *Kriegsereignisse*, 572–73; and Gommes, "Mennoniten," 7–10.

15. Lejoly, *Faymonville*, 175–91 and 194.

16. Colignon, "Bataille," 271; Fagnoul, "Märtyrerstadt," 317 and 333.

17. "Extraits," in Rivet and Sevenans, *Civils*, 239–40; Chambre des Représentants de Belgique, Projet de Loi, 6 June 1996/Amendment No. 1, 595/3–95/96; Hubert, "Après la bataille," 255–56.

18. Gillard, "Vesqueville," 18–31 January 1945, microfilm 46, CEGESOMA; Karen, *Kriegsereignisse*, 613.

19. Schetter, *Saint-Vith*, 37–38; "Extraits," in Rivet and Sevenans, *Civils*, 243; Heintz, *Perimètre*, 176; and Dropsy, *Mon village*, 102 and 105.

20. Lombard et al., *Nos démineurs*, 28; author interview with Charles Hilgers, 5 August 2002; Fagnoul, *St. Vith*, 131–32; "SEDEE: Des héros tranquilles" and R. Dumont, "Le SEDEE aujourd'hui," BB B 14/150, CEGESOMA; and "Extraits," in Rivet and Sevenans, *Civils*, 243.

21. Meurisse, *Croix Noires*, 251; "Extraits," in Rivet and Sevenans, *Civils*, 244; and Dropsy, *Mon village*, 134–35.

22. "Lierneux: Faits de guerre," Folder "Lierneux et vallée de la Lienne," Box VI-VIIIA, AA 1207–1208, CEGESOMA; Moërynck, "Marques commémoratives," no. 1 (2001): 23–24.

23. "Extraits," in Rivet and Sevenans, *Civils*, 243–44; Fraternelle des Démineurs de Belgique, *Nos démineurs*, 36, BB B 14/150, CEGESOMA; Lombard et al., *Nos démineurs*, 94–96; and Milmeister, *Chronik*, 125.

24. Heintz, *Perimètre*, 175–77; Hoyois, *L'Ardenne*, 155. For the casualties in the Luxembourg Ardennes, see the reports compiled for each parish in Rasqué, *Oesling*.

25. Gennen, *Burg Reuland*, 76; Toussaint, *Bittere Erfahrungen*, 538–39.

26. Toussaint, *Bittere Erfahrungen*, 405–608. For the Nidrum case, see Toussaint, 565 and letter from the Minister of the Interior to the mayors of Eupen-Malmedy-St. Vith, 26 July 1972, R 261, GAB; and Karen, *Kriegsereignisse*, 575.

27. Laby, *Stavelot*, 146 and 293. On the controversial Malmedy trial, see Weingartner's *Crossroads of Death* and *A Peculiar Crusade*.

28. Dropsy, *Mon village*, 140–45.

29. Heintz, *Périmètre*, 209–12.

30. "Il y a trente ans–L'Offensive des Ardennes: Cet Américain qui m'a sauvée," *La Libre Belgique*, 18 December 1974; Joseph Maertz, "16. Dezember 1944: Ardennenoffensive und Ihre Folgen," *Luxemburger Wort*, December 1984; and D.R., "Le souvenir ne s'estompe pas," *L'Avenir du Luxembourg*, 21 December 2001.

31. Schaffer, *Wings of Judgment*, 43 and transcript interview Nelly Simon, 4–5, A 363–64, AA 1593, CEGESOMA. For the civilian debate on this and similar Allied bombardments see, for example, Grandjean, "Ardennes," 204–5.

32. Dubru, *Houffalize*, 274.

33. Copeman, "Schönberg," 2, AB 1912, CEGESOMA.

34. Engels, *Circuit Historique*, 3; Guy Blockmans, "Un hommage aux oubliés de la bataille des Ardennes à Baillonville," *L'Estafette!*, no. 221 (2003): 3–4; and "Avis de recherche," *Le Pays de Bastogne*, no. 1 (1992): 6.

35. Hanlon, "Draps de Hemroulle," 15–18; Heintz, *Périmètre*, 155.

Bibliography

Works and archival collections that are frequently cited have been identified by the following abbreviations:

ACSL   Archives Communales Somme-Leuze
ARA-AGR   Algemeen Rijksarchief—Archives Générales du Royaume
BRK-CRB   Belgische Rode Kruis—Croix-Rouge de Belgique
CEGESOMA   Centre d'Études et de Documentation Guerre et Sociétés
            Contemporaines—Studie en Documentatiecentrum
            Oorlog en Hedendaagse Maatschappij
DOS-SVG   Dienst voor de Oorlogsslachtoffers—Service des Victimes
            de la Guerre
DVI   *Der verhängnisvolle Irrtum: Hitlers Fehlkalkulation in den
            Ardennen beschleunigte vor 40 Jahren das Ende.* Eupen:
            Grenz-Echo-Verlag, 1984.
EuW   Kurt Fagnoul and Hubert Jenniges, eds. *Ende und Wende
            im Lande zwischen Venn und Schneifel: Augenzeugen
            berichten von ihren Kriegserlebnissen 1944/45.* St. Vith:
            Geschichts und Museumsverein "Zwischen Venn und
            Schneifel," 1995.
FNSS   Fonds National de Secours aux Sinistrés
GAB   Gemeindearchive Büllingen
JdS   Christian Kraft de la Saulx, ed. *Jours de Sursaut.* Vol. 21 of
            Jours de Guerre. Brussels: Dexia, 2001.
KS   *Kriegsschicksale 1944–45: Beiträge zur Chronik der
            Ardennenoffensive zwischen Venn und Schneifel.* St. Vith:
            Geschichtsverein "Zwischen Venn und Schneifel," 1969.
RTBF   Radio Télévision Belge Francophone

Primary Sources

Archival Materials

Central Archives

Algemeen Rijksarchief–Archives Générales du Royaume

Brussels, Belgium
Commissariaat Generaal voor's Lands Wederopbouw–Commissariat Général à la Restauration du Pays.

Belgische Rode Kruis–Croix-Rouge de Belgique

Brussels, Belgium
Executive Committee reports, 21 September 1944–21 April 1945.
General Board reports, 14 October 1944–22 November 1945.
Reports from provincial committees and local sections to Brussels Headquarters.

Centre d'Études et de Documentation Guerre et Sociétés Contemporaines–Studie-en Documentatiecentrum Oorlog en Hedendaagse Maatschappij

Brussels, Belgium
AA 4
"Civil Affairs/Military Government. 21 Army Group. Operations North West Europe 1944/1945."
AA 16
Department of the Army. Office of the Chief of Military History. "History of the Civil Affairs Division, War Department Special Staff, World War II to March 1946: Civil Affairs Division Activities with Respect to Belgium."
AA 17
"First U.S. Army G-5 Reports: Civil Affairs and Military Government Summaries." Biweekly Reports, 15 December 1944–26 January 1945.
AA 20
"First United States Army. Report of Operations, 1 August 1944–22 February 1945. Annex No. 3: G5 Section Report."
"First United States Army. Report of Operations, 1 August 1944–22 February 1945. Annex No. 12: Provost Marshal Section Report."
AA 120
Belgische Commissie voor Oorlogsmisdaden–Commission Belge des Crimes de Guerre
Folder 2, Group II: "Libération Ardennes septembre 1944."
Folder 2, Group IX: "Libération, groupe français."

AA 145
Letters, circulars, and notes from and to Belgian municipal councils regarding Allied requisitions, 1944–1947.

AA 484
Postwar reports from German military commanders on unit actions in Belgium, 1940 and 1944/45. B-Series.
023: Generalmajor Heilmann. "Ardennen-offensive. 5. Fallschirmjäger-Division."
678: Oberstleutnant i.G. Hans-Hubert Voigt. "Bericht über die Kämpfe der 340. Volks-Grenadier-Division seit Weihnachten 1944 (Bastogne, Clerf, Westwall)."

AA 757
André de Lilienfeld Papers. Intelligence agent, Ministère de la Défense Nationale, Liège sector.
Folder 2: "Du 17–9–1944 au 5–4–1945."

AA 1207–1208
RTBF-Namur Papers. Correspondence, notes, and interview transcripts for the radio series La Bataille des Ardennes.

AA 1211
Survey of Belgian municipalities for the 40th anniversary of the liberation.

AA 1230
SHAEF Mission to Belgium and Luxembourg. Fortnightly reports. 26 December 1944–6 February 1945.

AA 1456
Survey of French-speaking municipalities for the 50th anniversary of the liberation.

AA 1593
RTBF-Mons Papers. Correspondence, notes, and interview transcripts for the radio series Jours de Guerre.

AB 30
Ruchenne, Marcel. "Témoignage, décembre 1944." Letter to the Confédération Nationale de Résistants Civils de Belgique, 8 February 1949.

AB 758
Chardome, Emile. "Aventures de guerre (Grune 1944–1945)."

AB 1912
Copeman, Andy. "Radio Documentary Proposal: 'Silent Night over Schönberg.'"

BB B 14/150
Dumont, R. "Le SEDEE aujourd'hui."
"SEDEE: Des héros tranquilles."

MICROFILM 46
Gillard, Jules. "Vesqueville: Guerre 1940–1945 et la bataille des Ardennes 1944–1945 (20 ans après)."

Dienst voor de Oorlogsslachtoffers–Service des Victimes de la Guerre

Brussels, Belgium
Fonds National de Secours aux Sinistrés. "Rapport présenté à l'Assemblée générale de l'Oeuvre tenue le 13 septembre 1945."
Hohengarten, André. "Vor vierzig Jahren: Die Gestapo in der Ardennenoffensive." (Rap 429–tr. 272 406)

Local Archives

Archives Communales Somme-Leuze

Belgium
"Memorandum de la Guerre à Noiseux."
"Réclamation de la Commune de Noiseux."
"Séances du Conseil Communal de Noiseux."

Gemeindearchive Büllingen

Belgium
B600: "Kriegsschäden, 1944–48."
R239: "Minenräumer, 1945–9."
R240: "Evakuierung–Viehverpflegung."
R261: "Sprengkörper u. Munition."

Published Materials

Bastin, Florence. "Sibret: Journal de l'offensive." *Cahiers de la Haute-Sûre* 3 (1985): 141–51.
Bastogne–Hiver 44–45: Des civils témoignent. Bastogne: Cercle d'Histoire de Bastogne, 1994.
"La bataille des Ardennes: Myriam y était." *Femmes d'Aujourd'hui,* 1 and 8 January 1985.
"Beim Fliegerangriff auf Malmedy die Mutter verloren: Aus dem Tagebuch von Richard Andriessen-Nemery." In *DVI,* 233–34.
La Belgique sous les bombes, 1940–1945. N.p.: Commissariat Général à la Protection Aérienne Passive, n.d.
Breuer, Josef. "Erinnerungen an die Rundstedt-Offensive im Raume Faymonville." In *KS,* 115–17.
Brill, Charles. "Met de panzers van von Rundstedt te Beauplateau." *Essen!* 16, no. 3 (1973): 99–108.

Burnotte, André. "Noël 1944 à Chenogne." *Cahiers de la Haute-Sûre* 3 (1985): 153–65.

Caster, Monique van. "Petit Spay: Décembre 44." *Segnia* 19, no. 4 (1994): 225–28.

Celles: Noël 1944. Les Cahiers de la Lesse, no. 4. Houyet: O.D.P.H., 1994.

Chevron: A Belgian Village. An Annotated English Version of the Diary of Mr. Walthère Jamar (December 18, 1944–January 12, 1945). N.p.: Jamar Sneiderman Historical Fund, n.d.

Collette, Ghislaine. "Souvenirs de l'offensive des Ardennes, 1944–1945." *Segnia* 19, no. 4 (1994): 184–86.

Collette, Henri. "Ma guerre à moi." *Info-CRIBA*, no. 2 (2001): 19–37.

Collin, Auguste. "Décembre 1944 à Mabompré." *Segnia* 19, no. 4 (1994): 216–17.

Commission des Crimes de Guerre. Ministère de la Justice. Royaume de Belgique. *Les crimes de guerre commis lors de la libération du territoire national, septembre 1944: Forêt.* Liège: Georges Thone, 1946.

———. *Les crimes de guerre commis lors de la libération du territoire national, septembre 1944: Région de Huy-Namur.* Liège: Georges Thone, 1948.

———. *Les crimes de guerre commis pendant la contre-offensive de von Rundstedt dans les Ardennes, décembre 1944–janvier 1945.* Liège: Georges Thone, 1948.

———. *Les crimes de guerre commis pendant la contre-offensive de von Rundstedt dans les Ardennes, décembre 1944–janvier 1945: Stavelot.* Liège: Georges Thone, 1946.

Coune, Denyse de. "Souvenirs de guerre: Assenois 1944–1945." *Cahiers de la Haute-Sûre* 3 (1985): 111–33.

Dries, Josef. "Streiflichter aus dem Frontbereich." In *DVI*, 159–91.

Dropsy, Paul. *Mon village dans la tourmente: Grand-Halleux, décembre 44–vallée de la Salm–janvier 45.* N.p., [1994].

———. "Quelques documents de 44–45." *Info-CRIBA*, no. 3 (2001): 13–17.

Dumont, Bernadette. *Bastogne, 1944.* Jumet-Gohissart: privately published, 1974.

"Extraits du rapport d'activités du Haut Commissariat dans la province de Luxembourg." In Luc Rivet and Yvan Sevenans. *La bataille des Ardennes: Les civils dans la guerre.* Brussels: Didier Hatier, 1985.

Fagnoul, Kurt. "Im Angesicht des Todes: Die Erlebnisse des Bauernführers Heinrich Maus." In *EuW*, 157–68.

———. "Ein gebürtiger Eupener und überzeugter Europäer berichtet: Kriegserlebnisse bei der 'Big-Red-One-Division.'" In *EuW*, 169–76.

———. *St. Vith im Schatten des 'Endsiegs': Augenzeugen berichten vom grossen Treck durch die Eifel, 1944/45.* Eupen: Doepgen, 1980.

Fecherolle, Paul. "Souvenirs des deux guerres." In *Contribution à l'histoire de Bastogne: Bastogne dans le temps.* N.p., n.d.

Flemings, Peter. "Unvergessliche Erinnerungen an die Offensive in Rodt." In *KS*, 277–81.

"Le 424e Régiment de la 106e Division d'infanterie: *After Battle* et *Personal Reports*." *Info-CRIBA*, no. 1 (2002): 22–36.

Fourny, Paula. *Hiver 1944–1945. Moircy-Jenneville-Bonnerue: Des civils confrontés aux horreurs de la guerre*. Libramont: privately published, 1995.

Frankort and Wilkin, comps. "Décembre '44–Janvier '45, souvenirs personnels: L'offensive von Rundstedt dans la région de Manhay." *Segnia* 9, no. 2 (1984): 21–24.

Frühbuss, Ernst von. "Hohe Gäste in Wallerode." In *KS*, 204–6.

Gaillard, Albert. "Mon Noël 1944." In Jean-Louis Giot. *Verdenne 1944: Les événements de septembre et les opérations militaires pour le contrôle de la route Marche-Hotton (20–26 décembre 1944)*. Marche: TOP Magazine, 1994.

Gennen, Emil. "Augenzeugen berichten aus dem Raume Burg-Reuland." In *KS*, 262–70.

Greindl. "Bastenaken in de greep." *Mooier Leven* (Christmas 1945), 13–16 and 36.

———. *Noël 1944 à Isle la Hesse*. Bruges: Desclée, De Brouwer, 1945.

Hanlon, John D. "Les draps de Hemroulle." *Info-CRIBA*, no. 2 (2003): 15–18.

Heinen-Drees, Maria. "Die Flucht ins Ungewisse." In *EuW*, 113–22.

Heinrich, Paul. "Zwangsrekrutierte der 2. deutschen Panzerdivision auf heimatlichen Boden." In *Ardennen 1944/45*. Luxembourg: CEBA, 1983.

Hinckels, Elie. "A Mageret, décembre 44: L'offensive." *Le Pays de Bastogne*, no. 1 (1992): 5–6.

Jenniges, Hubert, ed. "Eine Frau zwischen Einsamkeit, Trauer und Todesangst: Tagebuchaufzeichnungen der Maria von Monschaw-Buschmann." In *EuW*, 43–101.

Kauffmann, Gabrielle. "Mont-Houffalize: De la première libération à la seconde invasion." *Segnia* 19, no. 4 (1994): 180–83.

Kettels-Crémer, Marie. "Un mois d'offensive allemande à Tavigny." *Segnia* 19, no. 4 (1994): 191–94.

Kirch, Klara. "Wie ich die Ardennenoffensive erlebte." In *KS*, 123–30.

Kirch, Klara, ed. "Wie ich als Hilfspolizist die Ardennenoffensive erlebte: Nach Berichten von Johann Niessen aus Bütgenbach." In *KS*, 108–11.

Kubiak-Hoffmann, Catharina. "Harte Zeiten in Weckerath." In *DVI*, 225–26.

Laurent, Louise. "Une Jemelloise se souvient." *Pays de Namur: Pages d'Histoire et de Folklore du Namurois*. No. 97 (1985): 19–20.

Lechat, J. J. "La chronique de la Maison de Farnières, 16 décembre 1944–8 février 1945." *Info-CRIBA*, no. 3 (2003): 21–38.

Lozet-Gustin, Maria. "Journées tragiques de décembre 1944 à Chaumont." *Cahiers de la Haute-Sûre* 3 (1985): 135–39.

MacDonald, William. "Erinnerungen eines amerikanischen Jeepfahrers." Transl. Walter Reuter. In *KS*, 215–16.

Maniura, Leonhardt. "Erinnerungen eines Landsers an die Kriegsereignisse in Amel, Ondenval, Thirimont 1944/1945." In *EuW*, 145–56.

Martin, Michel. *Les Tailles et environs: D'une libération à l'autre, 1944–1945*. N.p.: privately published, [2003].

Meurisse, André R. *De croix noires en étoiles blanches: Un enfant du terroir bastognard se souvient des années 1940–1945*. Bastogne: Cercle d'Histoire de Bastogne, 1994.

"Meyerode, Medell: Aufzeichnungen in der Pfarrchronik von Meyerode und Medell von Pfarrer Leuffen." In *KS*, 206–13.

"Nidrum: Tagebuchaufzeichnungen von Michel Peiffer." In *KS*, 183–88.

1944: Un Noël en enfer. Des Malmediens racontent. Malmedy: Royal Syndicat d'Initiative et de Tourisme 'Malmedy Hautes Fagnes,' 1993.

Offergeld, Jean-Pierre. "'L'offensive,' comme je l'ai vécue." *Info-CRIBA*, no. 2 (2003): 19–38.

Peters, Heinrich. "Der Tod von St. Vith." In *EuW*, 139–44.

Peters, Josef. "Das Massaker von Holzheim (1945)." In *EuW*, 177–82.

Picalausa, Louis C. "Het Roode Kruis in de Ardennen." *Mooier Leven*, nos. 1/2 (1945), 3–7.

Rasqué, Fritz. *Das Oesling im Krieg*. [1946]. Reprint, Christnach: Éditions Emile Borschette, 1991.

Reuter, Walter, transl. "Aus den Erinnerungen des GI's Frederick W. Mack im Ourtal." In *KS*, 259–61.

Reuter, Walter. "Aus den Tagebuchaufzeichnungen von Frl. Tafniez, Weywertz." In *KS*, 133–37.

Rivet, Luc, and Yvan Sevenans. *La bataille des Ardennes: Les civils dans la guerre*. Brussels: Didier Hatier, 1985.

Rossignon, Jacques. "Voici quarante ans! Il a fait chaud à Fraiture. Louis Lesenfants, Marie et Louise Lehaire se souviennent." *Luxembourg Tourisme*, December 1984, 10–11.

Schetter, Joseph. *Saint-Vith, ville holocauste: Reportage*. Malmedy: Éditions 'Journal de Malmedy,' 1948.

Schiltz, Will. "Ein Kellerleben in Kaundorf: Erlebnisse aus bösen Tagen." *The Bulge*, no. 2 (2002): 20–27.

Schütz, Günther. "Unsere Flucht aus St. Vith." In *DVI*, 227–30.

Theissen, Josef. "Die Kriegsereignisse in Wallerode." In *EuW*, 103–12.

Thill, Albert. *L'insaisissable patriote des Ardennes*. N.p., 1979.

Toussaint, Heinrich. *Verlorene Jahre*. Vol. 1 of *Schicksale einer Kriegsgeneration im Grenzland*. Eupen: Grenz-Echo, 1987.

———. *Bittere Erfahrungen*. Vol. 2 of *Schicksale einer Kriegsgeneration im Grenzland*. Eupen: Grenz-Echo, 1987.

"25 jaar later: Een wonderlijke ontmoeting." *Ons Land*, 2 January 1970.

Villenfagne, Jacques de. "Belges dans la bataille des Ardennes (Décembre 1944)." *La Belgique Militaire/Militair België* No. 170 (May 1985): 27–33.

War Crimes Commission. Ministry of Justice. Kingdom of Belgium. *War Crimes Committed during von Rundstedt's Counter-Offensive in the Ardennes, December 1944–January 1945: Bande.* Liège: Georges Thone, 1945.

Warnaffe, Marie du Bus de. *Journal des tristes jours, 1944–1945.* Bastogne: Cercle d'Histoire de Bastogne, 1994.

Weynand, Margret. "Ein Mädchen erlebt die Front: So war es vor 50 Jahren in Bütgenbach." In *EuW*, 131–38.

Electronic Materials

Jamar, Emile. "How the Bigger Part of My Day of 19 December 1944 Was Spent." Interview by Joseph Dejardin. www.users.skynet.be/bulgecriba/merriken.html

Jeanpierre, Marcel. "The Battle of Grand-Halleux, 21–23 December 1944." www.users.skynet.be/bulgecriba/beaty.html.

Lange, Horst. "Auszug aus den Erinnerungen von Horst Lange, damals in der 5. Fallschirmjäger-Division." www.geocities.com/rguy.geo/lange_de.html

Lion-Lutgen, Sophie. "Erinnerungen an die folgenschweren Tage der Rundstedtoffensive: Aus meinem Tagebuch." www.geocities.com/rguy.geo/lutgen.html

Warnock, Frank. "The Story of a Small Town in Belgium: Stavelot, December 1944." www.users.skynet.be/bulgecriba/warnockfrank.html

Whitehill, John A. "Reports of the Liberation of Bondorf, Luxembourg." www.geocities.com/rguy.geo/reportwi.html

Secondary Sources

Books and Articles

"Amerikanische Bomben auf Malmedy." In *DVI*, 63–84.

Bartov, Omer. *The Eastern Front, 1941–45: German Troops and the Barbarisation of Warfare.* 2nd ed. Houndmills: Palgrave, 2001.

Bertin, François. *La ruée de von Rundstedt à travers nos Ardennes.* Bastogne: Musée de la Parole au Pays de Bastogne, 1988.

Binot, Henri. "Malmedy am Kalvarienberg." In *KS*, 157–65.

Blockmans, Guy. "Les Britanniques dans la bataille des Ardennes." In *JdS*, 218–45.

Blumenson, Martin. *Breakout and Pursuit.* United States Army in World

War II: The European Theater of Operations. Washington, D.C.: Office of the Chief of Military History, Department of the Army, 1961.

Bourgraff, Lucien, and Robert Guillot-Pingue. *Ourthe dans la tourmente von Rundstedt.* N.p., 1994.

Bovy, Marcel, and George R. de Lame. *La bataille de l'Amblève: Les combats sur le front nord du saillant des Ardennes, 16 décembre 1944–28 janvier 1945.* Liège: Les Amitiés Mosanes, 1947.

Cailloux, André. "Elsenborn: Le saillant nord de la bataille des Ardennes." In *JdS*, 24–45.

Cailloux, Lucien. "A propos de la libération de Bastogne en septembre 1944." *Le Pays de Bastogne*, no. 4 (1991): 4–5.

———. *Du 15 au 21 décembre 1944.* Vol. 1 of *Ardennes 1944: Pearl Harbor en Europe.* Liège: privately published, 1969.

———. *Du 21 décembre à la réduction du saillant.* Vol. 2 of *Ardennes 1944: Pearl Harbor en Europe.* Liège: privately published, 1970.

Cavanagh, William C. C. *Krinkelt-Rocherath: The Battle for the Twin Villages.* Norwell, Mass.: The Christopher Publishing House, 1986.

Chalon, P. "Saint-Hubert dans la bataille des Ardennes." *Luxembourg Tourisme*, December 1989, 17–21.

Cirillo, Roger. *Ardennes-Alsace, 16 December 1944–25 January 1945.* Vol. 16 of *The U.S. Army Campaigns of World War II.* Washington, D.C.: U.S. Army Center of Military History, 1995.

Cole, Hugh M. *The Ardennes: Battle of the Bulge.* United States Army in World War II: The European Theater of Operations. Washington, D.C.: Department of the Army, Office of the Chief of Military History, 1965.

Coles, Harry L., and Albert K. Weinberg. *Civil Affairs: Soldiers Become Governors.* United States Army in World War II: Special Studies. Washington, D.C.: Office of the Chief of Military History, 1964.

Colignon, Alain. "La 'grande bataille d'Ardenne,' pour mémoire." *Segnia* 24 (1999): 265–306.

———. "Ostkantone." In *Les dix-huit jours.* Vol. 2 of *Jours de guerre*, edited by Francis Balace, 105–13. Brussels: Crédit Communal, 1990.

Craven, Wesley F., and James L. Cate, eds. *Europe: ARGUMENT to V-E Day, January 1944 to May 1945.* Vol. III of *The Army Air Forces in World War II.* Chicago: The University of Chicago Press, 1951.

Crouquet, Roger. *La bataille des Ardennes au jour le jour.* Brussels: Éditions Libération 44, 1945.

Delvaux, Jean-Michel. *La bataille des Ardennes autour de Celles.* Celles: privately published, 2003.

Dermience, Victor. *Bataille des Ardennes, 1944–1945: Bonnerue et environs. Libramont-Chevigny. Saint-Hubert. Sainte-Ode.* Brussels: privately published, 1995.

Didier-Robert, Linda. *La mémoire de Sainlez: L'offensive von Rundstedt vécue au village.* Bastogne: Cercle d'Histoire de Bastogne, n.d.

Doucet, Jean-Marie, and Lucien Gillet. *Hotton (1939–1945): La guerre au village.* Arlon and Brussels: Les Presses de l'Avenir, 1994.

Drossart, André. "Bastogne en enfer." *Le Vif,* 22 December 1983, 154–57.

Dubru, Alfred. "L'anéantissement de Houffalize par les bombardiers de la Royal Air Force." *Glain et Salm, Haute Ardenne,* no. 48 (1998):17–39.

———. *L'offensive von Rundstedt à Houffalize (décembre 1944–janvier 1945).* Erpe: De Krijger, 1994.

———. "Offensive von Rundstedt: Les pertes et les dégâts dans le doyenné de Houffalize." *Segnia* 19, no. 4 (1994): 195–96.

Eisenhower, John S. D. *The Bitter Woods: The Battle of the Bulge.* New York: Da Capo Press, 1995.

Ellenbecker, Germain. "Recht im Mittelpunkt des Kampfgeschehens." In *KS,* 310–24.

Ellis, L. F., and A. E., Warhurst. *The Defeat of Germany.* Vol. II of *Victory in the West.* London: Her Majesty's Stationery Office, 1968.

Elstob, Peter. *Hitler's Last Offensive: The Full Story of the Battle of the Ardennes.* New York: Macmillan, 1971.

Engels, Emile. *La bataille des Ardennes: Le choc des armées.* Brussels: Didier Hatier, 1984.

Engels, Emile, ed. *Circuit historique des combats dans la région de Vielsalm.* N.p.: FTPN/FTLB, [1994].

Fagnoul, Kurt. "Aspects de la Seconde Guerre Mondiale au pays de Saint-Vith." *Cahiers d'Histoire de la Seconde Guerre Mondiale* 7 (1982): 185–211.

———. "Chronik der Ardennenoffensive: Thirimont." In *KS,* 141–44.

———. "Engelsdorf: Tiger-Panzer mit dem amerikanischen Stern." In *KS,* 147–51.

———. "Iveldingen-Montenau in der Zange." In *KS,* 300–5.

———. "Die Märtyrerstadt Sankt Vith im Zweiten Weltkrieg: Ihre Vernichtung und der Wiederaufbau." In *Destruction et reconstruction de villes, du Moyen Age à nos jours: Actes.* Collection histoire, no. 100. Brussels: Crédit Communal, 1999.

———. "Mürringen die Todesfalle." In *KS,* 176–77.

———. "Rocherath im Feuerhagel." In *KS,* 168–72.

———. "Schönberg." In *KS,* 84–87.

———. "Sie lebten in der Hölle von Büllingen." In *KS,* 103–8.

Fickers, Adolf et al. *Honsfeld: Ein Dorf geht seinen Weg.* Honsfeld: privately published, 1990.

Gaul, Roland. *The Germans.* Vol. 1 of *The Battle of the Bulge in Luxembourg: The Southern Flank, December 1944–January 1945.* Atglen, Pa.: Schiffer, 1995.

————. *The Americans.* Vol. 2 of *The Battle of the Bulge in Luxembourg: The Southern Flank, December 1944–January 1945.* Atglen, Pa.: Schiffer, 1995.

Gavroye, Joseph. *Haute Ardenne 1944/1945: Bataille des carrefours, Baraque de Fraiture–Manhay. Villages sacrifiés . . . et les civils?* N.p.: Éditions J.A.C., 1994.

Gehlen, Norbert. "Elsenborn fiel nicht." In *KS,* 179–83.

Gennen, Emil. *Wie der Krieg zu Ende Ging: Berichte und Dokumente über die Ardennen-Offensive in der Altgemeinde Burg Reuland.* St. Vith: Aktuell, 1985.

Georges, Paul et al. "Fors l'oubli: Petit guide des monuments et plaques commémoratives des deux guerres 1914–1918–1940–1945 situés sur la commune de Houffalize." *Segnia* 19, no. 3 (1994): 1–84.

Giot, Jean-Louis. *Verdenne 1944: Les événements de septembre et les opérations militaires pour le contrôle de la route Marche-Hotton (20–26 décembre 1944).* Marche: TOP Magazine, 1994.

Gommes, Karl. "Mennoniten bauten in Büllingen auf." *Zwischen Venn und Schneifel,* no. 1 (1980): 7–10.

Gosset, Pierre. "La poche de Saint-Vith: Victoire défensive des blindés americains." In JdS, 99–121.

Graf, Raymund. "Die Kriegstoten 1940–1945 der Stadt Sankt Vith." *Zwischen Venn und Schneifel* (1990): 41ff.

————. "Märtyrerstadt St. Vith." In *KS,* 229–52.

————. "Vor 30 Jahren: Hitlers letzte Offensive verwüstete unsere Gegend." *Grenz-Echo,* 14 December 1974–14 January 1975.

Grailet, Lambert. "Hemingway parmi les libérateurs de Houffalize." *Segnia* 14, no. 2 (1989): 48–67.

Grandjean, Albert. "Ardennes 1944–1945." *Segnia* 19, no. 4 (1994): 198–206.

Grégoire, Gérard. *Décembre 44: Les Panzer de Peiper face à l'U.S. Army.* Stavelot-Malmedy: J. Chauveheid, n.d.

Guillaume, P. *Marche-en-Famenne aux jours périlleux de 1940–1945.* Liège: Imprimerie de l'École Professionnelle Saint-Jean Berchmans, 1955.

Hanlet, C. *La tragédie de la Maison St-Edouard à Stoumont, 19–22 décembre 1944 et histoire du préventorium, 1912–1944.* Liège: H. Dessain, 1945.

Hasquin, Hervé et al. *Gemeenten van België: Geschiedkundig en Administratief-Geografisch Woordenboek.* 4 vols. Brussels: Gemeentekrediet van België, 1981.

Heintz, Joss. *Dans le périmètre de Bastogne, décembre 1944–janvier 1945.* Arlon: Les Presses de l'Avenir, n.d.

Hemmer, Albert. *L'offensive von Rundstedt dans la vallée de l'Ourthe: Les combats décisifs de Hotton.* Hotton: privately published, 1994.

Hoyois, Giovanni. *L'Ardenne dans la tourmente.* Marcinelle-Charleroi: J. Dupuis, 1945.

Hubert, André. "Après la bataille." In *JdS*, 247–63.

Iterson, A. van. *L'antique porche de l'abbaye de Saint-Remy à Rochefort.* Rochefort: privately published, 1978.

Jacob, Jules. "Sur le front des Ardennes en 1944." *Revue du Cercle Sportif et Culturel du Ministère de la Santé Publique* (1969).

Jenniges, Hubert, and Kurt Fagnoul. "Manderfeld." In *KS*, 76–84.

Karen, Fred. *Kriegsereignisse im Frontsektor der Untersauer, September 1944–März 1945: Erlebnisse-Berichte-Schicksale.* Luxembourg: Sankt-Paulus-Druckerei, 1989.

Kartheuser, Bruno, ed. *Documentation crimes de guerre Stavelot, décembre 1944.* N.p.: Édition Krautgarten, 1994.

Kohn, Camille P. "Der historische Flankenstoss von General George S. Patton, Jr." In *Ardennen 1944/45.* Luxembourg: CEBA, 1983.

Kohn, Camille P. et al. *30 Jahre im Dienst der Erinnerung: CEBA 1972–2002.* Clervaux: CEBA, 2002.

Küches, Hubert. "Zivilcourage bewahrte Amel vor der Zerstörung." In *KS*, 289–91.

Laby, Hubert. *Ardennes 44, Stavelot: 18 décembre 1944–le tournant dramatique.* Faimes: privately published, 1999.

Lambert, Florent. *Von Rundstedt dans nos vallées d'Ourthe et Aisne et les verrous du Nord-Luxembourg.* Aye: privately published, 1997.

Laurent, Gotti. "Un Noël en enfer!" *Folklore: Stavelot-Malmedy-Saint-Vith* 66 (1982): 5–39.

Lefèbvre, Louis. *La bataille de Bastogne, 19–12–1944–15–1–1945.* Bastogne: n.p., n.d.

Lejeune, Carlo. *Hünningen: Heimat an den Grenzen.* Hünningen: privately published, 1995.

Lejeune, Rudi. "Hünningen/Büllingen." In *KS*, 99–103.

———. "Wirtzfeld war leer." In *KS*, 178–79.

Lejoly, Guy. *1940–1945 Faymonville: Années sombres d'un petit village.* Faymonville: Syndicat d'Initiative de Faymonville, 2000.

[Lesage, Jean-Marie]. *Houffalize: Ville martyre–Martelaarsstad.* Houffalize: privately published, 1984.

Levy, Paul M. G. *Les heures rouges des Ardennes.* Brussels: Les Éditions Nouvelles, 1946.

Lierneux 1884–1984: Psychiatrie d'hier et d'aujourd'hui. Herstal: Province de Liège, 1985.

Limbrée, Christian. *45 ans après: L'offensive von Rundstedt à Rochefort.* Monograph Series, no. 38. Rochefort: Cercle Culturel et Historique de Rochefort, [1989].

Lombard, Laurent et al. *Nos démineurs.* N.p., 1946.

Lucas, P. *Wavreille par la lorgnette. Historique: Exposé chronologique des faits. Retrospective.* N.p., n.d.

MacDonald, Charles B. *The Last Offensive*. United States Army in World War II: The European Theater of Operations. Washington, D.C.: Center of Military History, United States Army, 1990.

———. *A Time for Trumpets: The Untold Story of the Battle of the Bulge.* New York: Quill/William Morrow, 1984.

Maertz, Joseph. *Luxemburg in der Ardennenoffensive 1944/45.* Luxembourg: Sankt-Paulus-Druckerei, 1981.

Marche, souviens-toi! Septembre 1944–janvier 1945. Marche-en-Famenne: Cercle Historique de Marche-en-Famenne, 1994.

Margraff, Willy. "Born vergass das Luziafest." In *KS*, 306–9.

———. "Die Rundstedtoffensive in der Gemeinde Heppenbach." In *KS*, 281–88.

———. "Verhängnisvolle Tage für Eibertingen." In *KS*, 292–94.

———. "Verirrte Kugeln in Deidenberg." In *KS*, 294–300.

Marloie, 1944–1994. Marloie: privately published, 1994.

Marquet, Roger. "La bataille pour Bastogne: Les larmes de la liberté." In *JdS*, 168–217.

Marshall, Samuel L. A. *Bastogne: The Story of the First Eight Days.* Washington, D.C.: Infantry Journal Press, 1946.

Mayérus, René. "Die Rolle der Gendarmerie in der Ardennenoffensive." In *DVI*, 135–56.

Melchers, E. T. *Bombenangriffe auf Luxemburg in Zwei Weltkriegen.* Luxembourg: Sankt-Paulus-Druckerei, 1984.

———. *Luxemburg: Befreiung und Ardennen Offensive.* Luxembourg: Sankt-Paulus-Druckerei, 1982.

Milmeister, Jean. *Chronik der Stadt Vianden, 1926–1950.* Vianden: Veiner Geschichtsfrënn, 1976.

———. "Zum Einsatz von Kommandos der deutschen Sicherheitspolizei in Luxemburg während der Ardennenoffensive." *The Bulge*, no. 2 (2002): 3–9.

Moërynck, Robert. *L'immédiat après guerre.* Bastogne: Musée de la Parole au Pays de Bastogne, 1985.

———. "Les marques commémoratives de la Seconde Guerre Mondiale dans notre commune, Bastogne." *Bulletin d'Information du Centre Liégeois d'Histoire et d'Archéologie Militaires.* 7, no. 12 (2000): 5–26 and 8, no. 1 (2001): 17–42.

Monfort, Eddy. *L'offensive des Ardennes: Les combats pour les carrefours de la Baraque de Fraiture, Manhay et le village de Malempré du 19 décembre 1944 au 7 janvier 1945.* Manhay: Syndicat d'Initiative et de Tourisme, 1994.

Murray, Williamson, and Allan R. Millett. *A War To Be Won: Fighting the Second World War.* Cambridge, Mass. and London: The Belknap Press of Harvard University Press, 2000.

Neu, Peter. "'Der Gegner verteidigte sich zäh und tapfer': Bericht über die Einnahme Echternachs in der Ardennenoffensive am 19. Dezember 1944." *Hémecht* 48, no. 1 (1996): 41–46.

Nilles, Leon. "Breitfeld lag auf dem Vormarsch nach St. Vith." In *KS*, 226–27.

———. "Dreihütten: Der Feldherrnhügel." In *KS*, 221–22.

———. "Lommersweiler." In *KS*, 222–25.

———. "Neidingen." In *KS*, 255.

———. "Schlierbach." In *KS*, 261–62.

———. "Steinebrück: Schicksalsschwerer Tag." In *KS*, 219–21.

———. "Umleitung Galhausen." In *KS*, 253–54.

———. "Die Winteroffensive im Ourtal zwischen Weppeler und Heuem." In *KS*, 256–59.

Nollomont, Charles, Jr. *Ardennes '44–'45: Résumé des opérations militaires dans la région de La Roche-en-Ardenne.* La-Roche-en-Ardenne: Commune de La Roche-en-Ardenne, 1995.

Nos démineurs. N.p.: Fraternelle des Démineurs de Belgique, n.d.

Parker, Danny S. "Order of Battle." In Charles B. MacDonald, *A Time for Trumpets: The Untold Story of the Battle of the Bulge*, 630–55. New York: Quill/William Morrow, 1984.

Peterges, Jakob. "Andler." In *KS*, 87–91.

Pottier, Georges, ed. *Cinquante ans après Stavelot se souvient, 1944–1994.* Stavelot: Comité Communal du Souvenir, 1994.

Ramscheid, Peter. "Ondenval." In *KS*, 137–39.

Remacle, Gaston. *Vielsalm et ses environs.* Vielsalm: 'Val du Glain, Terre de Salm,' 1993.

Reuter, Walter. "Vor Weywertz kam der Angriff zum Stehen." In *KS*, 119–23.

Reuter, Walter, and Kurt Fagnoul. "Harte Kämpfe um Schoppen." In *KS*, 112–15.

Robert, Linda, and Denise Raths. *La mémoire de Sibret.* Bastogne: Cercle Historique de Bastogne, 2003.

Rogister, Henri. "Le massacre de Baugnez." In *JdS*, 46–77.

Rossignon, Jacques. "Voici quarante ans! Houffalize survivait sous un déluge de bombes." *Luxembourg Tourisme*, September 1984, 24–26.

"Ruines et résurrection." *Alumnat de Marie-Médiatrice Bure-Grupont.*

Schaffer, Ronald. *Wings of Judgment: American Bombing in World War II.* New York: Oxford University Press, 1985.

Schorkops, Martin. "Auch Herresbach gehört zum Schicksalsraum der Kriegswirren." In *KS*, 194–97.

Schrijvers, Peter. *The Crash of Ruin: American Combat Soldiers in Europe during World War II.* New York: New York University Press, 1998.

Schütz, Valentin. "Der amerikanische Rückzug führte durch Crombach." In *KS*, 273–76.

Senonchamps se souvient. Senonchamps: A.S.B.L. 'Les Foyans,' 1994.

Signon, Henri. "Honsfeld." In *KS*, 92–95.

Taghon, Peter et al. *La bataille d'Ardenne: L'Ultime Blitzkrieg de Hitler.* Brussels: Éditions Racine, 1994.

Toland, John. *Battle: The Story of the Bulge.* Lincoln and London: University of Nebraska Press, 1999.

Urbain, Eric. *Un front méconnu: Bataille des Ardennes dans les régions de Libramont, Saint-Hubert, Sainte-Ode.* Libramont: privately published, 2002.

Veiders, Leo. *Möderscheid im Wandel der Zeit.* Möderscheid: privately published, 1999.

Velge, Henri. *L'activité de l'Oeuvre Nationale de l'Enfance pendant la guerre, 1940–1945.* Brussels: Oeuvre Nationale de l'Enfance, n.d.

Verbrugghen, Jo. "Aide et solidarité." *Segnia* 19, no. 4 (1994): 208–15.

Weber, Paul. *Geschichte Luxemburgs im Zweiten Weltkrieg.* Luxembourg: Victor Buck, 1948.

Weingartner, James J. *Crossroads of Death: The Story of the Malmedy Massacre and Trial.* Berkeley and Los Angeles: University of Califonia Press, 1979.

———. *A Peculiar Crusade: Willis M. Everett and the Malmedy Massacre.* New York: New York University Press, 2000.

Electronic Materials

Carter, William R. "Air Power in the Battle of the Bulge: A Theater Campaign Perspective." www.airpower.maxwell.af.mil/airchronicles/apj/apj89/carter.html

Gaul, Roland. "A Brief Historical Survey of the War Years in Luxembourg (1940–1945)." www.luxembourg.co.uk/NMMH/waryears.html

Unpublished Materials

Limbrée, Christian, ed. "La résistance à Rochefort." School project, Athénée Royal Rochefort, 1980.

Index

Index of Military Units

United States Army

British Army

German Army